BUSINESS COMMUNICATION

Dr. Urmila Rai

Former Principal
Narsee Monjee College
Vile Parle, Mumbai
and
Former Director
Pillais' Institute of Management Studies
New Panvel
Mumbai.

S.M. Rai

Former Principal
Hinduja College of Commerce and Economics
Mumbai.

Himalaya Publishing House

ISO 9001:2015 CERTIFIED

First Edition : 1999
Edition : 2000, 2001, 2002, 2003, 2005, 2007
Second Revised Edition : 2008
Edition : 2009, 2010, 2011, 2012, 2013, 2014
Edition : 2015, 2016, 2017, 2018, 2019, 2020
Edition : 2022, 2023
Edition : 2025

Published by : Mrs. Meena Pandey
for **HIMALAYA PUBLISHING HOUSE PVT. LTD.,**
Ramdoot, Dr. Bhalerao Marg, Girgaon, Mumbai - 400 004
Phone: 022-23860170/23863863; **Fax:** 022-23877178
E-mail: himpub@bharatmail.co.in; **Website:** www.himpub.com

Branch Offices :

New Delhi : "Pooja Apartments", 4-B, Murari Lal Street, Ansari Road, Darya Ganj, New Delhi - 110 002. Phone: 011-23270392, 23278631; Fax: 011-23256286

Nagpur : Kundanlal Chandak Industrial Estate, Ghat Road, Nagpur - 440 018. Phone: 0712-2721215, 2721216

Bengaluru : Plot No. 91-33, 2nd Main Road, Seshadripuram, Behind Nataraja Theatre, Bengaluru - 560 020. Phone: 080-41138821; Mobile: 09379847017, 09379847005

Hyderabad : No. 3-4-184, Lingampally, Besides Raghavendra Swamy Matham, Kachiguda, Hyderabad - 500 027. Phone: 040-27560041, 27550139

Chennai : No. 34/44, Motilal Street, T. Nagar, Chennai - 600 017. Mobile: 09380460419

Pune : "Laksha" Apartment, First Floor, No. 527, Mehunpura, Shaniwarpeth (Near Prabhat Theatre), Pune - 411 030. Phone: 020-24496323, 24496333; Mobile: 09370579333

Cuttack : Plot No. 5F-755/4, Sector-9, CDA Markat Nagar, Cuttack - 753 014, Odisha. Mobile: 09338746007

Kolkata : 3, S.M. Bose Road, Near Gate No. 5, Agarpara Railway Station, North 24 Parganas, West Bengal - 700 109. Mobile: 09674536325

Printed at : Geetanjali Press Pvt. Ltd., Nagpur. On behalf of HPH.

PREFACE

In business, communication and relationships are very important. Words and sentences must be effective and clear. If words are vague and meanings not clear, business is hampered and relationships may be affected.

In a market that is widening rapidly, sellers must strive to maintain good long term relations with both their customers and their suppliers.

Communication is at the heart of business. Technological edge over one's competitors does not remain for long. Technology can be learnt and developed by others. It is Communication and Relationship that gives one an edge over competitors. Communication is a skill; it can be learnt and improved by practice and experience.

This book deals with the techniques and skills of communicating effectively, both orally and in writing. Everyone, whatever the profession or occupation, needs skills in speaking in official and formal situations and in writing letters, email messages, reports and memorandums.

The structure, layout, form and style of communication in various situations are explained with illustrations. There are also exercises for practice.

The authors have several years of wide ranging experience of teaching students, training managers in companies, and writing books on Business Communication. Feedback from users of the book is welcome and will enable the authors to add to the usefulness of the book.

DR. URMILA RAI

S.M. RAI

CONTENTS

Part I : Communication Theory

Part II : Oral Communication

Part III : Written Communication

PART I

COMMUNICATION THEORY

Chapter 1

BASIC ELEMENTS OF COMMUNICATION

The word "communication" (which comes from the Latin word "communicare" meaning to make common) is used in common talk, usually, to mean speaking or writing or sending a message to another person. Communication is really much more than that. It involves ensuring that your message has reached the target audience, (that is, the persons to whom it is sent) and that the receiver understands and responds as you want them to. It also involves ensuring that you yourself take care to receive, understand, interpret, and respond to messages that are sent to you.

Communication is an important aspect of behaviour; human communication is affected by all factors that influence human behaviour.

Role of Communication in Business

Entry into a good organisation requires excellent communication skills. The primary element in the skills of management is competence in communication. It is the tool with which we exercise influence on others, bring about changes in the attitudes and views of our associates, motivate them, and establish and maintain relations with them.

Communication is central to everything that we do. Our city/town are the organisations in which we live and act. Our activities in our family, school/college, office, hobby group, community group, succeed or fail, and our goals are achieved or not achieved, according to our ability to communicate effectively with other members.

Communication is the mortar that holds an organisation together, whatever its business or its size. Without communication an organisation cannot function at all. Without effective communication, information cannot be collected, processed, or exchanged; words and data would remain isolated facts. With effective communication, multinational organisations that are spread all over the world can function like a single unit.

The most important foundation skill for anyone in the new world of work is the ability to communicate. This means being able to express your ideas effectively in writing and in speech. Employers have always emphasized the importance of communication skills, and the current trends in the business environment make these skills even more critical.

Owing to advances in information technology, organisations need smaller staff. Owing to globalisation, an organisation may be spread in many locations in the world. Companies also decentralize, and work is increasingly carried out by teams. Team members must be able to work together to identify problems, analyse alternatives, and recommend solutions. They must be able to communicate their ideas persuasively to others. Ability to work well in teams, to manage your subordinates and your relationships with seniors, customers and colleagues, depends on your communication skill.

Production of goods is of no use if potential buyers have no information about the product. Communicating to the public about the product is the essence of business. A large amount of communication in the form of advertisement and public relations is needed in order to inform the public and to persuade potential customers to buy the products.

Business Communication

The term business communication is used for all messages that we send and receive for official purposes like running a business, managing an organisation, conducting the formal affairs of a voluntary organisation and so on. Business communication is marked by formality as against personal and social communication.

It includes both written and oral communication. Letters, reports, memos, notices are all formal and part of commercial and business activity; so are interviews, meetings, conferences, presentations and negotiations. Some of these are more formal than others; a group discussion would be less formal than a company meeting; a letter is less formal than a report.

Friendly chatting, letters between friends and family, reciting poetry for one's own pleasure or telling stories to entertain friends, are not included in business communication.

The study of communication and efforts to develop skills of communication are needed because communication is absolutely necessary for business. And there is no one who does not have to engage in some kind of business activity. Persons in all professions need to cultivate skills as needed for their work. Doctors, engineers, chartered accountants, actors and others in the entertainment industry, managers of all kinds of organisations, educators, besides persons engaged in business enterprises have to engage daily in some kind of business communication.

CHARACTERISTICS OF COMMUNICATION

Understanding the characteristics of communication helps us to improve our competence and skills in communication.

Communication is unintentional as well as intentional

We do not always succeed in conveying exactly what we want to; the target receiver may receive less or more, or even something other than what we intended to convey. In fact, communication does not happen exactly as the sender wishes. It often fails.

Communication takes place even when we do not plan it and when we are not conscious of it; we may communicate something that we had not intended to communicate. Our non-verbal behaviour, which is always present, conveys something about us.

Communication is a dynamic process

A process is an ongoing activity. Communication is a process and is always changing, always in motion; it grows and develops. Even if the same two persons exchange the same ideas again, the communication will not be exactly the same as it was the first time, because the two persons have grown and developed and changed since then. Every time we engage in an act of communication, we bring to it all our previous experiences, feelings, thoughts, attitudes which have been formed by other communication events.

Communication is systemic

Every component of the process is affected by every other component. The source, the environment, the goal, the medium, the nature of the message, the receiver, the feedback, all affect one another. If the audience is inattentive or uninterested, the source is not able to communicate effectively. If a wrong medium is chosen, the message may fail to have the intended result; if the sender's goal is not clear, the message will be confused. Disturbance at any stage in the communication process affects the entire process.

Communication is both interaction and transaction

The two participants, the source and the receiver, exchange ideas and information and influence each other during the process of communication. They also come to a shared and common meaning as a result of the communication. They share as well as exchange thoughts and meanings.

DEFINITIONS OF COMMUNICATION

There are many definitions of Communication given by many theorists; some of these definitions are quoted here.

* Communication is a process of passing information and understanding from one person to another.

  — *Keith Davis*

* Communication is any behaviour that results in an exchange of meaning.

  — *The American Management Association*

* Communication may be broadly defined as the process of meaningful interaction among human beings. More specifically, it is the process by which meanings are perceived and understandings are reached among human beings.

  — *D.E. McFarland*

* Communication is the process by which information is passed between individuals and/or organisations by means of previously agreed symbols.

— *Peter Little*

A wider and more comprehensive definition is given by National Joint Committee for the Communicative Needs of Persons with Severe Disabilities:

* Any act by which one person gives to or receives from another person information about that person's needs, desires, perceptions, knowledge, or affective states. Communication may be intentional or unintentional, may involve conventional or unconventional signals, may take linguistic or non-linguistic forms, and may occur through spoken or other modes.

— *Julia Scherba de Valenzuela, Ph.D.*

These definitions show that communication involves exchange of thoughts between two parties. Communication is the transmission of information and meaning from one individual or group to another. The crucial element is **meaning.**

Communication is successful only when the receiver understands an idea as the sender intended it. Both parties must agree not only on the information transmitted but also on the meaning of that information.

In order to transfer an idea, we must use symbols (words, signs, pictures, sounds) which stand for the idea. The symbols must be understood by the person or persons with whom we intend to communicate. Both must assign the same meaning to the symbols used; otherwise, there is miscommunication. Unless there is a common understanding of the symbols, it is not possible to communicate.

ELEMENTS OF COMMUNICATION

In order to analyse the activity of communication, we must know the process and the elements involved in the process of communication.

There are seven elements or factors which make up the process of communication:

1. Source/Sender, is the one who initiates the action of communicating.
2. Audience /Receiver is the person(s) for whom the communication is intended.
3. Goal/Purpose is the sender's reason for communicating, the desired result of the communication.
4. Context/Environment is the background in which the communication takes place.
5. Message/Content is the information conveyed.
6. Medium/Channel is the means or method used for conveying the message.
7. Feedback is the receiver's response to the communication as observed by the sender.

Each of these is complex; any analysis of communication has to take into account the various possibilities of each of these.

PROCESS OF COMMUNICATION

The process of communication involves decisions and activities by the two persons involved, the sender and the receiver.

The **sender** begins the process of communication. The sender has to be clear about the **purpose** (or goal or objective) of the communication and about the target audience (or receiver) of the communication; that is, the sender decides why and to whom to send a message. Conscious or intended communication has a purpose. We communicate because we want to make someone do something or think or feel in a certain way, that is, to influence the person.

The source has to decide what information to convey, and create the **message** (or content) to be conveyed by using words or other symbols which can be understood by the intended receiver. The process of putting the idea into symbols is called **encoding**; in order to encode, the sender has to select suitable symbols which can represent the idea, and can be understood by the receiver.

The sender also chooses a suitable **channel** or **medium** (mail, e-mail, telephone, face-to-face talk) by which to send the message. The choice of the medium depends on several factors such as urgency of the message, availability and effectiveness of a medium, and the relationship between the two communicants. Note that the choice of the medium/channel also influences the shape of the message.

Finally, the sender tries to note the effect of the message on the receiver; he checks whether the receiver has got the message, how the receiver has responded to the message and whether he has taken the required action; this information about the receiver's response is called **feedback.**

Sender's functions make up half the process of communication. The functions of the sender are:

1. Being clear about the goal/purpose of the communication.
2. Finding out about the understanding and needs of the target audience.
3. Encoding the required information and ideas with symbols to create the message to suit the receiver/audience.
4. Selecting the medium to send the message.
5. Making efforts to get feedback.

The **receiver** becomes aware that a message has arrived when he perceives it with his senses (he may see, hear, feel, etc). The receiver attends to the message and interprets it. The process of translating the symbols into ideas and interpreting the message is called **decoding.** Interpreting is a complex activity; it involves using knowledge of the symbols and drawing upon previous knowledge of the subject matter. The receiver's ability to understand, level of intelligence, values and attitudes, and relation with the sender, all influence his creation of meaning.

If the sender and the receiver have a common field of experience, the receiver's understanding of the message will be closer to what the sender intended.

The receiver also feels a reaction to the message; this reaction may be conscious or unconscious; it may cause some change in the receiver's facial expression. The message definitely leads the receiver to think. The receiver may take some action, if required. He may also reply to the message. The reaction, the response and the reply together form the **feedback.**

Receiver's functions complete one cycle of the process of communication. The functions of the receiver are:

1. Attending to the received message, that is, listening, reading or observing.
2. Decoding the received message.
3. Interpreting and understanding the meaning of the message.
4. Responding to the message.
5. Giving feedback to the sender of the message.

This is a simplified description of a single cycle in the process of communication. Communication really takes place in several cycles and the two persons take turns and alternately carry out functions of sender and receiver.

Both, the sender and the receiver have important functions in the communication process; it can be successful only if both are efficient and attentive.

Context and Environment: Context is the set of circumstances that surround an event and influence its significance. It is the background of events which lead to the message being sent. A message may acquire a different meaning in a changed context. If both have the same amount of background information about the situation and the issue, it is easier to communicate on the topic. The context influences the sender's encoding and the receiver's decoding, and also each one's interpretation.

The meaning of a sentence depends strongly on the circumstances in which it is said. For example, "How much have you had to drink?" asked of a patient by a nurse could mean "Do you have enough liquids?" The question would have a completely different meaning if asked by a policeman of a driver who had got on to the footpath.

The circumstances of each communicant, each one's position in the organisation, the usual work that each one does, and the present state of mind of each one, can all influence the communication process. The present relationship between the two is a part of the context; the receiver tends to interpret messages in the context of the relationship.

Communication takes place in an environment. Environment includes several things, The most obvious is the place in which the communication takes place; if it is pleasant and comfortable, the communication is better. Noise or disturbance in the environment usually hinders the flow of communication.

The political, cultural, legal, technological environment influences communication as these factors may affect each one's situation and attitude to the content of a message.

Time is also an element of the environment; it has three aspects:

(a) The time of the communication (first thing in the morning, just before or just after lunch, when it is almost closing time) affects the communication.

(b) The length of time taken by a communication event (how long the presentation or the meeting or the conversation goes on) influences the quality of the communication. Too long can be tiring and boring; too short may be inadequate and one of them may feel that insufficient attention was given by the other.

(c) There is a right time for giving some information. If it is given too late, it may be useless; if it is too early, receivers may not be ready for it and may not understand it.

The following figure shows the steps in the one-way process of communication in a linear form.

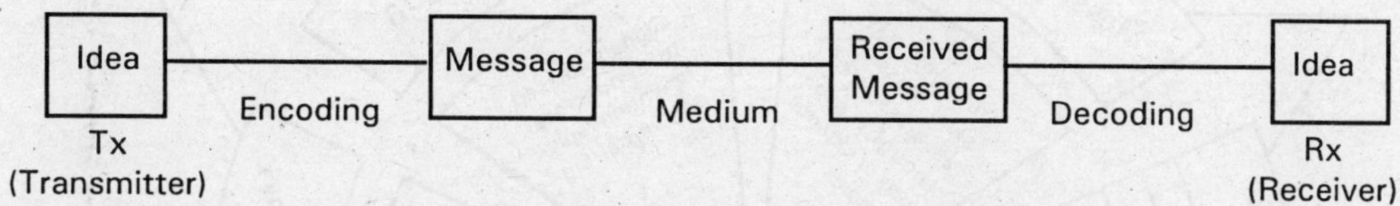

One-way communication process

This one-way routine is only a part of the communication process. For the communication to be complete, the sender must know whether the receiver has got the message, understood it in the way it was intended, and has received it well. The sender can find out this only on getting a chance to note the reaction and response of the receiver. The response may be in words (spoken or written), signs, or behaviour, both conscious and unconscious. The response or return message is feedback. When sender gets the feedback, one cycle of communication is complete. This may be represented roughly by the following diagram.

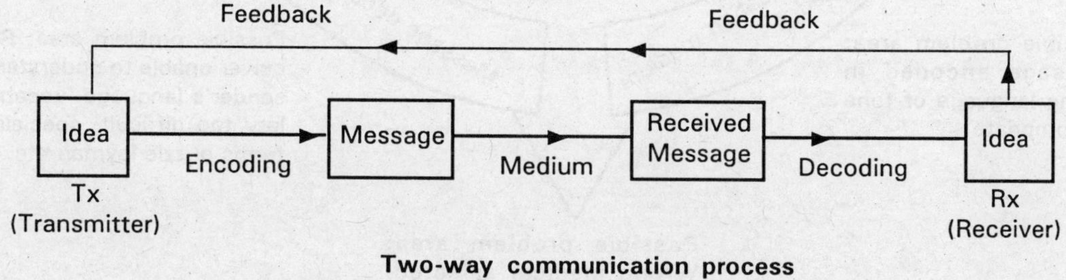

Two-way communication process

The following figure shows the process of communication in six stages.

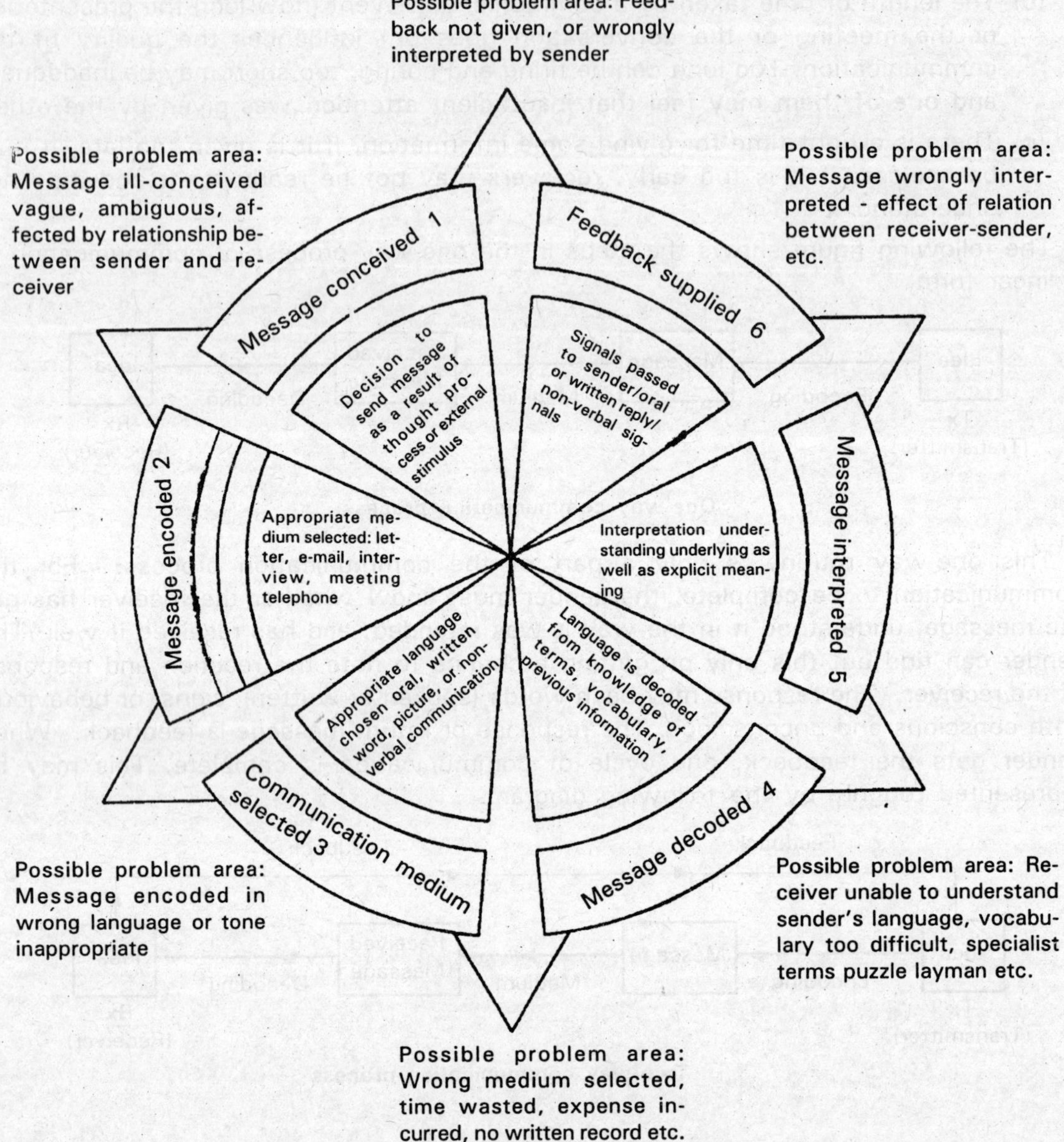

Figure slightly adapted from "People, Communication and Organisations" by Desmond W. Evans (Pitman).

EXERCISES

1. Name the factors of communication.
2. Explain the terms: *encoding, decoding*, *channel, medium*, *sender*, *receiver, context, feedback*, as they are used in describing the process of communication.
3. Functions of the source are: __________.
4. Functions of the receiver are: __________.
5. Give three examples of unintentional communication.
6. How does context affect the meaning of the message?
7. Explain the process of communication with the help of a diagram.
8. What is meant by "Communication is a two-way process"?

Chapter 2

OBJECTIVES OF COMMUNICATION

An objective is something that we want to get done by our efforts; it is the purpose with which we undertake an activity. When we communicate we have a reason for doing it. When we speak or write to our friends, our purpose is to keep in touch and to be friendly. But in a business or official situation, when we communicate with customers, or to our subordinates or our superiors at work, we have a specific objective or purpose; we want to accomplish something, that is, succeed in getting something done.

In business, we have many reasons or purposes for communicating. We may want to give information, we may want to make a request, give instructions, or make a complaint. We may also want to ask for information or learn. Many times, we want to persuade someone to agree with what we say. There are also some more difficult purposes to achieve when we communicate.

A person who is a leader or manager, or supervisor who has to keep together a team of many persons, has the purpose of motivating them. Sometimes, a leader has to show appreciation and praise the members of the team. Sometimes, the leader has to scold and warn them to do their work properly.

Our communication is clearer and more effective when we know the objective of a particular message which we are going to send. It is also better when we make the objective clear to the receiver. We should be fully clear what we are trying to achieve when we speak to a customer or to a supplier.

All communication has the two broad objectives of information and of persuasion. Other objectives are aspects of these two broad objectives. Whatever we might be communicating, there is some information in what we say. There is also an element of persuasion, because we want the other person to believe us and agree with us and accept what we say.

The objectives of downward communication from seniors to subordinates are different from the objectives of upward communication from subordinates to seniors. Also, the objectives of lateral communication between persons of equal status are different.

Information

Information consists of facts and figures and data which can be arranged in different patterns as required for different purposes. Messages which give information contain data on which the conduct of business is based. Information does not include emotion.

For example, a list of customers' names, addresses and telephone numbers forms a customer data base. It becomes useful information for accounts and collections department when we prepare from it a list of customers who have not paid their dues. It becomes useful for the sales department when we prepare from it a list of customers who have not placed orders for a long time. Both lists are made from the company's data base of customers.

Other examples of information are: the syllabus for a course, a stock market report, a user manual, a signboard and a news report.

We need information to carry on our work. If we are in a new job, we need information about it in order to know what we have to do. If we are in a new situation, we need information to make sense of it and to know what to expect.

Information may be given orally or in writing. It may be given in a meeting, at airports and railway stations information is given over public address system. A large amount of information is available and moves about in an organization and in the world. We need to develop the ability to take what we need.

Companies give employees information about the company's goals, plans, progress and prospects, and also about working and service conditions, training and promotion opportunities, and the benefits available to them. For this purpose, there are organized channels; the notice board is used for fresh information; manuals and instruction sheets are used for information about procedures and regulations; house organs, bulletins, pamphlets, are used for periodical and general information.

Many companies give information to the public about their progress, products, and policies through the mass media like newspapers and television. This type of information forms the basis of persuasion and motivation which is the other important objective of communication.

OBJECTIVES OF DOWNWARD COMMUNICATION

Messages moving from seniors to subordinates in an organization or from persons with expert knowledge to lay persons, have several objectives like giving instructions and orders to carry out tasks, training people for the tasks and for general improvement, motivating people to put in their best effort, to maintain high level of discipline and conduct, giving advice and suggestions when needed and persuading others on various matters. Customers and the general public have to be educated on the use of products, business procedures; customers who do not pay their dues have to be warned, and potential buyers have to be persuaded to buy.

Instructions

Instruction is information about how to carry out a process or procedure. Supervisors instruct their staff on tasks that are to be performed from time to time. In most cases, this can be done orally, individually or in groups.

Oral instruction may be supplemented with written material and visual material. Actually showing how to do something is called demonstration; it is a method of instructing in procedures and in operating machines. Films can also be used for demonstration. User manuals which are given to customers with mechanical articles, have diagrams and pictures. This type of instruction is educational.

Orders

An order is formal assignment of a task. It is often in written form, and generally means that the matter mentioned in it is final. Simple orders to carry out certain tasks may be given orally. Subordinates who question or disobey orders are considered guilty of misconduct or insubordination.

An order must be clear and exact. Junior staff may not have enough understanding to be able to function usefully unless they are given clear and full instructions on their tasks. All communication must be in a style which the recipient understands.

Office Order is a formal written statement of any change to be made in office routine. It is a record and formal instruction to all concerned that the change is effected. It states the change and the date from which it comes into effect. Copies are filed in all the relevant files and sent to concerned persons who are expected to take action and who are affected by it.

Education and Training

Education is the development of the abilities of the mind. Training is practical education or practice in some skill, under the guidance and supervision of an expert. Both require an expert to teach and guide. Education and training are both informative as well as persuasive. Both lead to discipline and development through learning, and practice.

Special communication skills are required to accomplish these objectives. Oral communication in the form of lectures and discussions is most commonly used for this purpose. Written notes and handouts are used for training. Demonstration, films, and actual work experience are used for training in technical work and skills.

Training is also used for changing attitudes and developing a commitment among employees. It is meant to create an emotional commitment to service and high quality of performance.

Customer education is an important objective of the marketing department. Customers who buy consumer durables are given training to use them most effectively. Companies selling products like Xerox machines, computers, vacuum cleaners, cellular phones, etc., arrange for training of buyers. Some customer education communication is done for the purpose of building up goodwill and public relations; it is informative as well as persuasive.

On-the-job Training

When a new employee takes up a job, s/he needs some instruction and training, even if s/he has had previous experience. The person must be educated and trained to handle the work (especially if it involves handling a machine) and helped to understand the routine.

When a new employee is placed on the job, the supervisor, or another experienced employee watches, supervises, helps and corrects the new person till s/he learns the job. This kind of education/ training communication is informal. A supervisor or mentor who is given the responsibility for on-the-job training must have patience and the ability to teach.

On-the-job communication is oral; it may be supplemented by instruction booklets, policy statements, pamphlets and employee manuals.

Motivation

Motivation means providing a person with a motive, an incentive, an inner urge to make effort to do his best. Managers constantly try to improve performance in the workplace by motivating the staff.

Communication is the most important and critical element in motivation of employees. Managers use communication to improve employees' sense of self-worth by showing recognition and appreciating good work. We all have a need for recognition, prestige, esteem, status and reputation. When our seniors communicate to us that we have done well, we feel happy and good about ourselves. When we feel good about ourselves we are motivated to make better efforts.

Motivation requires regular and careful communication which managers and supervisors need to do skilfully. Subordinates and team mates can be motivated by managers, supervisors and leaders in several ways:

(i) Listening to them and showing respect for their views. People feel happy and important when their ideas and opinions are heard and respected by their supervisors.

(ii) Ensuring that credit is given where it is due. Expressing appreciation for achievement and effort is a good way to make people feel that they are recognized.

(iii) Avoiding personal criticism even when opposing their ideas. Persons must be shown respect and consideration even if specific ideas they express are not acceptable.

(iv) Maintaining an open communication climate. People should feel free to speak out their view even if they have complaints and criticism to express.

(v) Using friendly and co-operative style for giving instructions. Instructor and learner have to make co-operative effort to give and receive the communication;

authoritative style is not always effective. For example, after having explained something, the manager might say, "Let me make sure that I have not missed giving you information which you might need; will you summarize for me to make sure I've covered everything?" In this way, the manager takes the responsibility and encourages co-operation from the subordinate. It helps to meet the ego-needs of the juniors and establishes a co-operative climate. It is much better than saying, "Please repeat what I said so I can make sure that you have understood."

(vi) Making clear statement of expectations. The manager must give the subordinates a clear idea of what is expected from them so that they can make the required effort to achieve it. People generally try to meet the expectations that others have of them.

Raising Morale

Morale is the state of mind and of discipline and spirit of a person or a group. In a work place, it is reflected in the individual and collective actions of the employees; it reflects their level of discipline and confidence. People with high morale feel good about themselves and are highly motivated and have the courage to face problems and meet challenges.

Confidence is an important factor of morale. People need confidence —

(i) in themselves; they must feel that they can do their job well and have confidence that they can meet challenges;

(ii) in the management; they must feel confident that their company will support them, give them required training and give them information about plans, progress, changes and problems which affect their job, career, prospects;

(iii) in their company's ability; they must feel confident that their company can meet outside challenges like competition, crisis, business problems and other threats.

Raising morale cannot be done by a single communication; morale is affected by all communications, and by the manner and style of communications. The communication policy of an organization must be framed with this objective in mind.

An open communication climate helps to keep the morale high. Open communication climate means that there is good flow of information in the organization. For example:

(i) Information about programs, plans, policies, progress must be circulated

(ii) Details of welfare schemes and facilities must be publicized

(iii) Upward communication must be cultivated and encouraged

(iv) There must be consultations on proposed changes and assurances of job security before any major changes are made.

When morale is low, the performance is poor; there is lack of discipline, absenteeism, and general lack of interest in work. The grapevine is likely to become fast and thick, and there are many rumours. Sometimes, the morale of some employees or a group of employees begins to drop if there are rumours of retrenchment, close-down of a department, a take-over, or some such possibility which creates fear and anxiety. Morale also comes down if the managers cannot handle a crisis or a threat from outside.

Communications with employees must be increased if the morale goes down or is likely to go down. It is seen in increased rumours. Companies put up notices and distribute circulars giving the correct information in order to stop rumours. Meetings, including informal tea meetings provide a good channel for giving correct information and for improving morale. In case of a difficult or critical situation, a meeting of all staff may be held to explain the correct position and clear the doubts and anxieties of employees.

Such special morale-boosting communications must be carefully planned. Top managers may hold a conference to work out a program of morale-boosting communications in case a crisis appears.

Counselling

Counselling is a specialized form of advice; it is done by specialists. Persons who are experts in psychiatry, medicine, law, or other fields, give advise on matters related to their field of specialization. Companies which take care of employees' welfare have counselling services for their employees; they engage the services of specialists to give advice and career guidance to their employees. Stress, tension and some emotional problems can be sorted out, treated and corrected at the health counselling centre of the company.

Communication for counselling is oral, face-to-face and confidential. There may also be some printed material for the purpose of giving the required information. Counselling can be successful only if there is free two-way communication; the counsellor can give useful advice only when the person needing the advice is willing to explain and discuss the problem.

Advice

A manager or supervisor may advice junior employees on matters related to work or on personal matters if the relationship is close. A senior may give advice to a confused employee on how to be more efficient. Advice on purely official matters can be given with authority; but advice on personal matters can only be offered as a suggestion.

Communication for advice is oral, face-to-face, informal and confidential communication. The person giving advice must be tactful and have a sympathetic nature.

Persuasion

Persuasion means making efforts to change or influence the attitudes and behaviour of others. Persuasion is achieved by skilful appeal to emotions. The style and tone of persuasive communication is different from the style and tone of informative communication.

Persuasion means using the best arguments to win over and convince others. It requires the skill and ability to use the symbols of communication in an effective manner; the persuader should be able to use words, both spoken and written, as well as non-verbal methods in such a way as to have the most influential effect on the target audience.

Persuasion needs a basis of information; we cannot persuade customers to buy unless we give them information about our goods and services.

A great deal of communication in an organization is persuasive. We use persuasion to motivate employees to make better efforts or to accept a change; we use it to sell goods to customers and collect dues from customers. A company uses it to get the public's goodwill and investment. Government uses persuasion to make people pay taxes.

There are three factors of persuasion:

(i) The personal character and reputation of the persuader must be respected and accepted by others; people believe what is said or written by a respected and reputable person or organization. This is known as source credibility.

(ii) The emotional appeal made by the persuader must be suitable and effective. All persons have three types of needs: physical needs, social needs and ego needs. Social and ego needs are the emotional needs; social needs are the need to belong to a group, to have friends, to meet others and have social interaction; ego needs are the need to win, to be successful, to do well, to be appreciated and recognized and to feel good about oneself. If the persuader offers satisfaction of these emotional needs, people respond favourably.

(iii) The logic of the presentation made by the persuader must be reasonable. People must be shown how they will benefit by accepting the proposed ideas, views, or actions. The persuader needs knowledge of the background and the present attitudes/views of the people in order to use the right appeals and reasons.

Warning

Warning means advising or urging someone to be careful; it is meant to caution someone of possible danger. A warning is also an authoritative and formal notice of something unfavourable. Warning is given in special circumstances.

An employee who does not work properly is given a warning. Groups may also be given a warning; for example, workers' union may be given warning that their agitation might lead to closing of the factory, which is a loss to all parties. A customer who has bought goods or services on credit and does not pay his dues is given a warning of the dangers of not settling his dues. The warning is caution that credit facilities will be stopped, that other sellers would get information about his failure to pay, possible loss of credit reputation. Finally, there is a warning that legal action would be taken to enforce payment.

Warning is given only after milder methods have failed to achieve results. At first, an attempt is made by advice, request, instruction, or order; only if all these fail, a warning is given.

Warning may be given orally or in writing. A warning, whether oral or written, is always confidential. When severe disciplinary action, like dismissal, is to be taken against an employee, a warning notice must be given in writing. The termination of any contract requires that one of the parties should give a written notice to the other party. Similarly, an employees' union that intends to go on strike has to give a written notice of strike.

The purpose of a warning is not to break the relationship. You need good communication skill to be able to give a warning without beieng insulting. Courtesy, even while giving warning, is necessary to maintain one's dignity and proper relationships.

Appreciation

Appreciation means showing and expressing praise for the work of others. Appreciation by managers and supervisors when employees do good work and make achievements creates a good attitude among the staff.

Simple appreciation can be expressed orally, in writing and by non-verbal methods.

Oral methods are:

(i) The manager may tell the person or group personally, immediately, that has made the achievement that their work is appreciated.

(ii) If the achievement is big, appreciation can be expressed again at a meeting or a function.

(iii) It may also be mentioned at the time of introducing the person or group to a guest or visitor.

Important achievements are given written appreciation. Methods of written appreciation are:

(i) Letter of appreciation is issued to the person or persons

(ii) Notices on the notice board and bulletin board

(iii) It is mentioned in the minutes of a meeting of the staff

(iv) It is reported in the company's House Magazine.

Non-verbal methods of appreciation include:

(i) Award of a certificate at a function

(ii) Promotion

(iii) Invitation to a special meeting/function

(iv) Giving additional opportunity for career development (such as training courses)

(v) Assignment of more important and responsible tasks.

Appreciation always makes the recipient feel good and improves the motivation.

OBJECTIVES OF COMMUNICATION TO AUTHORITY

Most of the objectives discussed so far are related to communication from superiors to subordinates and from sellers to buyers. A good deal of communication also moves from subordinates to superiors and from buyers to sellers. Information moves upward by a system of periodical reporting and collection of feedback and users' evaluation sheets.

Also, people make requests, applications and appeals to those who have the power to grant them; aggrieved persons may make demands and representations and complaints; more creative and motivated persons make suggestions.

Request

Requests are made by staff for various kinds of permission or favours. There may be requests for leave, for permission to report late or leave early on a particular day, for permission to attend classes, a request to be sponsored for a special training course, or for an increase in salary. These are best done in two stages; first, orally with the immediate superior and then, through the immediate superior, a written request to a higher authority.

Application

Application is a written request, giving full details of the matter and supported with reasons, whenever necessary, for example, an application for a job, or for leave.

Appeal

Appeal is an earnest request for help or support or for something that does not fall within your privileges. Such special favours may be obtained by appealing to a higher authority with proper reasons. An appeal may be written or oral, by an individual or by a group. Power of persuasion is necessary for success in having an appeal granted.

Demand

A demand is formal and is put up through an employee union. It has to be supported by good arguments. Demands are usually collective and in writing. Requests and appeals for better service conditions may turn into demands if the management is unsympathetic or the union is aggressive.

Representation

Representation is always in writing. An employee who feels that he has not been given what he deserves, for example, a promotion, makes a representation.

A representation must contain full explanation of the case; evidence in the form of documents like an appointment letter, rules in the service-conditions book, government circulars, etc., may be quoted or cited.

A representation may be made by a group of persons; for example, a group of students may represent to the University Vice-Chancellor to get their grievances redressed; a group of citizens may represent to the city transport company to get bus services extended to their locality; a group of aggrieved employees may make a representation to top management to get redressal of their grievances.

Complaints

Complaint is made when there are faults or defects in the system or in the goods supplied or services rendered, so that they may be corrected. A complaint may be oral or written. Within an organization, minor complaints may be adjusted by oral communication. In commercial transactions, it is necessary to make complaints in writing. Customers can also make complaints by telephone.

If an internal complaint is of a serious and complicated nature, and if its correction is likely to involve action over a wide area, a written statement is necessary for circulation as well as for constant reference. Otherwise, good managements do not need written complaints because they are alert in correcting faults as soon as they are pointed out. There should be courtesy in making a complaint. Courtesy is not contrary to firmness; talking or writing with courtesy and normal respect due to other human beings does not dilute the strength of a complaint or of a warning.

Suggestion

A suggestion is a new idea proposed for consideration. Everyone develops ideas about better ways in which to do their work or to improve their conditions and environment. In an organization, employees at all levels may suggest to their supervisors and seniors, ideas on better procedures and methods. A suggestion is usually oral, and may come in a formal or informal discussion. However, a good suggestion which requires attention and careful consideration may be out up in writing so that it can be circulated to several concerned persons.

A suggestion can be made by any employee or customer. Suggestions from employees at all levels are greatly welcomed by modern managements. Many companies have suggestion schemes as an organized method to encourage suggestions from employees. A well-operated suggestion scheme is an effective morale-builder. This is discussed in detail in chapter 21 on Public Relations.

OBJECTIVES OF COMMUNICATION AMONG EQUALS

Communication among persons of the same status is very important for co-ordination and planning. Managers need to meet at regular intervals to ensure that the organization's activities are in harmony. While official issues may be taken up in formal meetings, requests, suggestions and advice may be exchanged informally.

The main functions of horizontal or lateral communication are:

(i) Exchange of information: Heads of departments and other peer groups need to share information about work, activities, progress and processes. Some information is conveyed formally through copies of documents like letters and reports; a good deal of information is exchanged orally by formal and informal meetings or over the intercom.

(ii) Requests: Informal and formal requests may be made among peer groups for suggestions, advice, favours and so on.

(iii) Discussion: Plans and projects require discussion and review; formal and informal meetings are held for this purpose. Daily routine matters may be settled by informal discussion. Discussions among persons of equal status have an educative value, and are used in training programs.

(iv) Co-ordination: Projects and tasks involve several departments; co-ordination needs lateral communication. Every department must know how the other aspects of a task are progressing so that all can make proper contribution. Members of a team need to meet regularly to review and understand the progress of their project.

(v) Conflict resolution: Conflicts are unavoidable when different personalities work together. Regular lateral communication is necessary for preventing and resolving conflicts that arise between departments or individual members of a team.

(vi) Problem solving: Problems may arise in the course of carrying out any task or project. Most of these can be solved by horizontal communication among all those who are concerned with the problem and affected by it. Brainstorming is often used for finding solutions.

(vii) Advice: Persons of the same status also exchange useful suggestions and advice in a friendly informal way.

(viii) Social and emotional support: One of the important and informal objectives of lateral communication is to provide social and emotional support among peers.

Persuasion plays a large part in horizontal communication, as matters are discussed and agreed upon and co-ordinated.

EXERCISES

1. What is meant by "objective of communication?"
2. Write notes on the following:
   (a) Raising morale as an objective of communication
   (b) Communication for Education and Training
   (c) Motivation as an objective of communication.
3. Fill in the blanks:
   (a) Complaint and application are objectives of communication to ____.
   (b) ____ and ____ are objectives of communication between persons of equal status.
   (c) Counselling and motivation are objectives of ____ communication from ____ to ____.

❑❑❑

Chapter 3

METHODS OF COMMUNICATION: VERBAL

Most of our communication is with words. Language is a common system of symbols which we use for sharing our experience with others. We do communicate a number of things by our facial expressions, movements, clothing, and so on, whether we speak or not. We can also use other symbols like pictures, colours, signs and sounds to communicate. Communication with words is called verbal communication; communication with other symbols is called non-verbal communication.

Verbal communication may be oral or written. Both are naturally accompanied by non-verbal symbols; facial expressions, gestures, voice quality, etc., always form a part or spoken language; paper quality, type, appearance of the document etc., form a part of written language. Both can be enhanced by careful and conscious use of non-verbal symbols; body language can be practised and cultivated for better oral communication; pictures, charts, graphs, colour maps can enhance written communication.

Written communication can greatly extend the field and powers of oral communication. Writing overcomes the limits of space and time which confine speech. A written message can wait for the attention of the receiver while speech requires immediate attention. This shortcoming of speech has been overcome by modern technology. It is now possible to use Dictaphones and leave voice mail on the telephone which will be heard by the other person later.

Attributes of Oral and Written Communication

Oral and written communication have different attributes which have to be taken into account in choosing which one to use in a particular situation. Some of the attributes are discussed below.

(i) Speed: Written communication is slower in preparation, in conveyance and in reception; it takes more time to draft, type, dispatch, and to receive and read a letter than it takes to speak, and to hear, listen to, and understand an oral message. Feedback is also slower in written communication.

(ii) Record: Written communication serves as a record and can be used for future reference. It is a documentary proof, and can be used as legal evidence. Oral communication may be taped for later reference, but the authenticity of the voice can be questioned; moreover, tapes can be edited and the message distorted. Written records and documents are more reliable and acceptable.

(iii) Precision and accuracy: Written communication is more precise and accurate than oral. Choice of precise words is possible in written communication because the writer has the time to look for suitable words and phrases, and to revise the draft, if necessary. Accuracy is necessary in written communication because the receiver is not present to ask for clarification. In oral communication, it is not always possible to be so precise in the choice of words. There is also no time to seek and consider words while speaking; however, the receiver can seek clarification on the spot. Besides, oral communication has the support of vocal tone and gestures and expressions which enrich the meaning of the words.

(iv) Length: A written message is usually shorter than an oral communication. The situation of oral communication requires some preliminary and closing remarks, while for written messages there are standard formats for opening and closing which can keep the message short.

(v) Expense: Written communication requires stationery, preparation, and transmission, all of which cost money. Oral communication can also cost a great deal since it requires simultaneous presence and attention of the two parties, and getting together costs money. Costs will depend on the availability of the required person(s) at the particular place. Each type requires different channels for transmission. Availability and cost of each of the channels is a factor to be considered. Modern technology like tele-conferencing, and video-conferencing has made it possible to use oral communication even when the two parties are separated by a great distance. The cost is high but certainly less than travelling when there is a need for interviewing or personal discussions.

(vi) Body language: Oral communication is supported by the speaker's body language and paralanguage. The speaker can control the style of delivery, giving meaning to words and sentences by voice inflexion and facial expressions and gestures. Written communication is separated from the writer's bodily presence and is more in the control of the reader. The reader can give to the words the sound, inflexion and stress as he chooses; and this may be affected by the reader's mood and state of mind at the time of reading.

(vii) Feedback: Oral communication allows immediate feedback; the listener's face gives some feedback and the speaker can modify the message on the spot. Clarifications can be sought and given at once. A conversation can be brought to a satisfactory conclusion by continuous exchange of ideas and views. In written communication the feedback is delayed; the reader's facial expressions cannot be seen by the writer; the reader's response is known to the writer only when the reader replies. The reader may give a cautious and guarded reply without letting the other see the really felt reaction.

Oral Communication

Oral communication occurs in situations like conversations, telephone talk, interviews, conferences, presentations, negotiations, group discussions and meetings. Each of these situations requires special oral communication skills, which are discussed in subsequent chapters.

Oral communication is more natural and immediate. It is natural to speak when the other person is present. We speak to communicate in informal situations. We also speak in formal and official situations like interviews and meetings and presentation. Many persons feel nervous and cannot speak easily in formal and official situations; it needs training and practice to speak effectively in a formal situation.

Oral communication requires that both parties should be present and attentive at the same time. The need of personal presence makes certain demands on the skills of both; each must be able to respond to the body language of the other, and must be able to respond immediately to what the other says.

Most persons in an organization are constantly involved in oral communication situations of all kinds. You need to be aware of the subtle, non-verbal communication which accompanies oral communication and take care to cultivate it. A person who has cultivated it to a high degree strikes the audience as a "polished speaker", and can convey meaning effectively.

Channels of Oral Communication

The different channels of oral communication are affected by the environment and the conditions of the situation.

Face-to-face conversation

Oral communication is best when it is face-to-face. A face-to-face setting is possible between two individuals or among a small group of persons at an interview, or in a small meeting; communication can flow both ways in these situations. There is immediate feedback, which makes clarification possible. Besides, a face-to-face setting offers a richer communication experience owing to the close presence of the living personality whose voice, tone, expression, eye contact, and movements add significance to the words.

Telephone conversation

Telephone has overcome the need for both parties to be present at the same place. Telephone conference facility allows three to five persons at different places to have a conversation together. Telephone talk depends entirely on the voice. It does not have the advantage of physical presence. Clarity of speech and skilful use of voice are important. There can be confusion between similar sounding words like "pale" and "bale", or between "light" and "like". Names and addresses communicated on the telephone are sometimes wrongly received. It is therefore customary to clarify spellings by saying C for Canada, D for Delhi and so on. Telephone skills and manners are necessary for everyone who speaks on the telephone; this is discussed in a later chapter.

Presentation

A presentation is a formal, well-prepared talk on a specific topic, delivered to a knowledgeable and interested audience; the audience may consist of just one or up to 50 or more. The larger the audience, the more difficult it is to make an effective presentation. If the audience is large, a microphone has to be used; old-fashioned microphones cause some restriction in the movement of the speaker, but modern collar mikes are more comfortable.

A presentation has a face-to-face setting, but it is largely one-way communication, and the speaker has to make careful arrangements for feedback and for interaction with the audience. A presentation is always followed by questions from the audience. The general tone of a presentation is serious and businesslike, though a touch of humour can enhance the presentation; visual aids are also used to support the oral communication.

A good deal of the success of a presentation depends on the environment and the arrangements in the room.

Public Speech

A public speech is given to a large audience through a microphone. It has a face-to-face setting but the distance between the speaker and audience is great; this distance increases as the audience gets larger, as in an open air public meeting. Feedback is very little as the speaker can hardly see the facial expressions of people in the audience. A public speech is followed by applause from the audience.

The purpose of a public speech may be to entertain, to encourage and/or to inspire. The success of a public speech depends on the arrangements and on the speaker's skill in using gestures and voice, and using the microphone.

Interview

An interview is a meeting at which one person or a panel of persons, who are the interviewers, discuss a matter with another person or ask questions of another person, who is the interviewee. An interview is structured, and is characterized by question and answer type of communication. The environment and the arrangements in the room influence the communication in an interview.

The purpose of an interview is, usually, to assess, to judge whether it would be worthwhile to enter into a business relationship with the other. Each side makes an assessment of the other.

Group discussion

A group discussion is a meeting of eight to ten persons for discussing a given topic. The group has a problem or a topic to discuss and find a solution or come to a conclusion within the allotted time of half hour to one hour. It is a joint effort of the group. While it is not a very formal situation, the communication has to be controlled and focussed on the task. There is no appointed leader, but a leader may emerge during the discussion. Often, several persons show leadership qualities, and control and guide the group to a conclusion. All participants need discussion skills.

A group discussion is a very stimulating and useful communication activity. It helps in understanding a situation, in exploring possibilities and generates a multiple point of view. Group discussion is used as a tool for selecting candidates by observing their behaviour and abilities in the group activity.

Negotiation

Negotiation is official discussion between representatives of opposing groups who are trying to reach an agreement. Buyers and sellers negotiate to settle the final price, management and employees negotiate to settle their differences. Negotiation is a very difficult form of oral communication and requires complex skills. Both parties have to be shrewd, intelligent, controlled and skilled communicators. Negotiation work is assigned only to experienced and especially skilled persons.

Meeting

A meeting usually involves many persons; there is a chairman or leader who leads and guides the communication and maintains proper order. A meeting is a highly structured event. There is a fixed agenda, that is, a list of items to be discussed at the meeting. Persons attending the meeting are informed of the agenda in advance and are expected to be prepared for a discussion. The items are discussed strictly in the order of the agenda, and other discussions are not permitted during the meeting.

A meeting is backed up by written communication in the form of notice of the meeting and agenda circulated before the meeting, taking of notes during the meeting, and writing of minutes after the meeting.

Meetings are of many types, from the small committee meeting of three or four persons to the large conference or the shareholders' meeting.

Channels of Written Communication

Written communication is used for many purposes. First of all it is needed for communicating with persons who are not present. Although the telephone overcomes the problem of distance between the two, it is not necessary to incur the expense of a telephone call unless the matter is urgent. Besides, many types of documents are required for official work and for record. Letters, circulars, memos, notices, reports and minutes are constantly prepared and exchanged in and between organizations. Each has a format and layout which is fixed by custom. Documents are printed out on the organization's official stationery.

Letter

Letters are the most widely used form of written communication. They are used mostly for external communication. A letter has a complex layout which has to be carefully followed as each part of the layout has a purpose and is needed for reference.

It is typed/printed on the company's letterhead. It may be sent by mail, speed post, courier or hand delivery.

Letters can also be faxed or sent by e-mail. Faxed and e-mail letters do not use the complex format since they are usually followed up by other communication.

Memo

Memo (short form of memorandum) is usually an informal message between members of an organization and generally relates to daily work. Information or instructions can be conveyed by a memo. Many organizations provide pads of memo forms (with blank sheets for carbon copies) for the exchange of short messages among individuals. Memo forms are usually small and are used for brief messages. The forms may have the company's name printed on the top; spaces are provided for date, sender's name and department, and the receiver's name and department. Top executives of an organization may have personal memo pads with their name printed on the top, for use within the department. A memo may or may not be signed.

Notice

A notice is used when many people in the organization have to be given the same information. It is the most common method of mass communication within an organization. A notice is short; the language is simple, and the type is large and well spaced for easy reading. A notice is put up on the notice board.

Circular

A circular is a detailed document giving information, instructions or orders on a specific matter. A circular has a number and a date for reference, and is signed by the authorized signatory of the issuing office. Circulars are generally issued by government departments and other official bodies like councils, universities, and Head Offices of organizations. Circulars are sent by mail or fax to the various offices that are to be given the information.

Report

A report is a document prepared by an individual or a committee entrusted with the task of collecting information on a given subject. It requires careful research, collection of data and presentation of the findings, conclusions and recommendations. Reports are of varying length and may be anything from two pages to a full book divided into chapters.

Minutes

Minutes are the written record of decisions taken at a meeting. Different bodies have their own convention of recording the discussion and the decisions. Minutes may be written by hand or typed and pasted in a minute book, or typed and filed in a minute file. Minutes are a legal document.

EXERCISES

1. Compare the features of oral communication and written communication.
2. List three situations in your experience where you would prefer to use written communication, and explain your reasons.
3. List three situations which could occur in your personal life where you would choose to speak rather than write. Explain the reasons for your choice.
4. Name five oral communication situations.
5. Name five types of documents used in business.

Chapter 4

METHODS OF COMMUNICATION: NON-VERBAL

We communicate by exchanging symbols to describe our ideas and experience. Language is a common symbol system which we use for sharing our experience with others. Communication through words is called verbal communication; communication through other symbols is called non-verbal communication.

Non-verbal methods of communication include all things, other than words and language, that can convey meaning. For example, graphics like pictures, maps, charts, graphs and diagrams in a written document, and body language and voice qualities in speech, are non-verbal communication

Non-verbal communication can be independent of verbal communication; but verbal communication is always accompanied by non-verbal communication. Non-verbal methods can be used as a substitute for words like the red colour to mean danger, or nodding the head to mean "yes." Or both may be used together as when we shake the head and also say "no." Sometimes, a gesture like slapping the hand on the table may be used with words like, "We must do it," to emphasise the point.

Sometimes, our body language or voice, or untidy typing may convey something opposite of what we want to convey. This discordant or inconsistent relation between verbal and non-verbal communication occurs when the person is not comfortable or is trying to say something different from what he or she really feels. Non-verbal communication is mostly involuntary and unconscious and difficult to control; it may sometimes reveal the truth which the speaker/writer is hiding behind the words. It is said, "non-verbal communication speaks louder than words." Thus, there can be unintended and unconscious non-verbal communication. On the other hand, non-verbal methods can be consciously created and used with both written and oral communication.

An understanding of non-verbal methods and aspects of communication helps a person to improve oral and written presentation by using the methods and by gaining control over body language.

Uses of non-verbal methods

(a) Non-verbal methods have almost instant effect because of quicker grasp by the receiver; it takes less time to see a colour or a picture and to hear a horn or a bell than to read or hear and understand words and sentences. Speed in conveyance and response makes non-verbal methods extremely useful in critical situations like traffic signs and signals.

(b) Visual non-verbal methods aid verbal communication; maps, charts and graphs are necessary for conveying information or plans related to geography, locations, data, and most of the sciences. A large amount of complex data can be presented in a compact form; one page can convey information that would need several pages of words. It makes information available conveniently, at a glance for comparisons.

(c) Response to visuals and plain sounds is more powerful than to language. A cry of agony arouses stronger response than a sad story; a film is more effective than a written story. TV news is more interesting than on radio.

(d) It is the best method to convey information to illiterate people. Containers of poisons are marked with a skull and cross-bones as a warning; illiterate drivers manage with the non-verbal traffic signals. Films are used to explain processes to people who may not follow oral explanations easily. Non-verbal communication can overcome the barrier of language.

METHODS OF NON-VERBAL COMMUNICATION

Non-verbal communication occurs mainly through visual symbols and auditory symbols. Visual symbols are those which are seen and auditory symbols are those which are heard. Our other senses like smell, taste and touch also take in meanings and can be used for non-verbal communication. For example, the fragrance in a room, the feel of the plush covering on furniture, the taste and aroma of the coffee served in the visitors' room of an office, make significant impressions.

Non-verbal aspects of written communication

A document has an appearance which is the consequence of font size and style, margins, spacing, quality of the paper,

Written communication can be enhanced by using various symbols and graphics. Written communication implies a document, and the paper (or synthetic plastic paper, or cloth or other material as for invitation cards) on which it is printed has characteristics like size, thickness, quality, and colour. The print also has characteristics like colour, font type and size, spacing, margins and general layout. The appearance and feel of a document convey impressions about the status of the sender and also make it more readable and attractive to the receiver.

A company's letter is carefully designed with attention to its visual aspects and the impression it conveys.

Besides, other visual symbols can be created and used to enhance the quality of written communication.

Colour

Colour is an important and powerful means of communication. Matters of life and death, as in traffic signals, are conveyed by colours. It is also used for classification and identification of different products and materials in industries; the cosmetics industry uses colour to make products attractive as well as to classify and differentiate types. Carbon copies of documents are on different coloured paper to distinguish copies meant for different departments. Teams have colour in their uniform to identify their members; countries have their colours on their flag. Colour gives an added dimension to maps, chart and graphs, and makes it possible to convey a greater amount of information within the same visual/graphic representation.

Colour is used in clothing, design, decoration and to enliven a dull environment. Colours are associated with different moods and feelings like, white with peace and purity, red with danger and black with death and sorrow.

Colour also has psychological effect. The state of mind of employees is influenced by the colour of their surroundings. Pleasant, cool colours in the work place have good influence on workers; black, dark, gloomy colours are known to reduce productivity; very bright, gaudy colours may be disturbing and over-exciting; softly blending colours are pleasant and soothing.

Pictures

Pictures, from simple drawings to coloured photographs, are used in brochures, posters and advertisements. Pictures can be combined with a very few words for persons who cannot read well as in posters. Besides, pictures are universally understood, more easily remembered and make an immediate impact because they are easier to "take in". Reading requires practised eye movement, while a picture may be tackled in any order. Pictures are used extensively in advertising because they attract the eye and convey instantly even when the reader just glances at them.

Diagrams

A diagram is a figure consisting of·simple line drawing made to accompany and illustrate the parts and the operation of something.

Graphs and Charts

Graphs and charts of different kinds represent statistical information. Special skills are needed to prepare and to understand a chart or a graph. Information presented in a chart or a graph allows the overall situation to be seen at a glance; the relationships between the figures are also seen easily. Every charts or graph must be properly titled to show what information it represents; it must have labels and a scale/ key to explain the symbols used and to indicate what the different bars or parts stand for. Every chart or graph must show the date of the information.

Charts can be made in many ways. There are **bar charts** and multiple bar charts like the one shown below. The use of colour can make charts more informative as well as attractive.

A **line graph** compares two variables. Each variable is plotted along an axis. A line graph has a horizontal axis (x-axis) and a vertical axis (y-axis). If you want to graph the height of a ball after you have thrown it, you could put time along the horizontal x-axis, and height along the vertical y-axis.

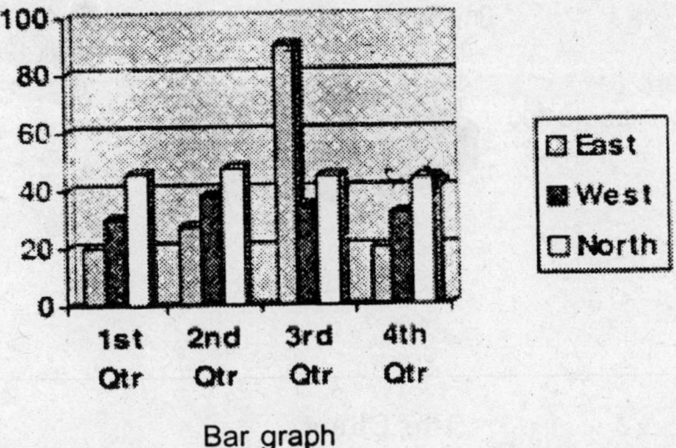

Bar graph

The line graph is used for showing trends in data. It enables the viewer to make predictions of possible future results.

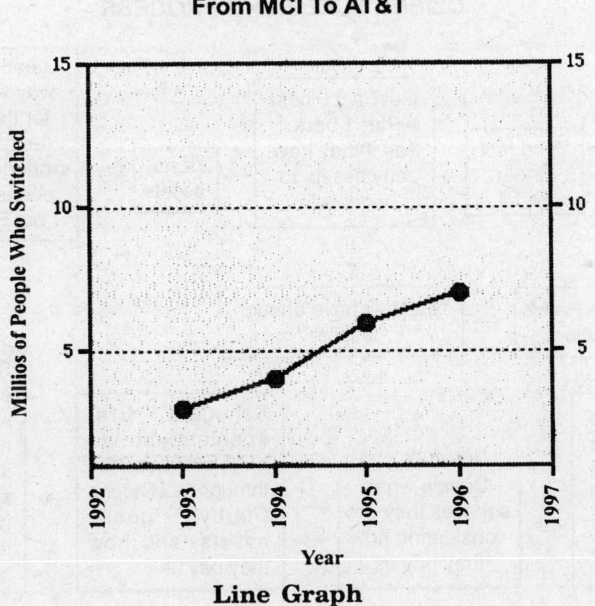

Line Graph

A **pie chart** or pie graph is a circular diagram for displaying percentages. It is used to compare different parts of the same whole. The circle of a pie chart represents 100%. Each portion that takes up space within the circle stands for a part of that 100%. The percentage values are represented as proportionally-sized slices of a pie. In this way, it is possible to see how something is divided among different groups.

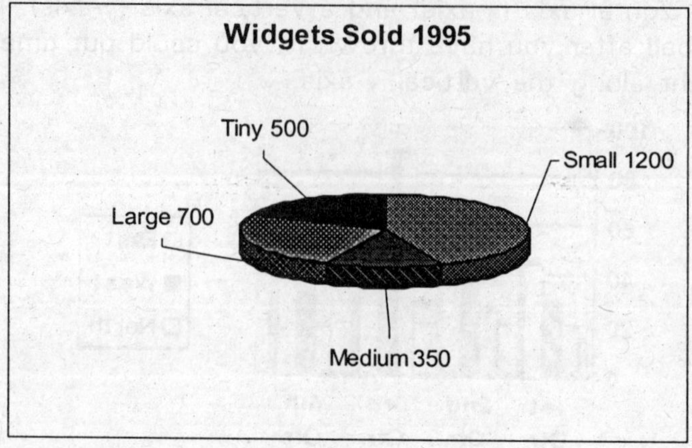

Pie Chart

Flow charts are used for indicating procedures in which alternative actions have to be taken depending on the result of the previous step. The following diagram is a flow chart.

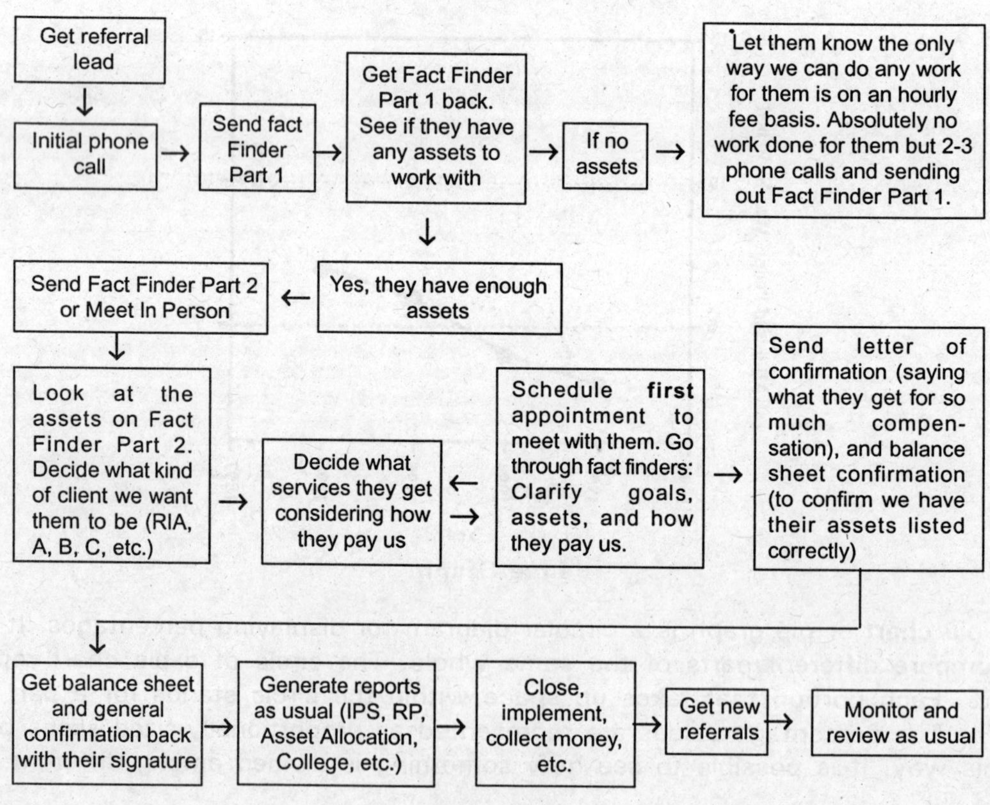

Flow Chart

Maps

Maps are representations of territory and are used for conveying the space relationships between places. They can convey geographical information like transport routes, climatic conditions, distribution of population, crops, animal life and vegetation; sociological factors like religion, literacy, health and nutrition. Maps of small areas are used to give information about routes and to locate places.

A map has labels to show the four directions; it must have a key to explain the meaning of the symbols used, and a scale to show how many kilometres are represented by one centimetre.

Signs and signals

A sign is a mark used to represent something; for example, + for "plus", skull and cross bones for "danger." It has a fixed meaning. A signal is a previously agreed movement which serves to warn, direct, or command; for example, the coming on of a green light is a signal to go ahead; the firing of a gun salute signals the arrival of a VIP. A signal may be visual or auditory.

Signs and signals used by members of a group may be made with hands, lights, cloth, smoke, drums, whistles or anything that can be seen or heard at a distance.

Auditory symbols

Sounds have very limited use as symbols; they can convey only very simple information. Sounds are used mainly for warning, like **sirens** to warn about enemy air raids in war-time or in factories to warn of fire or accident, and by police vehicles. **Whistles** are used by sport directors, the police/army to call members to assemble. Trains and ships use it as signal for departure and for warning. **Bells** and **buzzers** are used to indicate the starting and ending of work periods; bells and beepers are also used by special vehicles like the fire engine and the ambulance, to warn other road users to give way. A bell with a pleasant sound is used to call the faithful to prayer in many religions. **Beeps** are used by most electronic gadgets.

Tunes are often used as an identification mark. Programs on the radio/ TV have a signature tune; advertisements on these media have their tunes. Secret organisations whistle/hum tunes to identify and recognise members.

BODY LANGUAGE

Body language means the changes that occur in the body position and movements that show what the person is feeling or thinking. Much of it is involuntary and unconscious; most persons are not aware of their body language; but it makes a powerful impact on others. Body language can make or spoil a presentation.

Body Language always conveys meaning. It is:

- Omnipresent: it always accompanies spoken communication
- Emotionally expressive: it expresses mainly the feelings of the speaker and also of the listener

- Dominates interaction: it is more communicative than words
- Seems trustable: it is usually felt to be more truthful than spoken words

Non verbal communication can accent, complement, repeat and substitute for verbal communication. It can also contradict verbal communication.

It is complex and is influenced by many factors:

Biological: certain body shapes, skin colour and features cause persons to have some kinds of gestures, expressions and postures. Besides, we constantly try to adjust and adapt our body to our environment which we may or may not find comfortable. Some gestures or postures are related to this adjustment.

Habitual: Some movements and expressions are learnt as habits in the process of adapting oneself to the environment; they also arise from one's occupation which requires constant posture or movement of certain kinds. Certain speaking styles and phrases are also occupational habits.

Cultural: Customs like not sitting cross-legged before elders, not looking straight in the eyes of elders or superiors, are culture-specific. Customs of receiving guests, introducing, social conduct, also induce some gestures and stylistic features.

Body language can be divided into conscious and unconscious:

(i) conscious movements, postures and voice modulations are deliberately used. Actors are specially trained for this; skilled communicators, especially good presenters, also learn to make conscious use of body language.

(ii) unconscious movements are of biological origin, acquired habits and cultural customs.

No one can gain full control of one's body language, but it is possible to enlarge one's awareness of one's body and gain a good deal of control on one's posture, movements and voice modulation. If we develop increased sensitivity to our own body language, our ability to read others' body language is increased.

Body language consists of many aspects; it includes facial expressions, posture, gestures and other body movements; it also includes general appearance, clothing, accessories worn or carried in the hands, voice, and so on. It is an important factor in oral communication in face-to-face situations.

Appearance

A person's general appearance depends on several things. Two of the important factors that contribute to appearance are grooming, and personal hygiene. Care of skin, nails, feet and hair are expected standards; a person who neglects these aspects makes an unpleasant impression. Appearance makes the first impression; lack of neatness or cleanliness, carelessness in grooming, clumsy gait or clothes make a negative impression.

State of health is a very important factor in a person's appearance; no amount of cosmetics can hide lack-lustre eyes and poor skin. Poor health is easily reflected in the appearance.

Clothing and accessories

Clothing is a very important aspect of body language. It requires good taste/ judgement to make a subtle impression by what you wear. The colour, design, cut, and fitting combine to make up the dress. In India we have several choices as it is acceptable to wear clothing of national style or of Western style. Appropriateness for the occasion is essential; the formality of the occasion, the time of the day, the season, the cultural background of the people who will be present, and the conventions of your own organisation should provide good guidance. Many organisations have a dress code for occasions in order to ensure that its representatives convey the desired impression.

As a general rule, avoid wearing patterned clothing, especially on the upper half of the body, because it tends to shorten the attention span of the person with whom you are speaking.

Accessories like tie, footwear, jewellery need careful selection and should be comfortable to wear. Handbag or briefcase is included in accessories; so is an umbrella if it is necessary to carry one. Whatever you carry on your person or in your hands ought to look comfortable and gracefully carried; otherwise it will convey a poor image.

Posture

Posture is the way we hold ourselves, the way we stand or sit. It indicates something about our feelings and thoughts, attitudes and health. Stiff posture shows tension; comfortably leaning back conveys a relaxed mood; eagerly leaning forward shows the listener's interest. Posture can indicate disregard or disrespect for others; polite and well-bred persons are usually careful of how they stand or sit in the presence of visitors and in formal situations. Graceful posture is a great asset in any business.

Four Types of posture can be clearly identified: (i) forward lean indicates attentiveness and interest (ii) drawing back or turning away, expresses a negative or refusing; (iii) expansion suggests "proud," "conceited," "arrogant"; (iv) forward-leaning body, bowed head, drooping shoulders, and sunken chest usually convey "depressed," "downcast," "dejected."

Postures express attitudes, feelings, and moods more clearly than briefer gestures of hands or head. Slight movements and postures of the body wall are more basic, and more reliable as cues; they are not so easy to manipulate or control consciously as other body movements like fingers, hands, legs, and feet.

In a business meeting where feelings run high, the most truthful expression comes from the torso rather than arms and legs. Unconscious movements sideward, forward, and backward bending, reveal how people really relate to one another.

Angular distance reveals how we relate to and feel about people sitting, standing, or waiting nearby. Our upper body unconsciously squares-up, addresses, and aims towards those we like, admire, and agree with, but angles away from disliked persons with whom we disagree. In a conversation, formal interview, or staff meeting, a greater angular distance (turning away) substitutes for greater linear distance. Angular distance may range from 0 degrees (directly facing) to 180 degrees (turning one's back).

Facial expression

The expression on the face is the most obvious aspect of body language. A cheerful face or a gloomy face influences most people. A cheerful or appreciative smile, a displeased frown, a look of surprise, and several other expressions of the face can convey, with or without words, the attitude, feelings and reaction of the communicants. Expressions accompany the speaker's words and also indicate the listener's reactions. An alert speaker can judge the listener's reaction by the facial expressions that act as a constant feedback. Eyebrows and lips are the most mobile parts of the face; an eyebrow raised unconsciously can convey disbelief or surprise. A frown may convey displeasure or effort to concentrate, depending upon the context. Pursed lips certainly do not convey friendliness.

Smile

A smile is a universal gesture; it is understood by everyone, is generally unmistakable and clears the atmosphere; it is believed to release chemicals which create feelings of happiness.

Here is a quotation from an unknown author. "A smile costs nothing, but gives much. It enriches those who receive, without making poorer those who give. It takes only a moment, but the memory of it may last forever. No one is so rich or mighty that he can do without it, and none is so poor that he cannot be enriched by it. A smile creates happiness in the home, fosters good will in business and enhances friendship. Yet it cannot be bought, begged, borrowed, or stolen, for it is something that is of no value to anyone until it is given away. If some people are too tired to give you a smile, give them one of yours, as none needs a smile so much as one who has no more to give."

A smile can also be a useful non-committal gesture when it is better to be silent. And beware of an involuntary (sometimes one-sided) smile either on your own face or on the other's face; it could be sarcasm; it cannot be conducive to good relationships.

Eye contact

Eye movement is a key part of facial behaviour, directing others' attention or showing surprise or happiness and other emotional displays.

Eye contact is a very important communicative factor. Eye contact between speaker and listener is necessary for indicating that both are interested in the communication. While making an oral presentation it is important to create rapport with the audience with eye contact. Presenters make it a point to take in the whole audience with a sweep of the eye, making brief eye contact with as many as possible.

The comfort level for eye contact is three seconds; if eye contact is held longer than three seconds, it can cause discomfort to the other person. Aggressive persons try to fix others with a stare; anger may be expressed with extended eye contact.

It is commonly believed that avoiding eye contact indicates that the speaker is lying; yet, some liars may hold unblinking eye contact and watch to see your reaction. Persons who lack self-confidence also generally avoid eye contact. However, the rules and customs of culture influence how people use their faces and eyes. Several African and Asian cultures consider it impertinent for younger persons to look at elders directly in the eye.

Gestures

Gestures are movements of hands/ head/ body; they are a natural accompaniment of speech; a person who does not make any movement while speaking appears somewhat stiff and mechanical. Gestures may not have specific meaning; a clenched fist may emphasise an important point, or convey determination, or indicate defiance/ opposition. As gestures are closely related to personality, no two persons make exactly the same gestures; yet the general meaning is easily recognised.

The occasion, the size and nature of the audience influence speaker's gestures. On very formal occasions, like employment interview/ conference, speakers use fewer gestures (Note TV news readers). In a relaxed situation, gestures are used more freely.

Energy

Energy and enthusiasm as an aspect of body language is hard to describe, but most people have experienced the impact of a person with a high level of energy. Some impress with high level of physical energy which is almost infectious; some have high intellectual or emotional or spiritual energy. Whatever its source, energy conveys competence and inspires respect. State of physical and mental health plays a large part in body language. A healthy person is energetic and maintains a certain level of enthusiasm in work. A person's enthusiasm is reflected in the style; it is usually infectious and makes listeners also feel enthusiastic.

Space

The way we use space plays a subtle role in body language. Individuals naturally maintain a certain space between themselves in various social and interpersonal situations. The distance we keep from the other person while speaking, indicates the relationship; we keep a longer distance from a slight acquaintance and get closer to persons with closer relationship; we maintain a respectful distance from and allow more personal space to our superiors.

It is important not to invade others' space in any situation. Four types of distance indicate the relationships between persons: intimate space is 0 to 18 inches, personal space is 18 inches to 4 feet, social distance is 4 feet to 12 feet and public distance is 12 feet to hearing and seeing distance.

The way people structure the space around them also conveys meaning. A manager can use space to create an impression of status. A spacious office, a large office desk, a large car suggest important position. Efficient use of space without creating a clutter generates a sense of orderliness.

Time

Our use of time is an even more subtle non-verbal factor in communication. Time given to listen or to speak to people creates a sense of self-esteem in them; it is equated with care and concern.

On the other hand, a person who uses one's own time and other people's time wastefully, creates an impression of being inefficient and disorganised.

A sense of timing in conducting meetings (formal and informal), in conveying good or bad news, in making a presentation, generates respect and goodwill.

PARALANGUAGE

The non-verbal aspects of the spoken word are known as **paralanguage**. It includes the qualities of the voice, the way we use our voice, as well as the sounds we make without uttering words. It is possible to control and use paralanguage effectively by becoming aware of it and paying attention to one's voice and speech.

Voice has characteristics like tone, volume, and pitch. **Tone** is the quality of the voice. **Volume** is the loudness or softness, which can be consciously adjusted to the number of persons in the audience and the distance between the speaker and the listeners; speaking too loud shows lack of self-command or abrasive nature. **Pitch** is the high or low note on the scale; a high-pitched voice is often unpleasant, and suggests immaturity or emotional disturbance; a frightened person speaks in a high pitched voice. It is better to begin softly, in a low pitch and raise the volume and pitch as required.

Speed is factor of speech. Rapid speech indicates excitement; we increase speed of speaking to tell an interesting story, and reduce speed to explain a difficult idea. **Pronunciation** means the accepted standard of the way in which a word is said; correct and clear pronunciation is important and indicates that the speaker is careful and has consideration for the audience. **Accent** is the way a person pronounces the sounds of the language; every language has its own accent or way of forming the sounds; we carry our mother tongue accent to other languages we learn. Good accent in a new language is learnt by listening to native speakers of the language. Imitating American or British accent does not convey a good impression; it is more important to speak with clarity so that others understand what we say. **Intonation** is the sound pattern of sentences; like accent, each language has its intonation and we carry our mother tongue intonation to a new language we learn.

Stress on a particular word in a sentence can change the meaning and implication. Try reading the sentence, *"Were you there last night?"* by stressing a different word each time, and note the difference in the implied meaning.

Besides, there are hesitations and **non-fluencies** which form a part of spoken language. Sounds like *Er-er, Mmmm—*, indicate that the speaker is hesitating or cannot find the next word to say. Sounds like, *Ahem!, huh! Ah-ha! Ouch! Oh-oh!* are used to convey various ideas or emotions.

Silence can be a very effective way of communication. It is not a negative absence of speech but a positive withdrawal or suspension of speech. Silence is a difficult method of communication to use as it takes a good deal of self-control and self-confidence to be able to hold one's tongue.

Short silences or pauses are very effective in giving emphasis to words. A pause before or after certain words makes the words stand out from the rest. A skilfully placed pause has the power to make the listener more alert. In presentations, silence can be used effectively to emphasise a point; it is often far more effective than wild gestures or table-thumping.

In a face-to-face situation, silence may indicate several things. Facial expression and posture may indicate the feeling behind the silence. It may mean that the person is not sure what to say, or is so full of feeling as to be unable to speak. Sympathy with someone who has suffered loss is often best expressed by keeping silent rather than speaking. Some feelings like anger or displeasure can also be expressed by keeping silent. The terms "dead silence", "stony silence", "embarrassing silence," show that silence has a quality that communicates itself.

Silence can be very embarrassing if it is not possible to interpret it. It can be awkward in a group, if no onc knows how to break it. On the telephone, it can cause much discomfort, as one cannot see the other and therefore has no clue from facial expressions as to the reason for the other's silence.

In a dialogue, two persons take turns to speak. If one maintains silence instead of using his turn to speak, it can puzzle the other person. We expect a response from the other person to what we have spoken; if the response does not come, it belies our expectation and we do not know what to do. When faced with such silence, we may repeat what we said; the repetition is not likely to be in the same words and manner as before; it is possible that we may give additional information, soften what we said, try to explain more or make it more acceptable to the other. In a negotiation, silence, and non-response is a useful strategy; it could make the other person speak more.

Body language like eye contact, facial expression and posture can convey something of the silent person's thoughts. A person who can control all facial expression can really puzzle the other.

EXERCISES

1 Fill in the blanks in the following sentences.

(a) ______ and ______ are pictorial representation of statistical data.

(b) ______ and ______ are aspects of body language.

(c) ______ help to review geographical facts and comparisons.

(d) ______ is a good method for communicating to illiterate masses.

2. Are these statements true?

(a) Silence is always embarrassing in a communication situation.

(b) Body language is entirely unconscious and involuntary.

(c) Careful cultivation of one's body language can enhance one's oral communication.

(d) It is not possible to control non-verbal communication.

(e) Non-verbal communication can be completely controlled.

(f) Non-verbal communication may convey meaning that conflicts with the words used.

3. Explain what is meant by body language.
4. Write a detailed note on non-verbal communication.
5. What is the role of body language in making a presentation?
6. How can written presentation be enhanced by non-verbal methods of communication?

□□□

Chapter 5

MEDIA AND MODES

A medium (plural: media or mediums) is the means of transmitting or conveying a message. Some media carry written words and/or pictures/graphics (like the mail) and other media carry the voice (like the telephone). Electronic media can carry both voice and written material.

You can transmit a message by any suitable medium; there are many media to choose from. Each medium has its own characteristics which are advantageous in one situation but disadvantageous in another situation. Besides, each medium makes a different kind of impression and impact on the receiver.

Many messages in an organization have an emotional content, which influences the choice considerably; the emotional content is not carried equally by all media. In order to understand the importance of choosing the medium carefully, consider an occasion when you have to convey a tough message. People do not want to get bad news; employees do not want to hear about changes in practices which they have been following, and certainly do not want to learn that their job is in danger. Such message have high intensity and are very complex. How should you convey such messages? Which medium or a combination of media will be the best? Generally, the best method is to convey the information personally, face-to-face; the advantage of instant feedback and continuous two-way communication allows for a satisfactory closure to the communication. Since it may not be possible to do this with a large number, the next best thing is to choose a medium (or a combination) that is as personal as possible. The first decision is between oral and written and non-verbal.

Within each of these, there are further decisions to be made. Written messages are transmitted by the mail, courier, telegraph, telex, fax, E-mail, notice boards and bulletin boards, newspapers, magazines. Oral messages are carried by air vibrations, the microphone/loud-speaker, the telephone, cellular phone, voice mail and the radio. The cinema and the TV are the most powerful media as they can transmit all types of messages, written, oral, visual and auditory.

Conventional Modes

Media which have been in use for a long time and depend on traditional carriers are called conventional for convenience and to distinguish them from the modern media based on advances in electronics.

Mail

The postal service uses rail, road and air transport, and is usually a government-owned network with links with all other countries. Various types of mail services are available: ordinary mail, registered mail which may include A.D. (acknowledgement due), Quick Mail Service (QMS), Express delivery and Under certificate of posting.

Speed post is a service offered by the Post Office, it ensures delivery of letters and parcels on the same day within the city, within 24 hours to certain cities in the country and within 48 hours to cities in other countries. This service is not available in all cities.

The Post Office now offers electronic media for new services like hybrid mail in some cities.

Courier

Courier services are private; they collect and deliver packets door-to-door at any time during the day. Though the cost is high, this is a very quick service for the delivery of letters and parcels. Courier services are limited to the cities where they maintain their network. Their door-to-door service is a great advantage.

Courier companies are recognized as commercial companies. Courier services are the modern, sophisticated form of the messenger or runner of the old days before the postal service.

Hand delivery

Written messages and documents and parcels can be delivered within the city by an organization's delivery boys. The effectiveness and speed of this method depends on the organization's own system of messengers. It requires a number of employees for outdoor work, and may be expensive; but it ensures prompt delivery and acknowledgement from the receiver. It is most useful when proof of delivery is necessary for the record, as the messenger can bring back a signed copy, or an official receipt or a signature in the sender's peon book.

Telegraph

Telegraph is a government-owned network in most countries; it has links with all other countries. It works by transmitting sounds in the Morse code. Telegrams can be sent 'ordinary' or 'express'. There is also facility for reply-paid telegrams; you can send a telegram and pay for the other party's reply telegram at your telegraph office. This facility is used to impress upon the receiver that immediate reply is expected. The telegraph office registers special telegraphic addresses for companies, on application. This address is only one word; the only addition needed is the pin code number. Organizations which receive and send a large number of telegrams can thus save expenditure for themselves and their correspondents. The telegraphic address can also be used as signature of the organization in telegrams.

A telegram is used for external communication, for contacting customers, suppliers, travelling salesmen, branches, offices, etc. A telegram gives an impression of urgency, and therefore gets immediate response. It is used when there is an urgent message to be conveyed or urgent action is required. This medium's importance has been substantially reduced by fax and mobile phones in large cities, but it has an excellent net-work which reaches even remote parts of the country where the modern media have not yet reached. Hence, it will continue to be used for a long time.

Telex

Telex (short form of Teleprinter Exchange) is a world-wide teletype service providing instantaneous communication through a direct dial teleprinter-to-teleprinter system. Messages can be sent and received 24 hours a day.

The system of direct dial teleprinter exchange was introduced in 1958; within ten years it had more than 25,000 subscribers. It enabled subscribers to send messages and data directly to each other.

Telex connection is got through the Post Office; each subscriber has an Identification code for connection. The teleprinter has a key board for typing messages and a transmitter/receiver for sending and receiving messages. The machine is fitted with a roll of paper, and messages can be typed out continuously. When a message is typed on the sender's machine, the same message gets typed at the same time on the receiver's machine also.

The advantage of this machine is that it automatically types out received messages even if the machine is not attended; the received messages can be read later. When the receiver's machine is attended, the sender and the receiver can carry on a two-way "dialogue" by typing out in turn.

Telex messages are paid for on the basis of the time taken for transmission and the distance; the charge begins as soon as the connection is made. Telex users have developed a language of contractions and abbreviations for saving time.

As telex connects the two communicants in real time, it is not subject to problems like viruses.

It is used mainly by organizations like railways, ports, shipping companies, stock exchanges, banks and financial institutions, embassies, and major corporate houses which need constant international communication. Telex messages are relayed on a screen in newspaper offices, share markets, air ports, railway stations and places where moment-to-moment information has to be conveyed to many people.

Telex has an excellent international network and installation of good machines in good working condition. Recent developments have made it possible to use a computer instead of a teleprinter for transmission of telex. As technologies converge, the use of teleprinters may become outdated.

You can transmit a message by any suitable medium; there are many media to choose from. Each medium has its own features which are advantageous in one situation but disadvantageous in another situation. Besides, each medium makes a different kind of impression and impact on the receiver.

Emergence of Modern Communication Technology

Communication technology has made rapid strides in the past few years. A combination of wireless, telephone and computer technology has given many capabilities to communication tools. An important development is the portability of the cellular telephone and of the laptop computer, so that an individual has the power to contact anyone at any location from any location. The instrument is no longer tied to the transmitting equipment because of developments in wireless technology combined with telephone for the cellular (mobile) telephone. The laptop and other portable computers and the mobile telephone have freed the person from the office and the desk.

Secondly, the mobile telephone has acquired a large number of capabilities besides transmission of voice. It has become capable of storage; data which might be needed at important meetings at a far away location can be carried in compressed form in a mobile telephone, a laptop computer, palmtop computer or pocket computer. This data can be in the form of text, graphics or voice and sounds. The user can also edit the data.

The instrument is also capable of taking instant pictures and storing or transmitting them; these can then be transferred to other equipment like the desk top computer.

It allows access to the internet, thus making some information search possible from any location.

The main effect has been that you need not be at your desk all the time; and time spent in travelling for one task need not take you away from other tasks.

Communication Technology and Business Productivity

Business productivity has increased dramatically with mobile communication tools. The mobile telephone and the mobile PC have freed the business person from the desk and made it possible to work from anywhere, anytime.

With instant messaging, the capabilities of communication have become even more powerful. Regular Instant Messaging users have increased the number of people they contact and the frequency of such contacts, while decreasing the number of e-mail and phone calls they initiated.

Whether you have customers across the country or across the world, a sales force that travels near or far, or employees within the same building or on a sprawling campus, it is possible to share information quickly.

It builds customer and partner relationships. Clients and business partners get instant access to the company contacts they need, right when they need them. They do not have to waste time waiting for the operator or the EPBX system to put them through to the person they need to talk to.

It increases employee productivity since on-the-spot responses means that work gets done faster and more efficiently, right from your desktop.

It increases flexibility and decreases downtime. There is no need to spend time just waiting for information to be located and transmitted by some other person. Direct access to the needed information means ability to take decisions on the spot.

Within the organization, rigid and time consuming procedures of getting information through the organizational channels can be avoided. Using wireless connectivity gives users more flexibility to work from a variety of locations, resulting in productivity gains and efficiency savings.

The time saved by eliminating or expediting specific business tasks adds to efficiency. With instant messaging it is possible to reply to urgent queries, eliminate the need to make copies, eliminate travel in many cases. All this leads to faster decision making.

Productivity gains are measured by the *amount of additional time available that is used to perform business tasks.* Productivity increases when managers and employees can

- Hold one-on-one conferences online and hold "virtual meetings" where others can join in
- Discuss sales deals on-the-spot
- Get immediate answers to urgent questions
- Stay in close touch with employees who are on the road
- Send personal, timely congratulatory notes to boost staff morale
- Get the facts in a fast two-minute exchange — not a lengthy meeting
- Work from any location without having to be idle while travelling between locations
- Locate data all in one place
- Access data from many sources at any time
- Improve time spent with clients

Electronic media transmit signals instantly from any source to any destination in the world by modern electronic technology.

Telephone

This form of electronic communication has been around for nearly a century. It is the most useful and universal medium of oral communication with a person who is not present at the same place as the sender. The telephone instrument has evolved, over the years, into very sophisticated forms with many new facilities.

An answering machine can be attached to the telephone to take a message if you cannot answer it. Conference facility permits three or more persons from different parts of the world to have a discussion by telephone. Cordless telephone frees the handset from the hand-hold and allows the user to take it around within a range of 100 metres from the hand-hold. Caller identity device attached to the telephone can show the number from which the incoming call is being made.

Intercom is an internal telephone system which allows communication between persons in different parts of a building. It eliminates the need for visiting another part of the office and the need for a peon to carry written notes and messages. Information can be passed quickly from one person to another in the office. Most intercom instruments have facility to broadcast messages to the entire office over all the internal lines or a particular location on one line.

STD (Subscriber Trunk Dialling) allows a user to make call to a number in another city directly, without having to call the operator at the telephone exchange. This service is available to almost all cities in the country. Every city has a code number which you dial before dialling the personal telephone number. The code number for Mumbai is 022.

ISD (International Subscriber Dialling) allows the user to call a number to any of the major cities of the world, without calling the operator at the telephone exchange. Every country has an international code number which you dial before dialling the required city code and personal telephone number. The code for India is 091.

STD and ISD facilities can be locked with a number code.

Cellular (Mobile) Phone

The cellular (mobile) phone is based on a combination of the old radio technology and emerging telecommunication technology. Cellular phones have some of the characteristics of the home phones but there are several differences. Cellular phones operate through airways, much like a radio. This means that weather conditions, underground parking or passages, and fortified buildings may affect reception. There are some boundaries to cellular coverage outside metropolitan areas and away from major highways.

Air time is charged by 30-second units. The rates have been falling rapidly with the increase in competition among providers of cellular phone service.

Cellular phone instruments have facilities for storage of numbers, record of missed calls (calls which were not answered), for receiving text messages (SMS), for leaving voice mail, and for receiving information given by the network about the weather, about conditions on the road, and other vital news needed while travelling. Call conferencing allows up to five parties to hold a discussion, "Ask Me" information service, food and flowers ordering, airlines information, restaurant bookings, and so on.

Mobile phones now have the capacity for Multimedia Messaging. It allows you to add pictures, sound, colour, voice, animation, to messages which you send over the mobile phone. You can take a photo, edit it instantly and send it with text or a sound clip. Photos taken by MMS-enabled phone can be sent to other MMS-enabled phones, to e-mail addresses, can be published on the internet, used in a presentation, or just stored in a personal album.

The mobile has freed managers from their offices as they can be in touch with the office from wherever they are. It has become possible to contact persons who are travelling or are out in the open. Marketing persons who visit customers can instantly get in touch with their home office to consult. Most importantly, travelling representatives have instant access to data and information from the home office as well as other information through the internet which can be accessed from the mobile phone.

SMS

SMS (Short Message Service) is sending and receiving text messages to and from mobile telephones. The text may include words or numbers or a combination of both. SMS is also known as text messages, messages, or more colloquially, SMSes, texts or even txts.

Messages are sent by a store-and-forward mechanism to a Short Message Service Centre (SMSC), which sends the message to the recipient; it may retry sending the message if the user is out of reach at a given moment. There is no guarantee that a message will be delivered to its recipient; delay or complete loss of a message can occur, especially when a message has to move from one network to another. Users can opt for delivery reports, which gives positive confirmation that the message has reached the intended recipient.

Message length is bound by the limitations of the signalling protocol to exactly 140 bytes. Longer messages have to be sent segmented as multiple messages; each segment starts with a user data header and segmentation information. The receiving phone has to reassemble the message and present it to the user as one long message. Theoretically, 255 segments can be sent, but in practice, people use only 3 to 4 segment messages. Long messages are billed as equivalent to multiple SMS messages.

Owing to the small keypad and the small screen of the mobile phone, the message length is limited. Hence, people have made a number of adaptations in SMS spelling, and developed new abbreviations such as the use of numbers for words ("4" in place of "for"), the omission of vowels, as in the phrase "txt msg", and the use of capitalization to indicate space, as in "ThisIsVeryCool".

This type of language first developed in Internet chatrooms. It became much more pronounced in SMS, since the mobile phone does not have the QWERTY keyboard and it takes much more effort to type each character on the small, limited keyboard.

There is predictive text software that guesses words (AOL's T9) or letters and can reduce the labour and time of typing. It makes abbreviations less necessary. But it makes the text longer; it may have to be sent in multiple parts and therefore costs more.

Voice Mail

Voice mail is a communication service on a telephone line. The simple answering machine which can be attached to a telephone is a form of voice mail; it allows a caller to leave a name/number and message if you do not answer the phone. The message can be retrieved and answered later, at a more convenient time.

Cellular phone companies offer voice mail service as a part of their network offerings; the service is inexpensive and available 24 hours a day. A voice mail device can be attached to a telephone directly or through a computer. Fax machines have voice mail facility.

Some voice mail services add the date and time to each message so that you know exactly when the call was left.

Voice mail has many advantages. For the organization, it helps to make better use of time; it can help to prevent interruptions in office work.

Sometimes just trying to communicate a simple message can entail a series of phone calls back and forth because the other person was not available when you called. The result is wasted time and lost productivity. Voice mail systems are meant to address this problem. It acts as a corporate answering machine, relaying messages from people both inside and outside the company. It reduces paperwork since messages do not have to be taken down to be passed on.

Callers can leave a detailed message up to three minutes long, even while you're talking on another call. As each message is in the voice of the caller/user it avoids miscommunication and misunderstanding which can occur if the message is conveyed by a telephone operator/attendant. It increases communications capability of the organization.

For individuals, voice mail avoids the constraints of answering a telephone call on the spot. The call can be retrieved and answered at a time convenient to yourself, after you have had the time to think and decide what to say in reply. It allows you to avoid taking a call if necessary, and also relieves you from the anxiety of losing a call. Since you can hear the caller speak, you can pick up the receiver and answer if you want to speak to the person.

You need to develop the skill to use the voice mail. Make a clear statement of purpose after you have identified yourself. The voice mail carries the tonal quality of your voice and your feelings; speak as you would, if the other person was present at the other end of the line. You may feel uncomfortable delivering a monologue, but you have the advantage that you are not interrupted.

Fax

The facsimile machine is a device for transmitting copies of printed images over telephone lines. The machine is connected to the telephone through a modem (modulator-demodulator). The sender has to dial the receiver's fax number, insert the documents into the machine and press the start button. The machine scans the page and makes an electronic representation of the text and graphics, compresses the data to save transmission time and transmits it to the dialled fax machine. The receiving machine decrypts the signals and uses its in-built printer to produce an exact photocopy of the original page. The cost of the print-out is borne by the receiver.

Fax permits quick exchange of information and documents between offices and organizations and individuals. Important decisions and instructions can be quickly conveyed to branches and other offices.

Fax is used only for documents which are not confidential. The machine puts out a printout which is open and can be seen by anyone. However, you can arrange (by telephone talk) to be alone with the machine, when a confidential message is being sent. The printout contains the time and date and the fax number of the sender's machine. The sender gets a confirmation printout showing the receiver's fax number, the date and the time of transmission and the number of pages transmitted.

ometimes the received copy is not clear. It is customary to telephone the receiver to make sure that the fax has been received.

The fax machine can be set to function as a telephone or as a voice mail (answering machine) by pressing relevant buttons. It can also make one or two photo copies of a document.

Fax can be sent through a computer. The latest models of computers have an in-built modem, and software for fax is included as a part of Windows. Fax through a computer can transmit only messages which have been created on the computer; it cannot transmit a document as it is, as the fax machine can. However, a scanner can copy a document, both text and graphics, into the computer, which can then be transmitted by fax.

E-mail

Electronic mail requires a computer, a telephone line and a modem (if a modem is not in-built in the computer). The connection is given by the VSNL, the MTNL and other e-mail and Internet Service Providers (ISP). E-mail is the most frequently used application of the Internet.

The communication is almost instantaneous; besides sending a message you can send whole documents (which are on your computer) as attachments with the message.

It is easy to send e-mail; you can prepare the message on a word processing program, log onto your e-mail, copy-and-paste the message on the "compose" frame; or you can write the message directly on the compose frame after logging on and send it by clicking on the "send" button. The message remains in the receiver's e-mail inbox and can be read (or deleted) at any time.

In order to send an e-mail, you must know the recipient's e-mail address. This has the form: someone@someplace; "someone" could be the person's real name like geeta or it may be a word/letters chosen by the person, like gverma or gmd3 or anything else; "someplace" is the address of the computer and network on which the person has an account, like hotmail.com, yahoo.co.in or vsnl. net. An error in a single letter or number or punctuation or space will prevent your message from being sent. You will receive a notification that the message could not be sent.

An important capability of e-mail is its ability to create ongoing electronic conferences. People all over the world, interested in a particular topic can "meet" to hear new ideas, new papers, and discuss them in a group. E-mail provides "discussion groups" or "lists" for electronic conferences.

An important advantage of e-mail is that it makes information more accessible and permits faster procedures in an organization.

E-mail respects the receiver's time; the message need not be answered at once as with the telephone. Although in speed of transmission e-mail comes close to the telephone, it does not demand instant reply; there is time to think before replying.

Within the organization, e-mail by-passes the chain of command for vertical communication. A subordinate's query or observation may be simultaneously on the computer of the immediate supervisor as well as a higher level manager. Information which would take time moving through the chain of command and may get edited on the way, can go straight to the intended recipient. The e-mail democratises the organization.

Issues of confidentiality and security pose the greatest problem; many organizations restrict access to the e-mail and the internet because of security risks and the possibilities of abuse. It is worth considering what kind of messages should not go by e-mail. You would not expect to get a firing from the boss or to give a firing to your subordinate by e-mail. But congratulatory and other social goodwill messages are actually made easy by e-mail which offers free electronic greeting cards which can be sent.

Efficacy of the e-mail depends on the user's regularity in checking mail; you cannot know how often or at what time the receiver checks the e-mail box. The message could lie there for days if the person does not check the e-mail regularly.

Teleconferencing

Teleconferencing can bring people together without anyone having to spend time and money on travel. There are three types of teleconferencing: (a) audio teleconferencing (b) audio graphics teleconferencing (c) video teleconferencing.

Audio teleconferencing is conference by telephone; it is the most frequently used, most productive and inexpensive medium. It is also called "phone meeting"; it does not need any special equipment other than the ordinary telephone.

The main factors for its wide spread acceptance are:

- easy to use—everyone can use a telephone
- easily available—telephones are available anywhere
- easy to participate from any telephone line in the world
- takes only a few minutes to set up a conference call
- costs little

Audio Graphics Teleconferencing provides the facility to move text, computer-generated images, photographs and large files over ordinary telephone lines (like the Internet). It is not as expensive as video conferencing but still requires going to the location that has the equipment or investing in the equipment.

Video Teleconferencing allows people at different locations to see and hear each other at the same time; it is fully interactive and almost like a face-to-face meeting. Depending on the level of technology used, it may connect two locations interactively or it may be Broadcast video with the broadcasting site transmitting its image to many sites that may be able to communicate back through standard telephone lines. With more complex systems and equipment it is possible to have more than two locations connected together so that they can all see and hear one another, very much like an actual meeting.

The cost of the equipment is high; only a few companies with international operations have their own video-conferencing facilities. The facilities are also available with MTNL and other service providers on rent.

Videoconferencing is made possible through merging a variety of complex modern technologies. The equipment is becoming less expensive and more user-friendly as more manufacturers compete in the market.

The benefits of video teleconferencing are remarkable. First of all, it is almost like communicating face-to-face. The interaction allows people at distant locations to understand one another better. It makes discussion more meaningful. It helps people feel connected and goes a long way in building relationships in a way that telephone and e-mail cannot do. It improves appeal and retention by including diverse media like video and audio clips, graphics, animation, and computer applications, for demonstration and explanation. It saves the time and cost of travelling to meet, and allows people to keep in touch more frequently. It enriches communication in several ways.

Use of Websites in Business

Internet is the most recent, the most powerful of all media. It has a growing audience, and most people use it for finding information. Even small firms now have a web site whose address is indicated on their letterhead, in their brochures, advertisements and other publicity literature.

A website can be used for publishing all information about the company; it addresses a multiple audience by giving a different page for each category of information.

It is used for publishing the company's catalogue with images and description of the products. Companies that have provision for buying online, give information about how to order on line. Others give information about retail outlets and whom to contact. More advanced websites include provision for existing and new customers to contact them for more information and for queries. Companies that have full-fledged online sales also provide for making payment by credit card online; however, concerns about security make many buyers prefer to pay without using the website.

Information about the companies history, owners, staff, and so on is provided on other pages of the web site. The web site can be used as a medium for maintaining Public Relations; information about the social and environmental concern and work of the company, is also publicised with pictures and descriptions.

It is worth visiting web sites of Amul Dairy (www.Amul.com), Godrej (www.godrej.com) Indian Railways (www.irctc.co.in) to see how the web site has been used for various purposes.

Choice of Medium

Communication media available to business people have mushroomed in the past few years. You can select from the traditional oral and written channels and from the new electronic media which have some of the characteristics of the older media. People who need to communicate will have to keep up with the technology of communication which is developing rapidly to bring communicating parties closer to each other. Some older channels and media may become outdated as new methods become available. Your selection of the medium can make the difference between effective and ineffective communication. You have to do your best to match your selection to your message and your intentions.

Every medium has limitations which filter out parts of the message. Every medium influences the receiver's perception of the sender's intentions. Different cultures favour one medium over another. In short it is said that the medium is a comment on the message.

You need to consider several aspects in choosing a medium for a particular message. The main aspects are:

(a) The type of audience you want to reach.

(b) The speed with which the message should be conveyed: The pressure of time and the distance between the sender and the receiver influence the choice of the medium. Some media are faster and can travel distances rapidly, like the telephone, the fax and the e-mail; these media also have the advantage of being person to person.

(c) Need for confidentiality of the message is an important consideration. The choice will certainly be influenced by requirement of secrecy; all media do not ensure the same secrecy of the message. Messages like warning memo, report on a customer's credit standing, demand for overdue payment, and so on, are confidential. They cannot be sent by media like telegram or telex or fax even if they are urgent.

(d) Need for accuracy in transmission is not the same for all messages. If the content to be transmitted is mainly data, you make the choice for accuracy and speed in transmitting.

(e) Need for reliability of the medium is an important factor. Sending a message by hand delivery is more reliable than ordinary mail; registered post is more reliable than ordinary mail.

(f) Cost of the medium and its relative importance and urgency.

(g) Availability of a particular medium to the sender and to the receiver is obviously an affecting factor. You can use only those media which both you and the intended receiver can access. You may have a fax machine but if the receiver does not have one and has no arrangements for receiving a fax message, you cannot use that medium.

(h) Feedback capacity of the medium: For some messages, you need immediate feedback; you have to use a medium which will enable you to get it at once, like the telephone.

(i) Availability of hard copy for record.

(j) Formality of the medium must be suitable to content of the message. A letter of congratulation is more formal and has a different effect from conveying the same message orally.

(k) Intensity and complexity of the message is a major factor.

Many messages in an organization have an emotional content, which influences the choice considerably; the emotional content is not carried equally by all media. In order to understand the importance of choosing the medium carefully, consider an occasion when you have to convey a tough message. People do not want to get bad news; employees do not want to hear about changes in practices which they have been following, and certainly do not want to learn that their job is in danger. Such message have high intensity and are very complex. How should you convey such messages? Which medium or a combination of media will be the best? Generally, the best method is to convey the information personally, face-to-face; the advantage of instant feedback and continuous two-way communication allows for a satisfactory closure to the communication. Since it may not be possible to do this with a large number, the next best thing is to choose a medium (or a combination) that is as personal as possible.

MEDIA OF MASS COMMUNICATION

Mass communication is communication from many to many. The messages are prepared by teams (as in newspaper, radio, TV, cinema) and reach a large number of people all over the world. The distance between the sender and the audience is very great.

Notice board

Notice board and bulletin board are media for public communication within the organization. A notice board is placed at a location where it can be seen by the persons for whom it is meant.

Notice boards need care and attention. They must be attractively laid out; overlapping notices and crowding of too many notices gives the notice board a poor appearance and makes it difficult to read. An up-to-date notice board, which is neatly laid out and does not carry stale notices, looks attractive and gets attention. Notices typed in double spaced lines, in large font, with wide margins are easy to read.

Hoardings and bill boards

These are meant for mass communication like advertisements. They are used for posters conveying simple ideas. They usually have a short message in large letters and also include pictures. Location of the boards is important; they are usually placed high up and can be seen from a distance.

Newspapers and magazines

These media of mass communication are used by business houses for inviting tenders, for recruitment information and other public notices and advertisements.

Radio

The radio is a medium of mass oral communication. News, notices, advertisements are transmitted to the public by radio. Like other mass media it allows only one way communication. The transistor set has made it possible for radio to reach all parts of the country and all sections of the population.

Film

The film is the most powerful medium of communication. It is the audio-visual medium which combines all possible forms: written, oral, visual and auditory. A film can be shown in a cinema theatre or projected on a small screen in a room with a film projector, or projected on the TV screen through a video player or transmitted by television. It can now be viewed on the computer monitor through the internet.

The film is a highly versatile medium and can be used for many purposes, and adapted to different conditions.

Television

Television is a powerful medium, which, like the film, is audio-visual. Its ability to transmit live events as they are going on makes it the most powerful medium for mass communication. With teleconferencing, the television can transmit things happening at more than one place at once. A news reader in Mumbai can take the audience to a view of what is happening in Los Angeles or hold a live discussion with a reporter in Paris.

Internet

This is the most recent, the most powerful of all media. It has a growing audience, and most people use it for finding information. Even small firm now have web sites which are indicated on their letterhead, in their brochures, advertisements and other publicity literature.

Communication media available to business people have mushroomed in the past few years. You can select from the traditional oral and written channels and from the new electronic media which have some of the characteristics of the older media. People who need to communicate will have to keep up with the technology of communication which is developing rapidly to bring communicating parties closer to each other. Some older channels and media may become outdated as new methods become available. Your selection of the medium can make the difference between effective and ineffective communication. You have to do your best to match your selection to your message and your intentions.

Every medium has limitations which filter out parts of the message. Every medium influences the receiver's perception of the sender's intentions. Different cultures favour one medium over another. In short it is said that the medium is a comment on the message.

EXERCISES

1. Write a note on the advantages and disadvantages of the conventional media of transmission.
2. Discuss the advantages and limitations of e-mail.
3. What factors will you take into account in making a choice of a medium?
4. Name the factors that influence choice of a medium for transmission.
5. Name the media of mass communication.

6. Are the following true of false?
   (a) Telegram allows two-way communication.
   (b) Telex allows real time two-way dialogue.
   (c) Hand delivery is the cheapest method of sending written messages.
   (d) You can transfer files by e-mail.
   (e) A fax machine can transmit a document as it is.
7. Briefly explain the difference between:
   (a) E-mail and fax
   (b) Courier and hand delivery
   (c) Speed post and courier
   (d) Cordless telephone and cellular phone.
8. Explain briefly:
   (a) Telegraphic address
   (b) E-mail address
9. Find out the telephone code numbers
   (a) for New Delhi
   (b) for all the capitals of the States in India
   (c) for the major cities in Maharashtra
   (d) write your own telephone (or your college telephone) number as you would give it to a friend in the USA.
10. Find out
    (a) the rates of the different mail services available at your nearest post office.
    (b) the telephone numbers of two couriers nearest to your house or college.
11. Discuss the advantages and limitations of e-mail.
12. What factors will you take into account in making a choice of a medium?
13. Name the factors that influence choice of a medium for transmission.
14. Are the following true of false?
    (a) Telex allows real time two way dialogue.
    (b) Hand delivery is the cheapest method of sending written messages.
    (c) You can transfer files by e-mail.
    (d) A fax machine can transmit a document as it is.
15. Briefly explain the difference between:
    (a) E-mail and fax
    (b) Cordless telephone and cellular phone
16. Find out the telephone code numbers
    (a) for New Delhi
    (b) for all the capitals of the States in India
    (c) for the major cities in Maharashtra
    (d) write your own telephone (or your college telephone) number as you would give it to a friend in the USA.

❑❑❑

Chapter 6

CHANNELS OF COMMUNICATION

Communication networks have taken on a new pattern because of recent advances in information technology. In some organizations, employees are allowed to work from any place and at any time. As a result, task groups may be scattered and may be working at different times. Communication with and between persons who are not located in the office is carried out by electronic media.

Computer-mediated communication is replacing many of the traditional forms of internal communication in many organizations; memos, queries, instructions, exchange of ideas and even discussions may be on electronic media instead of by movement of papers or holding meetings. Information can be made available to all simultaneously, clarifications may be sought at once and employees may discuss their work or other things via the intranet.

Computer-mediated communication is quick and tends to be informal, without the need for traditional polite forms of address. The formal hierarchical structure for achieving co-ordination and managing relationships within an organization is likely to be replaced by the more informal and faster exchange of messages. Information, which used to be limited and controlled and was a source of power, is now freely available to the entire organization. These changes in communication flow channels result in changes in organizational structures.

Nevertheless, most organizations still have the traditional channels of communication flow. Channel of communication refers to the way along which a message flows from the sender to the recipient. An organization has well-ordered network of channels along which communication flows. Formal communications move along the established channels.

The direction of the flow of communication is described in terms of the formal power and authority relationships among the members of the organization. Communication from superior to subordinate is called downward; communication from subordinate to superior is called upward; and communication between persons at the same level is called horizontal or lateral communication. In addition to the formal channels of communication, an organization develops informal channels which satisfy various human needs of the members of the organization.

An organization has internal and external communication. Communication with those outside the organization is external; communication within the organization, among its members is internal;

EXTERNAL COMMUNICATION

Messages that go out of the organization are outward communication; messages that are received from outside are inward communication. Organizations have office procedures and systems for handling external communication; both, the incoming and the outgoing messages are recorded and filed.

Outward

Messages go out of an organization to customers, suppliers, banks, insurance companies, government departments, the mass media and the general public. They may be in the form of letters, faxes, telephone calls, telegrams, reports, advertisements, press handouts, speeches, visits and so on. The style, format and tone of the company's outgoing communication affect its public image and public relations. Therefore, most organizations have a policy about the style and appearance of the company's messages that go out.

Copies of outgoing written documents are filed for reference. A written note or summary of oral communications is also filed by many companies.

Inward

An organization receives letters, telegrams, fax messages, telex messages, reports, brochures, circulars, journals and magazines, telephone calls, and personal visits. These may be from customers, suppliers, other organizations, government departments and so on. These inward communication messages are filed for record and reference. A written note or summary of visits, meetings, telephone talks may also be filed.

INTERNAL COMMUNICATION

There is a large volume of communication within the organization. The flow of communication within an organization forms a complicated pattern. The volume and the direction are usually determined by the pattern of hierarchy, the levels of authority and also by the requirements of tasks.

Formal Channels

Formal channels are those which carry the official messages in the organization. The efficiency of an organization depends on a regular flow of messages. The flow of messages needs to be organized into a well-ordered network, to ensure that communication flows easily and reaches the persons who need the information. If communication by passes the channels, someone who needs the information may not get it; the managers may not get information about what is going on in other parts of the organization. This can lead to gaps in information, and failure to take the required action. If the channels are not well organized there can be a communication gap which causes confusion and failure to take action.

Information has to go through proper channels. Clerks from one department are not supposed to exchange official papers directly with clerks from another department; the papers move must through the supervisors or section heads. A clerk can approach the manager only through his own supervisor or officer. Messages are made to move through fixed channels so that the executives concerned are kept informed of what is going on.

Messages within an organization, between managers, supervisors and workers, are varied and numerous. They move up and down the chain of authority as well as sideways between persons at the same level of authority, and among teams. Messages that move up and down the authority line are called vertical communication and those which move among persons of the same level are called horizontal or lateral communication.

Vertical Communication

This includes all the messages that move between subordinates and their supervisors. Messages going from superiors to subordinates are downward communication; messages going from subordinates to superiors are upward communication.

Downward

Messages going from the higher authority levels to the lower levels may be written or oral. Written messages are notes, circulars, notices, e-mails; oral messages may be face-to-face, or by telecom or telephone, or announcements over the public address system.

The common purposes of downward communication are to give:

(i) instructions about a specific task;

(ii) information about the practices and procedures followed by the organization;

(iii) information which creates understanding of the task in relation to other tasks of the organization;

(iv) feedback about subordinates' performance;

(v) information about the ideology and the goals of the organization which would help them to develop a sense of belonging to the organization.

Earlier, when business companies were authoritarian, employees were only told about their task, and how to do it. Now, many organizations realize the importance of giving employees a general understanding of their task's relevance to the organization's work; employees are also given feedback about how they are doing. Such communication makes them feel a sense of identification with the organization's goals.

Downward communication must be simple and carefully explained; persons at the lower levels of the hierarchy may not have sufficient knowledge or understanding of the organization's work; hence they need explanation. Long circulars, written in an official and legal style are not easy to follow. Instruction sheets and employee manuals should be written in a simple style.

A great deal of information is lost as messages move downward. When a message is passed from a senior to a subordinate down the line of command in a chain, it passes through many levels of authority. There is delay in the movement of the message. Also, the message gets changed and modified and there is distortion of the message. Each person along the line edits it, filters it, and simplifies it for the understanding and needs of the next person who is to receive it. If the chain of communication is very long, there may be much change and distortion in the message.

Information is also lost because sometimes, some members of the organization may misinterpret a message, or may not understand it properly, or may neglect it. Even when there is very active downward flow of communication, information that is passed down may not be is accurate; it may not be received and understood and accepted by subordinates.

Many organizations avoid long channels to ensure that information moves directly and fast. In a rapidly changing work environment, communication must move fast to keep up the efficiency of the organization. Passing messages down the line in a chain causes the greatest loss of information. It is more effective to communicate downward in a cluster as in a meeting; everyone receives it at the same time, in the same environment. The recipients of the information may be of different levels of hierarchy. This method gives opportunity to everyone to seek clarification; loss of information is avoided. Organizations that have linked and networked computers (LAN and WAN) are able to send messages at once to all concerned persons; the flow of information is more easy and efficient.

Upward

Messages which go from subordinates to supervisors and to higher levels of authority are upward communication. These may be written or oral. Written messages are in the form of reports, letters, representations, notes and e-mail messages. Oral messages may be face-to-face or by intercom or telephone.

The common purposes of upward communication are:

(i) to give information to the management;

(ii) to enable the management to learn about and understand the concerns of the subordinates;

(iii) to enable all employees to contribute ideas and make suggestions;

Communication does not move upward easily. Subordinates may be too shy or afraid to communicate their ideas to higher authorities. Superiors may be too impatient to listen to their subordinates. The resulting gap in communication can be harmful to the organization.

When messages pass upward through official channels, some information is lost. At every level there is some editing and filtering. There may also be a deliberate suppression of information because of self-interest and jealousy; a supervisor may not pass upward, a good suggestion from a subordinate, or he may change it so as to get the credit for himself; a senior officer may prevent information about discontent in the department from reaching the manager because it reflects on his/her human relations skills. As a result there is an information gap; this can be harmful because the upper level of management may not find out the true state of affairs until it is too late. Therefore, cutting across the official chains of communication is sometimes necessary for the sake of speed and efficiency.

Open and free upward communication also helps to maintain good staff relations. Employees work better when the managers listen to their ideas. Persons at any level in an organization may have good ideas and suggestions for the improvement of the organization; these ideas are encouraged when the organization has good upward communication channels.

Organizations set up special formal and informal channels to encourage and ensure upward movement of communication. Most organizations have these channels:

(a) Regular reporting systems exist in all organizations. There are forms for periodical reports and progress reports of different activities in the organization. These reports convey factual information to the management.

(b) Periodical review meetings are held with individuals and groups of employees; these meetings are conducted in an informal style. They provide an opportunity for employees to express their opinion about work, problems, solutions, ideas, budget allocations, etc. They give an opportunity to subordinates to talk to the superiors.

(c) Suggestion scheme is a formal and well-organized system for making ideas move up from the lower level employees to the management and decision makers. A suggestion scheme requires elaborate set-up, committee meetings, a well-planned award system, and a good deal of time and energy. The employees feel happy when their ideas are respected and valued. The company also benefits from the ideas of people who are actually on the job.

(d) "Open door" policy provides an informal upward channel. It gives every employee an access to higher authority. Managers allow free access to any member of the staff without prior appointment, during a fixed hour everyday, or on a fixed day of the week. Thus, any employee can approach the manager directly. This system prevents distortion by avoiding the chain of authority. Feelings and attitudes of staff are conveyed to the managers this way.

(e) Informal gatherings, picnics or weekly tea meetings bring together all members of the organization. Some organizations call it the "Happy Hour". This is an opportunity for socializing and getting to know one another more closely. Such occasions encourage employees to overcome their shyness and talk freely about their work and their ideas and their life. Closer relationships are built up and there is better interaction among all levels.

(f) Standing Committees (like grievance committee, welfare committee, counselling committee) provide a channel for problems, unhappy feelings, troubles, complaints and grievances to be made known to the upper level of the organization where they can be given serious attention.

Upward communication provides two main types of information: one is feedback about the official work which is necessary for the working of the organization; the other is personal information about staff's performance, views, ideas, feelings, which is vital for employee relations and morale.

Horizontal or Lateral Channel

Messages that flow between persons of equal status or same level of authority in the organization is horizontal or lateral communication. A large amount of communication flows laterally in an organization. Horizontal communication can be oral or written. Written communication may be in the form of letters, memoranda, notes, reports, and copies of documents. Oral communication may be in the form of face-to-face talk, intercom, meetings, committee work or conferences.

There is more horizontal communication at higher levels of authority. The clerks in one department may have no dircct contact with the clerks in another department, but section heads and managers have closer contacts. The higher level managers have to be in constant consultation and communication with one another. Horizontal communication is more interactive than vertical communication.

Horizontal communication is needed for several purposes in an organization. It includes both information and persuasion. Besides exchange of information and suggestions, lateral communication is required for persuasive purposes like discussing plans, solving problems, resolving conflicts, negotiating, and co-ordination of work. It serves an important function of providing emotional and social support to one another.

Conference is a form of organized horizontal communication. At a conference, common problems are discussed, and the ideas, information, knowledge and experience of several persons are pooled for common benefit. It serves as a training tool among persons of equal status.

Consensus

Consensus is a method of decision making that reflects the ideas and thought of all the team members. Reaching consensus ensures that decisions are explored thoroughly and strong disagreements resolved. It is used by task forces, teams, departments, work groups and so on.

Consensus is a decision that is acceptable to everyone. It is **not** unanimity; (the conclusion may not be everyone's first choice) nor is it a majority vote.

Decision making by consensus involves discussion and accountability of view points rather than power struggles. The idea behind consensus is to empower not to overpower. Everyone must act as a member of the group.

It requires:

- Time
- Communication skills especially listening, probing and conflict management
- Considering disagreements and conflicts as part of the process
- Keeping an open mind and thinking creatively

At the end, everyone must be able to support the decision even if they do not feel it was the best one. Underlying the consensus decision there must be some shared values which are:

- Unity of purpose – the decisions are made in the best interests of the group or organization
- Co-operation – the participants look for a solution that best meets everyone's needs
- Mutual trust – all believe that others will be fair with them, respect them and care about their feelings
- Common ownership of ideas – personal attachment to an idea hinders the process
- Feelings are valued
- Conflict is valued
- Equal power — everyone has equal power and no one is made to feel "conquered " (not respected as a person) or compromised (values not respected)
- Time and process – the process is respected and given the time it needs
- Willingness to learn skills – skills of communication, meeting participation, etc., are learnt willingly by everyone.

GROUP NETWORKS

Most organizations have small task groups and teams working together. Certain patterns of communication network evolve among the members of work groups based on the power structure and relationships among them.

The **chain** pattern allows only vertical movement of communication and is strictly hierarchical. Messages are passed up and down the chain of authority. There can be loss of information at every level of authority because each person edits the content according to his/her own understanding of what is needed by the person at the next level. The content may be simplified or edited in other ways. This pattern is useful for tasks that have to be performed within given time and without any deviation.

In the **wheel** pattern the person at the centre or hub of the wheel co-ordinates all the communication; persons around the wheel do not interact with one another. All messages have to be addressed to the central person by each member; the central person then passes the required messages to the others. It represents a two-level hierarchy.

The **circle** pattern allows each member of the group to interact with those on either side, but not to the others. In a group of five persons, it may have three levels of hierarchy in which there is interaction between supervisors and subordinates and lateral interaction at the lowest level. In a larger group, this pattern limits the flow of information.

The **all-channel** system allows everyone to communicate with every-one else. It is the least structured group, and tasks can be delayed because of too much unstructured communication.

The wheel pattern has been found to be the most efficient in arriving at good solutions. The other patterns can become efficient if they develop a hierarchy, though this takes time. Whether the communication is vertical or horizontal, hierarchical patterns develop among the group.

INFORMAL CHANNELS

In addition to the imposed organizational arrangement, members of groups that work together construct their own communication networks. These informal networks have two basic purposes.

(a) They compensate for inadequacies in the formal network by establishing new links which bypass obstacles that come up in the formal structure. In many groups there is someone who can expedite the matter at hand; often, the expeditor is not the person holding official responsibility. By locating the right person (who may be anyone in the organization), the informal network can be used to serve organizational goals.

(b) They serve the needs of the individuals involved; these needs may or may not be the same as the goals of the organization. These informal networks link persons with similar interests and experiences and those who simply like one other.

Informal networks serve a valuable organizational function: they protect the individual from becoming isolated from professional colleagues by stimulating him/ her to more creative thinking and by supplying a psychological support group. Quite often, an informal work relationship completely obscures the formal organizational structure.

Informal networks are sure to arise in any organization. In examining the advantages or problems of an organizational unit, informal communication networks must be considered as carefully as formal communication networks.

Grapevine

Grapevine is an informal channel of personal, unofficial communication which exists in every organization in addition to the formal organized channels. It has no definite pattern or direction though it is largely horizontal. It is a complex web of oral communication flow, linking all the members of the organization one way or other. It may sometimes move along in a chain, passing information from person to person; and sometimes in clusters, that is, groups, at meal-times or other free time.

There may be more than one grapevine channel in an organization, and individuals may be on more than one grapevine. People whose places of work are close together, people who come into contact with one another in official work, people who travel to work together, or people with similar temperaments are likely to be on the same grapevine.

It is not related to organizational goals; it does not arise because of the need to expedite one's work or to by-pass the slow official channel.

This informal channel carries unofficial information about the management's policies and plans, individual managers, work programs, the company's performance, and such matters related to the company. Naturally, the talk is coloured by the ideas, prejudices and feelings of the persons engaged in it. The grapevine can become quite powerful and influential though the stories and information are not fully correct. It often carries more information than the formal official communication channels. It moves much faster because it is not hindered by the delays of the official channel.

Grapevine can affect an organization's working by its influence on the opinions, beliefs and attitudes of its members. Attitudes have a direct effect on people's willingness to work. The nature of the talk among the employees affects their attitudes and efficiency. Excited talking and bad tempers lead to poor performance; so does excessive fun. What employees hear and say affects their relationship with the management, and this has a direct effect on productivity. Hence, grapevine cannot be ignored.

The presence of the grapevine is recognized and accepted as a part of an organization. Since it can influence the efficiency of the organization it needs to be skilfully controlled. Efficient managers learn to listen to the grapevine and can find out who are the talk-leaders; they can give the leaders desirable information so that good information spreads.

There is a close relationship between the grapevine and the morale of employees; when the morale is high and employees are well-motivated, the grapevine is usually thin and slow; when the morale drops, grapevine becomes thick and fast. Bad news and unpleasant stories cause excitement; they travel faster and are discussed more extensively than good news. A manager has to keep eyes and ears open; managers encourage upward communication to find out what the employees talk about and how they feel.

Grapevine cannot be destroyed. The management has to watch it. If a harmful half-truth begins to travel around, the management has to take quick action to convey correct information. This can be done in many ways: by giving the information to talk-leaders, by mentioning it at briefing and routine meetings, by putting up notices on notice boards, and by distributing bulletins and circulars. If the matter is serious, a meeting may be called.

Sometimes, a bit of information may be planted in the grapevine in order to test the possible reaction to a proposed decision or plan. Grapevine can be used constructively because of its speed in moving.

EXERCISES

1. Fill in the blanks using as few words as possible:
   (a) Downward communication moves from ____ to ____.
   (b) Horizontal communication moves among ____.
   (c) Freely moving informal communication in an organization is called ____.
   (d) ____ means arriving at a general agreement of opinion.
2. Mention five methods by which communication can be kept moving upward in an organization.
3. Are these statements true?
   (a) Communication does not move upward easily.
   (b) Grapevine can be used productively by the management.
   (c) There is no loss of information in downward communication.
   (d) There are no barriers to horizontal communication.
4. What is downward communication? What causes loss of information as communication moves downward?
5. What is meant by upward communication? How can upward communication in an organization be improved?
6. Write a note on the informal channels of communication in an organization.
7. What is 'grapevine'? How can management use it to influence the morale of the employees?
8. Write notes on the following:
   (i) Internal Vertical communication
   (ii) Horizontal or Lateral communication
   (iii) Consensus
   (iv) Grapevine
   (v) Upward communication
   (vi) Downward communication
   (vii) Communication networks
9. Write a note on formal communication channels in an organization.

□□□

Chapter 7

BARRIERS TO COMMUNICATION

Communication is not always successful. Several things can prevent the message from reaching the intended recipient or from having the desired effect on the recipient. As noted in chapter 1, there are problem areas at every stage in the process of communication. The circular figure in chapter 1, showing the stages in the process of communication, shows the possible gaps in the process which can lead to a failure of communication between two persons.

Besides these pitfalls, there are other things that can hinder or distort communication.

There may be some fault in the communication system which prevent the message from reaching. Some of these defects are in the mechanical devices used for transmitting, that is, the medium. Some are in the symbols we use for communicating, that is, language or other symbols used for encoding. Some are in the nature of the persons who are engaged in communication, that is, the sender and the receiver. In an organisation, these barriers can become quite complicated and can cause information gaps leading to problems in its working.

Barriers can be divided into broad groups: Physical barriers, Semantic and Language barriers, Socio-psychological barriers and Organisational barriers. Besides, there are Cross-cultural barriers which distort communication between persons or groups belonging to a different cultural background.

PHYSICAL BARRIERS

Obstacles that prevent a message from reaching the intended recipient may be outside and beyond the control of the persons concerned. Some can be controlled by the management; some cannot be controlled because they are in the environment.

Defects in the Medium

Defects in the devices used for transmitting messages are external and usually not within the control of the parties engaged in communication. The telephone, the postal system, the courier service, or electronic media may fail. Messages can get delayed, distorted and even lost while being transmitted.

A partial failure of the mechanical equipment is more harmful than a total failure because a partial failure may carry an incomplete or distorted message. A fax message can be wrongly delivered as a wrong number can get dialled on the telephone. The printout may not be clear at all. It is advisable to call up and check that the fax has been received.

If a medium like the telephone is out of order, the communication may have to be postponed or sent by an alternative medium.

Noise in the Environment

Noise is any disturbance which occurs in the transmission process. In face-to-face communication which is carried by air vibration, the air may be disturbed by noise such as traffic, factory work, or people talking. In a factory, oral communication is very difficult because of the noise of the machines.

Organisations that can afford sound-proof rooms can overcome this barrier to some extent.

Information Overload

When there is too much information, some of it is blocked in transit and may not reach the intended audience. Advertising and sales information is an example of overload; so much communication about products floats through so many media that a good deal of it does not reach the potential buyer.

SEMANTIC AND LANGUAGE BARRIERS

Semantic means pertaining to or arising from the different meanings of words or other symbols.

Language is our most important and powerful tool of communication; and yet it is a tricky tool that needs skill in handling. First of all, many words have multiple meanings. Just look into a good dictionary and see how many meanings you can find for some commonly used words like "charge", "spring", "check", "suit", "ring". The meaning that comes to your mind first depends on your occupation ("charge" may mean electrical charge to an engineering student, but fee/rent to a commerce student).

Words like "minute" and "wind" are pronounced in two different ways to mean two entirely different things. Some words like "present", "transfer", "record" are used as verb and as noun with a difference in stress in speaking, but no difference in spelling. A person may be **present** at a function and receive a **present** (stress on **pre-**), and **present** (stress on **–sent**) some thoughts on the budget.

Similar sounding words like "access" and "excess", "flour" and "flower", "cite", "site" and "sight" can cause misunderstanding in speech. Many people confuse "week" and "weak," "steal" and "steel" in writing.

Adjectives and adverbs like "fast", "far", "few", "early", "easy", convey different meanings to different persons depending on their daily activities and way of life. The meaning of descriptive adjectives like "beautiful" and "ugly" depends entirely on personal taste.

Even a concrete noun like "table" may suggest a writing table or a dining table or a statistical table to different persons; similarly, "chair" could be something to sit on, or a position to occupy. How many ideas does the word "home" convey?

Emotional and cultural attitudes towards something can evoke different responses in people; for example, "dog" will evoke responses according to a person's past experience with the animal as well as cultural attitudes towards the animal.

Phrases can be more tricky; 'a red and a blue carpet' signifies two carpets: one red and one blue. 'A red and blue carpet' is one carpet in two colours.

Sentences can convey entirely different meanings depending on how they are spoken. Consider the sentence, *"What can I do for you?"* It means something different with every shift of emphasis from one word to another. In oral communication, the speaker can signify the meaning by emphasising particular words; but in written communication, the reader is in control and may read with different emphasis.

Technical terms can be a barrier to communication. Such terms are limited to the group of persons who work together, or work in the same kind of occupation; they need to use technical terms in their work. Often, these words have other meanings in ordinary language, and are differently understood by people who do not belong to that occupational group. Consider the new meanings given to ordinary words by computer technology; to people who are not familiar with computers, "mouse" is only an animal.

New words are being coined almost everyday; everyone does not understand them and many of them are not in the dictionaries yet.

More importantly, semantic barriers arise because words mean different things to different persons. It is said, "meaning is in people, not in words." Age, education, cultural background and many other factors influence the meaning we give to words.

SOCIO-PSYCHOLOGICAL BARRIERS

All persons are not skilled communicators. Skill in communicating has to be cultivated. Most people have problems which come in the way of good communication. In order to be a skilful communicator you have to watch yourself constantly and make an effort to overcome your deficiencies or problems in communicating. It is useful to understand how barriers develop in persons, and what problems prevent communication from being successful.

People have personal feelings, desires, fears and hopes, likes and dislikes, attitudes, views and opinions. Some of these are formed by family background and social environment; some are formed by the individual's own intelligence, inherited qualities, education, and personal experiences. They form a sort of emotional filter around the mind, and influence the way we respond to messages that we receive and to new experiences. Factors like the time, the place and the circumstances of a particular communication also influence our understanding and response.

Problems of understanding, interpretation and response to communication arise partly from our socially-learnt attributes and partly from our personal attributes. These are called socio-psychological barriers.

In order to understand these barriers, you must know how we deal with a received message. We receive a message at three levels:

(i) Noticing is at the physical level. We notice the message with our senses; when we become aware that a message is addressed to us, we focus attention on it. It is quite possible that our eyes or ears miss it on account of other competing messages which claim our attention. Sometimes we may not notice a message addressed to us.

(ii) Understanding is at the level of intelligence. We must be able to understand the language or any other symbols used in the message. Also, the ideas and concepts in the message must be within our understanding and knowledge.

(iii) Acceptance is at the emotional level. There is usually an emotional response of pleasure or dislike or indifference to every message that we receive. If the message arouses an unpleasant feeling, we may reject it, resent it or forget it. Emotional blocks may even make us fail to understand the message correctly.

Most of the socio-psychological barriers discussed below operate at the emotional level.

Self-centred Attitudes

We tend to see and hear everything in the light of our own interests and needs and desires. We pay attention to messages which are useful to us, and often do not pay enough attention to those messages which do not interest us. Self-interest may prevent us from seeing the point of view of others. If we look at everything from the point of view of our own interests and desires, we miss some useful information and develop narrow ideas. A person who is highly self-centred also fails to build up good relationships with other people. In order to win the goodwill of others with whom we work, we must be able to understand how other people feel and think.

Group Identification

Our values and opinions are influenced, in some matters, by the group to which we belong. All persons have a sense of belonging to a group, like family, the larger family of relatives, people of our locality or city, our religion or language group, age group, nationality, economic group and so on. Many of our ideas, attitudes and values are picked up from the group. We tend to reject an idea which goes against the interests of the group. Sometimes it is difficult for parents and children to agree because of the different age group ideas; there are disagreements between women and men because of different gender values and attitudes; employees and the management cannot come to an agreement because the interests are different. It is difficult for persons of one group to understand how persons of another group think and feel. This becomes a barrier to communication.

Self-Image

We have a certain idea of our self; some persons even take care to project an image of themselves. Self-image is our idea about what we are, what we look like and what impression we make. It is usually based on some truth and some exaggeration of our good points.

A self-image is built up over the years, and it is quite difficult to accept any idea which goes against it. This makes it particularly difficult for us to give and take feedback. If you make a good self-assessment, it will be easier for you to endure the stress of an assessment by others. A systematic self-assessment gives you a balanced self-image.

Selective Perception

Sometimes, we fail to get the complete message which is sent to us. We see, read or hear selectively according to our own needs, interests and experience. We project our expectations into the communication as we interpret the message. We may not perceive some of the aspects and information content of the message.

Defensiveness

If we feel threatened by a message, we become defensive and respond in such ways that reduce understanding. We may question the motives of others or become sarcastic or judgemental. Such defensive behaviour prevents understanding. This is a particularly harmful barrier in handling complaints and grievances and in resolving conflicts.

Filtering

Filtering is the process of reducing the details or aspects of a message. Each person who passes on a message reduces or colours a message according to his/her understanding of the situation. In the role of sender, we tend to edit information so that it will appear favourable to ourself; some information is changed and lost in this way. Information which has to be sent up the levels of hierarchy has to be condensed and integrated so that the senior managers at the top are not overloaded with information. At each level, the information gets edited according to what the person thinks is important for the boss. The more the levels of hierarchy in an organisation, the greater is the filtering and loss of information.

A common barrier to horizontal communication is organisational politics; one manager may withhold information from another since possession of information usually has benefits and advantages.

Status Block

A "boss" who is conscious of status finds it difficult to receive any suggestions from subordinates. People in senior positions often develop the feeling that they know everything about how to run the business. They do not agree that a junior may have some good ideas. Many good ideas are wasted only because they come from junior employees who are considered to be too young and inexperienced.

The ideas of workers are most likely to go unheard because of the social distance between them and the managers. A subordinate may be too nervous to speak to a senior manager. Social distance sometimes makes workers too shy or frightened to speak to their senior bosses. Social and official status distance can raise a difficult barrier which both may be unable to overcome.

Resistance to Change

This is a serious psychological barrier. Some people strongly resist new ideas which are against their established opinions or traditions or social customs. They may avoid new ideas because they feel insecure or afraid of changes in methods or situations. People bound by traditions have their own emotions, attitudes, standards and convictions and do not accept anything that goes against their cherished ideas.

Closed Mind

Limited intellectual background, limited reading and narrow interests can cause a person's mind to be narrow. This limits the ability to take in new ideas. Persons with a closed mind do not take any suggestions for change. Young employees with bright ideas and fresh approach feel frustrated by the closed mind of the senior people in an organisation. Persons with a closed mind have limited understanding of human nature; this makes it difficult for them to receive communications with sympathy.

This becomes a serious barrier to receiving grievances and appeals. Organisational procedures like grievance committees, counselling and suggestion schemes are meant to overcome this barrier.

Poor Communication Skills

Lack of skill in writing and in speaking prevents a person from framing the message properly. Oral communication can be handicapped by a number of problems; nervousness in facing an audience may affect a person's clarity in speaking. Even excitement about an achievement or a new idea may make a person's speech incoherent. Written communication can be handicapped by poor skills in using language.

Lack of skill in reading and in listening is even more common though these are really the more important communication skills. Poor reading habits and faulty listening are both psychological short-comings, and need careful training to overcome.

Since listening is an important skill in communication, it is discussed in detail in the chapter 9.

State of Health

Physical condition can affect communication efficiency. Pain or fever certainly makes a person disinclined to engage in communication; but even if the general state of health is poor, communicating ability is reduced. The mind is not sufficiently alert; there will be gaps in attention while reading or listening; there is lack of energy to think clearly and to find the right words. Perception is low when the state of health is poor. Emotions, which play an important part in successful communication, are easily disturbed.

ORGANIZATIONAL BARRIERS

In an organization, the gaps and barriers become more complex.

The movement of papers and of information gets held up by the system itself. A great deal of loss of information occurs as a message moves from senior management to lower levels. If it has to pass through many levels of authority, there is delay as well as distortion of the message. Each person through whom it passes edits it, filters it, and simplifies it for the understanding and needs of the next person who is to receive it. If a message passes down through many levels of authority, there may be much distortion in the message. The chances of such distortion are fewer in a flat organisation with few levels of hierarchy.

Loss or distortion of information as it moves downward may be caused by misinterpretation, lack of understanding, and neglect of messages by some of the members of the organisation. Even if there is very active downward flow of communication, it does not mean that the information is accurate, or that it is received and understood and accepted by subordinates. Studies have shown that employees at the lowest level receive only 20% of the information that they should get.

Too much dependence on written communication is one of the reasons for this. Circulars, bulletins, notices and even letters are not always read carefully. Many employees are unable to read and understand long messages. Even better educated persons at higher levels do not always give proper attention to all written communication. Oral communication has to be used to supplement written communication when the message is important.

Loss of information also occurs as messages move from subordinates to higher levels of authority. Messages are filtered at every level. There may be deliberate suppression of information out of self-interest and jealousy; a supervisor may suppress or change a good suggestion from a subordinate so as to take the credit personally; a senior officer may prevent information about discontent in the department from reaching the manager because it reflects on his/her human relations skills.

Deliberate withholding of information from peers who are perceived as rivals becomes a barrier in horizontal communication.

The resulting information gap can be harmful if the upper level of management does not find out the true state of affairs until it is too late. Therefore, cutting across the official chains of communication is sometimes necessary for the sake of speed and efficiency. The system of routine reports and the system of sending copies of documents for information, is meant to ensure that information is conveyed to the concerned persons, but some information may still not reach some persons.

Improving communication is the responsibility of all educated persons. The advantages of effective communication among members of a working team or any organisation, including the family, are such as to improve the efficiency as well as the quality of life. Ways and means to improve communication are discussed in another chapter.

CROSS-CULTURAL BARRIERS

Even in the best of conditions, communication can be difficult. Cross cultural factors naturally increase the possible problems of communication. If for historical or political reasons, the relationships between two countries are not friendly, there can be even greater problems of communication. Culture is a shared set of values and attributes of a group; it is the sum total of the ways of living built up by a group and transmitted from one generation to another. Culture is so much a part of an individual's manner of talking, behaving and thinking, that communication style and competence are influenced by it. In a world that is becoming global in its business, skill in communicating with people of other cultures is vital to success. Many international business training firms give courses in cross-cultural communication to company executives. Knowledge of some of the features in which cultures differ, provides a good foundation for any training you might like to take later.

Some of the most significant differences between cultures are:

National character/basic personality

Language

Values and norms of behaviour

Social relationships

Concepts of time

Concepts of space

Thinking processes

Non-verbal communication

Perception

Each nation has a character of its own. The Chinese are not like the Indians, nor the Pakistanis nor the Sri Lankans, although they are neighbouring countries. Neighbouring European nations like the French and the Germans and the Swiss are also different from one another.

The Language of any group directly reflects their culture. You only have to think of some of the sayings or proverbs or idiomatic expressions in an Indian language and in English to see that translation from one to the other is nearly impossible. Many words cannot be translated exactly. Even among countries that speak the same language like the British and the Australians, a word may not have the same significance. It has been pointed out that Russians cannot understand the concepts of free market, regulation, efficiency as the British or the Canadians do. Connotations of words differ in different cultures. When the Japanese say "yes" they mean "Yes, I'm listening." The Americans may take it to mean "Yes, I agree". Negotiations are made difficult because of this.

Values are our ideas of what is good and what is evil; they form the basis of our behaviour and actions. Notions of good and evil vary between cultures. Besides, norms, rules and manners of cultures differ. Behaviour expected from women in Eastern cultures is different from what is expected in Western cultures. Certain subjects which are not considered proper for talking about in polite society in one culture may be acceptable in another.

Social relationships depend on the groupings in that society. All societies have groups like families, classes, castes, and so on.

The Indian caste system, though officially abolished, still plays a significant part in social behaviour. Significance of family relationships in India is reflected in the elaborate system of words which can describe the precise relationship of two persons indicating the descent three or even four generations back. In Western languages, the all-covering word "cousin" describes a variety of relationships. Relationships between parents and children, between teachers and students, and the rules of behaviour that govern these relationships differ vastly between Eastern and Western cultures.

Concept of time is perhaps one of the most troublesome differences that cause barriers in cross-cultural communication, especially between Eastern and Western cultures. The Eastern concept of time is that it is circular, while the Western concept is that it is linear. Apart from this, time orientation varies; some cultures focus on the past, some on the present and some on the future. For some cultures, "time is money" and is more important than personal relationships; for others, time is subordinate to relationships.

As a result of perceiving time differently, work behaviour and social behaviour styles vary greatly. Ideas about punctuality and scheduling of activities depend on concept of time. In India, and other Eastern countries, lack of punctuality and not functioning to schedule is almost normal; in Western countries arriving late for an appointment is one of the worst things you can do. The idea of keeping work time strictly separate from personal time is a Western concept and is not easy for Eastern cultures to understand and follow. Attitude to time is one of the major problems in cross-cultural communication between Indians and people of Western cultures.

Concept of space influences design and use of shapes and colour in design. Besides, it has an important effect on behaviour and the distance between speakers during conversation; in some cultures, speakers stand close enough to touch often, while in others they maintain distance to denote respect. People in South Asian countries like India and Sri Lanka, maintain less inter-personal distance.

Thought processes vary between cultures; some are strictly logical and rational while others may be holistic and emotional. The frame of reference, that is, the higher perspective from which we view a situation makes a difference to the way we see it. Thinking process is affected by acceptance or rejection of superstition, belief in magic, miracles and so on; cultures where these beliefs are rejected are likely to view the world as logical, clear and law-based.

Non-verbal behaviour is another area of trouble in cross-cultural communication. Body language is a major factor that varies between cultures. Not only are gestures understood differently, but the amount of use of gesture varies. Indians use much more natural gesture than the British; the Japanese have many formal gestures for social interaction but less free body movements.

Appearance tends to be an unconscious basis for evaluation. We react unconsciously to the biological appearance (colour and texture of skin and hair, shape and colour of eyes, stature and body structure) as well as to the acquired appearance (style of dress and grooming) of persons we communicate with. Appearance of people of different cultures varies significantly; besides, there are multi-cultural nations like Canada which can present problems to Indians.

Ways of dressing and what is considered formal clothes is another problem area. The Indian saree which seems so formal in India, is not acceptable formal clothing in most American companies.

Use of Voice is another source of trouble with cross cultural communication. Cross-cultural confusion arises from the way we use our voice. People in many countries are put off by loud Indian voices, and noisy Indian tourists. Some Western cultures speak in such low voices that we can hardly hear them, and may wonder if they intend to be secretive. Difference between cultures in speed of talking makes the faster talking people consider the slow talking cultures as slow and lax. Some cultures expect formality and formal tone at work and are embarrassed or put off by the informal tone of another culture. The amount of silence that is considered as right during a conversation can cause confusion. The Japanese believe, "Those who know do not speak—those who speak do not know"; this is quite contrary to Americans who are embarrassed by silence and hasten to fill it by speaking. Closely related are the rules of turn-taking in conversation; most Western cultures consider interrupting as very impolite; each speaker is allowed to complete speaking; in India interrupting others in a conversation is acceptable. Also, "breaking into" a conversation between others is acceptable here, but not in Western cultures.

Perception is influenced by culture. We perceive some things and ignore others; we particularly perceive what is contrary to our own culture and what makes us uncomfortable. What smells "good" or "bad" is perceived differently. Rain means something different for Indians from what it means for the British. Differences of perception of the world can be amazing. Our world view and attitudes to life affect our meanings.

OVERCOMING BARRIERS

Constant organizational effort is needed to overcome the barriers which are unconsciously built up by different people in the organization. Persons in positions of authority, as well as subordinates, can be helped to overcome these barriers by training in effective communication. Periodical review and reorganization of communication networks is also needed to ensure that information reaches people in time.

Health centres: Many organisations provide medical aid, gymnasiums and recreation for the staff in an effort to keep down stress levels. Regulations like compulsory vacation after a certain number of months/years are also meant to ensure that employees avoid stress and fatigue.

The responsibility for overcoming barriers to personal communication and ensuring the success of every communication activity falls upon the senior and the better trained person. The higher your position, the greater is your need for effective communication. You have to cultivate all the communication skills including getting feedback and non-verbal communication. The external barriers of defective channels and faulty organizational systems are the Management's responsibility within the organization. The channels must be kept in good working condition; the intercoms, notice-boards, information meetings must be kept up-to-date. Many companies which can afford it, maintain soundproof rooms for meetings and take steps to reduce the noise level in the office.

Semantic and language barriers can be overcome only by being careful with the use of language, and by using words which have clear meaning, by using short and simple sentences, and also by using visual aid whenever possible. Whenever possible, feedback must be got and given to ensure that there is common understanding of a message.

Personal barriers can be overcome only by making a conscious effort, and by training for better communication. Persons in responsible positions are expected to improve their communication skills and overcome their particular blocks. Many companies organize training sessions for their staff for better communication skills.

Barriers can develop unexpectedly since emotions play a large part in communication. It is not easy to overcome all barriers; everyone has to make efforts to be aware of them and take care to avoid them.

To reduce misunderstanding when communicating with people from different cultures, these rules may be useful:

It is better not to assume similarity until you are sure. We tend to think others are similar to us and are often surprised to find they are quite different in their thinking. It is safer to assume difference till you are sure of similarity. Depend on description rather than evaluation or interpretation; persons from different cultures evaluate and interpret differently. Before communicating, try to feel yourself in the other's role, values and frame of reference.

Working in other cultures means understanding the hosts' conception of greetings, timing, hygiene, negotiation, agreement, politeness, personal space, gesture, meal etiquette, and closure.

EXERCISES

1. What is meant by barriers to communication? How and why do they occur?
2. What can be done to overcome the barriers to communication?
3. "The responsibility for the success of communication always lies on the senior person." Discuss the statement.
4. What are the problems of cross-cultural communication?
5. Fill in the blanks:
   (a) Barriers to communication can be classified into ____, ____ and ____.
   (b) ____, ____, and ____ are some of the socio-psychological barriers.
   (c) Responsibility for trying to overcome barriers to communication lies with ____.
6. Complete the sentence by choosing the correct alternative.
   (i) Semantic barriers are created by ____.
      (a) difference in age between sender and receiver.
      (b) disturbance in the environment.
      (c) divergence in individual understanding of meanings of words.
      (d) difficulties in accepting others' ideas.
7. Are these statements true?
   (a) Socio-psychological barriers can be overcome only by one's own effort.
   (b) External barriers can be overcome by individual effort.
   (c) Semantic barriers can be eliminated by acquiring an excellent command of the language.
   (d) There would be no semantic barriers if all people spoke the same language.
   (e) Semantic barriers can arise among people who speak the same language.
   (f) Organizations have to make regular efforts to prevent communication barriers.
   (g) Differences in rules of social behaviour contribute largely to cross cultural barriers to communication.
   (h) It is the responsibility of the sender of a message to overcome barriers to communication.
   (i) Continuous effort is needed to ensure that communication is successful.

❑❑❑

Chapter 8

PUBLIC RELATIONS

Public Relations is an organization's effort to establish and maintain its image with the public. It means carrying out activities and communication for the purpose of promoting goodwill with the community, the employees, the customers, and so on. A simple definition of Public Relations would be that it is good performance well communicated. It has two elements: action and expression; it begins with good acts and is expressed with good communication.

The Institute of Public Relations has defined PR as "the deliberate, planned and sustained effort to establish and maintain mutual understanding between an organization and its public." This shows that Public Relations work has to be carefully planned and carried out continuously. PR has also been defined as "the establishment of two-way communication to resolve conflicts of interest by seeking common ground of mutual interest based on truth, knowledge and full information." It cannot be just the organization's publicity and other mass communication. It has to be interactive; the public must have opportunity to interact with the organization and convey views and opinions to the organization.

It is the function of the PR department to watch the effect of the organization's activities on the public, to get feedback and to keep the management informed about public reaction and response. PR also has to explain the organizations' policies to the public, and gain acceptance and understanding of the public for the policies. At the same time, it also has to convey to the company's management, the needs, desires and expectations of the public. PR has been described as "the inward and outward seeing eye." It has to look outward to note public responses; it also has to look at its own organization's policies, activities and conduct from the public's point of view.

Every organization, whether a business firm, an educational institution, a public service, a club, a hospital, or a government department, is a member of the society in which it exists and functions. Just as an individual maintains good relations with other members of the society, an organization also has to maintain good relations with other organizations and people in the society. Its goodwill, the respect and confidence that it enjoys from the public, depends on its conduct and its relations with others as well as its products and services.

An organization needs to consider the effect of its policies on different sections of the public, and also to keep the public informed about itself and its work. It must get the right status in the public eye, and keep up its contacts. Lack of information among the public about an organization can itself be damaging; an organization may come into the limelight suddenly, and if the public knew nothing of its activities earlier, it might find the unexpected publicity difficult to bear.

The target audience of public relations communications is segmented into groups of persons who stand in different relationships to the organization, such as customers, suppliers, investors, employees, and so on.

Media of mass communication like the press, the radio and the film are extensively used for Public Relations; but mass communication tends to be one-way, and it is necessary to set up interactive systems and research to obtain feedback.

Objectives of PR

The objectives or goals of Public Relations are: building public awareness about the organization and its services, achieving acceptance, winning trust, co-operation and recognition, maintaining awareness and cultivating understanding.

PR aims at gaining credit for good performance and tries to create a good public image for the organization. It takes time to achieve the aims and hence, PR requires constant and continuous activity and monitoring.

Every organization competes for the attention and patronage of the public. Its services and products must be made known to the public. Information about the organization's performance in its field of activities like exports, research and social welfare schemes, and other contribution to society, enhances its respect and goodwill.

An organization draws its employees from the society around it, and is in competition with other organizations for efficient and loyal employees. A company with a good public image attracts better employees and staff if it is known for good administration, efficient management and employee policies; it can build up a good credit standing if it is known for good employee relations. Hence, its employee welfare and training programs must be made known to the public.

An organization needs various kinds of financial support. It needs credit from bankers and other financiers and investors. Credit standing, and public willingness to invest in the organization depends on how the public perceives its value.

It has a good image if it is known for supporting social causes, education, hospitals, sports, cultural activities, etc. A company can win respect by its contribution to research and development, and by sponsoring research even unrelated to its products or activities.

All these activities and social responsibilities contribute to the corporate image. PR has to see that information about these activities is widely known to the public.

PR is not propaganda; its aim is to achieve understanding and acceptance, while propaganda tries to push an opinion or an idea and may even try to brain-wash people into believing something. PR works by information, persuasion and adjustment, to win public support.

PR is different from advertising and marketing. It is needed and practiced by charitable institutions and voluntary organizations which do not sell anything. For a commercial organization, PR is an excellent support in marketing; the products of a company with a good public image are more easily accepted by the public. On the other hand, a bullying salesman, or a tasteless, unethical advertisement is a PR liability. There is a connection between PR and marketing, but PR activity has a much wider scope and purpose.

Public Relations is often called Corporate Communication. It is a separate department staffed by persons trained in communication and public relations. A Corporate Communication manual gives the company's guidelines for the conduct of relations and interaction with other institutions and the press and other media.

PR activity is essentially publicity. All Public Relations activities depend on active and effective communications. The Public Relations staff must be able to use all communication media and channels effectively.

Active PR practice requires that all publics are attended to and all media are used in good combination. It involves the skill to break down the vast public to manageable segments and groups, and using the most suitable medium for each.

The "Publics" of PR

PR activities are concerned with every section of the public with which the organization has any contact or association. PR extends its activities to various groups of people in the society and is concerned with all aspects of the organization. The function of marketing alone needs good communication with wholesalers, agents, distributors, importers, exporters, overseas agents, various kinds of retailers like chain-store owners, department stores, co-operatives, supermarkets, down to the smallest road-side stall-keepers, besides the service and technical experts and sales staff.

The success or failure of marketing is also affected by packaging, printing, transport contractors, advertising agents and media owners. To these may be added people concerned with testing and approving, various government officials, opinion leaders and consumer organizations. And yet, marketing is not the only activity of a manufacturing organization.

An organization has other concerns with the public; it needs finances from banks, credit societies and financiers and investors. It needs people for recruitment and co-operation from educational and training institutions for human resource development. And it needs the co-operation of various public services like telephones, electricity, municipal and government departments.

A good way to understand the "publics" of different types of organizations is to make a list of them. The lists given below are not complete or entirely accurate since there are bound to be individual variations.

Publics for the PR of a School

Teachers
Office staff
Staff and Trade Unions
Students
Parents of students
Past students
Hospitals and doctors in the neighbourhood
Trustees and Managers of the school
Ministry of Education
Government departments concerned with education Local authorities All people in the neighbourhood of the school.

Publics for the PR of a Voluntary Organization

Members
Office staff
Donors
Users of the services given
Municipal councillors and people's representatives
Local authorities
Government departments
Critics and opponents
Opinion leaders
Other voluntary organizations.

Publics for the PR of a Bus Service

Staff
Trade Unions
Schools and colleges
Tourist agencies and holiday trade
Hotels
Garages
Motor insurance companies
Traffic police and R.T.O.
Ministry of Transport
Ministry of Tourism
Advertising agencies

Banks and financiers

Dealers of vehicles

Petrol pumps.

Publics for the PR of a Cosmetics Manufacturer

Beauty Parlours

Wholesalers

Retailers

Staff

Trade Unions

Community around the factory

Laboratories and testing organizations

Food and Drugs Administration

Consumer Guidance Society

Doctors

Departments of Chemistry in colleges and universities

Government departments/Local authorities.

For each of these segments a different kind of communication is necessary. Communication activities required for PR with each of the groups/publics must be carefully planned.

An important segment of an organization's public is its staff, the internal public.

INTERNAL PUBLIC RELATIONS

An organization needs good internal public relations with employees and members as much as it needs good external public relations.

Employees of different categories form the internal public of an organization. They are the most concentrated and nearest public of an organization. This is also the smallest public.

There are several groups and several unions among employees. The workers' group is highly organized, and, being newly aware of their rights, they tend to be aggressive; since they have a low educational background, they have a limited understanding of the larger issues and problems involved in running a business.

Employee unions often cover more than one organization; for example, Textile Workers' Union is meant for all workers employed in textile mills. Such unions are independent of the employing organizations, and often engage in negotiations with one or the other employer on behalf of their members. Thus, employee relations expands into communication with the union's office-bearers who may not be the organization's employees. Good employee relations are essential for any business; it is even more important to create a feeling of loyalty among employees. For this purpose, companies have employee welfare schemes.

Communication plays a major role in this field. Information, education and training, counselling and advice, entertainment, appreciation and recognition, and opportunities to contribute to the organization's growth and improvement are some of the activities of internal public relations. Channels are set up for these communications.

Counselling and Advice: This is an important HR function. Companies have counselling services to help employees to adjust themselves to their jobs and their environment, and also give advice on personal matters.

Suggestion Schemes

A suggestion scheme is an opportunity for employees to contribute their ideas to the improvement of the organization. It is as an organized device to encourage suggestions from employees. It encourages employees to think and make suggestions for improvement of the organization; this builds up their sense of identification with and pride in the organization. The scheme recognizes the employees' ability; those who are actually involved in the work are better able to see any shortcomings as well as possibilities for improvement, and make useful suggestions.

The opportunity to make suggestions about their work and the equipment they handle gives psychological satisfaction to employees; this is as important for their morale as the satisfaction of material needs.

The suggestion scheme not only uses the human resources of the company productively, but also creates positive feelings. Employees feel happy when their ideas as well as skills and abilities are recognized and used by their organization.

A suggestion scheme must have:

(a) provision of suggestion forms and suggestion boxes;

(b) a set of rules indicating who is eligible, what is the procedure for examining and assessing suggestions, what is the basis for awards;

(c) a committee for working the scheme;

(d) a system of awards.

There are some difficulties in putting the scheme into practice. As supervisors and their subordinates are not put into competition with each other in the same scheme, more than one scheme is needed. The rules have to be worked out carefully. The committee must be representative but not too large. The greatest difficulty is with assessing the value of the suggestions and deciding the awards; it is not easy to decide which is a good suggestion and what award should be given to the good ones. Some suggestions may be long-term improvement ideas, some may be immediately useful. Which ones should be rewarded? and how? Suggestions may be in a variety of fields; for example, for improvement of the quality of a product, service, or public relations, for cutting costs, raising profits, or bettering the conditions of employees. Which is to be considered the best? These difficulties are overcome by inviting suggestions in a specific area in a particular month.

Allotting the rewards to different suggestions is as difficult as assessing the suggestions. Rewards may be given in the form of cash prize, or certificate or other benefits. In spite of these difficulties, many organizations have suggestion schemes because of the advantages.

1. Opportunity to contribute is favourable for employees
2. Negative feelings of complaint and grievance can be converted to positive feelings of suggestion
3. Bright ideas are not wasted.

The routine procedure for the working of the scheme varies from company to company. Suggestion boxes are placed at easily accessible locations. There is a suggestion form on which the suggestion is to be written. The suggestions are collected at regular intervals and examined by the committee. It is important to give immediate feedback to those who made the suggestions. If a suggestion needs clarification, the person who made the suggestion may be called for a discussion. If a suggestion is rejected, the reasons for rejection must be tactfully conveyed.

Decisions on awards may be announced on a Suggestion Bulletin Board.

To be successful, a suggestion scheme must attract a majority of the employees. The interest and enthusiasm of the employees depends largely on employer-employee relations and the confidence which the employees have in the management's fairness. A great deal depends on the regularity, efficiency and promptness of the committee in attending to the suggestions and announcing its decisions. Enthusiasm may be stimulated by naming areas in which suggestions are needed, and by holding competitions among the various departments.

Good publicity must be given to the scheme, its working, and to the winners of awards. A well-operated suggestion scheme is an effective morale-builder.

Publications

Publications intended specifically for the staff are house journals, bulletins, news letters. There may be regular posters, manuals etc. which inform, educate, and entertain the employees. The Public Relations Department is usually in charge of these publications.

Employees are given information about the company, its history, its activities and its policies. Having this information builds up a feeling of identification with the company.

House Journal is a periodical magazine of an organization, meant for distribution to its members. Every company has its own format and style for its house journal; the varieties range from a simple folded sheet to a well-produced magazine with photographs and art-work. The frequency also varies according to each company's policy and budget allocation. A house magazine is one of the best means of communicating with a known and selected public like the staff or members of the organization. It has also got the advantages of the direct mail medium since it is posted to individual addresses or given personally in the office premises. There is usually a special editorial board for the production of the house journal. Company news forms the major part of the contents of a house journal; activities of the organization, new products, executives and employees, information about family events like births, marriages and deaths, achievements of different members, all form a part of the company news.

There may be contributions from members and employees; this provides an opportunity for the development of creative talent among the members. There may be sections for entertainment, and special pages for women and for children; this makes it a family magazine.

The house journal can encourage participation in company activities by holding competitions and contests in story-writing, photography, cover-designing etc. The incentive of prizes and the opportunity to publish one's writing attracts many people to take part in the house journal activity. This kind of collective activity creates a sense of oneness and identification with the organization. It creates unity and togetherness among the different branches of the company.

Bulletin is a short publication for the purpose of announcing urgent or important or special official information to the public or members of an organization. If an announcement is short, it is put up on the bulletin board, which is a notice-board set aside for special notices and bulletins. A bulletin deals with a single item, and is published when the need arises. News can be more interesting when accompanied by photographs and details of events; members of the organization like to take such reports home to show to their families and friends. Bulletins are very good for creating a sense of unity and loyalty among the employees. They are a method of keeping up the morale of the employees.

Bulletins are published if a bad rumour begins to circulate. Correct and authoritative information is provided, and the company's policy or attitude is explained; if there are fears or other unpleasant feelings among the employees, an attempt is made to set them at rest by explaining the situation.

A bulletin can be effectively used as preparation for unpleasant decisions. For example, if the company is not able to give bonus to its workers, a bulletin might prepare the ground by giving facts and figures of sales, profits, etc., and also the Government regulations on bonus. A brief review of the company's bonus payments in the past, other employee welfare schemes etc., may also be included.

Newsletter is a written report, sometimes illustrated, and usually issued periodically. Its purpose is to present information to employees. A newsletter is prepared by and for an organization like a charitable institution, association, club, or a government agency, and distributed to members, shareholders, employees or contributors. It may be directed at a special audience, and may contain special or important items of news, with analysis, comments and sometimes even forecasts based on the news.

EXTERNAL PUBLIC RELATIONS

An organization's external public can be segmented for the purpose of specific PR activity.

Customers

Customers form the most various and widespread public. Their relationship with the organization is as buyers or users of the service provided; what they think of the organization will depend on their opinion of its products and its services. Service includes promptness in delivering goods, issuing receipts, giving after-sales service, besides courteous behaviour by employees. A company's courtesy is seen in all its communication; telephone calls, personal visits, correspondence, are all opportunities for a company to develop its image with its customers. An important aim of PR is to create a sense of loyalty and good feeling for the company among the members of the public. All communication is aimed at winning goodwill and the loyalty of the public.

Financiers

Developing confidence and positive relations for the organization with investors in the financial community requires financial strength and good accounting practices. Honest dealings, good reports to shareholders, well- conducted shareholder meetings, are a part of Financial Relations and Shareholder Relations.

This segment include banks, creditors, shareholders, investors, donors, sponsors, of the organization and its work. They receive the organization's annual reports, invitations to functions and celebrations, as well as letters.

Annual reports of companies are attractively got up; they contain not only the details of accounts and the chairman's report, but are adorned with photographs of the works, offices, products, annual gatherings, functions, etc. They are printed on high-grade paper and project a good image of the company. Some companies give gifts to shareholders at the annual general meeting.

Other organizations of various kinds are clearer groups than the general public; these are engaged in definite activities and have definite views and goals. Educational institutions, particularly professional institutes, are a source of trained personnel for a company. Companies may give donations for prizes and scholarships and special projects or special departments, to educational institutions and universities. Hospitals, orphanages and welfare institutions are also given help by companies.

The general public is the largest, the most diffuse and the least known of the groups that form an organization's public. It is the entire society in which the organization exists and functions.

There are various societies and associations like Environmentalists, Consumer Guidance Societies, etc., which are concerned with the protection of society from the malpractice and unhealthy activities of unscrupulous business houses. They mobilize public opinion against the harmful policies and activities of companies or the government through newspapers and other media, and even hold demonstrations and morchas. Public Relations has to defend and explain the company's activities to these groups.

Employees sometimes damage the company's reputation by discourteous behaviour to members of the public or by agitations and strikes. During times of labour agitations, which cause the customers to suffer, Public Relations has to step up communication with the public through the mass media, particularly newspapers, by explaining the company's side of the dispute, and publicizing its employee welfare activities.

The public is also influenced by the company's publicity campaigns and good taste in advertising. Artistic, interesting, and original advertising like that of Amul butter and Air India, goes a long way in impressing the public with the wit and humour of the company. False or improper advertisements make members of the public object and write letters to the press. The Public Relations Officer has to apologize through the newspapers for objectionable advertisements or objectionable behaviour by the company or its employees.

IMAGE BUILDING

An organization projects an image of itself upon the public. People develop and hold a collective opinion about the services, credibility, integrity, and dependability of an organization. This public opinion is formed by the perception of people about the behaviour and conduct of the organization as a whole and of the individuals who are members of the organization. The image can be actively built up in a positive way by monitoring and setting up communications and relationships with segments of the public through various media.

Open House is a time during which the organization is open for visits, by members of the public. Arrangements are made to receive and entertain visitors, show them around, answer their questions and give them information about the activities. It is an opportunity for people to get personally acquainted with the organization. Persons who have been welcomed, given hospitality, and treated like friends and guests feel friendly towards the organization; personal acquaintance by such a visit creates a sense of oneness and intimacy.

Exhibitions provide an excellent opportunity to display the organization's products and /or information posters and leaflets. It enables the organization to interact with members of the public. Persons attending at the stall distribute printed information to visitors and answer their queries. Exhibitions are usually supported by film shows, seminars, symposiums and presentations.

Fairs and Shows are festive occasions at which products are exhibited and sold. The atmosphere of a fair is informal and more intimate than that of an exhibition. It provides opportunity for interaction as well as to bring one's products and activities to the knowledge of the public. Flower shows, dog shows, farm product shows, etc., are the urban and sophisticated version of the traditional village farm fairs. Participating or organizing such fairs and shows helps to give visibility and status to the organization's image.

Sponsorships: Popular programs are sponsored on TV and radio not only for the purpose of advertising one's products but also to appear before the public as a friendly and socially responsible entity.

Books on interesting and useful subjects, biography of an eminent personality, the writings of an author, collections of articles on a subject, are sponsored by companies, as a part of PR activity. They need not be on subjects related to the company's products; the company's public image is enhanced by the fact of sponsoring a good and useful book.

Conferences and Seminars: In order to establish relations with other business organizations, conferences of specialists in various fields are hosted and attended. Hosting of a conference gives a boost to a company's image; the press is often invited to conferences, and the host company gets good publicity.

Visits: Some companies arrange group visits of shareholders to their plants and factories in order to keep them informed and to maintain good public relations. Groups of students are encouraged to visit and are received by the Public Relations Officer; the visitors are shown around, given presentations to inform them about the company, and may be given gifts or mementos. Visitors who have been treated well, given information and allowed to go around, and have received the organization's hospitality are sure to gather a good impression and to speak well of it.

USE OF MASS MEDIA FOR PR

The PR department has to use all the media of mass communication in order to reach out to the various publics. Each mass medium has its own power and the PR department has to evaluate each one and decide which ones are best for particular PR programs. The media can be listed as follows:

Press	Literature
Radio	Books
Television	Direct Mail
Exhibitions	Word-of-mouth
Films	Internet

All the media are not likely to be used for every PR program. After analyzing the publics which need to be reached for a particular program, the PR department has to consider suitable media. Every medium can be divided into classes which can reach different publics.

Press has many sub-divisions. These are: (a) Newspapers (b) News Weeklies (c) Magazines and Journals (d) Year Books and Annuals. Each of these can be further divided.

Newspapers

National daily papers (morning), Evening papers, Afternoon papers, Local papers, papers in different languages, Sunday papers and Weekly newspapers. The PR department maintains a complete list of every type of newspaper, with the names of one or two reporters with whom special relations have been established.

Press handouts or press releases are short reports prepared by the company, giving facts and figures about any matter that it may wish to publicize in the press. A press handout may inform the public about expansion projects, foreign orders secured, export performance, visits of technical personnel to advanced centres of training and research, new discoveries made in the company's research department, etc. A press handout is also used to keep the public informed of the company's action, attitude and position with regard to labour agitations. If there is a disaster like accident, gas leak, explosion etc., there are likely to be rumours. A press handout can give the company's statement of facts and the steps being taken to manage and control the disaster.

Press handouts are prepared by the Public Relations staff. Whenever it is necessary to give a long explanation to the public, as in the case of prolonged labour troubles and lock-outs, space is bought in the newspapers for the publication of the full statement. Short press releases are printed as news items. They may be edited and shortened to fit into the available space in the newspaper; if they are well-written and short, they are printed as they are; if they are badly written, they are thrown away.

The Public Relations staff has to be good at drafting reports for the press. A press handout is meant to give purely factual information. It tells what happened where and when, and who were the persons concerned or involved in the event. Some handouts may include the how and the why of the story, depending on the nature of the event. The report should have a short, clear title which indicates what it is about. The newspaper editor may change the title, if necessary.

The Public Relations staff has to draft good reports for the press as well as for the organization's own publications. It must also be able to draft good letters to the press, defending the organization if criticism appears in the press.

Magazines

Some magazines are of general interest. Sports, science, health, travel and women's magazines, are some of the subjects magazines. There are magazines for almost every kind of special interest and in different languages. Besides, industries and trades have their own specialized magazines and journals.

Executives and staff are encouraged to contribute to business journals and other specialist journals; the organization's public image is enhanced by the contributions of its members.

Radio and Television

Radio has a large morning audience of housewives; there are also businessmen and salesmen moving in cars. Outdoor workers in fields, construction and other people working outdoors form an all-day audience which has increased since the development of the transistor.

Television is best used for sponsoring programs of entertainment. Efforts are also made to get the company's executives to participate in discussions.

Films

Films giving information about the organization and its activities can be made interesting for the public if they are professionally well-made. They succeed very well if they are entertaining, informative and educational. Films can be used at in-house gatherings, exhibitions, annual functions, press visits, share-holders' visits etc., some PR films, like the one by ONGC, are so well made that they are shown on the National TV.

Educational and entertainment films of different kinds are a powerful medium for employee relations.

Literature

Literature for PR includes all the leaflets, pamphlets, folders, booklets and brochures which tell a story or give useful information. Typical examples are cookery recipe booklets, travelling guides, road maps, health care books etc. These do not attempt to highlight any product or service; they simply inform and educate and entertain. Limca Book of Records is an example of PR literature.

Direct Mail

Direct Mail is used for sending invitations to exhibitions, programs and functions and also for sending seasons' greetings and gifts. House journals and PR literature are also sent by the medium of direct mail. The style and tone of all the company letters has great effect on the company's public image; every letter should make a good impression on the receiver.

Word of Mouth

Word-of-mouth includes every oral communication from an informal conversation to a public speech addressed to an audience. The audience extends far beyond the people present to hear the speech directly; there is an invisible audience which gets reports and hears about the speech. Ability to express oneself clearly, intelligently and interestingly is essential for PR. All staff, besides the telephone operators, need to be trained to speak properly on the telephone. Executives have to be trained to address a press conference and face a TV interview. Oral communication is a powerful medium and poor speakers can damage the company's image just as much as skilled speakers can enhance it.

Internet

A website on the internet is the latest and a powerful method of getting yourself/ your company noticed and known. It takes you to the international scene at once. A small entrepreneur has as much chance of attracting visitors as a big company. With user-friendly software, it is possible for a person with reasonable competence on the computer, to put up a page on the web. Some providers give about five pages of website space free. A small entrepreneur can present a good deal of information within this space. A large company would prefer to use professional services and more space.

A website must be kept up-to-date. The appearance, the information given, the links provided, in short, the quality of the web page will itself speak for the image of the organization. The organization's size, experience, fancy offices, and finances need not play a part in this medium.

The website address has to be publicized through other media. Advertisements in all media, press releases and letterheads can carry your website address and a line requesting a visit. A great deal of PR is needed to get people to visit your site. You can provide a counter of the number of visits to find out how many the website is attracting.

If you have by chance arrived on a web page that gives nothing but the organization's name, no links at all, and some outdated information in a style that looks like a newspaper headline, you know how a poor website looks.

EXERCISES

1. Name the groups that form the publics of your college.
2. Name and describe the different groups which form the public of a business company.
3. What is meant by Public Relations? How is it different from propaganda?
4. Name the various media of communication that can be used for
   (a) internal Public Relations
   (b) general Public Relations.
5. How does the P.R. Department use house journals and bulletins?
6. Name and describe the publics of a computer class.
7. What is image building? What media can be used for building an organization's public image?

❑❑❑

PART II

ORAL COMMUNICATION

Chapter 9

LISTENING

Listening is the receiver's activity in oral communication. As the speaker has the responsibility to make effort to be understood, so the listener has the responsibility to be attentive and to make effort to understand the meaning of the speaker. Of all skills of communication, listening is the most important of all. The higher your position in an organisation, the greater is your listening responsibility. A manager has to spend more time listening to others than speaking. An executive's communication time is spent roughly in the following proportion:

Writing:	9%	Reading:	16%
Speaking:	30%	Listening:	45%

Although listening is so critical in our daily lives, it is not taught and learnt as a part of any course in schools or colleges; the other three basic communication skills, reading, writing and speaking get all the attention. Most people are not good listeners; but fortunately, listening skill can be improved by understanding the steps involved in the process of listening and by following some basic guidelines.

The Four Steps of Listening

Hearing is the first step of listening. At this stage, the listener simply attends to the speaker to hear the message. If you can repeat the speaker's words, you have heard the message. This step may fail if there is a great deal of noise or if the listener is occupied with something else.

The second step is interpretation. This depends on the listener's vocabulary, knowledge, experience and so on. If the listener fails to interpret the words correctly, the message is misunderstood. People misinterpret words because of varying knowledge, vocabulary, experience, attitudes, culture and background. A listener may also fail to note or may misinterpret the speaker's body language.

The third step is evaluation. At this stage the listener decides what to do with the received information. When you are listening to a sales talk, you may choose to believe or not to believe what you hear. The judgements you make at the stage of evaluation are crucial to the listening process.

The final step is response. The listener's response to the message may be in words or in body language. The response lets the speaker know whether the listener has got the message and what his/her reaction is.

The Activity of Listening

Listening is not being passive; it is positive activity. It needs a good deal of hard work, and is often accompanied by a slightly raised heart-beat indicating that there is increased activity. It takes a good deal of effort and self-discipline to listen attentively. Listening can make a person quite tired.

Listening involves making effort to get the speaker's full meaning. It involves not only understanding the content of the message, but also understanding the feeling of the speaker. Understanding the feeling is called empathetic or active listening.

Listening is an intellectual and emotional activity; our faculties function in different ways according to the kind of listening required by the occasion. Listening to music and poetry requires appreciative listening; listening to presentations, lectures, instructions, requires attentive listening so that the information and ideas received are understood and stored in the memory. Listening to political speeches, sales talks or elocution contests requires evaluative and critical listening.

IMPORTANCE OF LISTENING

Any interaction with others, whether at home, with friends, at college or at work, depends for success on your ability to listen. In working with people, skilled and sympathetic listening is the most effective tool.

The importance of listening carefully to the instructions given by one's supervisors is obvious. Unless instructions are carefully listened to, understood and remembered, one cannot carry out the assigned work.

Inefficient listening affects interpersonal relations as well as decision-making and employee relations. In a company where the supervisors are poor listeners, there can be problems of human relations. A number of grievances of workers are either imaginary or only a vague expression of discontent; if the supervisors listen with empathy, some of these grievances disappear.

It is not enough to listen during a speech; you have to remember, what you have heard. You have to think over the communication received and, sometimes, note it down immediately after the communication has been completed.

Benefits of listening include being able to:

- find out more information
- learn about people and how their minds work
- improve relations with people
- raise morale of employees/subordinates
- obtain suggestions and new ideas

- discover why employees perform as they do (well or poorly)
- help with solving problems.

Blocks to Effective Listening

Unfortunately, most of us are unable to listen with full concentration for more than one minute at a time; attention lags and returns. There are many reasons why people's ability to listen is not as good as it should be.

If you want co-operation and willing response from your team, listen to their ideas, suggestions and problems. Keep aside your pet ideas and discuss their ideas, not yours. If you want to win their respect, you must show them respect and listen with attention while they speak.

We can overcome many of our defects in listening by making effort. It is useful to know what prevents people from listening efficiently.

The common barriers to listening are given below. Which ones are your specific problems?

Distraction in Your Mind

This is a great barrier to listening and must be firmly checked. If you allow your mind to go on a joy-ride, thinking of the next vacation or the last week-end's party, there will be no listening. It takes a great deal of self-control and discipline to stay tuned to another person, particularly when your own mind is excited about something.

Wandering Attention

There is a natural difference between speaking speed and listening speed. Average speaking speed is about 150 words a minute; the listener's mind can process about 500 words a minute.

This gives rise to something like the tortoise-and-hare race, especially if the speech is long. The listener's mind goes off on various expeditions, returning now and then to check up on the speaker's progress; if the hare gets quite lost or falls asleep, the tortoise will get too far ahead for the hare to catch up.

While listening to a speaker, your mind has excess time. You can learn to keep your mind usefully occupied in reviewing the talk and connecting the various ideas that are put across by the speaker.

Planning a Reply

In most cases, the listener's mind is busy planning what to say when the speaker stops. If the speaker makes a controversial statement which conflicts with your views, you may get much excited and engage in mental argument. In preparing an argument, or a question to ask, you might miss the rest of the speech. The speaker may even raise the point of objection and answer it, but the mentally busy listener does not hear it.

Lack of Interest

Not being interested in the topic can cause faulty listening. It might make you reject the speaker or the subject as dull or boring. Such an attitude to the speaker arises from narrow interests and a closed mind. Very often, uninteresting speakers communicate useful information and ideas, while interesting and amusing speakers may have very little useful matter. A responsible listener must make an effort to be interested in the communication.

Pretending to be attentive is usually not possible as body language will show the boredom. In a social situation it is discourteous to look or behave bored; in an official situation, it can have very bad consequences.

Tendency to Criticise

Criticizing the speaker's appearance, manner, voice and so on, is another cause of poor listening. No doubt, style adds to the effectiveness of speech; but the content is always more important than the appearance or the style of the speaker. There are many worthy persons who do not cultivate style but have good matter to give; by paying too much attention to the speaker's style, you may lose the matter.

Being Self-centred

Some persons are self-centred and like to keep on talking themselves rather than share a conversation with others. They want others to listen to them, but are not willing to listen to what others have to say. They listen selectively; only to what interests them, and ignore everything else. A word or an idea that the speaker expresses makes them start off on their own talking, and the speaker loses the chance to say what s/he wanted to say. Naturally, the speaker feels frustrated and will not take ideas or problems to such a person again.

Avoiding What is Difficult

If you are mentally lazy, you may switch off attention when you find the subject difficult to follow; if this becomes a habit, it makes the mind more and more lazy. Make every effort to follow discussion programmes on the TV. A little daily effort to follow a serious discussion on the TV is useful for improving listening ability.

Excessive Note-taking

Trying to take down extensive notes is a sure way to disturb your listening and to miss some points. No matter how fast you write, you cannot write as fast as the words are spoken. Cultivate the art of taking notes and limit it to writing down the general ideas. Lecture notes or meeting notes can never be in final form; they have to be expanded and filled out after the session.

Emotional Blocks

Most people have "deaf spots"; this is a tendency to ignore and block out ideas that disturb your emotional comfort. This defect can prevent a person from taking in and retaining certain ideas. Some people find it difficult to listen to figures or to descriptions of surgical operations or stories of horror. A deep-seated inability to endure going through something which we find painful causes us to block it out of the mind.

Another type of deaf spot is inability to face an idea that goes against a prejudice or an opinion that we have held for a long time. We may hear it wrongly or it may get distorted in our mind if we do not pay careful attention.

Emotional Excitement

You may get disturbed by the speaker's use of certain words. Words and phrases acquire different meanings and connotations in different cultures; a perfectly good word may appear loaded with prejudice or ill-feeling to a person from another culture. Feeling angry in the name of gender bias, or racial prejudice, or some other cause, may bar you from giving attention to the speaker. It is important to guard against getting upset by words which may have been used quite innocently by the speaker.

Impatience

Lack of patience to listen is the commonest barrier to listening. We often have no patience to wait until another has finished speaking. We want to answer or add our own points to the discussion, or narrate our own experience. In a competitive culture, conversation often turns into a story-telling match, each one vying with others to narrate one's own experiences of being cheated, of medical treatments, of bargains, and what-have-you. This competitive desire to talk indicates lack of maturity and an inability to listen to others.

Poor Health

Poor state of health reduces listening efficiency. No doubt, any physical pain demands all your attention in coping with it, and you cannot be expected to pay attention to work; it is better not to attend a meeting or a conference if you have a headache or some other physical pain. But besides pain, poor state of general health makes a person impatient, inattentive and unable to concentrate; it impairs listening ability. It is important to take care of your health at all times.

Personal Anxieties

If you have a serious personal worry or anxiety, it is difficult to get away from it. In such circumstances, it is better not to engage in any important listening responsibility. The responsibility may be delegated to someone else. It is often worth seeking co-operation and requesting the other person to excuse you until you are out of the worrying situation.

External Noise and Disturbance

If there is noise in the environment, it makes hearing difficult and distracts attention. If noise cannot be avoided, seek the speaker's co-operation in overcoming this problem.

Do you allow disturbance by other people or by the telephone while someone is speaking to you? It surely disturbs listening and frustrates the speaker. A good manager avoids it by insisting on discipline in the office and making it a rule that a meeting should not be disturbed.

Exercise:

Examine each of the barriers to listening listed above, in relation to yourself. Which ones are yours?

List all the listening problems that you have found in yourself. Then choose your worst problem and analyse it.

How did you become aware that you have this problem?

What goes on in your mind when someone speaks to you?

Write a full description of the situation:

Who was talking to you?

What is that person's relationship to you?

What kind of emotional, social, or power relationship do you have with this person?

What was the topic of conversation?

What was your mind doing when this person was talking to you?

Write down every thought honestly; you don't have to show it to anyone.

Do you think it is the topic or the person that caused you the problem?

Think the problem through.

Is it possible for you to get the co-operation of this person?

What is your attitude to the person and/or to the topic?

Write down your plan of action to overcome the problem.

Becoming aware of one problem and trying to overcome it, will help you to identify and overcome others.

Remember that you cannot achieve this in one day; it takes continuous effort.

As you must have seen, it takes time to identify which of these blocks we suffer from. But it is worth making the effort to watch oneself and check one's mind if it behaves irresponsibly.

It is possible to learn and cultivate some positive listening habits. First of all, pay close and full attention to the speaker. This may need determination to concentrate. Concentration is helped by alertness of the mind and of the body. If you are determined to pay attention, you can train and discipline your mind and body to get into the listening mode.

Importance of Listening to Non-verbal Messages

Use your eyes as well as your ears to listen. A spoken message does not come only through words. Research has shown that non-verbal signs make up over 90% of the message. In order to get the whole message you have to pay attention to the body language, which carries 55% of the meaning and the tone of voice which carries 38% of the meaning. Words carry only 7%. The speaker's body language and voice can tell about the speaker's state of mind and feelings. How many times have you been influenced by the way a person looks at you? And by someone's tone of voice?

The non-verbal part of a person's communication is largely unconscious and cannot be controlled or hidden by the speaker.

(a) Facial expression, gestures and posture are important carriers of meaning. Over-enthusiasm or excitement can be seen in a person's face and gestures. Posture shows the level of interest a person feels in the current activity. Lack of eye contact, looking away, turning the corners of mouth downward shows that the speaker is unhappy; frowning and sharp steady eye contact can be disturbing to the listener. We can affect others without saying a word.

To be a good listener, you have to be aware of your own body language as a listener as well. Your body language can affect the speaker. Remember you can hardly disguise your body language.

Here is an **exercise** to sharpen your awareness of a listener's body language. Write down your answers to these questions.

1. From what physical signs do you know when someone is not listening to you?
2. What signs make you feel that the listener wants to stop the conversation?
3. How do you know when the listener is not interested in what you are saying?
4. What body language shows that a person is day dreaming?
5. Have you ever noticed that your listener is upset by some words you said? How?
6. How do you know when someone has a problem?

Do any of your answers describe your own listening behaviour? What do you need to change in order to make yourself a better listener?

(b) Tone, pitch of voice and speed of speaking can show excitement, anger or fear. Speaking fast and jerkily may come from nervousness or impatience.

How do you respond to these? Do you try to complete the speaker's sentence if he hesitates or cannot find the words? Do you look impatient or bored? Can you reflect the feeling with a simple, non-critical statement like, "I can see that — has been a disturbing experience."

Try saying "Hmm..." in different ways and with different emphasis. Working in pairs, try to interpret each other's feeling from the way it is said. This is a fun exercise, but it can throw light on the power of the tone of voice.

(c) Omission of facts, failure to explain or to illustrate or failure to give proof and evidence shows gaps in the speaker's knowledge or ability. It may also indicate an emotional problem of not being able to face something. Sometimes, individuals say things in an indirect way if they feel embarrassed about saying it directly.

If you, as the listener, can summarise what the person says, just reflect back and look expectantly for more information, the chances are that the person may add some information. If your attitude and body language appear interested and empathetic, the person is likely to speak up.

Try this with a role play partner. You have a class picnic next Sunday; the class representative managed to persuade everyone to join the picnic and this is the first time that the entire class will be going. This person (your practising partner), who often collects a lot of work to do on a Sunday, says to you on Friday, "It looks like I won't be able to join the class picnic this Sunday." What would your response be?

(a) Why? Have you collected work to do on Sunday?

(b) You always seem to drop out of things at the last minute. Didn't you agree to join and even pay the contribution?

(c) You feel that you won't be able to join the class picnic, and you're feeling sorry about it?

(d) This is not the first time you have backed out of a class activity.

Profile of an Effective Listener

Research has shown that good listeners:

- Consider listening to be an opportunity to learn something new.
- Are aware of their personal prejudices and can avoid judging the speaker.
- Are not influenced by words filled with emotion.
- Are not upset by the speaker's use of any words.
- Listen to the ideas behind the speaker's words.
- Use the time lag to evaluate what they hear.
- Consciously notice the speaker's non-verbal behaviour.

The following behaviour indicates that you are a good listener:

- Making and maintaining good and comfortable eye contact.
- Reflecting appropriate feelings in facial expressions.
- Sitting/standing in an attentive posture.
- Tuning in to the speaker's line of thought.
- Using nouns and verbs in the same constructions and in the same tenses as the speaker.
- Reflecting the speaker's terminology.
- Using empathic questioning technique.
- Asking open-ended questions, seeking information and clarification.
- Summarising what the speaker has said.

For an executive, the aim of good listening is not only to follow what the speaker is saying but also to get at the problems of customer relations, employee relations and motivation.

Guidelines for Effective Listening

The following guidelines for good listening require practice.

1. Stop talking. Be attentive. Make the speaker feel important.

2. Put the speaker at ease. Create a positive atmosphere through body language. Your non-verbal behaviour must show that you are interested; the speaker must see and feel that you are listening. Make eye contact and keep still. Tapping with the foot or a pencil, shuffling papers, attending to other work, makes the speaker feel that you are not attending.
3. Be patient. The speaker may need time to say what s/he wants to say; some people are shy or nervous or cannot easily find words. If they are interrupted or hurried, they get more nervous.
4. Show that you are listening. This can be done by (a) using encouraging, non-committal expressions like "Hum", "Uh-huh", "I see", "Oh" and so on. (b) nodding the head, appropriate facial expression, eye contact, touching. (c) invitation to say more such as, "Tell me about it," "Would you like to talk about it?" "Sounds like you have some ideas or feelings about this." Try to match the speaker's mood by appropriate response.
5. If the speaker has many things to say, write down the main points and get them checked for correctness; this makes the speaker more responsible and clear in what s/he says, because s/he realises that s/he is receiving serious attention.
6. Do not create or allow distractions. Some important ground rules are:
   (a) Do not interrupt
   (b) Do not give advice
   (c) Do not question
   (d) Do not take the conversation in a different direction
   (e) Do not criticise.
7. Keep your temper no matter how angrily the speaker speaks. Allow the speaker to let off steam. An angry person cannot speak and cannot listen.
8. Listen "between the lines."Think of what is not being said as well as what is being said. Remember that many clues to the speaker's meaning come from body language.
9. Ask questions only after the speaker begins to feel more comfortable and only to get a clear understanding. If you are not sure what the speaker is saying, check your understanding by saying "Do you mean...?" and state what you understood. It is a good idea to repeat, in your own words, what the speaker said in order to confirm that you understood.
10. Keep an open mind; do not jump to conclusions. Avoid making any judgement until the speaker has completed speaking. A hasty judgment is a prejudice, and it closes the mind; a proper evaluation can be made only after getting full information and understanding it.

The power to listen is a very sensitive skill; it is the skill that makes interpersonal relations effective.

Importance of Silence in Communication

Have you noticed that the word LISTEN is spelt with the same letters as the word SILENT?

To listen effectively, you have to be silent; it is not enough that you close your mouth. You must also stop your mind from chattering. You have to be really silent.

If your mind is filled with questions to ask, your own points to make, your own arguments to bring against the speaker, or criticism of the speaker's style, appearance, manners, clothing, etc., your mind is not silent. If your mind is engaged with all these or other things, the speaker's words cannot enter your mind fully.

Being silent does not mean being struck dumb or being half asleep; it means keeping aside all your thoughts and concentrating on the words, the tone and the body language of the speaker. It also means responding with your own body language.

Whatever questions you want to ask, must wait for the appropriate time and stage of the conversation.

A few minutes of complete silence everyday is very useful for developing your communication skills. It will help you to clarify your goals. Silencing your mind is useful so that you can listen to yourself and become aware of your self-talk. Your self-talk affects your self-esteem and your ability to listen to other people's opinions and point of view. Make sure you talk to yourself respectfully, and with honest pride in your talents and abilities, whatever they may be. If you feel sure of your own worth, you will feel more secure and not get angry and excited when you hear views contrary to yours. This is an important way to develop your ability to listen.

EXERCISES

1. Are these statements true?
   (a) Listening is a natural skill and cannot be trained.
   (b) You can make a speaker feel good by listening attentively.
   (c) A senior manager spends most of his communication time in speaking.
   (d) Listening attentively can be tiring.
2. Why is listening the most important of the communication skills?
3. What prevents good listening?
4. How can we improve our listening skills?
5. In your experience, what problems prevent you from listening efficiently in the classroom? What do you plan to do to overcome them?

□□□

Chapter 10

GROUP COMMUNICATION

A group is defined as a number of persons engaged in interaction with one another. The interaction may be during a single meeting or a series of meetings which may be formal or informal. In the course of the meetings, each member receives some impression of every other member and develops acquaintance. A group has a common purpose and develops norms for interpersonal relations; it also develops leaders and followers. Group communication takes place in a meeting. A meeting may be formal or informal, and it may be conducted in different ways depending upon its purpose and the size of the group. Statutory and conventional meetings like Annual General meetings or Board of Directors' meetings etc, which are held at fixed intervals, usually have a fixed agenda and business to be conducted; such meetings are very formal. Meetings of committees which are assigned specific tasks are held as frequently as required for their work, and may be informal. Groups of persons connected with different aspects of a job, or having similar responsibilities may be called for a conference meeting to discuss common problems or plans. Trainees and learners meet to discuss topics and learn from one another.

A group discussion can be a very stimulating communication activity for those who have the skill. It is a very useful activity in organizations. It helps in understanding a situation, in exploring possibilities and in solving problems because it allows a multiple point of view. It also gives a sense of participation to all those who participate in it. A meeting is an education for all persons who take part in it, including the leader/ chairman. Participants get an overview of the organization and the different aspects of its activities. The discussion enables the participants to see and appreciate other people's point of view. The business meeting has been described as continuing education in business management.

Participating in group communication requires skill and training; multiple barriers can come in the way of useful discussion and spoil the meeting. But a meeting costs money and time; an organization needs people who have the skill to make the best use of meetings. Ability to participate effectively in a group discussion is an important asset for anyone; many companies select candidates for personal interviews after testing their ability to participate in a group discussion.

Problems of Group Communication

There can be problems in communication even when only two persons are involved. Various barriers operate and are multiplied when more persons are involved. The participants as well as the leader need to have meeting skills, otherwise, a meeting can be very frustrating and a waste of time.

Problems are created by various personalities among members of the group. Some persons are shy or nervous of addressing a group; even if they have good ideas or good analytical ability, they may not speak up. Some are aggressive and prevent others from speaking; they take up all the time and insist on following their own agenda. Some do not participate at all because they have not applied their mind to the agenda or discussion topics. Members may get excited and turn hostile to one another. Even a cohesive group may have problems occasionally.

If the leader cannot control the meeting, or guide the discussion, the group's communication may go off the track or become diffuse and not arrive at a proper conclusion.

One of the worst problems in group communication is not being able to come to a conclusion within reasonable time. Meetings that go on for too long do not produce good decisions and are very frustrating to members of the group.

In order to overcome problems and to ensure success of group communication, the leader must have the required skills to conduct a meeting and lead a discussion; the other members must have the commitment and the skills to take part in the discussion.

MEETINGS

A meeting is a formally arranged gathering for the purpose of discussing an issue that concerns a large number of persons.

The method of conducting a meeting depends on the type of meeting.

Types of Meetings

Meetings can be classified on the basis of their formality as:

(a) Very formal meetings, like parliament, state assemblies, company shareholders meetings, management-union negotiations, university senate, councils and executive bodies.

(b) Formal meetings, like committees, managing councils and general bodies of voluntary organizations, briefing sessions, advisory bodies and management meetings.

(c) Informal meetings, like group discussions, ad hoc meetings of task groups and brainstorming sessions.

Purpose

A meeting may have any of the following objectives:

- to arrive at a consensus
- to get feedback
- to solve a problem
- to collect ideas
- to understand the situation
- to learn and train
- to inform and explain

Meetings can also be classified on the basis of the purpose for which they are held.

Decision-making Meeting: Committees, boards of directors, and such specially appointed bodies with powers to take decisions on behalf of the parent body or appointing authority, hold decision-making meetings.

Executive Meeting: Some committees like the board of directors or the executive council have powers to implement decisions; they may review recommendations of other bodies, or take decisions on their own. They hold meetings at which they pass orders and give instructions for carrying out certain work.

Consultation Meeting: An advisory body, which may consist of experts, holds meetings to discuss and advise other bodies. They do not have powers to take any decisions or action. Joint consultations between different departments, sections, or other related bodies/groups are an example of consultation meetings.

Problem-solving Meeting: A meeting of all those concerned with a particular activity where the problem is found may be called for the specific purpose of solving the particular problem. Everyone contributes by looking at the problem from his/her point of view and task. Any snags and blocks can be dealt with in co-ordination.

Briefing Meeting: Giving information is the main function of a briefing session. A prepared note of briefing may be read out, and questions or requests for clarification are answered; but there is no discussion at briefing meetings. Companies may hold a briefing meeting to inform the press/media. Within a company, seniors at every level hold briefing meetings for their subordinates. These briefing sessions are an addition to the formal information system of the company.

Negotiation Meeting: This is characterized by the presence of two clearly competing sides. When parties with competing interests like buyer-and-seller, or two separate organizations which want to collaborate, or employer-and-employee, need to settle their differences, they meet to discuss and arrive at an agreement.

Various other meetings of management with the staff, like interviews for selection, reprimand, appraisal and exit interviews and meetings for discussion of grievances also have an element of negotiation.

Group Discussion: This type of meeting is usually informal. It can be a very stimulating and useful activity in organizations. It helps in understanding a situation, in exploring possibilities and in solving problems as it generates a multiple point of view. It gives a sense of participation to all those who participate in it.

It is used as a tool for selecting candidates by observing the behaviour and abilities of the individuals taking part in it.

Conference: A conference is a meeting of a large group of persons assembled for the purpose of discussing common problems or activities. The number of participants may be anything from 10 to 500 or more; a large conference is divided into small groups for the purpose of discussions. The participants may not be from the same organization.

A conference may last a day or a few days, depending upon the subject of the conference. Participants are expected to pay a participation fee to cover the expenses. The conference is a tool of learning and training and development; members pool together and share their knowledge and experience, and discuss their problems. It is an enriching activity. It does not have a task to complete; any conclusions that are arrived at during the discussions are included in a report of the conference.

Copies of the report are given to the participants and their organizations, and may be sent to various authorities concerned with the subject of the conference.

A conference does not have any authority but it may make recommendations since the participants are persons who have experience and are engaged in the activity and are directly affected by the state of affairs in the field.

Committee Meetings

A committee is a small group of persons entrusted with a special business task appointed by a bigger group or someone in authority. A committee is a tool of administration and management and is expected to complete a given task in the given time. It meets as often as is required for the task, and maintains the minutes of its meetings. It is expected to prepare a report of its conclusions and submit it to the appointing authority. The size of a committee usually affects its working; sometimes a large committee may not arrive at decisions owing to too many differences of opinion; on the other hand, a very small committee may find that it lacks the information it needs.

There are several types of committees:

1. Ad hoc Committee is a small group selected on the spot, sometimes during a meeting, for looking into a troublesome problem: it may have members from among those present at the meeting as well as others. Persons who are knowledgeable about the problem are usually chosen for the committee.

2. Standing Committee is a part of the organizational set up. Membership of a standing committee is by position and title and office held; for example, Labour Welfare Officer, Health Counsellor and other office holders may be on a Grievance Committee. Whoever holds the particular post becomes a member of the committee. The committee is permanently in existence, but its membership may be for one or two years, and may change by rotation. A standing committee has a permanent recurring task assigned. It meets periodically to examine recurring problem, in the given area. Usually, a standing committee has high powers and can implement its decisions.

3. Special Committee is appointed for handling a special task. Its members are carefully selected for their special knowledge and experience in the field of the task.

4. Sub-committee is a smaller body formed by a large committee from among its own members, for the purpose of completing an aspect or a part of the larger task assigned to the committee.

There are advantages as well as disadvantages in using a committee for decision-making. The advantages are:

(i) the decisions are more acceptable to all concerned since they are impersonal and democratic;

(ii) a committee can examine the matter from several angles and put together more information, knowledge and experience than a single person can do;

(iii) it spreads the responsibility to the members of the committee, and relieves the manager of sole responsibility. The disadvantages of using a committee for decision-making have attracted some humorous and sharp remarks like: "A committee is a group that keeps the minutes and loses the hours," and "If you want to kill an idea, get a committee working on it."

The disadvantages are:

(i) a committee takes more time than an individual; sometimes, a manager may appoint a committee as a delaying tactic when he is faced with a troublesome situation;

(ii) committees are expensive; the members have to take time out of their work to attend committee meetings. Secretarial help, stationery, refreshments are further expenses of a committee;

(iii) committees sometimes fail to arrive at any useful conclusion.

But, in spite of the disadvantages, committees are extensively used for administration and management because the advantages are so many and so important.

Advantages and Disadvantages of Meetings

Group work has many advantages. Some of them are given here.

(a) There is an enormous amount of information and knowledge in every field. Activities have become complex and it is difficult for one person to handle tasks which have several aspects. Discussion permits a multiple point of view; it enables an organization to benefit from the expertise of specialists in technology, law, taxation, personnel and so on.

(b) Being involved in group activity and discussion provides social and emotional support to the participants. Employees who have a chance to contribute and take part in decisions are known to be more loyal.

(c) Discussing ideas and problems in a meeting is a democratic way of functioning. It shows respect for individuals and their opinions and views.

(d) As technology develops there will be easier access to information in organizations. It will be advantageous for managers to keep in touch with members of the organization and to have open discussions of various concerns.

On the other hand, meetings have disadvantages like these:

(a) Both, formal and informal meetings can be time-consuming and expensive. A great deal of money and time has to be spent on making preparations and on the actual conduct of a meeting.

(b) A meeting may end without any useful conclusion if there is much disagreement among the participants.

(c) There may not be any useful outcome. Several persons take meetings lightly and attend without preparation, just for the sake of spending some time away from their work place.

(d) If the chairperson is not skilled in conducting a meeting, there may be a great deal of useless talk from the Chair, causing others to feel frustrated if they do not get an opportunity to respond or to express their views.

Recent research in group activity has shown that leaders and participants can be trained in group activity and discussion. The disadvantages can be overcome with training of organization members.

Making Preparations for a Meeting

A meeting needs the support of written communication in the form of notice of the meeting, agenda of items to be discussed at the meeting and minutes which are a record of the proceedings of the meeting. These are discussed in a later chapter.

The seating arrangements and the duration of the meeting depend upon the number of participants, the subject of the meeting and the objective of the meeting. It may be a small committee meeting or a large conference meeting, or a group discussion meeting; its success depends on the preparation and arrangements made by those in charge and responsible for calling the meeting and conducting it. The convener, chairman or leader has the responsibility to ensure that the arrangements are made properly. A secretary or P.A. or any member of the staff may be assigned the duty of arranging for the meeting; the person making the arrangements must be briefed properly and given a check-list to work from. The arrangements begin with an agenda, the list of participants and the date, time and venue of the meeting. Notice of the meeting, with the agenda, should be sent out to members/participants so as to reach at least a week before the meeting to enable them to prepare themselves for a discussion. It is better to notify the complete program, with timing of each item, if possible.

Making arrangements in the room is the next step.

- Proper ventilation/air-conditioning, lighting, and also microphones must be ensured.
- Chairs and tables must be suitably arranged so as to provide face-to-face situation for everyone as far as possible. The arrangement will depend upon the size of the meeting and the purpose of the meeting. A square or rectangular table is suitable for a small group. A long rectangular centre table arrangement is suitable for a group of less than 20. A U-shaped arrangement is suitable for

a group up to 50. A class-room type arrangement can be made for larger groups. Very large groups may have to be seated in theatre type arrangement which has no writing facility for the audience. Participation by members gets much reduced as the number grows larger in spite of arrangements for movable mikes.

- Place-cards or boards must be placed to indicate seating arrangements, if it is necessary; otherwise, name-plates may be handed to each participant; it is advisable that participants should know one another's names.
- All visual aid equipment like overhead projectors, slide projectors, etc., must be checked, set up and focussed and an operator should be attending. Pointers and easels for flip charts must be provided. Blackboard, chalk and duster may be enough for some meetings. It is useful to check with the chairman as well as with the participants if any special material would be needed for their presentations.
- Stationery must be provided; this includes note-pads, pens or pencils, paper-weights, clips, pins, staplers, punches, files.
- The presence of a secretary to take down the proceedings in short-hand greatly adds to the efficiency of the meeting.
- It is very important to provide for drinking water and make sure that there are enough glasses. If the meeting is to be of long duration, arrangements must be made for refreshments, tea, lunch, as may be required. These arrangements must be checked carefully on the day of the meeting.
- *If there are outstation participants or guest speakers,
- There must be a team of persons to look after their accommodation, tickets, and other needs.

A meeting depends a great deal on the comfort of the members/participants. If they are uncomfortable or anxious about their arrangements they cannot pay attention to the proceedings. Every care must be taken to ensure that participants are comfort-able.

Checklist for meeting arrangements

1. Sufficient number of chairs, properly arranged
2. Name plates for participants and name boards for seating arrangement
3. Writing material (note-pads, pens, pencils) and pointers
4. Pins, clips, paperweights, paper-cutters, staplers, punches
5. Sound equipment to be tested
6. Projection equipment

(a) Plugged in, tested,

(b) Focussed and properly levelled (actually checked)

(c) Properly cleaned lenses

(d) Spare lamps and fuses

7. Facilities for display
   (a) Screens
   (b) Blackboard (cleaned), chalk, dusters
   (c) Easel (set up), crayons
8. Extension cords placed properly so that no one will trip over them
9. Provision for darkening the room if necessary
10. Exhibits, projection material, arranged in required sequence
11. Water and glasses.

CONDUCT OF A MEETING

A meeting of any kind is conducted by the convener or the chairman of the meeting or by a leader/moderator. The three represent a slightly different job description. A convener is one who calls and arranges for the meeting; the convener may conduct the meeting personally or have someone else to conduct it. The chairman usually has statutory powers and duties; s/he has to keep to the rules and regulations of the conduct of the meeting and maintain correct procedure. Many organizations have a rule book for the conduct of meetings, and the chairman has to see that the rules are followed. In case of controversies and wrangles, voting and ties, the chairman has to give a ruling and may have a casting vote. A leader or moderator is generally the one who conducts a group discussion or a conference session.

Chairman's Responsibilities

A person acting in any of the three capacities needs to be a skilful leader of a discussion; whether appointed by statute or selected for the occasion or elected from among the group, the leader has to carry out the function of guiding the discussion, keeping it on track and arriving at a useful conclusion at the end of the given time.

The leader must work up the agenda before the meeting, and check that all requirements are made available in the meeting room, and that the needed staff is in attendance, to assist at the meeting.

The given time must be strictly observed; that is, the meeting must be started at the scheduled time and closed, with useful conclusions, within the stated time, or at least within reasonable time. Time is an important factor in communication; long-drawn out meetings tire out participants and create a sense of wasted time. Delay in beginning the meeting usually has a bad effect.

The meeting leader should ensure that there is someone to take notes; if one has not been arranged for, someone from among the participants can be appointed to be the raporteur; in a large meeting it is better to have two or three. The success of the meeting depends, in a large measure, on the chairman/ leader.

Opening the Meeting: The opening remarks or introduction by the chairman sets the tone of the meeting. A good leader begins on a positive note even when the situation does not inspire optimism. The chairman/leader must outline the goal and objectives of the meeting, explaining any required details like the procedure to be followed in the discussion, the break-up of the discussion topic and the time allowed. The chairman's introductory remarks should be limited to two or three minutes, and the discussion should be passed on to the participants.

Running the Meeting: The discussion can be passed on to participants by putting a general question to the group; if this does not work, a specific question may be addressed to a particular person. Some leaders take pains to brief a member, in advance, to raise certain points to get the discussion started. The leader should talk as little as possible, and not take up more than 20% of the total meeting time; the leader's job is to guide the discussion, to see that it does not get out of point, that it does not get stuck, or limited to just two or three persons.

The leader must never pose as an expert or authority on any matter. The group must be encouraged and helped to take the decision as far as possible. The leader can direct their thinking through skilful use of questions, summaries and examples. A major task of the leader is to deal with difficult participants; there may be the professional opposers, the non-contributors, the show-stealers, complainers and ramblers. The leader must master the art of asking questions and the art of interrupting without giving offence or being discourteous; the leader needs patience, alertness, knowledge of the subject and a cool head. If some members do not speak, the leader must draw them into the discussion by addressing a question to them like:

"Mr. Agarwal, how would your section be affected by this?"

"What has been your experience in this, Mrs. Mehta?" If the discussion goes off the track, the leader may have to interrupt:

"That is an interesting side-light, Mr. D'Souza, and we ought to discuss it separately. Shall we return to this question of...?"

If one participant tends to talk too often or too long, or if the discussion gets limited to two or three persons, the leader will have to intervene with a remark like:

"Shall we hear some other points of view on this before we put down an agreed conclusion?"

"Let us also hear the views of other members on this. Miss Parikh, I can see you want to say something."

"You have brought up an interesting point, Mrs. Irani, and I'm sure several other members will want to discuss this. What's your experience, Mr. Raval?" (This may be said at a suitable point in the endless talker's speech).

If the discussion seems to come to a stop, the chairman may put a question to stimulate more ideas, or summarize the points brought out so far; a summary often provides a sort of review and may bring out a few more points or indicate a satisfactory conclusion.

Closing the Meeting: When the time allowed for the meeting (or for the topic/item) is over, and the meeting has arrived at a good conclusion, the chairman should re-state or summarize the conclusion and ensure that it is noted down. The closing remarks should have a positive note of accomplishment, so that the participants feel that they have achieved something by their effort at the meeting. The leader/chairman should also thank the participants for their contribution.

Post-meeting Activities: Whatever the type of meeting, the conclusions reached at the meeting must be recorded. The chairman/leader may write the report or get it written by the secretary. In the case of a formal meeting the secretary prepares the minutes in consultation with the chairman. Copies of the report are sent to all the participants.

It is also necessary to send information in the form of notices, letters, office notes, etc., to others who may be affected or are required to take action to implement decisions. Reports may also have to be sent to higher authority and to the press. All the follow-up communication should be completed as soon as possible after the meeting.

Responsibilities of Participants

Every participant has a stake in the meeting. In fact, the alert participant finds that a meeting is an opportunity for continuing education in business management.

If you are an attentive participant you gather much knowledge in your own field from the other participants, who present different points of view. The meeting also enables participants to learn about the total function of the department or the organization, and get an over-all company view.

The meeting forces the active participant to think carefully. Besides, it offers you the opportunity to develop your own skills of presenting your point of view before a roomful of critics who will review your thinking.

Active participation serves to demonstrate your talents to superiors. The ability to think clearly, to discuss rationally, to make positive contribution and to maintain courteous conduct is sure to be noticed in a meeting.

A person who has learnt to be a good participant generally becomes a good leader of a meeting. The following are some suggestions for effective participation:

(i) Never fail to do homework. Study every item on the agenda, collect information and gather points of view for each item. Any papers distributed with the agenda must be read thoroughly.

(ii) Keep an open mind. However well-prepared you may be, there is a possibility that you may be wrong. Be prepared to learn and correct any mistake in thinking or information.

(iii) Do not disturb other participants or yourself by talking on the side or by shuffling papers.

(iv) Have a sporting spirit. If your idea/suggestion is defeated in the discussion, be graceful and thank others for helping you to clarify your ideas.

(v) Show interest in what others say. When someone makes a good point, show appreciation even if it demolishes your point.

(vi) Never personalize a difference of opinion. If it is necessary to disagree with something that is said, first re-state or summarize it and then explain why you disagree.

(vii) Speak up if you have something to say, especially on a topic on which you have knowledge. Willingness to contribute and share is necessary. But keep your comments short and precise. There is no need to make a lengthy speech to make an impression.

(viii) Do not be carried away or swayed by emotions. Problems cannot be solved by anger, jealousy, revengefulness or spite. Willingness to examine the ideas presented will be more useful.

(ix) Be a good listener. You will learn a great deal about matters and about human behaviour if you listen carefully and intelligently.

(x) Be courteous at all times. Your meeting manners must be at least as good as your social manners when you are the host, or a guest in someone's house.

EXERCISES

1. Discuss the importance of learning group communication skills.
2. What are the different types of meetings?
3. What arrangements need to be made to ensure the smooth conduct of a meeting?
4. Distinguish between committee and conference.
5. What are the advantages and disadvantages of using committees for administration and management?
6. What are the responsibilities of the participants in a conference?
7. What skills does the leader of a meeting need?
8. What is the difference between convener, chairman and leader of a meeting? What communication skills does a person need in order to be successful in any of these positions?
9. Prepare a series of questions to serve as a guideline for a conference on each of the following subjects:
   (a) Should all office work of our company be computerized?
   (b) How to reduce accidents in the factory?
   (c) What makes a good website?
   (d) Rejections of our products.
   (e) What should be our policy on requests for financial aid from hospitals and educational institutions?
   (f) Is the present examination system satisfactory?
10. How does an organization benefit from group communication among its staff?
11. Are the following statements true?
   (a) The chairperson should do most of the talking in a meeting.
   (b) A lengthy speech makes a good impression in a meeting.
   (c) A committee may be a part of the administrative structure of an organization.
   (d) Conferences are useful for learning by sharing experiences.
   (e) Participation in a meeting is an educative experience.

❑❑❑

Chapter 11

INTERVIEWS

An interview is a formal meeting in which a person or persons question, consult or evaluate another person or persons. Reporters and writers have meetings with eminent persons to ask questions to gather material for a media story or broadcast. It is an oral, face-to-face communication.

An interview reveals the views, ideas and attitudes of the person being interviewed as well as the skills of the interviewer. Both, the interviewer and the interviewee must be well prepared for an interview.

While the interview for publication is confined to outstanding personalities and journalists, the interview for employment is an inevitable experience for everyone. The employment interview needs a good deal of preparation by both the interviewer and the candidate, and is discussed here in detail.

TYPES OF INTERVIEW

Interviews are classified by the purpose for which the interview is held.

The interview is used in an organization for several purposes besides selection for employment. Interviews of present employees are a channel of upward communication. Employees' attitudes, opinions and views, ideas and suggestions, feelings of fear, hopes and ambitions are revealed during an interview. Rumours which circulate among employees do not move upward through regular, routine channels; they can be made to move upward through interviews.

Besides, the interview is used for getting feedback in specific situations and for finding out information.

Promotion Interview

Persons due for promotion are interviewed even if there is no competition. The interview is likely to be informal and serves as induction into a new team, with new responsibilities. Clarifications about nature of duties and responsibilities and expectations are made during a promotion interview. If there is competition for promotion, the interview helps in the selection process and may also serve as an opportunity for a discussion of career opportunities for each candidate.

Grievance Interview

A grievance is resentment or complaint against some injustice which may be real or imagined. It is unhealthy for an employee to nurse a grievance. Human Resources staff sets up an interview with a person who has a grievance. The employee is given the opportunity to air the grievance, and efforts are made to correct any injustice. If the grievance is imaginary, efforts are made to make the employee see the situation differently. This type of interview is successful only if the person with the grievance is given full opportunity to speak and state his point of view. The interview needs patience and empathy to listen attentively.

Appraisal or Assessment Interview

An appraisal interview is one of the methods of periodical assessment of employees. There are other methods like completion of self-assessment forms and assessment by supervisors. But annual appraisal interview is the best method for judging employees' attitudes. A face-to-face confidential talk is an opportunity for both, the employee and the supervisor to discuss several issues.

This interview is more a discussion than question-answer. The focus is on the career development of the employee; short-comings, areas which need improvement, areas which can be further strengthened, training needs, job enrichment and opportunities for promotion, etc, may be discussed at the interview.

Problem Interview

A problem interview is a meeting with a problem employee. An employee whose performance or behaviour is unsatisfactory in spite of warning represents a problem. An interview is more likely to suggest a solution than warnings and notices. The reason for the employee's poor performance can be found out in a face-to-face talk; it may be domestic problems, ill health, lack of training or dissatisfaction with the job, failure to adjust to the environment, etc. Many organizations have facilities for counselling staff; the employee may be offered a session with the counsellor.

If the employee's behaviour is unsatisfactory, the interview can be used for giving a clear understanding of what is expected, and what will be the consequences of unacceptable conduct. The interviewer needs persuasion and negotiating skills for such interviews.

Reprimand Interview

A reprimand is a warning; it is given after efforts have been made to correct the employee's work and behaviour. The purpose of this interview is to let a seriously erring employee know that his/her behaviour or work is unsatisfactory and the management is displeased with his/her conduct. Usually such an interview is given after the employee has been given an opportunity to explain himself and the explanation has been considered unacceptable. A report of the interview is filed in the employee's personal service file.

Exit interview

An exit interview is given to an employee who has resigned. Several things can be accomplished in an exit interview. The organization can—

1. —find out the precise reason for the employee's decision to leave. If there has been any misunderstanding or ill-feeling, there is an opportunity to clear it. It is better for an organization's public image to maintain good relations with past employees.
2. —get feedback on employees' attitudes to and opinion of the organization's policies. An employee who is leaving has no fear of the bosses' displeasure and is likely to express his opinion of the organization's employee relations, public relations, sales policies etc., quite freely.
3. —check all the details and information in the employee's personal record file to make sure that they are up-to-date.
4. —give the final pay cheque, or information about when it will be ready and how it will be handed over.
5. —give information about accrued benefits like sick leave, earned leave which has not been used by the employee. The employee will also have made some calculations and may be anxious to know if the boss concurs.
6. —give information about Provident Fund, Group Insurance or any other benefits, and how and when the dues will be paid.
7. —check that all books, manuals, tools, equipment which were issued to the employee have been returned. When the exit interview is handled carefully and tactfully it can be an asset to the organization.

Stress Interview

As the name suggests, a stress interview puts the candidate into difficult situations in order to test her/his reaction to stress. This method is used for selection for positions in which the person must be able to face difficult situations without getting upset. A stress interview tests such qualities as courage, tact, cool temper, and self-command, which are needed when confronted by employees or people in big or small groups.

Several methods are used to throw the candidate out of balance:

rapid fire questions on several topics at once; questions asked by different members of the panel together; cross questioning and arguing, disputing the candidate's statements, ridiculing the answers; subjecting her/him to silence and inattention. Only a cool-headed and self-possessed candidate responds appropriately and passes the test. Interviewers need practice and training in taking a stress interview.

The candidate must be informed at the end that it was a stress interview.

Panel Interview

There is a panel of three or four persons who interview the candidate. They belong to different fields of expertise; one may be a technical or function expert. Assessment is made by the panel together, using rating scales or other assessment tools. The candidate has to communicate with all members of the panel.

Telephone Interview

Preliminary assessment of a proposal (for a job or a deal) may be made by holding a telephone conversation. Each side may ask questions to collect information about the proposal. While it is possible to make a fairly good assessment of some kinds of deals by telephone, a face-to-face interview is essential for a final decision on recruitment. For jobs in which the interviewee's telephone voice, skills and etiquette are the most important, as in a BPO, final decision may be taken on the basis of the telephone interview.

EMPLOYMENT OR SELECTION INTERVIEW

The most important objective of the selection interview is to assess the suitability of the candidates for specific jobs. The interview is the basis for important decisions for both, the employer and the candidate. The interviewer has to decide whether the candidate should be appointed; an organization wants to find the right persons for employment and the selection can affect the organization. The candidate has to decide whether he will accept the job; this decision will influence his career.

Employment interviews are usually taken by a panel of interviewers. The panel may have expert interviewers who can draw out and reveal aspects of the candidate's personality which are important for the job. There would also be technical experts and departmental heads and other senior officers to whom the person in the post would report.

For announced vacancies, interviews are taken in a suitable room in the organization's office. Many organizations recruit promising candidates by holding campus interviews in professional colleges and institutions.

An interview may take anything from ten minutes to forty-five minutes or even longer. Interviewers spend more time on good candidates; they have to gather enough information about the candidates to be able to assess their suitability to join the organization. The candidates too must find out about the organization, its employee policies and culture, what it expects the recruits to do and what opportunities for career development it offers. Both, the candidate and the interviewer must be well prepared for the interview.

Candidate's Preparation

The candidate must be physically, mentally and psychologically prepared for the interview. It is not only information and knowledge of the candidate that is assessed at an interview; the whole personality is assessed.

(a) Physical preparation:

(i) The candidate is expected to be properly groomed and formally dressed. Clean and well-cut nails, properly combed hair and general personal hygiene are very important. Well-laundered and well-fitting clothes, neat footwear, and a suitable hand-bag or brief case are the normal requirements of formal appearance.

(ii) Posture, that is, carriage and bearing, develop over the years; it cannot be changed in a short time. Those who find their posture is poor, must practice to improve it. The way a candidate carries himself while standing, walking and sitting reveals a good deal about him. Self-confidence, nervousness or over-confidence, are all reflected in the posture and bearing of the candidate. Note your body movements, and take care to stop any bad habitual movements.

(iii) Good manners and conduct are necessary. The candidate must know what is the suitable greeting for the time of the day. Indian style greeting of "namaste" is acceptable if the company is Indian and all interviewers are Indian.

- Do not offer to shake hands unless it is offered by an interviewer.
- Do not sit until you are asked to sit down; if you are not asked to sit, ask for permission to sit: "May I sit down?" should be said politely and without embarrassment.
- Take care while handling the chair; it should not be dragged noisily or clumsily. Sit comfortably and with good posture.
- If you have a large brief case, put it down on the floor near the chair. If you have a small hand bag, keep it on your lap. Be comfortable and well practiced in handling your bag or brief case.
- Do not put elbows or hands on the table. Practice keeping hands comfortably when you are not using them.
- Maintain comfortable posture throughout the interview.
- At the end of the interview, remember to thank the interviewers and wish them Good day.

(b) Mental preparation:

(i) For new job-seekers, it is necessary to revise subjects studied for the completed examinations and courses. Knowledge in the field of specialization must be up-to-date. It is absolutely necessary to take a look at your bio-data, and be prepared to give more information about all items including hobbies and other interests mentioned in it.

(ii) Current events, important current issues in the country and in the world will be subjects at the interview. Regular reading of newspapers, listening to TV news and discussions on current issues are useful in being well-informed. Some personal views and opinions on current issues may be asked for; candidates must be able to discuss issues intelligently and support their opinions with well-considered reasons.

(iii) Information about the interviewing company, its owners/directors, its products, its turnover, share capital, etc., are available in the company's annual report. The candidate must find out as much information as possible about the company whose employment she/he seeks.

(iv) A number of biographical questions and general questions are asked at an interview. Questions listed later in this chapter are representative of questions asked and it will be useful to be well prepared with them.

(c) Psychological preparation:

Several situations or questions during an interview can cause discomfort or embarrassment to the candidate. It is better to anticipate some, and be prepared to handle such situations or questions. Balance of mind is needed to deal with a discouraging situation. Psychological preparedness has to be built up slowly and gradually. It is a part of personality and character development during education.

(i) Honesty in answering questions is the best policy. Dishonesty generally shows up, and makes a bad impression. It is better to admit inability to answer a question than to pretend and guess answers. No one is expected to know everything; it is more important to know the sources of information. Being able to admit lack of information on a topic without loss of face is a strong point.

(ii) Inability to discuss a topic makes a bad impression. If there is any topic that seems too embarrassing to talk about, it is useful to read up information on it and talk about it objectively to a few friends for practice. Inhibitions can be dealt with only by facing them.

(iii) Salary is a topic that must be discussed at the interview. It is important to talk about the compensation package without appearing to be bargaining, or being driven or defeated. Information about salaries given for such jobs and one's qualifications, and a good self-assessment should give a candidate the confidence to negotiate the compensation package.

(iv) A candidate must have the clarity of purpose and determination to want to know her/his prospects in the organization. Information about the nature of duties, future prospects, other benefits, and any other desired information must be got before leaving. The information is necessary for taking a decision, especially if there are other job offers.

(d) Self-assessment:

Anyone who wants to be successful in life, must make a good self-assessment. Knowledge of one's strong points and weaknesses is very useful in gaining self-confidence. Self-assessment takes time and should be done carefully and patiently. Parents and close friends can help in pointing out faults and in correcting them and also in finding out strong points and strengthening them.

Coming to terms with oneself, knowing how to deal with one's faults, and how to make good use of one's talents and skills is excellent preparation for an interview. It adds a great deal of self-confidence and poise to the personality.

SELF-ASSESSMENT FORM

1. My favourite activities are: (i) .... (ii) ....
2. My best skills are:
   (i) Describing, narrating, explaining, discussing, elocution
   (ii) Drawing, cartooning, photography
   (iii) Writing letters, summarizing, reports, stories, poems
   (iv) Solving problems, settling conflicts, persuading, listening
   (v) Figures: geometry, maths, accounting, statistics,
   (vi) Singing, dancing, craft, languages, time management, Yoga, interaction
3. I like to work alone/ in a group
4. My contribution to—
   (i) family:
   (ii) friends:
   (iii) my school/college:
   (iv) society
5. The skills I have acquired from this are:
6. What are my hobbies?
7. What kind of activities do my hobbies involve?
8. What have I learnt from my hobbies?
9. What are my interests? (Travel, photography, sports, craft)
10. How can I do these activities purposefully?
11. What kind of room/environment do I like to work in?
12. What makes me
    (i) angry
    (ii) happy
    (iii) sad
13. What is my height (cm), weight (kg), state of health and history of health, posture, state of mind, (all facts about myself) date and place of birth, languages I know, family background, places I have visited.
14. What advantages and disadvantages do I have from each of these? Do any of them make me especially fit or unfit for specific tasks/ positions/ jobs?
15. What achievement have I made in the last one year, (in my life so far) of which I am proud? Why am I proud of it?
16. What are the things I hate doing?
    (i) ....
    (ii) ....

17. What frightens me the most?
18. What subjects do I hate and why?
19. What kind of work do I tend to avoid/ put off?
20. What kind of TV programs do I dislike? Why?

A. List at least 10 skills which you have developed in each of the following areas: Education/Work/Internships or Volunteer/Extracurricular. Use "action words" to write one-line summaries.

B. Circle each of the skills listed in part A that you would like to use in your job. If there are other talents you have that you would like to use on the job, add them to the list of circled skills. Then rank the skills in order of those you most want to use.

C. Make a list of what you consider to be 3 great accomplishments in your life. What personal qualities helped you reach each goal?

The Interview

Candidates should arrive at the place of interview at least ten minutes before the given time. It helps to look around the place and get a feel of the organization.

An interview can be considered as having four parts, all of which must be properly performed: Entry, Answering questions, Asking questions, and Leaving. A candidate is under observation from the moment of showing up at the door till she/he goes out of the door.

Entry: The candidate walks into an unfamiliar room; s/he must be able to adjust quickly to the size and appearance of the room. Manner of opening and closing the door, walking, greeting, and taking the chair will show whether the candidate is clumsy or graceful and well-mannered, nervous or composed and confident. An inexperienced candidate might feel nervous at the time of entry; being nervous is not a shortcoming and it usually disappears when the interview begins.

Entry takes only a minute, but it makes the first impression and impact. A natural pleasant expression makes a better impression than a grim, tense expression or a vain attempt to appear relaxed.

Answering questions: This takes the major part of the interview time. Good interviewers take care to make the candidate feel comfortable because they are interested in finding out the qualities and suitability of the candidate for their job; a nervous and uncomfortable candidate does not show his best qualities. It is in the interest of both that the candidate should be composed and calm

Questions range from details of education and experience, special abilities, personal interests, family background and circumstances, to any problems faced and handled in the past. The questions are meant to test the candidate's information and knowledge as well as personal qualities, character, attitude to work and life, career goals, motivation, and circumstances. The list of questions given later will be useful in making a self-assessment as well as in preparation for an interview.

Asking questions: The candidate is often invited to ask questions. If not invited, you may seek permission to ask for information by saying, "May I ask a few questions?" or "May I ask for some information?"

The questions you ask will depend on your situation, the position you are applying for, and your relationship with the interviewer(s) and the organization.

The questions should arise out of clarity of purpose, motivation and career goals. You may ask about working conditions, prospects of career growth in the organization, working relationships, etc. Some examples are given below:

- Will this job involve travelling?
- Does the company provide any training or other educational opportunities for staff?
- What are the avenues for promotion?
- When can I expect to hear from you?

The questions must be asked politely and with sincere desire to get information to assess the opportunities the job offers.

Depending on the company, a candidate, especially an experienced person, may ask more confident questions like the following:

- May I see a copy of the job description?
- Why has this job become available?
- Why did the person who held this position leave?
- What qualities are you seeking in a person for this job?
- What is the next step?
- When will you make the selection?
- What would a normal working day be like?
- Can you explain the position and the type of candidate you would like to hire?
- What do you expect from the successful candidate in the first two months?
- Is this a newly created position? If not, what happened to the person who held this position?
- Who will the new employee report to?
- Do you see any major changes within the company that will affect this position?
- How often are performance reviews given?
- Is it possible to tour the facility?
- What is the dress code?

Leaving: Interviewers generally indicate when the interview is over. They may say something like, "Thank you, we'll get in touch with you later." Like the entry, leaving takes a very short time, but can be confusing and uncomfortable for an inexperienced candidate. Leave taking should be responsive to the interviewers.

- Thank the interviewers.
- Collect and pack all papers and files quickly and neatly.
- Get up gracefully, without scraping the chair.
- Wish them Good day.
- Do not offer to shake hands; but be alert; if anyone offers to shake hands be quick to take it.

- Put the chair back in its place.
- Walk away with good bearing.
- Shut the door carefully and noiselessly.

On the same day or the next day, send a personalized thank-you letter to the interviewers (or HR Manager or the person to whom you had addressed your application) to refresh their memory of you. This gives you an opportunity to briefly mention any experience or skills that were not discussed in your interview. If possible, mention something that happened in the interview.

Make a "post-interview assessment", that is, a careful analysis of what you did well and what you could improve on during the interview.

QUESTIONS COMMONLY ASKED IN INTERVIEWS

Some commonly asked questions are given here; the list is not comprehensive. Well prepared interviewers ask some very probing questions.

1. Tell us about yourself.
2. In what school/college activities did you take part? Which did you enjoy the most?
3. Do you think the extra-curricular activities were worth the time you spent on them? Why?
4. What college subjects did you like the most (least)? Why?
5. Did you earn any part of your college expenses? How?
6. How did you spend your college vacations?
7. How often have you been absent from school/ college/ work/ training?
8. What is your opinion of the education and training you have received?
9. What have you learnt from your extra-curricular activities in school/college?
10. Did you enjoy the years you spent in college?
11. Which of your college years were the most difficult? Why?
12. How were your relations with your fellow- students? with your teachers?
13. Would you choose the same college again? Why?
14. How did you spend your free time while in college?
15. What contribution did you make to NSS /any other social service while in college? What did you learn from it?
16. Why did you choose your particular specialisation (professional course/career)?
17. Why did you choose this particular field of work?
18. How has your education (training) prepared you for a career in this field?
19. How has your college experience prepared you for this job?
20. Have you ever changed your major field of interest while in college? Why did you make the change?

21. Do you think examination grades should be considered by employers? Why?
22. What qualities do you have that might make you successful in this field?
23. Why do you think you would like this particular job?
24. What personal characteristics are necessary for success in this job/field?
25. What do you know about the opportunities in your field of training?
26. What are the disadvantages of your chosen field?
27. What are the most important rewards you expect in your career?
28. Why do you think you would like to work in our company?
29. What do you know about this company?
30. What do you think determines a person's progress in a good company?
31. Do you prefer any specific geographic location? Why?
32. Do you prefer working with others or in a team (or alone by yourself?)
33. What are your career plans?
34. How do you plan to achieve your career goals?
35. What kind of work interests you?
36. What are some of the things you find difficult to do?
37. How do you work under pressure? Can you describe a situation in which you worked well under pressure?
38. What causes you to lose temper?
39. Under what conditions do you work best?
40. Why did you (do you want to) leave your previous job?
41. How did your previous employers treat you?
42. What kind of trouble have you had with other people on the job?
43. What have you learned from the jobs you have held?
44. Are you looking for a permanent or a temporary job?
45. Do you like regular hours? routine work?
46. How would you describe the ideal job for you?
47. What criteria do you use to evaluate the company you want to work in?
48. Can you take correction without getting upset? How do you know?
49. What is your father's occupation? your mother's occupation?
50. Which of your parents has had the greater influence on you?
51. What part does family play in your life?
52. What has been the most painful experience of your life?
53. What two accomplishments have given you the most satisfaction?
54. What do you consider your most proud achievement?
55. And can you describe a situation when it was not so good?

56. What do you consider your worst failure?
57. How long do you expect to work here?
58. What do you really want to do in life?
59. Define cooperation.
60. What preparation did you make for this interview?
61. What does the name ___ mean to you? (anyone currently in the news)
62. What is your major weakness?
63. What do you do to keep physically fit?
64. How do you spend Sundays and holidays?
65. Have you had any serious illness or injury?
66. Are you willing to go where the company sends you?
67. What type of books do you read?
68. What is the last book you read? What is it about? Why did you like (not like) it?
69. What type of TV programs do you like best?
70. Name two or three things most important to you in life.
71. Tell me about your family background.
72. Tell me about your personal life.
73. What type of persons seem to rub you the wrong way?
74. What jobs have you enjoyed the most? the least? Why?
75. How do you get on with persons whose background and interests are different from yours?
76. Have you ever taught a student of a lower class?
77. What are your special skills/abilities?
78. What kind of work interests you? bores you?
79. Have you got an analytical mind? How do you know?
80. What do you consider the highest form of praise?
81. Do you enjoy sports as a participant? as an observer?
82. Would you prefer to work in a large company or a small company? Why?
83. What is your idea about the pressure under which industry operates today?
84. What have you done so far which shows your initiative and willingness to work?
85. How would your best friend describe you?
86. How would an enemy describe you?
87. What are you salary expectations?
88. What did you earn in your last job?
89. What do you expect to earn in five years from now?
90. What major problems have you encountered and how did you deal with them?

91. What have you learned from your mistakes?
92. Did you ever have problems with your supervisor?
93. Why should we hire you?

Role of Interviewer

Good candidates have the option of choosing the organization they want to work for, and to accept or reject a job offer. With changing times, organisations have less power to select or reject a candidate. Interviews have the dual role of attracting candidates and selecting candidates.

The impression that an organization makes on candidates is important. The manner in which the waiting candidates are treated influences the public image of the organization.

The following aspects make an impression and must be arranged properly.

- Candidates should be received with proper welcome and directions to go to the right room. They must be treated respectfully like clients and other visitors. Arrangements must be made for their reception, seating, tea and so on.
- The given schedule should be followed; delays make a negative impression.
- The environment where the candidates wait, and the room in which they are interviewed must be pleasant. Crowding, noise, chaos, poor ventilation, lack of cleanliness make a poor impression. .
- The interview itself must be a well-organized process. Clear information on job description, required qualifications, emoluments, organization's mission or goal, and other information about the organization should be readily available.
- Candidates should be given information on the result of the interview as soon as possible so that they are not kept waiting.

In order to make an interview fruitful, the interviewer must be adequately prepared. The interviewer must have a clear idea of the qualities and skills required for the particular job. Job description which gives all the details of the elements of the job must be kept in mind.

Job description gives: 'Title of the post' and its 'position' in the organization; that is, to whom the person reports and who reports to the person holding it. 'Duties and responsibilities' are indicated by a list of the tasks which must be carried out by the person in the post. 'Working conditions' indicates the working hours, physical conditions of the place of work, especially if they are different from the normal; very high/low temperature or lighting, unusual hours, night duties, requirement of high mobility, or any other stress conditions are indicated. 'Economic conditions' indicates salary, allowances, benefits, leave, bonus, retirement benefits, etc.

The job description is used to prepare a description of the personal qualities required of the person who will do the job. This is called Personnel Specification; it is an outline description of the kind of person who would be suitable for the job. It is not used for a value judgement of a candidate; it is a way of finding the most suitable person to match the job requirements. A personality sketch of a person can be developed by assessment in five areas.

(i) Impact is the effect of the candidate's personality on others. It depends partly on the appearance and clothes, and largely on the bearing and self-confidence. Communication skills are a very important factor. Different types of jobs need different levels of impact; a PRO needs it in large measure, while an accountant needs a lower level of impact.

(ii) Qualifications include education, training and experience. The details of qualifications are stated in the bio-data. Interview questions on this aspect probe what the candidate has learnt from the experience, and exactly what skill the candidate has acquired.

(iii) Abilities and skills are developed by training and experience; there are also natural abilities. Quickness of understanding, response and reaction to questions and situations at the interview are usually noted. Questions may be asked to find out the level of skill attained in a particular field. Different jobs need different levels of various skills and abilities.

(iv) Adjustment is the emotional balance which a person maintains. This is an important quality for a person to be able to work and get on with others, and to endure difficult or stressing situations. Some jobs require a higher level of stress tolerance than others.

(v) Motivation is indicated by the goals a person sets for oneself and the standards maintained by the person in all activities. Determination to achieve goals and skill in overcoming difficulties also indicate motivation. A person with high motivation is a misfit in a routine job without challenges. The level of the selected candidate's motivation should be suitable for the nature of work.

Interviewer's preparation

Preparation for the interview has to be made well in advance. The received applications are sorted and scrutinized, and qualified candidates are selected for interviewing. If the number of candidates is large, some are eliminated by examining and assessing the presentation of application letter and bio-data.

A panel of interviewers is selected on the basis of requirements of the job and the assessment which has to be made at the interview. A date for the interview is fixed, and the interviewers as well as the selected candidates are sent letters informing them of the date, time and place of the interview. Interviewers may be sent copies of the candidates' bio-data, job descriptions, etc. The candidates' names and other details are tabulated for use during the interview. A copy of the tabulation is provided to each member of the interview panel.

On the day of the interview, the room in which the interview is to be conducted is suitably arranged. The interviewer must see that all conditions are suitable for fair assessment of candidates so that the purpose of the interview is fulfilled.

Another room near the interview room is also arranged for candidates to be seated while waiting to be interviewed. A senior office staff and a peon attend to the needs of the waiting candidates.

Preparing questions: Besides these physical preparations, each panel member has to examine the bio-data of candidates and pre-pare questions based on the bio-data for each candidate.

Questions can be asked in three ways; each requires a different type of answer and also makes a different impression on the candidate, who tries to answer accordingly.

Can you prepare a trial balance? requires yes or no for answer, and makes the candidate think this skill is one of the requirements of the job.

You can prepare a trial balance, can't you? suggests that it is an essential skill for the job and may put the candidate on the defensive.

How far can you take the books of accounts? makes the candidate describe his skill. Questions which begin with What, How or Why make the candidate speak and give more information; questions which begin with Where, When and Who require limited information.

Conducting the Interview

The interviewer requires several social and interpersonal communication skills.

Welcoming: The interviewer(s) or chairman of the panel must welcome the candidate when he enters, offer him a seat and make him comfortable. A nervous and uncomfortable candidate is difficult to assess; suitable conditions for assessment must be created in order not to waste time and the opportunity of finding suitable staff. A relaxed atmosphere can be created by having a brief conversation unrelated to the interview and by using the candidate's name. A social question or remark like, Did you have difficulty reaching here? if the place is far from the candidate's address, or How do you find the weather in Mumbai (or whichever city it is)? to an outside resident, or You have come a long way for this interview; are you comfortable? can encourage the candidate to be communicative. These can be pre-planned on the basis of each one's bio-data.

Asking questions: This is the most important and longest part of the interview. A good strategy will help to obtain valid and accurate information. The strategy includes these steps:

Develop rapport to encourage the candidate to feel involved; a candidate is more willing to speak openly if the interview shows respect and understanding of his/her needs.

Focus attention and show interest in the candidate's answers and any questions he/she may ask. Using the candidate's choice of terms and phrases for comments, further questions and to answer questions demonstrates that the interviewer is tuned in.

Note non-verbal and verbal indications of the candidate's emotional state such as defensiveness or resistance to open communication.

Re-phrase the conversation if doubts or resistance appear.

For example, you may say, "What you are saying is —. Is that so?" or "I understand that what you mean is — —. Am I right?"

Watch for phrases that try to establish credibility. "I'll be frank with you" "Well, to be quite honest...", "I wouldn't say this to everybody," are often preludes to an attempt at deception.

Friendly responses to what the candidate says make the candidate comfortable and encourage him to speak. While some of the communication at an interview is discussion (not just question-and-answer) the interviewers must take care to see that the candidate speaks the most; if the interview panel begin to discuss among themselves, assessment opportunities are reduced.

It is important not to be sneering or sarcastic; a candidate must never be humiliated even if is obvious that he is unsuitable. Humiliated candidates speak badly of the organization and spread word that it insults visitors. This is bad for the organization's public image and can damage its prospects of attracting good staff. Insulting interview candidates also demonstrates poor organizational culture.

If a candidate is subjected to "stress" interview to judge his stress tolerance, the candidate should be told at the end of it that it was stress interviewing and that he need not feel anxious about it. The candidate should never be made to leave with a stressed, anxious feeling.

Giving information The candidate needs information about the job, the organization, about his prospects, etc and might want to ask questions. The questions must be answered clearly and fully; if any information cannot be given the candidate should be told so, with justification whenever possible. Openness in communication is healthier than secretiveness.

Concluding When all required information has been satisfactorily exchanged, the interviewer (chairman of panel) must conclude the interview with a suitable remark to indicate to the candidate that the interview is over. Leave taking must be pleasant and sociable, with response to the candidate's wishing.

The most direct way to end the interview is simply to say, "Well, I've asked the questions I needed to. Is there anything more you'd like to say or ask?"

If the candidate is to be called for a second interview, it is worth addressing these points:

- Make sure that the candidate is interested enough in the position to justify further discussion.
- Briefly indicate the decision making process for filling the post; for example how many more persons are to be interviewed and how long it will take.
- Inform the candidate approximately when to expect a call for scheduling another interview.

Thank the candidate for his/her time and interest in the organization.

For those candidates that are clearly not to be called for another interview, inform them that interviews will take up the next few days/weeks and that all candidates will be contacted at the end of the process whether they are called for second interview or not.

Assessment: This is a continuous process during an interview. Every candidate is assessed individually for personal ability and performance and also in comparison with other candidates. Members of the panel discuss each candidate and also grade them according to their suitability for the job. The assessment and grading is constantly reviewed as more candidates are assessed. At the end, a final ranking is made.

EXERCISES

1. You have been called for an interview next week, for a job as market research assistant. What preparation would you make? Write your answers to these questions which may be asked at the interview:
   (i) What makes you think you will be successful in a market research job?
   (ii) What do you do to keep yourself physically fit?
   (iii) What is your idea of market research?
   Write two questions which you would like to ask the inter-viewer.
2. Write answers to five of the questions given in this chapter, everyday till you have answered all the questions.
3. Read your answers six months later, and see if you would like to revise any of them. Give reasons for making changes and also for not making changes.
4. What questions would make you uncomfortable in an interview?
   Write down your three most uncomfortable questions.
5. Write down three questions that you would like to ask the interviewers at your first interview for a job.
6. What preparation does the interviewer have to make for an interview?
7. What aspects do interviewers assess when they interview candidates?
8. What is an interview? For what purposes is it used?
9. Write short notes on:
   (a) Appraisal interview
   (b) Exit interview
   (c) Stress interview
   (d) Candidate's preparation for employment interview
10. Fill in the blanks in as few words as possible.
    (a) An exit interview is taken when—
    (b) In a — interview, the candidate is often made to feel uncomfortable in order to —.
    (c) An appraisal interview is —.

□□□

Chapter 12

SPEECHES

A speech is a talk given to a large gathering. It is given on occasions like an anniversary or an inauguration or some such social occasion. Its content is light. Its purpose is usually to encourage, appreciate, congratulate or entertain; it is followed by applause from the audience. The tone of such speeches is cheerful and congratulatory. Controversial ideas and views are to be avoided.

Almost everyone has some occasion for making a short speech. It is an asset to be able to speak well to an audience. Following a few steps and practising delivery of the speech enables anyone to be competent at making the required speech on any occasion.

Preparation work has to be done in four stages:

- Finding out about the surroundings in which the speech is to be delivered
- Preparing the text
- Taking care of one's physical appearance and body language
- Practising delivery of the talk

FINDING OUT ABOUT THE SURROUNDINGS

You should know the venue, the occasion, the time available to you, the organisers, other speakers if any, the audience and your own position in relation to the audience.

The Venue

Be familiar with the physical environment. Is it in the open air or in a closed hall? What is the seating arrangement and how far from the audience will the speaker stand? What is the lighting and ventilation?

The Occasion

It is important to know the occasion. It may be an anniversary, or a celebration or an inauguration or a farewell. You will have to refer to it in your speech. The tone and style of your speech must be suitable to the occasion.

Time Available

Always check before hand, the time that has been allotted to you. Check this when you are invited and before you accept the invitation. Preparation work depends on the given time. Keep strictly within the allotted time. An average person speaks about 100 words a minute. A four to five minute speech needs 400 to 500 words; that is, double-spaced typewritten copy, with 250 words on a page. This is only a guide; find out your own speed by practising.

Find out the right time to arrive at the venue and the right time to leave. It is courteous to keep time to interact with organisers and other speakers.

The Organisers

Find out everything possible about the organisers; name of the organisation, names of the president, the secretary, office-bearers and any other important persons who will be sitting on the dais. You will have to address them by their names and designations at the beginning of your speech. You can begin with,

Mr. Chairman Dr. XYZ , Honorary Secretary Miss PQR, Honorary Treasurer Mr. ABC, and other office bearers of the SPCA, Ladies and Gentlemen:

It has become fashionable to address a lady in the Chair as "Madam Chairperson", but this implies that a lady is a person and a man is not a person. A man in the Chair can be addressed as "Mr. Chairperson." It is also acceptable to address a lady in the Chair as "Madam Chairman".

The audience may be addressed as "Friends" on informal occasions.

Other speakers

Find out if there are other speakers, and their names and their background. If there are only one or two and they are seated on the stage, you will have to address them by their names.

The audience

Knowledge of the audience is the most important for any speaker. The speech must be in a form and style that suits and interests the audience; the content and the tone of the speech depend on the nature of the audience.

Factors to be taken into account are:

Size of the audience: Will there be 30 (tutorial batch-mates) or 300 (all your class-mates) or 2000 (on College Day)? The size makes a great difference to the speaker.

Age group of the audience: Will they be teenagers (college audience), or adults (college teachers), children (school students), mixed group (in your housing society)?

Status: Economic status, educational status, professional status, cultural background (as in all-India student audience at University Youth Festival) are also important.

Choose suitable and appropriate words and phrases which should not give offence to anyone in the audience.

PREPARING THE TEXT

The most important thing is to decide exactly what to say, find out the required information, and give it a proper shape. It must have a smooth flow from one point to the next. For beginners, it is advisable to write down the whole speech, including the address, the opening sentences and the ending sentences.

Style: A talk must sound like conversation, not like a written text. The style of speech is different from the style of writing. In speaking, use short sentences to enable the audience to grasp them at once.

Use simple everyday words, which are easily understood. You can use short forms like *don't*, *couldn't*, and so on as in ordinary conversation.

The tone of speech is informal, but there is a formality in official speaking as distinguished from social or personal style of speaking. Never allow bad conversational habits to come into a speech; repeating phrases like "you know," "you see," or "basically" can be irritating to the audience. Avoid slang terms like "dough" for money, "grub" for food, or colloquial terms like "chap," "guy."

Humour: Humour makes a speech more interesting and personal, and the audience more attentive; but it is not easy to be humorous. Tell a joke only if you are definitely good at it, and can tell it without feeling nervous or self-conscious.

Never introduce a joke by saying "That reminds me of a joke..." Humour should arise naturally in the course of the speech. It must be light and enjoyable, relevant to the topic, and above all, it should not embarrass or hurt the feelings of any listener. Never make or tell a joke that makes fun of any group. Also, see that humour is appropriate on the occasion. Humour is not quite suitable for a farewell speech and it is extremely unsuitable for a condolence speech!

Style of addressing: A speech is presented at an organised meeting; the meeting has a chairman who must be addressed first; other members of the organisation who are seated on the platform are addressed next, in order of their seniority.

Check who all will be present, get their names and titles in advance and see that you address every important person, before addressing the audience. The audience is addressed as "Ladies and Gentlemen," (formal) or "My Colleagues" or "Friends," (informal).

In a condolence speech, there is no elaborate address. "Friends" or "Members of —," should be sufficient.

Composition of Speech

Opening: Your first words are: greeting, self-introduction, and expression of pleasure for the opportunity to speak.

You have 10 seconds in which to make a good starting impression. Smiling helps. Don't start with a joke; it can backfire. Don't begin with apologies for anything.

Build rapport by pointing to a common bond between yourself and the audience. For example, refer to the chairman's or the previous speaker's remarks, or to the occasion of the meeting.

Your confidence, friendliness and sincerity in saying these first few words will set the tone of your speech and the audience's attitude towards you. Read these sentences. Change them to suit your own style. Make sure the grammar is correct and get the correct pronunciation. When you find comfortable sentences practice saying them till you get them naturally.

- *I'm very happy to be here on this occasion of —. Let me thank the organising committee for giving me the opportunity to be a part of the function.*
- *Let me express my gratitude to — for giving me the privilege of participating in —.*
- *I must say how grateful I am that I've been invited to share in the festivities on the occasion of the 25th anniversary of this Institution.*
- *We've assembled here today to celebrate the centenary of our University and I am intensely aware of the honour given to me in being asked to address this distinguished gathering.*

Focusing attention can be done in a number of ways. Decide on a central point for your speech according to the occasion. Focus attention on the central point of the talk. You can adapt the devices given to suit the occasion and the central point of your speech.

(a) **One or two questions**. This can be used in different ways according to the size of the audience and the occasion and central point of the speech. Questions produce thinking, but no answer is expected.

- *What was the population of Mumbai at the last census? And how many are added every day?*
- *In 19—, there were 37,000 vehicles in Mumbai and there were 850 kms of roads. Today the number of vehicles has gone up to 13 lakhs and the road length has merely doubled to 1,870 kms. The density of vehicles in Mumbai is 800 vehicles per km; the international norm is 300.*

(b) A pointed **statement of facts and figures**

- *The average noise level in Delhi, Mumbai and Kolkata is 100 decibels, more than double the prescribed international limit of 45.*
- *In 1972, in Mumbai, the intensity of noise was 101 to 104 decibels during the day and 93 to 98 during the night. If this intensity was to increase by 1 decibel per year it might reach 150 decibels by the next century. (in a speech in 1979)*
- *Fifty percent of the road accidents in Maharashtra, occur in Mumbai.*
- *You can choose from a hundred exciting careers according to your interest and ability.*

(c) An appropriate quotation or proverb.

Tact is the act of making a point without making an enemy. - Clarence Darrow

(d) An **anecdote or historical story** narrated briskly and related quickly to the topic. Use this method only if you have a good story telling style.

Body of the Presentation: The main text depends on the occasion and the objective of the speech. The objective of an inaugural or annual function is to encourage and felicitate; the speech may mention the highlights of the achievements, elaborate on the value of the effort, and express faith in the participants' ability to do even better.

Conclusion: The closing must leave a clear message. For a speech of encouragement, a good conclusion is to express confidence in further achievement. For a persuasive speech, conclude with a request for co-operation or action.

The closing must not be abrupt. A graceful and smooth closing can begin by highlighting main issues. Interesting devices are similar to the attention-focusing sentences used at the beginning. A quotation or a parable or questions can mark the conclusion.

- *We need competition in business, but co-operation on the road.*
- *An exhibition is to be seen, not just to be talked about.*

The ending consists of only two or three sentences. The purpose is to thank the organisers once again, to thank the audience for their attention, and to express forward looking good wishes and/or to invite questions from the audience.

- *Let me once again thank — for inviting me to share your annual celebrations. And thank you for listening to me. I wish you all the success and prosperity you deserve so well.*
- *I thank you for the interest you have shown in —. I thank the organisers once again for giving me this opportunity to spend a pleasant evening with you. I declare the — formally open.*
- *Thank you for giving me your time and attention.*

It is important not to drag on the concluding sentences; the audience gets restless if the speaker does not know how to stop.

SPEAKER'S APPEARANCE AND PERSONALITY

Oral communication comes with the speaker. Your physical appearance and personality make an important impact. Your body language is noticed by the audience before you begin to speak.

Body language includes good grooming and clothing and movements. Personality is greatly influenced by posture, that is, the manner of standing, sitting and walking, and by what you carry in your hands. Whether you have a handbag or papers or a file, carry and handle it comfortably. Self-confidence is an important aspect of personality; it comes from being well prepared.

Here are a few suggestions for taking care of body language while making a speech.

Comfortable posture: While standing, balance your body weight on both feet. Standing with your weight on one foot, leaning on the table or the podium, or constantly shifting the weight from one foot to the other, looks uncomfortable. Never put your hands into your pockets while speaking; it is considered bad manners. Practice a good standing posture and pose; you should not get uncomfortable if you are required to stand free of any furniture and have no mike to hold.

Eye contact: Eye contact is important for creating rapport with the audience. Hold eye contact, for a second, with a person in one corner (say, right-back) of the audience; then, move your eyes to the opposite corner (left-front) of the audience, taking in the whole audience as you move your eyes, making brief eye contact with as many persons as possible. After some time, do it on the other corners of the audience.

Movements: Too much movement or walking around distracts the audience's attention. Movements must be natural and only as much as needed for establishing lively rapport with the audience and for handling visual aids.

Facial expressions and gestures: We all naturally make gestures and have expressions on our face while speaking. While making a speech, gestures and expressions should be natural and friendly. Needless movement of the hands distracts the audience's attention. A pleasant, cheerful face is always an asset.

Voice: Speak just loud enough to reach those sitting at the back. A very loud or very soft voice makes the audience inattentive. Volume and pitch should suit the room and the audience. If there is a mike, hold it six to nine inches away from the mouth. The voice should have variations and modulations to suit the matter and content of the speech.

Pauses: Speak at a comfortable speed. Fast speech, without pauses, overload the listeners. A short silence before making an important point helps to emphasise it. A pause after making an important point gives the listeners time to absorb it.

Health affects body language. If you are in good health your speech has energy and confidence. Your state of health affects your voice.

PRACTISING DELIVERY OF THE SPEECH

Beginners have to practise actual delivery of the speech. No matter how much time and care you have spent on preparing the text, the delivery is largely responsible for the success of the speech.

Rehearsal enables you to test if the language and style are suitable for speech. Reading out aloud is not enough. Only an attempt to deliver it to an audience will show whether the words are natural and comfortable in speech.

Practise till you are "conversationally comfortable" with the material.

Practice also helps to check the timing; you can shorten or lengthen the speech as required. In the beginning, the written text will be longer than required for the given time. If you are a beginner, you should practise speaking out several times; first practise in front of a mirror; then practise in front of any helpful audience that can be collected, such as a group of close friends or family who will give useful feedback.

It is worth making full dress rehearsal for your comfort. Never learn the speech by heart; it creates dependence, and if you forget even a single word it can cause you great confusion.

COMMEMORATIVE SPEECHES

Speeches for different occasions have different requirements. Some of the occasions are discussed here.

Welcome and Introduction

In a welcome speech, the speaker gives the audience information about the guest speaker(s), giving a brief history or report of the organisation which is holding the function, and information about the function itself.

The speech opens with expressions of welcome to the chief guest, other important guests and speakers and the invited audience. This is followed by an introduction of the chief guest. The introduction is prepared with the help of the bio-data which is acquired as soon as the guest accepts the invitation. If there are many guests or speakers to be introduced, the length of introduction is the same for all of them. The introduction is partly biographical and partly narration of one or two personal experiences of the person's interesting qualities.

A short history or report of the organisations' achievements, its plan for future activities, and the purpose of the present function can be included in the introductory speech. The amount of information to be included depends on the time available and the purpose of the function. Your best guide to length is the audience's interest; the worst thing a speaker can do is to bore the listeners with a speech too long for their tolerance. A good rule of thumb is to keep the introductory speech to five to seven minutes.

Inaugural Speech

After the opening sentences, a few remarks on the social relevance of the present activity can lead to the main body of the speech. For example, a speech at the inauguration of an exhibition may include something about exhibitions.

- An exhibition is a kind of stock-taking of the achievements in the field. People from different places can come together and present their work before the public. Members of the public can see what has been done in the field.

The body of the speech can be built around a topic related to the occasion. For example, the pleasure of growing roses is a good topic for an inaugural speech at an exhibition of roses; or the importance of maintaining safe and courteous behaviour on the road can be a topic for inaugurating a Road Safety Week.

For anniversary celebration speeches, there may be a few paragraphs on an organisations' social responsibility, the position of a business or industry in society and the particular organisation's accomplishments.

Towards the end of the speech, there may be some sentences of recognition for work done by the organisers of the present function, those who are engaged in the activities, the donors if any, and those who have contributed in different ways.

The concluding paragraph briefly requests co-operation, or action or encourages further achievement and ends with the customary closing sentences.

Vote of Thanks

A vote of thanks speech is usually the last speech in a function. You have to make special effort to hold the audience's attention.

First of all, find out very carefully, who are the persons, parties that have to be mentioned. Also find out what order you need to follow in listing them. The list will include many persons and parties who may not be present; for example, donors, sponsors, advertisers, and well-wishers. Everyone must be included.

Secondly, collect enough phrases and words that indicate graceful acknowledgement It is boring if you say, "We thank —, we also thank —-, " repeatedly.

For example, you can use:

We appreciate — given by—

We gratefully acknowledge —

We are grateful to — for —

We are indebted to —

Many thanks to —

We are happy to record our gratitude to — for —

Farewell and Send-off

A farewell is a slightly emotional occasion. Speeches on such occasions are short. The content is a summary of the achievements and contribution of the person who is leaving, some of the person's best and most notable qualities and the speaker's own personal experience of the person.

The speech can be made lively by narrating a specific incident to illustrate the person's qualities; good humoured reference to a well known foible like short temper, or avoidance of a particular type of work, may be made provided it will not offend the person. The content of the speech depends a great deal on the relation between the speaker and the person who is being given a farewell; the tone should be appropriate to the occasion; too much emotion or too much humour are both unsuitable. If the occasion is a send-off to a person going to a higher position or on a special assignment, the tone is congratulatory. The speech ends with good wishes for health, success, happiness and further achievement, for example:

- *A man of Mr Yadav's wide interests and capabilities is hardly going to sit idle because he has retired. I have noticed that he has already planned to work on a number of interesting projects which he has assigned to himself. I wish him excellent health and all success and happiness in whatever he chooses to do.*
- *We shall miss Dr .Nair very much. But we also rejoice in his good fortune and his abilities which have brought him this opportunity to serve in an important and responsible position. We wish him every success and all happiness in his new assignment.*

Condolence

A condolence meeting is a solemn occasion. Speeches on such occasions are brief and in a serious tone. Humour of any kind or reference to any humorous incident is out of place. There is no elaborate address even if there are many persons on the dais. The speech opens with a brief address like,

- *Friends, it is a sad occasion for us today when we have to mourn the loss of — who was with us for so many years.*

The cause and circumstances of the death are mentioned after the opening sentence. A brief life sketch of the person, a reference to the person's contribution to his/her organisation and to society, and a personal memory or incident, form the content of the speech. The speech ends with an expression of a sense of grief and loss.

- *In the demise of —we have lost a friend and the company has lost a loyal member.*
- *It will be hard for us to adjust ourselves to the office which no longer has the friendly presence of —*

It is customary to end a condolence speech with the words, "May his/her soul rest in peace."

EXERCISES

1. Write the opening paragraph of:
   (a) a speech on the occasion of a school annual function
   (b) a farewell party to the final year students of your college
   (c) a farewell to a retiring teacher (or colleague at your work place)
   (d) a condolence speech at a meeting to mourn the death of a classmate.
2. Write the closing paragraph for the speeches in 1 above.
3. As the Secretary of a college association, prepare a welcome speech to be given on the occasion of the inauguration of the year's activities.
4. As the General Secretary of your college, prepare a speech to be given at the farewell to the T.Y class.
5. The school/college in which you had studied is celebrating its golden jubilee. You have been invited as chief guest to inaugurate the celebration as you are now a successful person in your profession/business. Draft the speech.

6. As the year's Best Student Award winner of your college, you have been asked to introduce the chief guest at the annual gathering. Draft the speech introducing the guest.
7. As the secretary of your sports club, prepare a speech of welcome and introduction of an eminent sports personality who is the chief guest at your annual sports day.
8. An outstanding sports person among your college students had a fatal car accident. As the secretary of the college gymkhana, prepare a condolence speech.
9. Collect the bio-data of an important personality and prepare a speech introducing him/her.

❑❑❑

Chapter 13

PRESENTATIONS

A presentation is on a serious topic; its purpose is to inform, to explain, and to persuade the audience or present a point of view. It may introduce a product or explain a process or narrate an experience; it is delivered to a small, knowledgeable audience at a conference, a seminar or a business meeting. It is followed by questions from the audience.

Presentation skills can be cultivated and developed with some knowledge of the formal aspects and with practice. You don't have to be a brilliant speaker to make a good presentation.

As in the case of public speaking, preparation work has to be done in four stages:

- Finding out about the environment in which the presentation is to be made
- Preparing the text and the required visuals
- Taking care of one's physical appearance and body language
- Practising delivery of the talk.

FINDING OUT ABOUT THE ENVIRONMENT

The environment includes the venue, the organizers, the occasion, the time available, other speakers if any, the audience and your own position in relation to the audience.

The venue

If it is on your home ground, that is a place with which you are familiar, you will be more comfortable; but all the same, check the room and all the required equipment a few minutes before the talk. If it is outside, you must make efforts to get familiar with the room, the seating arrangement, the speaker's position. Is there a platform? How will it be arranged? Will there be others sitting on the platform while you speak? Is there a mike? Is there a podium? Is its height comfortable?

Check the visual aid equipment carefully. Note its position and the projection.

The organizers

Find out everything possible about the organizers; the name of the organization and names of the important persons in the organization.

The occasion

Is it a business meeting or a conference or a seminar?

Time available

Check before hand, the time allotted to you. Preparation work depends on the given time. You have to keep strictly within the allotted time.

Other speakers

Find out who else will be speaking. Will there be persons from competing organizations? What is their organizational position? Be careful not to make any unfavourable remarks about competitors whether they are present or not.

The audience

The talk must suit the needs and interests of the audience. The content and the tone of the speech depend on the nature of the audience. Take care of the words you use in the presentation; do not refer to anything that might be inappropriate.

Age group of the audience is one of the factors to be taken into account; the following may provide a clue:

- children love to listen to stories and are interested in dramatic presentation; emotions of joy and sorrow can be aroused through stories; ideas must be built up from familiar surroundings.
- high school and college students (teenagers) like to be treated like adults; they are responsive to new ideas; appreciate an honest straightforward approach; can be roused to idealism, but are also likely to be critical; they expect well prepared, informative presentations. Visual aids are effective.
- Young adults are the most sophisticated audience, with a wide range of interests and progressive attitude; they like new projects and ideas, but they are also very critical.
- Middle-aged audiences are conservative and do not accept new ideas easily; they have more knowledge and experience of life, but may not be very enthusiastic about changes or new ideas; they listen with interest but do not easily accept.
- Senior citizens are usually interested in information about new developments and what is going on in the world. They also like to be reminded of the good old days.

- Status: What is the educational and economic status of the audience? Highly educated audiences of any age group are more critical. The rich, as a class, do not favour social changes.

Relationship with audience: Consider your own relationship to the audience. Do they think of you as an expert on the topic, as a colleague sharing experience, as a role model, as a company representative wanting to sell ideas?

PREPARING THE TEXT

You need one hour of preparation for every minute you will talk.

The most important thing is to decide exactly what to say, find out the required information, and give it a proper shape. It must be logical and have a smooth flow from one point to the next.

Write down the whole speech, including the address, the opening sentences and the ending sentences. Then practice, edit and correct it till you get a good presentation to fit within the time.

Length: The average speed of presentation is 100 words per minute; find out your own speed by "delivering" a speech. An A4 size sheet typed in one and a half line spacing in 12-point font size makes a two-minute speech. A four to five minute presentation is 400 to 500 words.

Style: A talk must sound like conversation. Use short sentences to enable the listener to grasp. See that the words and terms you use are suitable for your audience. Specialists in your own field will follow the technical terms, but others will not.

Keep the style formal. There is a formality in official speaking as distinguished from social or personal style of speaking.

Humour: Be sure that you can be humorous without being nervous or looking silly. Humour should be natural, light, enjoyable, and relevant to the topic. It should not embarrass or hurt the feelings of any listener.

Style of addressing: A presentation begins by addressing the audience. A formal style is:

Ladies and Gentlemen,

If there is a Chairperson, she/he must be addressed.

Madam Chairperson, Ladies and Gentlemen,

A presentation does not have an elaborate address style.

Composition of Presentation

Opening: You get about 10 seconds to make a good impact and impression. Create (write it down) a good, strong, solid introduction, and rehearse it till it comes naturally. State your name even though you have been introduced; it reinforces your presence, and helps people to remember you.

Try "delivering" these opening sentences. Change them to suit your own style.

- *Good morning, Ladies and Gentlemen. I am — from — (organisation / your class and division). I'm going to speak on — .*
- *Good evening, Ladies and Gentlemen. As — has already said, I am — from —; and I am here to share with you the results of my experiment with —, (my experience of conducting—), (the background of the case of Messrs. A and B from the point of view of their credit dealings with us.)*
- *Good morning to all of you. I am —, and I intend to share with you the information I have gathered on the topic of "Barriers to Communication".*

The introductory remarks must build rapport and focus attention of the audience. It gives the audience the time to adjust to your personality; they size up the speaker while the introductory sentences are being spoken.

Use any of the methods to focus attention, discussed in Chapter 16.

(a) **Questions** can be used in different ways. In the following examples, the first is rhetorical and no answer is expected. The second directly addresses the audience and a few hands may be put up. The third is an invitation to each one (of a small audience) to speak up.

- *What is the average noise level in Mumbai? And what is the tolerable limit?*
- *Do you know what you are going to do after you pass your B.Com.? How many of you have already planned your career?*
- *What would you like to find out about — during the next 30 minutes? Will each one of you tell me your expectations so I can address your concerns as I go along?*

(b) A pointed **statement of facts and figures**

- *The persons at the lowest level in an organization get only 20% of the information in the organization. 80% is lost on the way downward.*
- *Words carry only 7% of the meaning of what we say, while body language carries 55% and paralanguage carries 38%.*

(c) An appropriate quotation or proverb

- *A man is known by the company he keeps. A company is known by the customers it keeps.*

Body of the Presentation

Plan the body carefully. Choose three main points and elaborate each one briefly.

Make one visual for displaying your three main points. And one each for elaboration of each point.

Using Visual Aids

Visuals focus audience attention. Learn to handle your visuals properly, without getting confused.

They help both, the speaker and the audience; the speaker has them for orderly presentation of points, to illustrate with a diagram, to exhibit data; the audience get a re-inforcement through the eyes for what they hear, and can see a visual summary of points.

You can use any one or more of the following:

Posters can be displayed almost anywhere. Though this is old-fashioned, marketing persons going to rural areas have found this a very dependable method.

Flip chart requires an easel or stand. It is most useful for interactive presentations. You can put up on it ideas that come from the audience. And work on it with audience participation. People in the audience love to see their ideas written up during the presentation.

Overhead Projector (OHP) is very popular and available in most places. Make slides on good quality transparencies. Put only 6 lines or less on one slide. Write or type large enough for the whole audience to see. (You have found out how many, and what seating arrangement and equipment) You can get computer printouts or xerox copy out of a book to put on the OHP slides. Use large font size like 24 and a clear face type like Bookman Old Style.

Powerpoint projection can be used if available. Keep the slides simple. Avoid too much movement (animation) or too much colour (keep to a single colour print). Do not use sound to accompany the slides.

Visuals must fit well into the speech. Prepare them carefully, to enhance a point with illustration or to lay out the main points, or to display a chart or graph.

Conclusion: For an informative speech, give a short summary of the main points. For a persuasive speech, make a request for co-operation or action.

It is important to invite questions from the audience. Introduce the Questions Session well so that people are encouraged to ask questions. Say pleasantly, "I'll be glad to answer any questions."

The concluding sentences should never be dragged; they should be vigorous and businesslike.

- *Thank you for listening to me..*
- *I thank you for the interest you have shown in —.*
- *I have gathered an impression that you have enjoyed this presentation. The attention with which you have been listening certainly made me enjoy sharing my ideas with you. I'm sure you have a lot of questions to ask, and I'll be happy to try to answer your queries.*
- *Thank you for giving me your time and attention. Any questions?*

YOUR APPEARANCE AND POSTURE

Your physical appearance and personality make an important impact.

Be formally dressed; practice it before the actual presentation if you are not used to wearing formal clothing. Make sure you are well groomed from head to toe. Audience notices your body language before you begin to speak.

Practice standing comfortably, being still and quiet. Stand firmly and take a deep breath.

Decide what to do with your hands (**never** in the pockets!). Holding a paper, a bunch of cards (loosely strung together with a string or chain through a punched hole in one corner), and/or a pencil may be helpful.

Relax your face; this may need practice.

Eye contact is very important. Cast your eyes over the entire audience in five seconds. Remember to take in everyone in your glance. If you feel relaxed, smile naturally and say "Good morning".

Keep movements and gestures to the minimum. Move only as much as needed for establishing lively rapport with the audience and for handling visual aids. Too much movement or walking around distracts the audience's attention.

Speak loud enough to reach those sitting at the back. A very loud or very soft voice makes the audience inattentive. The voice should have variations and modulations to suit the matter and content of the speech.

Use pauses; when too many sentences or ideas are given, listeners get overloaded. They need time to absorb ideas. A short silence before making an important point emphasizes it. A pause after making an important point gives the listeners time to absorb it.

A pause is also useful to regain the attention of any distracted persons in the audience; unexpected silence causes most people to focus attention on the speaker.

Take good care of your health. If you are in good health you will be energetic, enthusiastic and confident. Besides, the state of health affects the throat, the tongue and the entire speaking apparatus.

Profile of a good speaker

A good speaker—

- is lively, enthusiastic, interested in the topic and considers it vital to the audience and so speaks with enthusiasm;
- has a sense of responsibility to the audience and tries to say something that will be worth the listeners' time;
- has a sense of responsibility to the others in the programme and, if allotted 5 minutes, does not squeeze others off the programme by taking 10 minutes, thus showing respect for what they may have to say;
- has sense of responsibility to the subject; does not speak on something s/he does not know;
- has a sense of leadership; stands tall, makes eye contact, speaks responsibly and with authority; is positive, friendly, straightforward;
- keeps head on shoulders; does not let confidence turn into over-confidence;
- can accept feedback and benefit by it.

Practising Delivery of the Presentation

Recall the suggestions given in Chapter 12 and practice carefully. In your study group help one another by being the critical audience and giving useful feedback.

EXERCISES

1. Prepare a good self-introduction to be used when you have to make a presentation. Practise delivering it till you are comfortable with it.
2. Write the opening paragraph of: a formal presentation on the topic of "How extra-curricular activities contribute to your personality development."
3. Prepare a closing paragraph of 2 to 3 sentences which you can use for any presentation.
4. Make five-minute presentations on:
   (a) How body language communicates in a interview;
   (b) Participants' responsibility in a meeting;
   (c) Using visual aids in a presentation.

Chapter 14

DIALOGUE SKILLS

Dialogue is talk between two or more persons. In business, dialogue means an exchange of ideas and opinions between two persons, groups or countries, on a particular issue. The purpose of the dialogue is to reach a friendly and amicable agreement.

Dialogue in business is not the skill of debate where you have to defend your position. A debate has a "win-lose" spirit; one side can win only by making the other side lose. Losing gives rise to unhappy and bitter feelings in the loser. Business dialogue aims to win and keep friends; this can be done only by creating comfortable and happy feelings on both sides. Both sides must feel that they gained something.

You need interpersonal skills for business dialogue. Both parties need to tune in, build rapport, have a clear goal, and focus on the goal; they have to aim at reaching a closure which is satisfactory to both.

If the subject of the dialogue is agreeable, it is not difficult to carry on a dialogue. But sometimes, the subject may be unpleasant; there may be controversial issues, there may be hostile feelings; there may be fear and discomfort. In such conditions, the dialogue can be difficult and requires a great deal of skill.

You can create an atmosphere of friendliness, by **being inclusive** and **having empathy** with others. Being inclusive means making the other person feel that his/her contribution, views, ideas are as important as your own; it means including the other person's point of view fully in the discussion. Empathy means showing your understanding of how the other person feels; it does not mean agreeing; it means showing that you understand and appreciate and respect the other person's point of view. This can create a "win-win" atmosphere and the dialogue becomes more fruitful and leads to a comfortable closure.

Situations in which conversation skills are needed

Dialogue skills are needed in any oral communication situation, whether face-to-face or over the telephone.

In meetings there may be clarifications required and given, questions asked and answered, dissatisfaction expressed and pacified.

Interview appears to be a question-and-answer session. But it is a dialogue in which the two parties assess each other and come to conclusions and decisions. There is also some negotiation of terms and conditions between the two parties that plan to work together.

Negotiation is the most difficult type of dialogue. There are clearly opposing interests (especially in employer-employee negotiations) and most often hostile feelings as well.

SKILLS NEEDED FOR DIALOGUE

Dialogue skills require self-control. You cannot control how or what other people talk, but you can control what you yourself do. The only way to control others' talk is to control your own.

Clarify to yourself, the purpose of the dialogue and be sure of what outcome you desire, so that you can aim at it and work towards it.

Besides this, there are other personal and thinking skills you need.

Appearance and clothing

Always practice impeccable grooming (even in a jeans environment). It is insulting to others, colleagues and clients, to show a lack of concern about your appearance.

Speak clearly and pleasantly

This is a primary requirement. It takes practice to be clear in your purpose and ideas and to state them clearly.

Cultivate a pleasant and friendly way of speaking. Speak in a low voice, with controlled gestures. Make eye contact with the other person(s), when speaking as well as when listening. Respond by nodding your head, maintaining an upright posture. If appropriate, put in an occasional comment such as "I see" or "that's interesting" or "really?" to show that you are interested and really listening.

Vary the voice to avoid a monotone. A good command of paralanguage is valuable.

Ask people about their interests. This keeps them involved in the talk.

Do not interrupt others; wait and listen politely till they complete what they are saying; speak only when they stop. If by mistake you interrupt, stop at once and apologise.

Be well-informed on business environment, cultural events, or sports. Never use slang terms.

Good manners and etiquette

You need knowledge and practice of proper etiquette. Learn how to introduce and how to pay compliments.

Introducing: Introductions are the few moments in which critical first impressions are made. Generally, impressions are made within 20 – 30 seconds upon meeting someone.

The person making the introduction and the two persons being introduced must all be able to do their parts well.

Here are some rules:

- Business introductions are based on hierarchy; a person of lesser authority is introduced to a person of greater authority. In business etiquette, gender has no place and does not affect the order of introductions.
- A client always comes before anyone in your organization. Introduce someone from your firm to a client or customer. Example: *"Mr. Dhawan, this is Miss Soonavala, our Chief Accounts Officer. Mr. Dhawan our client from Delhi."*
- An elected official comes before a non-official. Introduce a non-official person to an elected official. An important point to note is that, whenever you introduce someone from the Press, include this information in your introduction in order to warn the person, especially a public official, that the conversation may be on record. Example: *"Mr Walia, allow me to introduce Michael D'Mello of The Tribune."*
- Introduce a junior executive to a senior executive. Example: *"Miss Senior Executive, I'd like to introduce Mr. Junior Executive."*

While introducing people, help the newly acquainted persons to start and carry on a smooth, friendly flow of conversation. Comment briefly on the background of each. A remark on a hobby or interest common to both helps to get a conversation started.

Practice

In class, stand in a group of 4 to 5; introduce another who joins the group.

Introducing Yourself: If no one introduces you, just introduce yourself to the other guests. Extend your hand, smile and say, *"I'm Hilla Vakil, David's partner."* Avoid saying things like "Mr. Mehta works for me;" it sounds arrogant. Instead, say, *"Mr Mehta and I work in the same office."*

Always use both, your name and surname when introducing yourself. Be clear and concise in your introduction; speak in an engaging tone. Construct an introduction that is interesting and easy to remember, and yet professional. It should not take more than fifteen seconds to deliver.

Consider what information about yourself will be of interest to the others. At a business function, it is appropriate to say where you work; it may be sufficient to say *"I'm in public relations at Infosys."*

At functions that are not strictly business, there is no need to give much job information. At a special interest event like environmental protection work, you can mention your connection to the organization that has organized the event. If there is a common interest, mention it but keep the focus on the other person. For example *"Kunal mentioned that you are a member of the Indo-Canadian Business Association*

I'd be interested in learning how the association has benefited you; I'm also engaged in international trade."

> **Practice**
>
> Join a group of 4 to 5 persons standing together and introduce yourself.

Paying Compliments: Paying compliments is an art; some persons do it naturally well, but most persons can learn the art with a little effort and practice.

A compliment is an expression of appreciation. To improve any personal or business relationship, find something about the other person(s) that you honestly appreciate, respect, or agree with — and find a graceful way to say it. You can make a complimentary remark on any of these: an attractive neck-tie or scarf, brief-case or handbag, a well-argued case, competent collection of data, a well-planned meal, a well-conducted meeting, a neatly turned out phrase; or simply say, *"You're looking very well."*

Get a good stock of positive adjectives to be able to compliment well.

Keep the following points in mind.

- A compliment should be moderate and genuine appreciation. Flattery is exaggerated expression of praise.
- A genuine compliment sounds true. Express it in a positive, sincere and friendly manner. Maintain good eye contact with the person to whom you are paying the compliment, and smile appreciatively while speaking.
- Compliments should have no other motive than to recognize someone for something special. Never give a compliment in order to get a compliment or a favour in return; people soon find out the ulterior motive.
- Do not ask where they bought it (whatever you appreciate) or how much they paid for it.
- Never boast about your own clothes or possessions or achievements.

Responding to compliments: How do you respond when you get a compliment? When someone pays you a compliment, acknowledge it and thank the person graciously. Don't feel embarrassed or reject the compliment saying "Oh! It's nothing" or "Sorry, I could not do much."

Respond positively by saying, *"It's very nice of you to say that"* or *"I'm glad you like it,"* or a simple, *"thank you"* and a smile.

> **Practice**
>
> Work in pairs or groups of 3 (sitting or standing). After the introductions, pay a compliment to the other member of the group.
>
> Practice the response equally carefully.

Self Control

Gaining self-control takes time and patient practice. Too often, we speak without thinking of the effect of our words on others. In a business dialogue, it is important to control your impulse to talk. It is particularly important to control the impulse to interrupt another person whose statements you do not agree with. It takes a great deal to remain cool when your own views are attacked in an unmannerly style. But, after all, you cannot control the other person's manners or style; you can only control your response. Holding one's tongue is difficult, but if you have the ability to maintain peace, and keep silent till you reach the right moment to speak, you will save yourself a great deal of energy.

Listening

The skill of listening is very important for the success of dialogue. You need a broad mind to tolerate various styles of speaking, a thorough knowledge of the topic of discussion, a genuine desire to reach a satisfactory conclusion.

The benefits of listening include

- Finding out more information
- Learning about people and how their minds work
- Improving relations with people
- Obtaining suggestions and new ideas
- Being able to help with solving problems

If you do not listen and keep talking only about your own needs and experiences, the conversation becomes one-sided. It frustrates the other person and leaves out his needs. To listen well, concentrate on the speaker's line of interest, try to understand the speaker's framework. In responding, use nouns and verbs in the same constructions and tenses, and use the same vocabulary.

Silence

It may seem strange, but maintaining silence — in fact, holding one's tongue — is a valuable and powerful communication skill. It takes a great deal of self-control.

Most persons have a strong desire to express their ideas, state their point of view, make themselves heard. A more mature person is able to keep silent and let the other person talk first. First learn to gain control over your desire to express yourself while someone is talking on your favourite topic.

Slowly, you can learn the more difficult skill of maintaining silence in the face of aggression, verbal attack and interruptions.

Be aware and remain in control of your body language. Posture, facial expression and eye contact must show that your silence is deliberate. Otherwise it will look as if you are struck dumb by the aggression of the other person.

If you can learn to hold silence, you will be able to puzzle the other person. If you do not speak when the other person expects it, the person feels uncomfortable. In order to fill in the uncomfortable gap, he may begin to repeat what he has said; since exact repetition is not quite possible, the repetition is likely to be accompanied by explanation and elaboration. In the process, he may speak out more than he had intended to say. Sales persons are known to bring down their quotation when faced by the client's silence.

On the other hand, you need the ability to endure the other person's silence and the skill to break it.

There are significant cultural differences in people's tolerance and use of silence in interpersonal communication.

Non-verbal behaviour

Remember that 55% of meaning is carried by body language, 38% is carried by the voice (paralanguage) and only 7% by the words. In a conversation, both need the ability to sense the feelings behind the words by observing the body language. Listen with eyes as well as with ears. Also, be aware that your own body language is being watched by others. Pleasant appearance and friendly body language are a great advantage.

Asking questions

The question is a powerful tool in dialogue. Questions can make people uncomfortable. Think of all the tones of voice in which a question can be asked (try them out on friends and class-mates). A simple question like "What can I do about it?" may be shrugging off responsibility or a request for advice, or an offer to help. Questions must be asked for clarification in a non-threatening tone, showing genuine desire to understand better. Questions asked in an aggressive style can make the other person withdraw from the conversation or feel hostile.

- Ask open-ended questions which cannot be answered with a simple yes or no. If you want to get the other person to talk, ask, "How could we do this?" "What do you think?"
- Do not ask questions that make others feel uncomfortable and defensive. For example, "Why?" is intimidating; it is softer to ask, "how come?"
- Ask "What if...?" For example, "What if we did it this way?"
- Ask for their advice. "What would you suggest we do to resolve this?" Everyone loves to be asked for advice.
- Offer alternatives and ask, "Which way would you prefer?" This demonstrates your respect for the other person.
- Ask about their feelings. "How do you feel about this?" People love to have their feelings respected.

- Repeat back what they said. "Let me be sure I understand what you're saying. You're saying that...?" This technique prevents misunderstandings and convinces them that you really are listening.

Practice

Take any question that you want to ask. Frame it in as many ways as you can. Note the difference in tone.

Try asking the question in different styles and see how the response varies.

Assertiveness without aggression

Assertiveness is reasonable behaviour. Assertive persons hold their own ground and work to find reasonable working compromises, so there are no losers. Use phrases like:

Let's agree that...

Shall we follow the rule that .....

Being assertive is being neither passive nor aggressive. Passive people give in too easily; they give up their rights and needs in order to avoid conflict. Aggressive persons are overbearing and try to lead others to agree to things that are either wrong or disadvantageous to them. Both these have negative effect on the dialogue. Don't get pushed around, but don't be the pusher either. Being assertive is neither passive nor aggressive.

Say what you think and feel calmly and clearly, without giving offence, and without denying the rights of others to have different views or expectations. Try to find solutions that recognise everyone's needs, and try to reach a constructive compromise that gives everyone something.

Assertiveness is not just a set of techniques. It requires self-knowledge, understanding of one's own the skills and limitations, a sense of self-worth and recognition of one's own and other people's rights and responsibilities.

When someone shouts at you and you don't like it, resist the temptation to withdraw (may be slamming the door on the way out). Resist the temptation to shout back to stop the attack, and deal with your own rising anger.

This is the time for assertiveness. Take a deep breath. Stay centred, feet firmly planted on the ground, and get your mind into "I" statement mood. The three elements of an "I" statement are:

When... I hear a voice raised at me

feel... humiliated (upset, hurt, distressed, disturbed)

And what I'd like is that I... can debate an issue with you without ending up feeling hurt.

The best "I" statement is free of expectations. It delivers a clean, clear statement of how it is from your side and how you would like it to be.

Take this quiz to assess yourself.

ASSERTIVENESS QUIZ

1. Do you buy things you do not want because you cannot say no to the salesperson? Yes/No
2. When you do not understand the meaning of a word, do you ask about it? Yes/No
3. Do you feel that you are responsible when things go wrong, even if it is not your fault? Yes/No
4. Do you look directly at others when you talk to them? Yes/No
5. Do people often ask you to speak more loudly in order to be heard? Yes/No
6. Do you feel intimidated by people in authority? Yes/No
7. Do you generally have good posture? Yes/No
8. Do you often feel so angry you could scream? Yes/No
9. Do you know how to ask for help without feeling dependent? Yes/No
10. If someone cuts in front of you in a line, do you usually tell them off? Yes/No

(Answers and explanations at the end of chapter)

Expressing disagreement without being offensive

If you disagree with someone's statement, you may feel tempted to express yourself aggressively. If you learn to be positively assertive, you have an effective way to respond when you do not agree with someone. An aggressive response like, "I don't agree with you," can provoke those who hear it. Also, an artificially polite statement like, "I beg to differ," is not friendly (it is a put-down).

If you are assertive, you can express disagreement without being offensive. When you disagree, instead of not keeping silent or responding aggressively, try positive assertiveness. Listen carefully and summarise what the other person has said. Only after summarising or restating the other's views, state your own position, and do it without attacking. It is useful to say something like, *"I would like to state another point of view."*

Summarising

It is important to summarise the previous speaker's view, especially when you disagree with it. Summarising must be done in your own words; it is a restatement without any comment and must be spoken in an objective tone and manner without indicating any opposition by tone of voice or facial expression. It demonstrates that you have understood the statements and also helps you to be objective and clear.

Closure

Ending on a pleasant note is always beneficial for relationships. Leave-taking is as important as greeting; it leaves the final impression. Whether the conversation has been smooth and easy or difficult and bumpy, the final words must pave the way for continuing relationship.

The main points and conclusions should be summarised. If there are any unsettled issues they are also mentioned and may be scheduled for another dialogue. Each side must thank the other for the time given and contribution made towards reaching the conclusion.

A cheerful and pleasant tone can relax the mood, and mark the conclusion of business. For example:

- *"This calls for a cup of tea. We have all worked hard, and have been able to arrive at a comfortable conclusion."*
- *"So, shall we all have some coffee now? Even though we have had some tense moments, we have been able to sort out most things."*
- *"Thanks for the contribution you made to this issue. It has been possible to make a satisfactory conclusion."*
- *"Shall we call it a day? Unfortunately, we have not been able to make any conclusions, but that need not keep us from having some coffee. After all, we have all worked hard."*

Feedback skills

A business dialogue can go on peacefully and usefully only when both parties clarify their points of view. If something that one party has said is not clear, or is not acceptable to the other, it is better to say so immediately and calmly, so that clarification or alternatives can be worked out. Relationships between persons are important for any joint effort, and communication forms the relationships.

Feedback involves three skills, getting or eliciting feedback, receiving and accepting feedback and giving feedback.

Getting feedback: Watch for glimpses of the listener's feelings from the expression on the face. Feedback on emotional reaction of the other person helps to achieve the most suitable style.

Seek feedback actively. Invite questions from the receiver, and encourage expression of response. If you have just spoken rather long and presented your statement of the situation, you may tactfully ask listeners to summarize by saying: "Will someone please summarize the main points of what I have said, so that I can check whether I missed any important points?" This way the listener co-operates in the success of the communication.

If you are a good observer and good listener, you can get feedback more easily. You must be able and willing to maintain silence and interest while others speak. You must be alert to see non-verbal feedback which is often given unconsciously and indicates emotional reaction.

Receiving feedback

Once you get feedback, you must be able to receive and accept it without feeling threatened. It is easy to feel angry when you find that the other person has not understood what you explained. It is even easier to feel offended if the other person expresses views contrary to yours.

Seek and receive feedback with a genuine desire to improve and facilitate the conversation.

Be non-defensive. There is no need to justify what you said or did. Feedback is to be used for taking a new look at the next step.

Listen attentively. Do not switch off attention because you do not like the feedback.

If the feedback is vague, seek clarifications and ask for specific instances. Check on possible misunderstanding ("Let me restate what I am hearing").

Giving feedback

As listener, you have the responsibility to give feedback. Check your own understanding by summarizing, by asking for clarifications, and whenever possible, by stating your own views and feelings in response to the communication.

Express your response honestly and non-emotionally, and without giving offence.

Give feedback in a positive manner so that the person feels prepared to accept it; negative feedback can put the person on the defensive.

Be specific, not general or vague. Don't make a general statement; say specifically what you are responding to.

Be descriptive, not evaluative. Describe what you see and hear and feel; do not bring in moral judgement of good or bad, right and wrong.

Be sure of your own motive in giving feedback. It should be given for a genuine reason and not to put down someone. If the feedback is given with a sense of power or superiority over the other, it has a bad effect.

Here is a **check list** for productive behaviour during a dialogue.

1. Am I using the appropriate question type? (open-ended to encourage discussion)
2. Am I leaving pauses for the other person to think and respond?
3. Am I really listening or just thinking about what I am going to say?
4. Am I responding with empathy, supportively to what I hear?
5. Can I get the other person to bring up the topics that I want to discuss?
6. Can I get the other person to see that we are reaching a conclusion together and not engaging in an argument?
7. Can I get the other person's ideas and use my own ideas as a back up for reaching a mutually satisfactory conclusion?
8. Do I use body language (nods, smiles, eye contact) well?
9. Do I use non-verbal sounds (uh-huh.. Hmmm) effectively?
10. Am I positively interested and energetic?

Answers to Assertiveness Quiz
Assertive Responses

1. No	6. No
2. Yes	7. Yes
3. No	8. No
4. Yes	9. Yes
5. No	10. No

Explanation of answers to the Assertiveness Quiz

1. An assertive person is not afraid to say no. She or he feels free to make choices.
2. An assertive person takes responsibility for getting his or her needs met. Fear of seeming ignorant does not prevent the assertive person from asking questions.
3. The assertive person takes responsibility for his or her own behaviour but does not take responsibility for the behaviour of others or for situations which are beyond his or her control. To feel responsible for things beyond your control leads to unnecessary feelings of guilt.
4. Direct eye contact is assertive and suggests sincerity, self-confidence and the expectation that others will listen.
5. An assertive person wants to be heard.
6. An assertive person does not allow status to intimidate him or her.
7. Good posture communicates a positive self-image. When posture is limited by a disability, good eye contact and facial expression can be used to express a positive self-image.
8. An assertive person works to get his or her needs met and does not let situations build to the point of crisis.
9. An assertive person is able to ask for help without feeling dependent because he or she maintains a strong sense of self-worth and self-respect.
10. Telling someone off is an angry, aggressive response. An assertive person would state that he or she does not like the unfairness and ask the person to move to the end of the line.

□□□

PART III

WRITTEN COMMUNICATION

Chapter 15

READING SKILLS

A large amount of reading material demands our attention everyday. Information technology, mass media an global business contribute to the increase in reading work. There is a flood of trade journals, house magazines, reports, and memoranda on all kinds of topics, besides the usual newspapers, books and magazines. People at work need a technique to cope with the task of reading quickly and understanding (comprehending) the important part of the contents.

Everything need not be read with the same attention and depth. Difficult subjects need careful study reading, but most business papers need routine reading to collect information. Some things, like a newspaper story or a light magazine, need only skimming, that is, going over it rapidly to see what it is about and whether it needs attention.

Techniques of Reading

Skill in reading comprehension can be acquired with systematic practice. Techniques for reading faster and more effectively can be learnt.

Speed-reading must be silent. The skill of silent reading is different from the skill of reading aloud. Silent reading can be very rapid because it is not constrained by physical movement of the throat and mouth muscles which is necessary in reading aloud. While reading, time gets wasted because of some poor reading habits like these:

- moving the lips
- making movements in the throat like reading aloud
- compulsively reading each word separately
- spelling out long words letter by letter
- going back to words you have already read (regression)

These habits can be controlled.

Eye movement needs training for fast reading. The eyes do not move smoothly along the printed line. Eyes cannot see while they are moving; they see only during short pauses of fixation linked by quick and sightless movements.

At each fixation pause, the eyes take in a certain number of characters. A fast reader takes in 10 to 16 characters including blank spaces; a slow reader takes in much less.

The eyes also have a small but troublesome backward movement, (regression) when moving along a line of print. A fast reader has less regression.

Fast reading requires concentration in the first place. For practicing silent reading, keep aside at least half an hour a day, sit in a comfortable chair with light falling over the shoulder; keep out any disturbance or noise of any kind. At the beginning, choose unimportant material to read, like the newspaper or a light magazine. Once you understand the technique, you should use average reading material like instruction manuals and articles of general information. Finally use study material.

Before beginning to read any material—

- Take a look at the heading, the sub-headings, any summary, table of contents, which give the general sense of the content and the train of thought.
- Be sure why you are reading the material. Do you intend to follow any instructions given in it? Or take a decision or an action based on the information collected from it? Or remember it for an examination? Summarize it? Report what is in it?
- Make sure that you keep your mouth shut so you do not keep mouthing what you read.
- Watch your throat; try not to move any muscles of the mouth or throat while reading.
- "Take in" familiar words at a glance. This will improve as you become familiar with more words, especially those which occur frequently in your work. Practice will also improve your span and enable you to take in more characters at a time.
- Make a careful effort not to let the eyes regress, that is, go backward every few words, instead of moving forward.

Overcome the compulsion to read every word. Use your knowledge of sentence patterns and information already gathered, to foresee the next few words. Every word in a sentence does not need reading; some words are only part of the language pattern; phrases like *that is, for example*, can be skipped. (See the exercise below to realize how many words are not even needed because we can "fill them in" as we read.)

Try carefully not to "hear" your reading in your mind (this can be difficult especially if you have developed a habit of doing it).

Skimming is a brief inspection of a text for general information. Look at the title, author, synopsis, contents page and date of publication to see if it has any relevance to your needs Also read the first few lines to see whether you find the style of writing suitable to you.

The following method is often used for skimming.

- Run your eyes down the middle of the text page.
- Skim from the top left-hand corner to the bottom right-hand corner of the page.
- Then skim from the top right-hand corner to the bottom left-hand corner.

If you feel that the book or article is not what you need, or is not of interest to you, you need not go further with it.

Scanning is examining the organization of a text to find specific information.

The point of scanning a text is to find required information quickly and efficiently. Avoid the temptation to read large amounts of material.

Suppose you have found a book whose title suggests that it might have the information that you are seeking.

Step 1: Look at the table of contents. It will list the following sections:

- preface
- list of diagrams or tables or illustrations
- introduction
- various chapters in sequence from 1 to the last one
- conclusion
- bibliography
- index

Step 2: Read the chapter headings. Do they contain the information that you are looking for?

If you find the relevant reference in the table of contents, go to that chapter or section of the book and read the first two paragraphs. These paragraphs often contain a statement about what information is covered in the chapter. This will help you to judge whether the material is useful to you. If you are still uncertain about the usefulness of the material, then read the last two paragraphs of the summary.

If you do not find anything useful in the table of contents, go to the index at the back of the book.

Step 3: Search the index for relevant topics or key words. If you find the relevant reference in the index go to the appropriate page or pages in the book. Find and read the paragraph in which the reference appears.

If you are scanning an article, read the first two paragraphs of the article and the concluding paragraph.

See if the article has sub-titles or is divided into sections. Read the sub-titles and the first two paragraphs and the last paragraph of the sections.

You will get the hang of the logic and organization of the article.

Reading Exercise

In the first paragraph of the passage given here, several words and phrases are in brackets. Read the first paragraph without the words in the brackets and see if you could gather the meaning. In the rest of the passage several words have been replaced by xs, and in the last paragraph by dots. While reading it, you will find that you can "fill in" most of the words to gather the meaning of the passage.

In early ages, man got his food, (shelter, clothing, weapons, and) tools from wild nature. When he had used up (all the) wild plants (in one place), or the animals (that he hunted) or the fish (that he caught), moved away, he left one place and (moved to another where he could) find new supplies (of what he wanted.) This meant he led a wandering existence, staying in a place only (as long as) it gave him (what he wanted), and then moving (somewhere else). Sometimes people (of this kind would) cover (close to) 2000 miles in a year, following (the) animals they hunted northwards (in the) spring (and then back) south (in the) autumn.

Later, xxxx men started xx collect xxx sow seeds, xxx this began xx keep them xx xxx place longer xxxx xxxxxx, because xxxx xxx xx wait until the seed grew into plants xxxxxx they xxxxx gather their harvest, and xxxxxxx xxxx xxx xx protect the plants xxxxxx xxxxxx while they grew. Those who began to live xxxx xxx xxxx on grain began to settle xxxx, xxx became agriculturists, while those who xxxx more and more xxx xx milk xxx xxxx became more xxx xxxx nomadic. But the life of primitive people living in one place was dangerous. ..... easy for enemies to find and destroy them (if they knew where they lived). It therefore often........ long time..... group .... finally settled down to cultivate the soil ....

Make a copy of whatever short passage you have in the computer, and replace the obvious phrases by xs; get a friend to read it. This exercise can be done by two persons for practice.

Coping with Figures: Figures can slow down reading. A technique is needed for coping with a schedule of figures and computer print-outs of details of accounts. If confronted with one, try these methods:

- first, read the headings across the top
- then read the lines down the side
- check at the bottom of the page to see if there are any notes or comments about the figures.

This will generally help you to decide which are the key figures that need careful attention. If the figures seem normal go ahead with reading the text.

If any of the figures looks abnormal, scan the column in which it occurs to see if its cause can be found. A computer print-out of the details of an item can take quite a lot of time to read as it contains every little detail. Before opening it, decide what you want to find out from it. For example, from a debtor print out, a manager may want to know only:

- if any customer owes more than Rs 100,000 for over 60 days
- if any customer owes more than his credit limit

But a person in charge of collecting dues and has to send reminders may want to know which customers have defaulted on the due date.

Illustrations and Non-verbal Material: Make yourself familiar with every kind of written presentation which forms a part of your work, in order to be able to deal with it speedily. Maps, graphs and charts may form a part of the reading material; reports and articles in journals often contain illustrations of different kinds.

To deal with these, read the titles, headings, key, scale and other guiding material and then quickly scan the illustration for details you want to check.

Reading Speed: We can develop three reading speeds depending on the material and our need of the information contained in it:

Study reading speed of 225 to 300 words a minute with 80% to 90% comprehension

Average reading speed of 275 to 500 words a minutes with 70% comprehension

Skimming speed of 500 to 800 words a minute with 50% comprehension.

We use study reading for complex material which is to be understood and remembered; average reading for simple, direct language, novels, stories, magazines; and skimming for material with which we are already familiar and only want to find out if there is anything new and should be given attention.

After practicing reading for some time, make a conscious effort to skim some pages of books on a subject with which you are already familiar.

EXERCISES

1. Read the first passage given at the end of Chapter17 for summarization, watching to make sure that your eyes do not regress.
2. Read the second passage as fast as you can. Write down the main points in the passage.
3. Read the third passage once, and answer the questions given at the end of it. What kind of reading is required for this passage?

❑❑❑

Chapter 16

ESSENTIALS OF EFFECTIVE LETTER WRITING

The letter is the oldest method of sending a message. Today, in spite of the telephone and the e-mail, the letter is still an important method of communication. The letter maintains the personal touch, serves as a record, and as a means of keeping other parties informed by sending copies.

Letters are written for getting and giving quotations, making and answering enquiries, contacting potential customers, persuading potential customers to buy, making and answering complaints, making credit inquiries, collecting dues, and maintaining relations with various members of the public. Maintaining customer relations and handling problems requires some very skilful letter writing. Good companies take every opportunity to write letters to customers in order to create and maintain goodwill.

Letters must aim at getting a favourable response from readers. In order to write good letters you need knowledge of language and a clear, concise style of writing. You also need knowledge of the working, procedures, policies and aims of your organization. As a person, you must be sincere, confident, self-respecting and friendly; these qualities are reflected in the style of the letter.

Electronic media like fax and e-mail have high speed and can transmit the written word instantaneously. Messages are now more informal and conversational in style. Letter writing style is changing as a letter may be a confirmation or a follow-up of an earlier message sent by telephone or e-mail or fax.

C's OF EFFECTIVE LETTER WRITING

The qualities which are essential for a good letter are collectively called the Cs of communication because most of them begin with the letter C. The main qualities are correctness, clarity, conciseness, and courtesy. Other related qualities are completeness, coherence, compactness, confidence, consideration, friendliness, directness and vigour; these qualities are found in any writing which takes care of the first 4 Cs.

Correctness

A letter must be correct in every respect:

(i) In spelling, grammar and use of language. Incorrect language spoils the message, distracts the reader's attention, and creates a poor impression of the sender; it may also convey a wrong meaning. All spellings must be checked; spelling of names must be checked with extra care; misspelt names always give offence. Note that the computer cannot check all spellings; it will accept both *steal* and *steel* as correctly spelt words.

(ii) In appearance and form of layout. Poor and untidy appearance, with corrections made in ink or carelessness in the layout, creates a poor impression of the company. Appearance depends on placing the parts of layout correctly on the letterhead and having proper margins on all sides. In manual typing, even space between letters, words, lines and parts of layout, must also be given attention.

(iii) In the information it conveys. Wrong or incomplete information is the most harmful thing in a letter; it leads to waste of time in making corrections and can lead to loss of goodwill and loss of business. All dates and days, time, numbers and facts must be in agreement. Nothing is more confusing than mismatched information. Correctness depends on completeness. A letter is complete only when it presents all the ideas and information required for the particular situation.

(iv) In tone, formality and style. The tone of every letter must be appropriate to the occasion, the content and the relationship between the writer and the reader. An overdone apology can sound childish or undignified; a grudging or patronizing agreement to grant a request can sound unpleasant.

Clarity

The message of the letter must be clear at the first reading. The information explosion of today takes up so much of everyone's time; people appreciate a letter that takes very little time to read and understand. Clearly written messages avoid misunderstanding and save time.

Consider the following examples of ambiguous writing:

- Please state from what date the patient was ordered to stay in bed and totally incapacitated by your instructions.

This has been caused by wrong placing of words.

- Certain remedies are available for this condition.

The ambiguity here is caused by the two meanings of the word "certain": definite and some; both meanings are grammatically correct in this sentence.

And here is another example of ambiguous language, probably an attempt to be non-committal.

- We feel that we are inclined to the position that the facts in the case point sufficiently strongly to disregard of basic rules of safe defensive driving as to make consideration of a much more severe penalty more appropriate.

To be clear is to be efficient; but unfortunately, few people take the trouble to be clear in their writing.

Clarity depends upon five factors:

(i) Simple, common everyday words which everyone can understand. Never send the reader to the dictionary. There should be no technical terms unless absolutely needed and if you are communicating within the profession. Abstract words like *beautiful* and *unjust* are often misunderstood as they convey different ideas to different persons. It is better to use concrete words with a definite meaning, or to give concrete examples and description.

Here are some big words often found in letters; the words in the right column are the short, preferable substitute.

Big word	**Substitute**
incombustible	fireproof
optimum	best
substantiate	prove
terminate	end
utilise	use

(ii) Short and simple sentences. Long sentences confuse the reader, and often confuse the writer also. Phrases and clauses should not be added on to a sentence. Each bit of important information should be given in a separate sentence.

Sentences with an average sentence length of 15 to 20 words keep the writing clear. This does not mean all sentences should have the same length. Longer sentences are balanced with shorter ones, but the average sentence length should be well below 20 words.

Using active verbs rather than passive verbs is the key to good writing. Sentences with passive verbs are long, ambiguous, impersonal and dull. Sentences with active verbs make your writing simpler, less formal, clearer and more precise. Here is an example:

Passive: It was agreed by the committee...

Active: The committee agreed...

(iii) Proper punctuation. It helps to provide pauses and stops and to break up groups of words into sensible units. Besides the full stop, there are other, shorter pauses like the semi-colon and the comma which help to break up a sentence into readable units. A sentence can often be made more easy to follow by using a punctuation mark.

(iv) Giving definite and concrete details with figures and names. Here are examples of vague or general phrases, with specific phrases in the right column.

General	Specific
high performance	95% efficiency
plant	oil refinery (or whatever)
unfavourable weather conditions	rain
structural degradation	leaky roof (or whatever)
in due course	in two weeks
at your earliest convenience	within three weeks.

(v) Logical sequence of ideas. Making a clear plan for the letter ensures that the ideas are in logical order; coherence, that is, logical connection of ideas makes any composition easy to read.

(vi) Consistency in the use of numbers, dates, units of measure, technical terms, abbreviations, hyphens, grammar, spelling, punctuation and capitalization. British or American spellings and style of writing the date vary. Hyphenation, punctuation and capitalization do not have absolutely fixed rules. Whatever you decide on, be consistent throughout the document.

Conciseness

Conciseness means expressing much in a few words; in business writing it means keeping to the point, using as few words as possible without sacrificing clarity or courtesy. It does not necessarily mean being brief; it means making every word count. Some companies lay down a limit of one page for inter-office memos in order to ensure concise writing.

Conciseness can be achieved by:

(i) Leaving out unnecessary modifiers; for example, some writers talk of "new innovation;" (can there be an old innovation?) or "very unique" (unique means only "one of its kind"). Other examples are: "advance plans", "actual experience", "cylindrical in shape", "three cubic meters in volume."

(ii) Reducing less important ideas to phrases or single words like,

Phrase	Short phrase /word
in the form of	as
in many cases	often
exhibits the ability to	can
on the event of	if
at a later date	later
at the present time	now
or the purpose of	for
have no alternative but	must
in addition to	besides, as well as, also
in order to	to
in relation to	about, in, with, towards, to
on a regular basis	regularly

(iii) Making sure that only the necessary and relevant details are included.

Using more words than necessary confuses the idea as in the following sentence:

- Our experience with having Mr. X as credit customer has been fairly favourable and we are of the opinion that he may be allowed to enjoy the benefits of a credit account of a moderate amount.

The writer may have been trying to be non-committal but the sentence does not convey any clear meaning. It is easier to understand if it is concisely written.

- *Our experience with Mr. X as credit customer has been favourable and we consider him to be safe for a credit account of up to Rs. 60,000/-.*

Conciseness and clarity are closely related; giving clear and definite details often reduces the length of a sentence; for example:

- We would appreciate receiving the goods as early as possible since arrangements have to be made for export so that they will reach our foreign customer within the required time.

This can be made concise by giving concrete details instead of vague phrases:

- *Please dispatch the goods so as to reach us by 7 September since we have to ship them to Mexico by the 17th.*

Check all messages to see if it is possible to cut out needless words. If you use ten words where two will do, you will waste the reader's time as well as yours. Readers are thankful for precise and clear messages.

Courtesy

Courtesy is consideration for other people's feelings. It is seen in an individual's behaviour with others. A well-mannered and courteous person shows consideration and thought for others. In a letter, the style, the manner and the choice of words reflect the courtesy of the writer. Some simple rules for courtesy are:

(i) Use the courtesy words *please*, *thank you* and *sorry* as the situation requires.

(ii) Express appropriate feeling according to the situation.

For example, sympathy when someone suffers, good wishes when someone begins something new, and congratulation when someone achieves something.

(iii) Make the other person feel comfortable. This is an important factor of courtesy. Care and consideration for the reader is reflected in the letter. The opening sentence itself shows the courtesy of the writer:

- *We appreciate your promptness in sending the goods.*
- *Thank you for sending your quotation so promptly.*
- *We are sorry to learn that you were inconvenienced.*

Requests must also be made courteously:

- *We would appreciate it very much if you could send your cheque within three days of receiving our bill.*
- *Will you please look into the matter at once?*

(iv) Be attentive and prompt in responding. Every letter (and missed telephone call) should be answered within twenty-four hours. If it is a letter of complaint, the response should be immediate; it is courteous to make a phone call or send a fax message immediately on receiving a complaint or hearing about a problem. Everyone appreciates prompt attention.

(v) Let the tone, the choice of words and the style of the message reflect your consideration for the feelings and needs of the reader. This is particularly important if the message to be conveyed is likely to be unpleasant for the reader. A courteous letter has the best chance of getting a favourable response. Seeing the situation as the reader sees it, and taking care of his/her needs, is courtesy. You must have an awareness of how the words sound to the reader.

LANGUAGE OF BUSINESS WRITING

Modern business language is simple, easy to understand, friendly and courteous. Personal relations with customers can be cultivated by writing friendly letters in a natural and informal style. Old fashioned business language is not suitable for modern business methods and practice.

Letters convey messages; letters must also build goodwill and create positive and pleasant feelings in the reader. Whatever the message of the letter may be, the writer must try to get a favourable emotional response from the reader. A large amount of written material reaches the desk of every businessman executive; there is a great deal of competition for the reader's attention and interest. The brief contact with the reader which a letter makes, must be pleasant and memorable. The manner in which a company's letters are written contributes a great deal to its public image.

Avoiding Business Jargon

Jargon means the vocabulary and phrases peculiar to a particular trade or profession. Business jargon or commercialese refers to the words and phrases which businessmen used in the old days for writing letters. Today, business people are well educated and write good English. Letters, memos and notes and reports are written in modern, simple style which is easy to understand.

Unfortunately, some companies still continue to write in the old-fashioned style. Given below, is a list of out-dated words and phrases which are found in the letters of some old-fashioned companies and government departments. They fail to make personal contact with the reader; they are to be strictly avoided. The following jargon phrases/sentences often occur in the opening paragraph of letters; change them to modern English.

* Referring to your favour of 17th inst. we have to state that ..
* Further to my recent letter ...
* I write in reference to ...
* In respect of the above ...

* I refer to previous correspondence
* This is to inform you...
* Attached/enclosed herewith please find...

In the closing paragraph the following jargon phrases/sentences are found; they fail to leave any friendly impression on the reader.

* Thanking you in anticipation
* Assuring you of our best services at all times
* Trusting to be favoured with further orders
* At your earliest convenience
* We hope that the position is now clear
* I trust this clarifies the situation
* Thanking you for your...
* Hoping for a prompt reply...
* Thanking you in advance for your assistance...
* Trusting this answers your questions...
* Please do not hesitate to contact me

In the contents of letters, the following jargon phrases appear:

* said matter
* deem it advisable
* as per your letter
* wherein you state
* please be advised
* we wish to state

Such terms are not used in modern letters. They ruin clarity; they are unfriendly and pompous; and they waste typing time.

Dealing with Technical Terms

The use of technical terms is not a problem if the letter is being written to a person who is in a related profession, e.g., a person who knows accounts understands the term "current liabilities" or "fixed assets"; a person familiar with computers understands "megabytes" or "64K". But when writing to persons who do not know the technical terms, they must be avoided.

If the technical terms are absolutely unavoidable in describing a product, the meaning should be given in plain terms. As far as possible the language should be adapted to lay persons; it should not have any technical terms which the non-professional or non-technical person would not understand.

Meanings and Associations of Words

Words do not have just a dictionary meaning; most words acquire associations and implications. Some words get additional meaning or power of suggestion because of being associated with certain ideas or activities; for example, *investigation* may suggest suspicion, *computerization* may suggest efficiency, speed and accuracy. *Profit* is pleasant suggestion to the seller but is disliked by workers and customers, who think of it as seller's benefit. *Competition* suggests risk and extra effort to the trader, but lower prices to the buyer.

Certain words like *debt, failure, complaint, deceive, cheat* are definitely unpleasant and should be avoided in letters. When such unpleasant matters have to be mentioned, it is better to soften them by saying, outstanding *bill* or *overdue payment;*. some unpleasant ideas can be softened by saying *oversight, not in accordance with the agreed terms*, or *not as we were led to believe.*

You must develop the skill of using the language so that the letter would never be offensive to the reader.

TAKING THE READER'S POINT OF VIEW

Looking at a situation from the reader's point of view helps you to frame the message in a pleasant and acceptable way. Presenting ideas, suggestions, proposals in such a way that the reader sees how it is advantageous to himself, is called the "You" attitude. "You" attitude is the secret of effective letters.

You must show understanding of the reader's needs and desires. What does the reader expect from the letter? Naturally, he expects to benefit in some way; to get some useful information, to find out what advantages are available to him. A letter usually proposes that the reader should take an action; the reader's action will ultimately benefit the writer in some way, but the writer's benefit should not be the main point of the letter. The main point and emphasis should be on the advantage of the reader.

Take the trouble to show the reader that it will be to his/her advantage to take the action you are suggesting in the letter. If you think only of your own advantage and offer none to the reader, you cannot get action from the reader. In order to be able to emphasize the reader's advantage, you must look at the situation from the reader's point of view, and try to realise how it feels to be in that situation.

In business transactions many difficult situations arise which need the cooperation of both, the supplier and the buyer, the debtor and the creditor, the employer and the employee. Co-operation is crucial; messages must be an effort to exchange views and share understanding in order to co-operate. In every communication, there are two points of view and therefore, two sets of ideas: one that interests the recipient and one that interests the sender; messages can be conveyed with the recipient's interest in mind, as in the following examples:

The seller's desires are to sell goods or services, to make profit, to collect his dues, to get a contract, to win a customer, to find a job.

These desires can be fulfilled only through the satisfaction of the buyer's needs, namely, to buy what is worth-while, to maintain a good credit reputation, to find an efficient employee. The letter writer must clearly show that he is offering to satisfy the reader's needs.

Organize the message to suit the reader's convenience. Appeal to the common human needs and desires like desire for security, status, leisure, comfort, need for sympathy, courtesy and consideration.

A customer who has not paid his dues can be approached by pointing out that he would be free of commitments and would protect his own reputation if he paid promptly. A difficult situation like refusing credit terms can be tactfully handled by stressing the customer's own advantage in buying on cash, such as freedom from commitments, gains in the form of discounts, and avoidance of risk.

The purpose of a letter is to create a response. The letter should try to influence the reader's feelings, thoughts and actions in such a way that the response will be beneficial to both the reader and the writer. The goal of writing is not merely to tell something but also to create a favourable reaction to the message.

It is important that the emotional response of your reader should be favourable to you. A sales letter may convince an executive of the value of computerizing the office work, but he may feel emotionally inclined to go to a competing firm. A collection letter may convince a reader intellectually that he will benefit by paying off his debt, but emotionally, he may feel dislike for the creditor who urges him to pay. The test of the effectiveness of a company's letters is the number of customers it retains even after collecting dues and refusing credit terms.

EXERCISES

1. Rewrite these sentences in simple modern English:
   - (i) If the occasion should arise, please do not hesitate to get in touch with us if we can be of assistance to you in similar circumstances.
   - (ii) Under the date of 14 September, we communicated to you by means of a letter our desire to have the meeting held in or around Mumbai.
   - (iii) We are in receipt of your cheque for Rs. 3000/- and wish to thank you for the same.
   - (iv) You are hereby requested to supply us with the serial number which you will find on the motor.
   - (v) Kindly advise us if the said premises have been vacated by you as per our agreement, and oblige.
2. Rewrite these sentences to make them clear in meaning:
   - (i) Please send us a supply of leaflets for distribution to our customers. We count on early delivery since our need is urgent.
   - (ii) Our local warehouse will handle your needs.
   - (iii) Rico Appliances have excellent relations with their Delhi distributors, but they are still not doing as much publicity as they want them to do. (replace the pronouns; they are confusing).
   - (iv) He returned the share certificates which he had received by mistake, by registered post. (did he return or receive by registered post?)
   - (v) Refusal by management to consider an outlined scheme for staggered working hours which had been put forward by the works committee was a cause of

grave dissatisfaction on the part of the latter (Make 2 sentences; use active voice).

3. Make these sentences concise:
   (i) It is obvious that it is becoming more and more important that top management should receive timely and up to date reports. It is therefore necessary that the methods of getting information from our branch offices should be improved.
   (ii) I would like to inform you about the policy of our company regarding adjustment of complaints. Since the inception of our company it has been the policy of our company not to charge for services and repair work from a customer who has purchased our products not more than one year ago.
   (iii) In view of the reasons explained above, and after subsequent talks with our director, we would like to inform you that it will not be possible to replace the machine as per your request.
   (iv) This is to acknowledge receipt of your letter sent under date of 16 March, which we are glad to answer related to information about our new vertical files which have just been introduced in the market.
   (v) We wish to inform you of the fact that it has come to our notice that your trucks are parked at our gate causing grave inconvenience to our office car drivers who cannot get through the gate because your trucks are in the way.
4. Rewrite these sentences making them courteous:
   (i) We have received your complaint that you received the consignment we sent, in a damaged condition. We have received no such complaints from other customers.
   (ii) I am surprised to learn that your kitchen grinder is not working properly. All our machines pass under strict quality control.
   (iii) Your failure to deliver our goods efficiently has caused us great inconvenience.
   (iv) Your typewriter has not been oiled for a very long time.
   (v) Taking care of the articles you buy is your own responsibility.
5. Describe, in 3 to 4 sentences, the customer's feelings and expectations from the seller in the following situations:
   (i) He has spent Rs. 1000 on buying a camera; owing to his inexperience his pictures are all spoilt.
   (ii) He has a fairly large debt to pay and finds himself unable to pay because of keen competition in business.
   (iii) He has asked for a quotation and is waiting for a reply.
   (iv) He had ordered goods for a sale; the goods arrived just in time but in a damaged condition, unfit for sale.
   (v) She finds that the kitchen gadget she bought a few months ago is not giving satisfactory service.
6. Write down the possible benefits to both, the writer and the reader, in the following situations:
   (i) Publisher of a news magazine asks for prompt renewal when subscriptions are about to expire.

(ii) Fresh graduate writes to a private company asking for a job.

(iii) Creditor reminds a forgetful customer to pay his bill.

(iv) Customer informs seller that goods he ordered have not arrived even 15 days after the order.

(v) Camera dealer explains to a customer that damage caused by accident is not covered by guarantee.

(vi) A firm informs its customers (a) that their office is to be shifted to more spacious premises, (b) that they are opening a new branch.

7. Rewrite the following from the reader's point of view:

(i) We hope that you will pay your bill of Rs.750 as early as possible. We have our own bills to pay, and it is expensive for us to keep sending reminders of past-due accounts. You can help us greatly by sending your cheque promptly.

(ii) We are surprised by your letter in which you claim that we did not dispatch your goods promptly. We maintain a policy of shipping all orders on the day they are received. However, we are looking into the matter.

(iii) It is our policy to send a wrist watch to customers whom we have served for fifteen years. Since you have now completed 15 years of buying from us, we are sending your watch by parcel post. If you do not receive it in the next five days please let us know.

(iv) This new microwave oven is our greatest achievement. We developed it in our own research department, and it will be distributed through our own dealers. We are so proud of this kitchen equipment that we would like you to see it working.

(v) Our business has been so successful that we are opening a new department for cosmetics and shall be stocking a varied selection of articles.

(vi) If we grant the adjustment that you ask for, we shall soon go out of business. The company from which we buy our stocks does not give us such adjustments.

8. Say whether the following statements are true or false:

(a) "Referring to your letter of 8th instant, the cheque could not be paid out" is a grammatically incorrect sentence.

(b) You can impress customers by writing letters in a legalistic style.

(c) "Assuring of our best services at all times" is a good closing sentence for a letter.

(d) "Please refer to the above-mentioned subject" is an effective opening sentence for a letter.

(e) Letters to customers should be written in polite language even if the content is not pleasant.

(f) Writing "you" when you mean "I" shows concern for the reader.

(g) Letters of complaint should be written in an angry and legalistic style in order to make an impression on the supplier.

(h) Sales letters should be written in a fresh and flexible style.

9. When dealing with an unpleasant situation, the reader may be most willing to see the writer's point of view if the letter ends with the sentence—
   (a) If there is anything that still needs clarification, we shall be happy to discuss this further.
   (b) If you consider this explanation carefully, we are sure you will find it satisfactory.
   (c) We hope and trust that the matter is now fully clear and satisfactorily explained.
   (d) If you find this explanation unsatisfactory, please let us know.
   (e) We are confident that you will now see this our way and consider this a satisfactory explanation.

❑❑❑

Chapter 17

WRITING TACTFULLY

Careful planning is the basis of success in most tasks. Thinking, reasoning, and planning before writing a letter has many advantages.

It gives you time to calm any emotions like anger which can spoil the communication if it is reflected in the letter. It helps to make sure that all information and ideas are included and are correct.

It enables you to compose the letter in a logical order and in the style most suited to the needs of the reader. It is a good method to separate the two elements of communication: planning the content and choosing the language/style for presentation.

Planning the Content

This involves thinking about why you want to communicate (the purpose), to whom the message is to be sent (the receiver), and what is to be achieved by the communication (the desired receiver-response).

Decide on the content and write it down in the form of notes. Make sure that all information is included, and number the points in the logical order in which you want to use them. A letter is a short composition and it is easy to arrange the collected notes in the structure of a letter.

Structure of a Letter

Many letters can be written on a framework of four points.

Opening/Introduction:
Giving the required information
Action/Response from the writer or the recipient
Closing

The first point takes one or two sentences; the second one forms the main content of the letter and may need more than one paragraph. The third and the fourth can be combined as they form the ending of the letter and each takes only a sentence. The main message of the letter should be carefully structured and the points arranged in a suitable order. Always put the reader's interests first; the order should be suitable to the reader's interest and convenience. Some possibilities are:

(a) In a reply, use the order of the original; this is courteous to the reader as it uses the order of the reader's priorities.

(b) In conveying a series of events, use chronological order; the events will be conveyed in the order in which they occurred.

(c) Ascending or descending order of importance may be used, depending on which will be more useful/comfortable/easy for the reader.

Composing the Letter

At the stage of composing, give attention to the language and style. Consider the recipient; a good deal depends on how much the recipient knows, what is the relationship between the sender and the recipient, what is the recipient's attitude to the issue being discussed in the letter; all these aspects can influence the recipient's response.

Opening and Closing a Letter

The first and the last paragraphs are important places in a short composition like a letter. Use them both to the maximum effect. Do not begin by repeating what is said in the subject line or end by making a flat or useless statement. Each of them has a definite function.

Opening Sentence

Consider these old-fashioned openings:

- We are receipt of your communication of 10 July.
- It has come to our attention that according to our records and in connection of...
- Reference is made to your memorandum of Feb. 6, same subject as above.

None of these sentences make direct contact with the receiver; there is no friendly feeling in them. Such sentences put off the reader at once.

The opening sentence has the important function of establishing good feeling and rapport, and drawing a favourable response from the reader.

- We are glad to say that we can deliver your shelves a week earlier as you requested in your letter of the 12th.
- We are extremely sorry to learn from your letter dated 23 September that you were not able to get good photographs.

Showing interest in the reader's needs and paying attention to his feelings and desires creates goodwill at the beginning of the letter.

If there is no subject line, the opening sentence has to indicate the subject of the letter; and it may have to refer to any previous communication on the subject, like telephone talk or letter or visit. But if there is a subject line, the opening sentence should not repeat it.

Avoid beginning with "Referring to your letter.." or "With reference to your letter." These openings lead to a grammar mistake or an incomplete sentence unless you have full command of these troublesome constructions.

Closing Sentence

Consider these poor closing sentences:

- May we again express our appreciation for the deposit balance.
- No doubt this account is now receiving your attention and we await your remittance in early course for which we thank you in anticipation.
- Hoping that the foregoing will meet with your approval.

They are almost meaningless; there is no pleasant thought or idea for the reader to remember.

Congratulation, appreciation, etc., are good ideas for either the opening or the closing but not for both in the same letter. If it has been expressed in the opening, it should not be repeated in the closing sentence.

Clarity, goodwill, courtesy, self-respect are most important in the last paragraph.

The last sentence has two functions: (i) to tell what is the next action to be taken and who is to take it, the writer or the reader; (ii) to win a favourable response for whatever has been said in the letter; or (iii) if the matter has been finally settled, and no further action or communication is to follow, a goodwill message is a suitable ending.

If the writer is to take the next action, the letter may end:

- Our representative will visit you on the 15th at 10 a.m.
- We shall let you know the result as soon as the test is completed.

If the reader is to take the next action, the letter may end:

- Please sign and return the enclosed card.
- We are expecting your cheque for Rs. 40,000/- within a week.
- May we request you to send us your cheque this week?

In letters which try to persuade the reader, the last sentence can add to or take away from the effect of the arguments stated. A firm, persuasive and convincing argument can be spoilt by a weak ending like, "We hope you will see the point" or "We trust the matter is now clear." A confident and lively ending has a better chance of getting action:

- We are sure you will take advantage of this offer and place your order before the 9th.

In the final letter after which there will be no further correspondence on the topic, the last sentence conveys a friendly goodwill message:

- We wish you all success in your new business venture.
- We sincerely regret the inconvenience which was caused to you.
- We shall be happy to give you any help which you may need from us at any time.
- Thank you once again for the help you gave us in this matter.
- We do hope we shall have occasion to be working together again.

The last sentence leaves the final impression on the reader's mind, and can be used to remind him about the last date for taking action or impressing upon him the advantage offered or for leaving a pleasant memory.

If you feel doubtful about the last sentence of your letter, cover it up, and see how the letter reads without it. If there is no loss of energy or strength, leave it out.

Review

1. It is grammatically correct to begin a letter with the sentence—
   (a) Referring to your letter dated 9 October, informing us that your washing machine is not working properly.
   (b) With reference to your letter of 9 October in which you informed us that your washng machine is not working properly.
   (c) We refer to your letter of 9 October informing us that your washing machine is not working properly.
   (d) Please refer to the above matter.
2. It is correct to end a letter with—
   (a) We look forward for receiving your order.
   (b) We are looking forward to receive your order.
   (c) Looking forward to receive your order.
   (d) We are looking forward to receiving your order.

TACTFUL USE OF LANGUAGE

There are several occasions when the content of the message needs tact in conveying, like insisting on action, refusing requests, or calling attention to mistakes. Some of these are discussed here.

Asking for Action

Most letters ask the reader to take an action. Imperative or command sentences are often used at the beginning and at the end of a letter. You can frame requests for action in several ways; each way has a different tone and can influence the receiver's response differently; choose a suitable style according to the need of each occasion.

Here are some ways of making a request for action:

- Please make the payment before the 15th.
- Please let us have your order by the 20th.
- Please dispatch the following, on the usual terms.

These are routine, polite requests for action; they do not draw particular attention. This kind of sentences occur in orders, routine requests for payment, and other instructions.

The following are direct commands, without even the word please; they sound brisk and businesslike.

- *Inform us immediately if the assignment is damaged.*
- *Book your order before the 18th.*
- *Don't forget to mail the enclosed card.*
- *Just post the enclosed postcard with your signature.*

They should be used only after explaining how the reader has a definite and clear advantage in taking the action.

These requests are formal; they are stronger and draw attention because of the opening words "I/We request."

- *We request you to allow us an extension of time.*
- *I request you to limit your purchases to cash.*

Such requests can be made stronger and more insistent by adding the word must.

- *We must request you to settle your bill in 3 days.*
- *I must request you to replace the damaged goods.*

Here is a question form of making a request.

- *Will you inform us as soon as you receive the goods?*
- *Will you arrange for a copy of the correspondence to be sent to us?*

These are polite but informal, and more suitable for oral communication. Such sentences do not usually occur in business letters unless the relationship between the writer and reader is informal, and the letter is addressed by name and written in informal style.

The same style is formal when used with the word please; it is considered even more formal when it begins with *Would you please...*

- *Will you please make the payment this week?*
- *Would you please arrange for an immediate inspection?*

Here is an indirect question form of asking for action.

- *May we expect your reply in a week ?*
- *May we have your cheque for our bill of Rs. 8200/-?*
- *May we request you to settle the account by the end of this week ?*
- *May I have a short interview at any time convenient to you?*

It is like a request for permission. It is very formal and very polite, and is suitable in upward communication, particularly in application letters, and in letters to strangers (e.g., status inquiries, letters to references) or to important customers.

Another indirect but common form is:

- *Please let us have your cheque/reply/order by this 15th.*

The following is a highly formal and indirect style.

- *We would appreciate receiving your reply within a week.*
- *I would appreciate it if you sent your cheque this week.*
- *I shall be grateful if you grant me an interview.*

- *We would be grateful for any help that you could give us.*

These requests are made in passive voice.

- *You are requested to pay your bills regularly.*
- You are requested to see me tomorrow morning.

This style is distant, impersonal and unfriendly and can damage customer relations. It is falling out of use and is best avoided.

Handling Negatives

Accentuate the positive. Most people respond more favourably to positive ideas than to negative ones. Your letters will be more successful if you focus on positive wording even when you have to convey a negative reply.

It is not always possible to grant a request; some requests have to be refused. What matters is the attitude the writer takes; the style and manner in which the negative is conveyed influences the reaction and response of the reader. A positive approach is more tactful and more effective in drawing a favourable response.

Be careful to avoid words with a negative connotation; these are the denying words like NO, DO NOT, REFUSE, STOP; or words with unhappy and unpleasant associations like, MISTAKE, ERROR, FAILURE, PROBLEM, NEGLIGENCE, DAMAGE, DEBT, CANNOT, UNABLE TO.

Try to express a negative idea in positive terms. Study the more acceptable and positive aspects of the situation before writing the letter. A positive approach is reflected in the choice of words and in the choice of details mentioned. If half the contents of a bottle have been used up, one may say that the bottle is half full or that it is half empty; both statements are true, but the attitude of the speaker— and the effect on the listener—are different. When you need to present negative information,

(a) emphasize what something IS rather than what it IS NOT

(b) stress what you (or product or company) CAN do rather than what you CANNOT

(c) start with positive ACTION rather than EXPLANATION or APOLOGY

(d) avoid words that convey unpleasant ideas.

There may be points on which agreement is possible, or parts of the request which can be granted; express these agreeable aspects first.

On the points where agreement or acceptance is not possible, think carefully of the reason. Reasons which are outside your control are emotionally more acceptable to the reader. Reasons based on personal opinion or judgement must be fully explained; reasons based on business policy must be carefully justified. A negative reply should never appear willful or arbitrary; genuine inability to agree or to grant a request is more acceptable to the reader and easier for you to communicate.

Support a refusal with: (i) an acceptable and well-explained reason, (ii) an apology, (iii) an alternative offer or a suggestion.

Your skill in the art of saying "no" without giving offence depends on your ability to use words well. Consider the following bad sentences which emphasize the negative aspect by the words used:

- We cannot dispatch your goods since you have not informed us where they are to be delivered.
- Our office closes at 5.30 p.m.
- We shall be careful to avoid delay in future.
- I cannot send the letter till Thursday.
- We cannot ship in lots of less than 25.

In order to emphasize the positive aspect, the sentences can be redrafted as follows:

- *We shall dispatch your goods as soon as you inform us where they are to be delivered.*
- *Our office is open till 5.30 p.m.*
- *We shall be careful to ensure prompt delivery in future.*
- *I can send you the letter on Thursday.*
- *To keep down packaging costs and help customers save on shipping costs, we ship in lots of 25 or more.*

Re-emphasize the positive by making effective use of position and space.

Position: Place positive and welcome ideas in positions of high emphasis: at the beginning and ending of a sentence, a paragraph, or a whole letter. Place negative, unwelcome ideas in low emphasis position like the centre of a sentence or paragraph or letter.

Space: Give more space to positive ideas and less space to negative ones.

See the section on Techniques of Emphasis, below, for examples.

Saying "no" and yet winning the reader's goodwill is one of the challenges of skilful letter writing.

Talking about Errors

A sensible attitude towards human error is necessary in official as well as personal life. It improves communication and interpersonal behaviour. When an error comes to light, it may or may not be possible to place responsibility for it immediately; but, sooner or later, the source of the mistake must be found out and steps must be taken to prevent repetition of such an error. The person who made the mistake must be told, corrected and, if necessary, warned not to repeat it.

It is important, while talking of mistakes, not to sound accusing, fault-finding, superior, victorious, or contemptuous. It is more useful to sound co-operative, courteous, patient, clear, and friendly. Choice of words and sentence structure is important. Each kind of sentence has its own value and emphasis, and can serve your purpose in different situations.

By using passive voice you can avoid mentioning the person who has committed the error. Sentences which include an object can be put into passive voice. A sentence is in active voice when the subject of the sentence is the doer of the action; it emphasizes and draws attention to the doer of the action. A sentence is in passive voice when its subject is the receiver of the action; it draws attention to the action, and usually leaves out the doer.

For example :

- *The goods were not packed properly.*
- *The crockery was handled carelessly.*
- *The order form has not been signed.*
- *The orders of two customers were confused.*

In active voice these sentences would be:

- You did not pack the goods properly.
- You have not signed the order form.
- Our new clerk confused the orders of two customers.
- Your packing department handled the packing carelessly

They sound accusing as they begin by mentioning the person who made the mistake.

Use of Active Voice and Passive Voice

Active voice is more direct and vigorous; passive voice is indirect and tame. An active voice sentence emphasizes the doer of the action while a passive voice sentence emphasizes the action. Each has its own effect and can be used as required for making the desired impression on the reader.

Active Voice

Active voice is more lively and vigorous than passive voice. Write most sentences in active voice.

Since active voice draws attention to the doer of the action, use active voice for talking about pleasant actions which the reader will like. Also use active voice to show that you will take responsibility for something, (like the customer's satisfaction) will improve the doer's image and goodwill, use active voice, for example:

- *We give discounts on these items if the order exceeds Rs. 5000/-.*
- *We ensure that our customers' interests are protected.*
- *We shall look into this matter immediately.*

Since passive voice keeps the doer of the action in the back-ground and emphasizes the action, it has other uses besides allowing tactful mention of errors.

When talking of unpopular decisions and policies like not giving credit terms or not revealing certain information, or not giving discounts on certain items, you can use passive voice instead of saying, "We do not...." For example:

- *Credit terms are not given to anyone.*
- *This information is not revealed to anyone.*
- *No discount is given on these items.*

Passive voice can also be used to protect the source of information. The impersonal passive voice is used for expressing general opinions on the credit standing of a customer; for example:

- *The firm is believed to have a small working capital.*
- *The new partner is believed to be quite enterprising and is expected to make good some of the lost position of the firm.*
- *It is believed that Mr. XYZ has a large commitment to his bank.*
- *We have been advised to be cautious in advancing credit.*
- *It has been brought to our notice that...*

Although passive sentences have their own uses and power, it is effective to make 80 — 90% sentences active.

Review

Are these statements true of false?

(a) Letters of refusal should end in a positive tone.

(b) Active voice is useful when talking about errors.

(c) Passive voice draws attention to the action rather than the doer of the action.

(d) "You are requested to see me tomorrow morning" is a friendly request.

(e) "Just send us an e-mail at docu@yahoo.com" is very formal style.

Techniques of Emphasis

You can emphasize an idea or a point by employing any of these four methods:

(i) **Placing:** An idea placed at the beginning of a composition or a paragraph, or a sentence, gets more attention than one which is placed later.

The following sentence emphasizes a negative idea.

- *We do not stock cotton shirts now as we have found that the demand for them has fallen.*

The sentence below emphasizes the reason for the decision, viz., the fall in demand, and de-emphasizes the negative.

- *As we found that the demand for cotton shirts has fallen, we do not stock them now.*

Just as the first sentence gets attention, a sentence which appears at the end of a composition or a paragraph gets greater emphasis than the middle sentences.

(ii) **Number of sentences (or amount of time) given to discussing the idea**: If you spend three or four sentences on the idea, the reader dwells on it longer; if you give it only one sentence, it gets less attention. If an idea or a point is to be de-emphasized or reduced in importance, you can give it in a subordinate clause or just a phrase. In the following examples, the idea of the colour can be given less or more emphasis by expanding the word to a clause and to a full sentence.

- *We want a dark blue carpet.*
- *We want a carpet which is dark blue in colour.*
- *We want a carpet. It should be dark blue in colour.*

(iii) **Type of sentence used:** An idea can be expressed in a number of ways, in different sentence constructions. Each way of expressing an idea and each type of sentence places the emphasis on a different aspect. Active voice emphasizes the doer, passive voice emphasizes the action; negative ideas can be expressed in positive terms; a request for action can be made in many of ways, with different emphasis; a change in the degree of comparison can shift emphasis from one aspect to another. Skill in transformation of sentences lends power to your writing.

(iv) **Mechanical devices**: An important idea may be underlined or typed in capitals or italicized for emphasis. This method is effective only if used very sparingly. Word processors have facilities for highlighting important ideas or words in a variety of ways such as colour, different font/type, etc. These methods are useful for sales letters.

EXERCISES

1. Rewrite the following negative ideas in positive terms:
   (i) We are sorry to inform you that the goods cannot be dispatched till Tuesday.
   (ii) We cannot ship the equipment you ordered till you give us the required specifications.
   (iii) Our office is closed on Mondays.
   (iv) We hope our customers will not be inconvenienced by our new order forms, which we have sent you.
   (v) Credit is not granted to anyone who has not been our regular customer for at least 3 years.
   (vi) I have no experience other than writing accounts in my father's garments store.
   (vii) We do not expect our employees to continue their education but we do have an excellent tuition fee re-imbursement scheme to help interested employees.
2. Make the following sentences more effective by using active voice:
   (i) You will be informed when the notice is received from our agent.
   (ii) This matter will be looked into immediately.
   (iii) The cancelled cheque was returned to you by us on 23 September.
   (iv) Care is taken to protect our customer's interests.
   (v) Prompt attention will be paid to your orders.
   (vi) You are requested to see me tomorrow.
   (vii) Your letter has been received and your complaint is being investigated. When all the facts are known a further letter will be sent to you.
   (viii) It is regretted that your new connection cannot be installed till next month.
   (ix) It is appreciated that an additional line is urgently needed by you.
   (x) It should be noted that the changed telephone numbers are published in a special supplement.

(xi) The inspection of the premises where the air conditioner is to be installed will be carried out by our technical supervisor.

(xii) Prompt attention to this matter is requested.

3. Improve the tone of the following statements by using passive voice:

   (i) You have returned the form without signing it.

   (ii) You damaged the camera by dropping it.

   (iii) The Transport Agent handled the goods carelessly and damaged them in transit.

   (iv) An inexperienced clerk in our dispatch department committed the error.

   (v) Messrs. A.B. & Co. have told us that Mr. X's credit standing is not very sound.

   (vi) Everyone believes that Messrs. Y and Sons have a high credit reputation.

4. Improve these statements so that they become sincere and friendly:

   (i) We are surprised that we have not received your order for a long time.

   (ii) We regret that we cannot hold ourselves liable for the damage.

   (iii) It is regretted that it is not possible for us to help you in this matter.

   (iv) We note with regret that you are not satisfied with our goods.

   (v) The inconvenience is regretted.

   (vi) While we understand your position, you must also realise that we cannot wait indefinitely for receiving our dues.

5. Say whether the following statements are true or false.

   (a) "Referring to your letter of 8th instant, the cheque could not be paid out" is a grammatically incorrect sentence.

   (b) You can impress customers by writing letters in a legalistic style.

   (c) "Assuring of our best services at all times" is a good closing sentence for a letter.

   (d) "Please refer to the above-mentioned subject" is an effective opening sentence for a letter.

   (e) Letters to customers should be written in polite language even if the content is not pleasant.

   (f) Writing "you" when you mean "I" shows concern for the reader.

   (g) Letters of complaint should be written in an angry and legalistic style in order to make an impression on the supplier.

   (h) Sales letters should be written in a fresh and flexible style.

6. When dealing with an unpleasant situation, the reader may be most willing to see the writer's point of view if the letter ends with the sentence —

   (a) If there is anything that still needs clarification, we shall be happy to discuss this further.

   (b) If you consider this explanation carefully, we are sure you will find it satisfactory.

   (c) We hope and trust that the matter is now fully clear and satisfactorily explained.

   (d) If you find this explanation unsatisfactory, Please let us know.

   (e) We are confident that you will now see this our way and consider this a satisfactory explanation.

❑❑❑

Chapter 18

LAYOUT OF A BUSINESS LETTER

A business letter has a distinctive structure and appearance. Each of the parts has a specific style, position and function which has been established by custom and is followed because it is convenient for handling and processing correspondence in an organization's office. A letter is usually an organization's first visual contact with another organization or person, and makes an important impression.

APPEARANCE OF A BUSINESS LETTER

A letter makes a visual impression before it is read, and the first impression is often decisive. Everyone is attracted by a good, presentable appearance.

The appearance of a letter depends on all the things that make up the letter.

Stationery must be of good quality. Most companies prefer to use pure white paper, with black print. The envelope must be of the same quality paper with the same type of print as the letterhead.

The printers and typewriters must be maintained well and cleaned regularly; the ribbons need regular attention. Good quality carbon paper must be used for making copies.

Typing must be neat, without cancellations or corrections. There should be equal spacing between words and between lines, and double spacing between paragraphs and different parts of the letter. The letter should be placed carefully in the centre of the page, leaving equal margins on the sides and at the bottom. The margins are usually one-and-a-half inch on the left, one inch on the right, and at least one inch at the bottom. If a continuation sheet is used, it must have the same margins as the first page.

A suitable style of layout is selected by every organization and all typists are expected to use the adopted style. Most word processing packages offer the choice of full block or modified block style of layout. Templates can be created and stored in computers.

Paragraphing is necessary for breaking up a composition into readable, logical and progressive units. It is also needed for a pleasing appearance. A large block of writing is not pleasant to see; it is restful to the eyes to see a good amount of white space between the reading material. In a business letter, paragraphing is important for appearance as well as for composition. Usually, a letter has three to four paragraphs: a short opening paragraph which may have only one or two sentences; one or two longer middle paragraphs which carry the main message of the letter; and a short closing paragraph which may be only one sentence.

Folding of the letter must be neat. It makes a poor impression if it is badly folded. The size of the folded letter must be such as to fit in the envelope leaving enough space for cutting the envelope open.

Address on the envelope is typed halfway down and one-third in from the left in order to ensure that the post office franking or stamping does not efface it. It is typed in block form. Its appearance is as important as that of the letter as it is seen before the letter. The practice of writing *To,* before the address is outdated.

PRINTED STATIONERY

Every office has certain standard stationery required for correspondence. The sizes of the sheets and envelopes are standard, but some organizations have distinctive sizes. The quality of the stationery, the designing of the letterhead, the layout and printing/typing together make the first visual impression on the receiver.

Letterheads

Letterheads can be got in several sizes. Most companies have letterheads of at least two sizes: the standard 8.5 x 11 inches for most letters, and smaller 5.5 x 8 inches for short letters. The appearance and the quality of the letterhead makes an important first impression on the receiver of the letter. Good quality, white paper should be used for letter stationery. Letterhead can be designed in consultation with a commercial artist or a computer graphics firm. Simple, elegant, streamlined designs are in keeping with modern style.

The letterhead includes the company's

(a) name and business
(b) emblem
(c) postal, telegraphic, and e-mail addresses
(d) telephone, telex, and fax numbers.

If the company's registered office is different from the one given at the top, it is printed at the bottom along with the company's registered number.

Some companies include the names of directors or of the Chairman or of the Managing Director. Most companies prefer to have letterheads with a streamlined appearance; the printed portion does not occupy more than one-fifth of the sheet. It is printed in a simple attractive design in a single colour, usually black. The printed sheet is called letterhead.

An illustration is given below.

> **Himalaya Publishing House**
> EDUCATIONAL PUBLISHERS
> "Ramdoot", Dr. Bhalerao Marg, Kelewadi, Girgaon, Mumbai 400 004
> Ref.... Date.....

Continuation Sheets

A continuation sheet is used if a letter does not fit on a single sheet. The continuation sheet is of the same size and quality as the letterhead. The company's name and logo are printed at the top of the sheet in the same colour as the print on the letterhead.

If a continuation sheet is used, it must show the name of the receiver, the page number, and the date of the letter; these details may be typed at the top in one line or each may be aligned at the left margin.

The top margin should be one inch, and the side and bottom margins should be the same as those on the letterhead on which the letter begins.

The following points are guidelines when using a continuation sheet:

It is not necessary to indicate anything at the bottom of the previous page since it is obvious that the letter has not ended.

There should be at least three of four lines of text on the continuation sheet before the closing section.

There should not be just one line of a paragraph either left on the previous page or carried over to the next page. As far as possible, a new paragraph should begin on a new page.

Envelopes

Offices usually have envelopes of several sizes for use according to the size and quantity of the material to be dispatched. The company's name and address are printed at the bottom on the left; some companies have it printed on the flap of the envelope.

The receiver's address is typed, or the address label is affixed neatly on the back of the envelope.

The quality of the paper and the colour of the envelope must match those of the letterhead. Some offices also have brown paper envelopes for dispatch of printed material.

Window envelopes have a transparent panel in the place where the receiver's address is to be written. The letter is folded and inserted in the envelope in such a way that the inside address can be seen through the window of the envelope. Window envelopes are most useful for sending out circulars as they eliminate the need for addressing the envelope. They are not generally used for confidential letters.

PARTS OF A LETTER

An official letter looks different from a personal letter and from other types of business documents. Convenience and custom have laid down certain requirements as parts of a letter. Since letters serve as records, some routine details are necessary in the make-up of a letter.

Different parts have their own fixed location on the sheet; there is a slight variation from left to right in the different styles of layout; their order of appearance from top to bottom is the same in all styles.

The main parts of the letter, apart from the text of the message are: Date, Inside address, Salutation, Complimentary close and Signature. In addition to these, the following details are included, according to the requirement of each letter: Reference number, Delivery mode, Subject line, Attention line, Enclosures, Courtesy copies, Sender's & Typist's initials. The letter wizard in most Word processors guides you through all the parts of the letter.

Date

Every official document must be dated. The date provides an important point of reference in further correspondence and in following up the issues dealt with in the letter. The date is placed two line spaces below the heading, on the right. In full block and NOMA styles, the date is at the left margin.

The date must always be written in full. The name of the month is spelled out in full and the year is written in all four figures. In British practice, the date is written in the order of day, month, year, with no commas.

16 June 2004

In American practice, the date is written in the order month, day, year with a comma separating the figure of the day from the figure of the year.

June 16, 2004

The practice of writing ordinal numbers, 1st, 2nd, 3rd, 4th, has fallen out of use.

Reference number

Reference number appears on the left on level with the date. The reference number gives the letter number, file no. and other filing details to make it easy to locate the file related to the issue.

Some companies include both, *Our ref. no.* and *Your ref. no.* both numbers in their letter. The words *Ref. no.* (and *Your Ref. no.*) are sometimes printed on the letterhead but this practice is getting outdated because, with modern word processors and printers, it is difficult to line up the printing on the pre-printed stationery.

Inside Address

Inside address is the name and address of the receiver as it appears on the envelope. The recipient's name should be exactly as they sign it in their letters. For example, if a person signs his name "Vishnu B. Kumar", he should be addressed "Mr. Vishnu B. Kumar" Addressing him as "Mr V.B. Kumar" is inappropriate.

For letters overseas, the name of the country is the last line of the address.

The inside address is typed in block form. In the block form all lines begin at the margin and there is no punctuation at the end of any line. This style looks neat and takes less time to type.

In the old indented form the first line began at the margin and subsequent lines were indented two spaces away from the beginning of the previous line; a comma followed each line and a full-stop followed the last line. The indentions and punctuation marks take more time to type, and also present a cluttered appearance. This form is now obsolete.

Block	**Indented**
Neil Publishing House	Neil Publishing House,
896, Mahatma Gandhi Road	896, Mahatma Gandhi Road,
Mumbai 400 001	Mumbai 400 001.

Remember that the practice of writing *To* before the address is outdated.

Special markings

If a letter is **confidential**, this is indicated above the inside address, either at the margin or in the centre. It may be either in all capitals or with initial capital and underlined :

CONFIDENTIAL or Confidential

Attention line is used only if, from previous communication, you know the name of the person in the organization who is handling the matter about which you are writing. The letter is addressed to the organization, but directed to the attention of the individual, by name, so that the letter is sent to that person without delay. It is not used if the letter is addressed to an individual by name.

The Attention line is placed after the inside address and before the salutation, either at the margin or in the centre. It does not affect the salutation. The salutation must match the first line of the inside address, e.g.,

The Blank Foods Manufacturers
Sir Dadabhoy Naoroji Road
Mumbai 400 001

Attention: Miss A.C. Patel

Gentlemen:

Subject line

Subject line gives a brief indication of the subject of the letter. It adds to the clarity of the letter, especially if the letter is long. It helps to focus the reader's attention. It is also used for classifying and filing the letter.

It is placed either above or below the salutation at the centre; in full block form, it is placed at the left margin. When there is an Attention line, the Subject line is placed after the Salutation. It is introduced by the word *Subject* or the Latin word *Re* but this is getting outdated.

In modern practice, the subject line is placed at the margin below the salutation, without any introductory word. It may be in capitals or initial capitals and underlined; e.g.,

> Dear Sir,
> YOUR INSURANCE POLICY NO. 88732265

Or

> Gentlemen:
> Your Order No. YA-42

(Note: *Re* is a Latin preposition meaning "in the matter of" or "in the case of"; it is not the short form of any English word; it is not correct to write ref. or reg. for the subject line.)

Salutation

The salutation begins at the margin, two line spaces below the inside address. It is followed by a comma; in American practice it is followed by a colon. In full block style it has no punctuation mark.

The salutation matches the first line of the inside address. If the letter is addressed to an organization, the salutation is plural: *Gentlemen* or *Dear Sirs* or *Sirs*. If the letter is addressed to a particular official mentioned only by designation, e.g., "The Sales Manager" the salutation is singular: *Sir* or *Dear Sir*. If the official is a lady, the salutation is *Madam* or *Dear Madam*.

It is quite common, now, to address business letters to an official by name and designation, e.g., *Mr. A.P. Shah, Sales Manager*, or *Ms A.B. Coelho, Finance Manager*. In this case, the salutation is *Dear Mr. Shah* or *Dear Ms Coelho*. *Ms* can be used before a lady's name as it stands for both Miss and Mrs.

Review

Fill in the blanks using the minimum number of words for each blank.

(a) A letter addressed to Tristar Computers Ltd. and directed to the attention of Mrs. Anita Dasgupta may have the salutation ____.

(b) The commonly accepted styles of writing the date are ____ and ____.

(c) The purpose of the reference number in a letter is ____.

(d) The attention line is used only when ____ in order to ____.

(e) In a letter which has an attention line, the subject line is placed ____; otherwise it is placed ____.

(f) If a letter is addressed to The Sales Manager, the salutation would be ___; if it is addressed to The Sales Department, the salutation would be ____.

Complimentary Close

The complimentary close is written two line spaces below the last line of the text of the letter; it is placed on the right and is followed by a comma. In full block style it is placed at the left margin and has no comma.

The first word begins with a capital letter.

The most common form is : *Yours faithfully*; Other common forms are: *Faithfully yours*, *Yours truly, Truly yours*.

If the addressee's name is used in the salutation, the complimentary close is *Yours sincerely*, or *Sincerely yours*.

Respectfully is used only when writing to a high public official.

Signature

The signature is placed just below the complimentary close. The name of the signatory is typed three or four line spaces below, to leave space for the actual signature; the designation/title is typed below the name.

Some companies include the name of the company just below the complimentary close, or below the name and designation of the person who signs; but most companies do not put the company's name in the signature as it is already in the heading.

Note that *Mr.* is not written before a man's name. If the signatory is a woman, *(Mrs)* is shown in brackets after the name.

Yours sincerely,	Yours faithfully,
William Lyle Marketing Manager	Raveena Murthy (Mrs) Finance Manager

When a letter is signed by another person on behalf of the sender, the word *for* is shown before the sender's printed name.

Letters with legal implications use the words *Per pro* or *pp* (per procurationem) which means "on behalf of."

Reference section

The reference section includes: enclosures, names of parties to receive copies, the type of delivery service to be used, and initials of the persons who dictated and typed the letter. The details are for the secretary or the dispatch department.

(a) **Enclosures:** Enclosures are related documents sent with a letter; bills, cheques, quotations, brochures, price-lists, etc., which have been mentioned in the letter and are sent as enclosures. If there are many enclosures, they are numbered and placed behind the letter in the order of their serial number.

Enclosures are indicated in the letter by writing *Enc(s)* or *Encls*: at the bottom left of the letter, after the signature. If there is more than one enclosure, the total number is also indicated, e.g. *Encs: 2*. Sometimes, the enclosure is named, e.g. *Encl: pro forma invoice*.

(b) **Copies:** When a matter concerns more than the two parties, a copy of letters related to the matter is sent for information to the other parties who are concerned. This is indicated by writing *copy* (or copies) or *cc* (copy circulated) followed by the name and designation of person to receive the copy :

copy: Mr. A.C. Sheth

or

copies: 1. Mr. A.C. Sheth 2. Accounts Manager, ABC Transport Service

If the receiver of the letter is not to be informed that copies have been circulated to others, *bcc* (blind copy circulated) is shown on the office file copy and on the 'bcc' copy; it is not shown on the copy to be received by the recipient of the letter.

(c) **Delivery service:** The type of delivery service to be used is indicated as Air Mail, Registered Mail, Express Delivery, Hand Delivery, Courier, Fax, etc. This detail is often placed at the top of the letter.

(d) **Initials:** The dictator's and the typist's initials are placed at the bottom. This is for future reference in the sender's office; the person who prepares or dictates a letter is not necessarily the person who signs it. The letter may be dictated by a senior clerk or a junior officer; it will be signed by the manager or a person who is authorized to sign outgoing letters of the company. The initials may be shown as: *PSW:rd* or *CRT gt* or *MRO/cs* or any such style.

Postscript

Postscript is a bit of writing, not more than three lines, added to the letter after the signature and after enclosures; it is signed again, without the complimentary close, by the same person. It is used for conveying a small bit of information which is not a part of the main message of the letter; it is an extra or unrelated point and is often written in hand at the time of signing the letter.

Postscript should never be used for adding something which was forgotten while preparing the letter. The idea of using P.S. to add a forgotten point is outdated with word processors. Even if a manual typewriter is being used, the letter must be typed again.

The postscript can be used to add a friendly personal note to a formal letter; it may be just a line, but it can successfully establish personal contact by referring to some common experience or by making a friendly personal enquiry. For instance:

- P.S. It was nice meeting you at the dinner last Sunday.
- P.S. How's your new venture in Pune coming up? Wish you the best of success.

The Postscript can be used effectively in a sales letter to impress an "action incentive" sentence on the reader's mind.

- PS: There's an early bird prize for the first seven orders.

It can also be used to make an impact at the end of a "stunt" collection letter.

- PS: Do clear your account before the fast approaching festival season.

Review

Complete the sentence by choosing the correct answer.

(1) An acceptable form of writing the complimentary close is ____

(a) yours Faithfully,

(b) Your's faithfully,

(c) Yours' faithfully,

(d) Yours faithfully,

(e) yours faithfully,

(2) When the salutation is Dear Mr. Gohel, the correct complimentary close is ____

(a) Yours obediently,

(b) Yours faithfully,

(c) Yours affectionately,

(d) Yours sincerely,

Fill in the blanks.

(a) The reference section includes ____, ____, ____, and ____.

(b) A letter addressed to Comfort Furniture, with the salutation *Gentlemen,* may end with *Yours* ____.

(c) Copies are sent to ____ for the purpose of ____.

(d) Any documents sent together with a letter are indicated by ____.

(e) Postscript is indicated by writing ____ and is used for ____.

STYLES OF LAYOUT

Layout means the design in which the different parts of the letter are placed on the letterhead. The parts are placed in the same order from top to bottom in all forms or styles; the variation is in the indention and the paragraph styles.

Indented Form

This old style is now outdated. In this form, the inside address was in indented style as shown earlier, and every paragraph began three to five spaces away from the left margin. The indention caused the letter to look uneven at the left margin. Besides, it took more time to type because of the indenting. This style is not used today.

Full Block Form

This is the most modern style. There is no indention from the left margin at all; every line, including the date and the complimentary close, begins at the left margin.

The address has no punctuation at the end of the line. The salutation and the complimentary close do not have a comma at the end. There is double line space between the parts and between the paragraphs.

This form takes less time to type because it requires no indention and has no punctuation in the layout parts.

Some companies do not like this form because it looks heavy on the left, and rather blank on the right.

A clear disadvantage of this form is that, after the letter has been filed, the date and the signature cannot be seen unless the file is fully opened. The date of a letter is an important item and is often referred to for many purposes. Quick reference to date and to signature in the filed letter is not possible in this form.

Modified Block Form

This style is a modification of the full block form. It eliminates the shortcomings of the full block style by keeping the date and the complimentary close on the right in their usual position. The inside address is in block form.

The salutation and the complimentary close are followed by a comma; however, many firms now do not use the comma after the salutation and the complimentary close.

All the paragraphs begin at the left margin, and there is double space between the paragraphs.

This is the most popular form as it has most of the advantages of the full block form without its disadvantages. Its appearance is balanced and neat.

Semi-indented Form

This form is also called Semi-block form. It has the inside address in block form but the beginning of every paragraph is indented. The date and the complimentary close are on the right side. The salutation and the complimentary close are followed by a comma as in the traditional style.

This style is getting outdated rapidly.

Hanging Indention Form

In this style, the inside address is in block form. The date and complimentary close are on the right. The beginning of every paragraph is at the left margin, but the subsequent lines of every paragraph are indented three to five spaces.

This style is adopted for sales letters, brochures and other documents in which striking appearance is useful. The opening line of every paragraph "hangs out", and can be used for high-lighting important points.

If this style is used, the opening words of every paragraph should be important and worth high-lighting.

NOMA Form

This is the most recent experiment in layout style. It is recommended by National Office Management Association of America (the name NOMA is an acronym). It has been accepted in the UK by the Institute of Office Management.

It has most of the features of Full Block form: all lines begin at the left margin, and the inside address is in block form.

The special features of this form are: (i) it has no salutation and no complimentary close; (ii) the subject line is in capitals, three lines below the inside address; (iii) numbered items of a list begin at the left margin, but if there is no number, the items are indented five spaces; there are no full-stops at the end of items; (iv) the writer's name and title are typed in capitals in one line below the space for signature; (v) the typist's initials are in the left bottom corner.

This style is not popular as it is too far removed from the familiar, conventional styles. Some people feel that this style saves time and sensibly omits meaningless salutation and close; but most people feel that this omission makes it impersonal and distant, and lacking in feeling.

Review

Answer in two or three sentences.

(a) What are the main differences between the full block form and the modified block form?

(b) What is the distinctive feature of the Hanging Indention form?

(c) How would you use the distinctive feature of the Hanging Indention form?

(d) Why do some people dislike the NOMA form?

An organization decides on its letter layout style and appearance after careful consideration and all typists are expected to conform to the standard of typing set up by the company.

Illustrations of all the styles are given below:

18 November, 2005

Excello Typing Institute,
    14, Green Avenue,
        Mumbai 400 053.

Dear Sirs,

This is the Indented form which is considered old fashioned now. The inside address is indented, i.e., each subsequent line is indented 2 spaces from the previous line; each line is followed by a comma, and the last line by a full stop. Each paragraph begins five spaces away from the margin.

This form was used in the days before the typewriter when all letters were hand-written. Today even hand-written letters are not written in this style.

The appearance of this style is not very neat; besides, it wastes typing time because of the indentions.

Yours faithfully,

Office Superintendent

Indented Form

May 2, 2005

Windsor Stationery Mart
86, Main Avenue, Santa Cruz
Mumbai 400 054

Gentlemen

This letter is in Full-Block form. Every part of the letter, including the date and complimentary close, begins at the left hand margin.

The inside address is in block form with no end-of-line punctuation. There is no punctuation mark after the salutation or after the complimentary close.

As there is absolutely no indention, this form takes the shortest time to type, and is very useful in a firm which sends out a large number of letters. It is the latest in styles of layout, but it has already become quite popular and is used in a number of firms.

The drawback of this form is that it looks rather blank on the right side and heavy on the left. Besides, when the letter is filed, it is difficult to refer to the date and the signature without taking out the file and opening it fully.

Yours faithfully

Correspondence Supervisor

Full-Block Form

10 September 2005

Pinto Commercial Institute
23, Rampart Row
Mumbai 400 001

Dear Sirs,

This is the Modified Block Form, and is in most common use today. Most companies adopt this form as the most convenient and also the most attractive.

The date and the complimentary close are at the right. The address is in block form, that is, all lines begin at the margin and there are no punctuation marks at the end of any line. The paragraphs begin at the left margin and are separated only by double spacing. As most of the lines begin at the left margin, this form saves the time of the typist.

This form is neat and balanced in appearance. It is a modification of the ultra modern Full Block Form.

Yours truly,

Supervisor

Modified Block Form

15 July 2005

Modern Typists
29, Mount Road
Mumbai 400 002

Sirs,

The Semi-Block form combines the indented and block forms. Some of its features are taken from the old style and some from the new style.

The date and the complimentary close are on the right. The address is in block form and the paragraphs are indented five spaces away from the margin. Many firms use this form although it does not look so streamlined as the modified block form.

This form will probably fall out of use for typewritten letters and will be used only for handwritten letters.

Yours faithfully,

Sales Manager

Semi-Indented Form

20 August 2005

Expert Advisory Service
Beach View
Warden Road
Mumbai 400 026

Gentlemen:

This is the Hanging Indention form. It has the address in block form, every paragraph starting at the margin, and subsequent lines of every paragraph indented a few spaces from the margin.

As the first line of every paragraph 'hangs' out, it attracts attention. Sales and stunt collection letters are written in this style in order to catch the eye. The opening words of every paragraph must be striking and the drafting must be done carefully.

Typing time is wasted in this form because of the large number of indentions. It is not used for routine letters.

Yours faithfully,

Sales Manager

Hanging Indention Form

11 May 2005

Expert Advisory Services
Beach View
Mumbai 400 026

NOMA LETTER LAYOUT STYLE

The name NOMA is an acronym of National Office Management Association. This American organization has recommended this style. It has been accepted in Britain with some modifications.

Most of its features are the same as those of the full block style. The address is in block form with no punctuation at the end of the line. All lines begin at the left margin.

This style has the following special features:

a. Salutation and complimentary close are omitted

b. Subject is in capitals three lines below the inside address

c. Enumerated item lists, like this one, begin at the left margin. Lists of items without number/letter are indented five spaces

d. There is no full stop at the end of the items in the list

e. The writer's name and title are typed in capital letter in one line at the left margin at the end of the letter, leaving space for the signature

f. The typist's initials are at the bottom left corner

Some people like this form as it eliminates the needless salutation and complimentary close, but it is impersonal, distant and too far removed from the familiar conventional styles.

KAMAL BHUTA - REGISTRAR
vsd

NOMA Form

EXERCISES

1. Fill in the blanks using as few words as possible.
   (a) A window envelope has ____; this saves office time because ____.
   (b) On envelopes, the sender's name is printed at ____ or ____.
   (c) On a continuation sheet, ____ is printed; you have to type ____, ____ and ____ at the top.
   (d) Companies have letterheads and envelopes in several sizes because —.
   (e) Appearance of a letter depends on ____, ____, ____.
2. Are these statements true?
   (a) Continuation sheets may be of a lower quality paper than letterheads.
   (b) Letterheads used for official letters should be colourful in order to be attractive.
   (c) Envelopes match the letterheads in quality, colour and printing style.
   (d) The manner in which a letter is prepared for dispatch affects its appearance and the impression it makes on the receiver.
3. How will you ensure that your letter makes a good visual impression?
4. Write notes on:
   (i) Letterhead and heading
   (ii) Date and reference no.
   (iii) First line of inside address
   (iv) Inside address and salutation
   (v) Attention line and salutation
   (vi) Subject line and attention line
   (vii) First line of inside address and salutation
   (viii) Salutation and complimentary close
   (ix) Complimentary close and signature
   (x) Reference section
   (xi) Enclosures
   (xii) Postscript

5. Write a note on the stationery required for letter writing.
6. Write notes on:
   (i) Advantages and disadvantages of full block form
   (ii) Modified block form
   (iii) NOMA form of layout
   (iv) Disadvantages of Indented form
   (v) Features of Hanging indention form of layout
   (vi) Semi-indented form of layout
   (vii) Continuation sheets
   (viii) Letterheads
   (ix) Envelopes
   (x) Window envelopes
7. Say whether the following statements are true of false:
   (a) A letter addressed to United Insurance Corporation with an attention line to Ms Radhika Sheth should have the salutation "Dear Madam".
   (b) In the modified block form, the date and the complimentary close are on the right.
   (c) It is acceptable to write the date in the form *23 Dec, '05*.
   (d) A letter addressed to "Omega Watches (Pvt) Ltd." should end with "Yours sincerely".
   (e) Hanging indention form of layout is most suitable for routine letters.
   (f) Postscript is used for adding a point which was forgotten while typing the letter.
8. Fill in the blanks in the following sentences using the fewest possible words.
   (a) In the Hanging Indention form, the paragraphs begin ____ and the rest of the lines of the paragraph ____.
   (b) The disadvantages of the full block style of layout are that ____ and ____.
   (c) If a letter begins with the salutation "Dear Sirs," the complimentary close should be ____.
   (d) Post script can be effectively used for ____.
   (e) The abbreviation Ms stands for ____.
   (f) The full form of NOMA is ____.
9. Choose the correct answer.
   In an official letter, the date may be written in the form ____
   (i) Jan. 12, 2005
   (ii) 12 Jan. '05
   (iii) 12 January 2005
   (iv) 12th January, '05
10. Discuss the advantages of the different forms of layout. Which form would you select for letters to be sent out by your office? Give reasons for your choice.

11. What is wrong with the following extracts from letters? Make the correction.

> Dear Sir,
>
> Sub: Negligence in delivering goods
>
> Thank you for delivering the two steel cupboards which we had ordered.

> Confidential
>
> Zen Graphics (Pvt) Ltd.
> Green Avenue
> Mumbai 400 004

> Sirs,
>
> Sub: Condolence on death of your partner

❑❑❑

Chapter 19

JOB APPLICATION

Written and oral communication related to employment is the first official communication that you will have to do. Prepare for it right now. The job application starts you on your career. Time and care must be given to the preparation of job application. Writing a bio-data is the first step. You will have to project yourself into a career. Make a careful self-assessment and find out what you are good at, and what you like doing. Take stock of all that you have done and can do in life.

The bio-data (also called resume or CV) and the covering letter, which goes with it, together make up the job application. The letter makes certain claims about the applicant's abilities, traits, and beliefs and offers to add value to the prospective employer's organization. The bio-data provides the credibility needed to support the claims by giving details of education (qualifications), experience, personal details and references. A job application is an offer of service; it must show the prospective employer that your services are worth employing. It must inform the prospective employer about your qualifications and persuade him that you are a desirable employee.

PREPARING BIO-DATA

Bio-data or resume is the most important document in the job-getting process; it is the first introduction of the candidate to the employer, and explains the candidate's background. It should be interesting and well laid out.

The bio-data gives credibility to the claims made in the covering letter. Write it with focus on the prospective employer's needs. The bio-data is not the story of your past achievements or just a list of what you have learnt and done; your past is the source material for the bio-data. It must tell what you can do and will do for the employer's benefit.

It is advisable to modify the bio-data for every new job; it should emphasize the details so as to support the claims you make in the covering letter for the job.

The following questions will help you to focus on the employer's needs before writing your bio-data.

1. What does the employer (the employing organization) want?
2. How will the work that I can do relate to the employer's objective?

3. What does the employer expect from an employee in this position?
4. What benefit can I offer in addition to what the employer expects?
5. What qualities and traits would describe a person that the employer would find desirable?

When you have answered these questions, you will be able to organize the details of your bio-data.

Bio-data is organized under headings. Tabulation permits orderly presentation of the varied items of information which have to be included in the bio-data. Usually, the information is classified under four headings:

Personal Data

Education

Experience

References

Personal data

This section gives the name, address, telephone number, date of birth, height and weight, marital status, religion, mother tongue, other languages known, interests and hobbies, participation in sports, and such other details. Applicants for overseas jobs should include nationality, passport number and foreign languages known.

The following must be kept in mind:

Name is written in the order of first name, middle name, surname. Keep to this order unless the company's application form requires the surname first.

Date of birth must give date, month (spelt in full), year in full, as in:

8 August, 1980.

Height and weight should be given in cms. and kgs. The item "other languages known" can be made interesting and informative by indicating the extent of skill in each, e.g., Gujarati—can speak; Marathi—can read and speak. Hobbies and interests are significant items. Include those that enhance your suitability for the particular job; highlight abilities and traits developed through hobbies.

Education

This section gives a complete record of academic qualifications and achievements. It is customary to begin with the latest degree/diploma and give the earlier record in reverse order. All details of institutions attended, degrees/diplomas obtained, scores/grades obtained, name of examining body, special subjects, etc. should be kept in mind. Include those details which are relevant to the job you are applying for. Select the details so as to support the claims you make in the covering letter. For example, include names of institutions attended if you wish to stress the quality of education and training received at reputed institutions.

The order of the details depends upon their importance and relevance to the claims made in the covering letter. Give names of institutions first if you intend to stress the point in the letter. If you intend to capitalize on specialization in a highly valued field, state the subjects first. If you have an excellent academic record, you would prefer to give the grades/scores first.

Further information to be included in this section can be given under three headings:

(i) Awards, prizes, scholarships with details. Mention the achievement or performance for which it was won, the year in which it was won and the number of competitors, and name of the organization that awarded it.

(ii) Participation in co-curricular activities like study circles, workshops, seminars, project work, and so on, points out your intellectual interests and development. Skills which cannot be developed in the classroom are developed in these activities. Give details of dates, organizers, subjects, etc.

(iii) Participation in sports and cultural activities in school and college reveals your range of interests. It also supports a claim that you have team work skills, inter-personal skills and organizational skills.

Inclusion of items and the details of the items depends on their relevance to what you say in the covering letter. The information must be narrated so as to support any claims of ability and traits that you make in the letter.

Projects done as a part of any course or undertaken independently, add a great deal to your bio-data. Give details of the project such as its full title, the company for which it was done, the coverage, conclusions, how it was received, etc. Young persons applying for their first job should emphasize their project work because it comes nearest to actual experience of work.

Experience

When you write about experience, mention the present position first; mention previous posts in reverse order, and state the first job last. Include the company's name, position held and the period of time (dates of joining and of leaving). Give a brief description of duties or nature of work or tasks done on the job; this should demonstrate qualities and traits claimed in the letter. Highlight any special achievements (like record of reaching targets before time).

Young applicants, in the early stages of their career can include voluntary work done for clubs, associations or charitable organizations, vacation jobs or any other informal experience. You must demonstrate that the experience has added to your ability to be useful to the prospective employer.

References

A prospective employer would like to verify the claims made in your letter; besides, an objective assessment of your personality can be obtained from persons who have observed you in different roles. Usually three references are given: a teacher, an employer, and a friend of the family, with a high social/professional status. The three references know you from different angles: academic aptitude, working habits and efficiency, and personal character and family background.

The name, title, complete address, and telephone number of the references must be given; it is preferable to indicate their social relationship to yourself.

You must take permission from the references to give their names. They might appreciate having a copy of the bio-data and some details of the job(s) applied for.

It is not advisable to write "references will be supplied on request." This phrase means that **letters of reference** will be produced by the candidate if the prospective employer asks for them. But the bio-data must give names of persons who can be referred to by the prospective employer.

Bio-data should be concise. It is a personal statement about your education and work life. It is also a sales tool. Here is a useful checklist for the bio-data.

Answer "satisfactory" or "needs improvement" for each item.

A. General

1. Is the layout/format pleasing to the eye? ....
2. Does it fit comfortably on one sheet? (without squeezing/ not too empty) ....
3. Is it neatly done, on good quality paper? ....
4. Is it easily readable? ....
5. Are important qualities highlighted? ....
6. Is important information placed near top and left of the page? ....
7. How is the overall appearance? ....

B. Specific Features

1. Goal focus: Does text support objective?
2. Length: Does it need shortening? Or expansion?
3. Relevance: Are the details in order of importance and relevance?
4. Format: Does the chosen format present you in the best light?
5. Precision: Does it focus on specific information about projects, experience, and avoid general statements?
6. Completeness: Is all important information included?
7. Bottom-line: How well does it achieve ultimate purpose of being called for an interview?

It is useful to give the prepared bio-data to someone who has not seen it before to examine for a minute and then ask the person to rate it on this checklist.

Here are some examples of bio-data/resume.

BIO-DATA

Name : Seema Shah
Address : Blue Heaven
35,B.Desai Road
Breach Candy
Mumbai 400 096
Telephone : 4468282
Date of Birth : March 16, 1964
Marital Status : Married
Education:

Year	Exam.	School/ College	Board/ University	Subjects	Marks	Class
April 1987	M.A. Department of Economics	University	Mumbai Electives: Industrial Economics, International Economics	Economics	65.6%	II
April 1985	B.A.	St. Xavier's College, Mumbai	Bombay University	Economics 6 papers major Other subjects: Book keeping & Financial Management, Sociology History	61.5%	I
April 1982	Std.XII Arts	St. Xavier's College, Pune	H.S.C. Maharashtra State	English French History Sociology Psychology Economics	80.67% 8th rank in the State	Dist.
March 1980	Std. X	St. Peter's School Mumbai	I.C.S.E. Board		67%	

Scholarships and Awards:

(i) Open Merit State Government Scholarship from Std. XII to Final Year B.A.
(ii) Dr. R.V. Bhagwat University Prize at B.A.
(iii) University Daxina Fellowship, in M.A. Pt.I and Pt. II.
(iv) Department Merit Scholarship in M.A. Pt. II.

Co-curricular Activities:

(i) Completed four courses in French at Alliance Francaise.

Took part in the class play, in French.

(ii) Completed a course in copy writing conducted by the Advertising Agencies Association of India in 1986.

Languages Known:

English — can read, write and speak very well

French — can read, write and speak

Hindi — can read, write and speak very well

Marathi — can read, and speak

Gujarati— mother tongue

Interests: Reading, Writing poems, Yoga, Travelling

Work Experience:

Name of Employer	Nature of work
Jayco Garments 322, Kaliandas Udyog Bhavan, Mumbai 400 025.	Office Co-ordinator June 1987 Duties include: Overall administrative responsibilities, client servicing and follow up, liaison with other departments like Production and Accounts.
Privately coached students in French.	

References:

Mrs. G.K. Doshi, Chartered Accounant
17/C Citizens' Cooperative Housing Society
Gulmohar Road
Andheri (W), Mumbai 400 058 — Tel. No. 2620xxxx

Dr. M.J.M. Kailash
Professor, Department of Economics
Bombay University
Vidyanagari, Mumbai 400 098 — Tel No. 2842xxxx

Father Correa
St. Xavier's College
'B' Road, Churchgate
Mumbai 400 020 — Tel. No. 2202xxxx

Here is a resume laid out in a different style. Change the layout style as you would like it. Write a covering letter to an employer to whom you would like to send it.

Suresh Barot
43, Plaza Road
Vashi, Mumbai 400 081
Tel. no. 743 xxxx

Date of birth: 6 October, 1973

Education

Presidency College, Mumbai
B.Sc., Botany, Environmental Studies, Economics, June 1993
M.A., Environmental Studies, and Industrial Economics, June, 1995

Business Experience

Entrepreneurial

* Developed and maintained substantial lawn service business, providing complete lawn maintenance, including rolling, aerating, cutting. * Originated lucrative week-end launch service in local harbour. * Wrote, published and sold a condensation of book readings and notes for college courses in Botany and Economics.

Management

* Reorganized the management of a 78 unit housing colony while on temporary duty as Resident Manager. * Supervised an award winning restaurant; monitored and dealt with customer service problems, resolved employee complaints. * Trained and managed 9 student workers in all job functions, including inventory, customer service, and scheduling for a prominent department store.

Sales/Merchandising

Entrusted with merchandising control for over Rs. 2,000,000/ worth of sales. * Negotiated with manufacturing representatives, introduced new products, and charted merchandising plans yielding 30% increase in profits. * Modelled and marketed lawn care products using creative packaging; tripled profits.

Employers

Jai Housing Society, Mira Road, Mumbai, Interim Manager, Summers 1995-present. * West side Restaurant, Malad, Mumbai, Maitre d'hote, 1994. * Consumers' Own Department Store, Sales Representative, Summer 1993-94. * Blue Waters Launch Service, Gateway of India, Mumbai, Owner, 1991-93.

Skills

Working knowledge of French, besides command of Marathi, Hindi and Gujarati; comfortable with spreadsheet, database and accounting software. Wrote weekly college news reports for college Wall paper; secretary of college co-operative store.

References and work samples will be provided.

Review

A newly established dotcom company needs young energetic persons to canvass advertisements for its website. The ad says, "Walk in for interview with a one-page statement of why we should hire you. We'll meet you at..." Prepare your one-page statement on the basis of your bio-data.

COVERING LETTER

A resume is always accompanied by a covering letter. It should briefly elaborate on your accomplishments, and highlight prior experience that will make the bio-data "come alive". Try to integrate your experience with your academic background. Before writing the letter, research the position for which you are applying and find out whatever you can about the organization. This will help you to present yourself as a perfect fit for the organization.

State what you can do and how you will be useful to the employer; writing in a fresh natural style gets more favourable attention than a letter which makes a request for "a job under your kind control." The letter must reflect an energetic, well-cultivated and poised personality.

Every detail of the covering letter needs careful attention; parts of the layout must be arranged neatly and framed accurately; names, designations, addresses, dates, and so on, must be absolutely correct. Even a small error tells the prospective employer about the applicant's carelessness. An employer is interested in the applicant's personal qualities like diligence, willingness to learn, ability to work with others, and motivation to achieve. Your covering letter must show that you have these qualities and that you fit the employer's needs. Show the employer how he will benefit by employing you. Writing about the employer's needs and interests is the art of using the "You" attitude in the application letter.

If a job is attractive, there will be many applicants with similar qualifications competing to make the best impression. An impressive covering letter with an individual style and tone has a better chance than a routine letter which is no different from a hundred others which state the same required qualifications. A successful letter reflects a personality that an employer would like to meet.

Use your own style; be concise,— not more than one page; use simple language without flowery phrases. Above all, show your distinctiveness and fit for the job/organization. Here is a useful format for a covering letter.

Your address
City and PIN code
State,

Date

Name/Title
Division/Organization
Address
City and PIN code
State

Salutation,

In the first paragraph, tell why you are writing, mention specific position you are applying for, how you learnt about the position.

Draw attention to anything in your background that makes you a sure candidate for the position. Elaborate on specific accomplishments given in your bio-data. Indicate how your experience or education/training fits the requirements of the position. Indicate your motivation for a career in the particular field/ industry/organization.

Say what you will do next; for example, make a telephone call to make sure that the employer is interested in setting up an interview. Or, if you prefer to be conventional, say that you will show samples of your work/answer questions at an interview.

Complimentary close,

Signature

(Your name typed/neatly written)

General Hints for Letter

- The applicant's address and telephone number are at the top right corner of the letter.
- Neat layout is necessary. Modified block form or semi-block form is the best. The full block form is not suitable for an application. Avoid the old-fashioned indented form.
- If the advertisement asks that the application must be written in the candidate's own handwriting, the covering letter should be neatly written in dark blue ink or ball pen.
- The letter should be addressed as indicated in the advertisement. If the letter is to be addressed to a company, the salutation is "Sirs". If it is to be addressed to an individual like The Personnel Manager, the salutation is "Sir". The complimentary close for an application letter is "Yours faithfully".
- If the given address is a Box No., the first line of the inside address is, "The Advertiser". The number and address should be carefully copied from the advertisement. The salutation is "Sir", and complimentary close is "Yours faithfully."
- Original documents like certificates are never enclosed with the application; only certified copies are enclosed. The original documents are produced at the interview.

Review

Complete the sentence choosing the correct alternative.

(i) When answering a recruitment ad. to be sent to Box No. 218, The Times of India, Mumbai 400001, the first line of the inside address should be—

(a) The Times of India

(b) The Editor

(c) The Advertiser

(d) Box No.218

(ii) An application is most effective if it ends by —

(a) promising to serve to the best of one's ability.

(b) referring to the enclosed bio-data.

(c) asking for a personal interview.

(d) hoping that you (the applicant) will be found suitable for the job.

Conventional Application Letter

Applications for jobs like that of typist, office clerk etc., with only a few required qualifications and details, can be written in conventional letter form.

The conventional form begins with a reference to the job announcement, and requests consideration as candidate for the post. The second paragraph states the qualifications and the last paragraph requests an interview.

Opening: Here are some traditional opening sentences:

**Please consider my qualifications, given below, for the post of Travelling Salesman, which you have advertised in today's Indian Express.*

**I wish to apply for the position of travelling salesman which you have advertised in the Times of India of the 7th....*

But even the conventional letter form can avoid a stale opening. Letters that open with a statement of the best qualification (rather than with a reference to the advertisement) are more attractive; such opening sentences are becoming more popular. For example:

**As a scholarship student and a prospective graduate in Sociology from the University of Mumbai this academic year, I should like to be considered for the position of research assistant which you have advertised in this morning's Times of India.*

**Since I have earned my way through college for the past two years, doing advertising work, I am sure that my knowledge and experience would be useful in your advertising department. I therefore offer myself as a candidate for the post of copy-writer which you have advertised in—.*

**My three years' experience as counter salesman in a children's garments shop has given me a good knowledge of customers, which will be useful in your newly opened shop. I request you to consider my candidature for the post of ....*

A letter which opens in this way can be brief.

Describing Qualifications: In describing qualifications, whether education or experience, select carefully, the items to be included; give specific details of the items. It is not useful to make vague statements like "I am a graduate of the Bombay University", or "I worked for the ABC Co. for 2 years." Such statements tell nothing about your ability. Give relevant details and show how the particular qualification or experience has helped you to develop valuable qualities that have a bearing on the job you are applying for.

Here are some sentences you can use.

**For 2 years I have worked as an assistant to the Librarian of Laxmi College of Commerce in Nagpur. In this job I got an opportunity not only to learn the various duties and responsibilities of a librarian, but also to observe the needs of various types of students who use the library. This experience will be useful to me in my relations with the members of your library.*

**After graduating in Hindi Literature from the University of —, I took a course in Conversational English at the Indo-American Society, Mumbai. Together with my knowledge of Gujarati, Hindi and Marathi, this training in speaking English should help me to build contacts with a wide circle of customers.*

If the advertisement requires personal qualities like tact, pleasant personality, poise, etc. there is no point in declaring, "I have tact." It must be demonstrated by stating some experience of work in which the quality was developed or proved.

**My one year's experience in modelling for The Perfect Cosmetics has helped me to develop self-confidence.*

**In my duties as personal secretary to the manager of The Blank Co., I was required to meet different kinds of people and also to answer telephone calls. This gave me an opportunity to develop tact and poise in contacts with people.*

Personal data such as age and marital status are necessary but not interesting items and can be stated in a single short sentence like,

I am 23, and single.

Hobbies and interests are important items. They develop abilities and traits in a person and are a part of the personality. Do not mention too many activities; it can give an impression that you may be a jack-of-all-trades or a scatter-brained person; there must be some relationship between the interests and the career you are planning and the job you are applying for.

I am interested in music, travelling and cricket.

is a good statement to make in an application for a job as a travelling salesman for products related to music or sports or for a job in a tourist agency. Of course, the statements you make about yourself must be true; there will be questions about them in the interview.

The names and addresses of References must be introduced in a separate paragraph:

** The following have agreed to give you information about my character and ability.*

** The names and addresses of my present employer, my college teacher of Mathematics and my family doctor are given below. You can refer to them for any information you might need about me.*

There are two sensitive items that may have to be included in an application: the question of salary and the reason for leaving the last job. It is better not to mention expected salary, but if the advertisement asks for it, you cannot ignore it. Stating a definite figure may put you at a disadvantage; the topic can be covered by saying something like the following:

**The question of salary could be discussed at the interview after you have had a better opportunity to judge my ability.*

**Until I have had an opportunity to prove my ability, I should be willing to start at the salary you pay for this post.*

Reasons for leaving a job need not always be given, but if it has to be given, nothing should be said against the job or the employer; expression of dissatisfaction will not be appreciated by a prospective employer. It is better to focus on a clear career plan and a search for better opportunities.

**I am seeking new employment because I feel I have gone as far as I can in this position and wish to gain experience in a larger company.*

**My present position is a job I took to earn my way through college, I am now looking for a post in my chosen career of marketing.*

Concluding Paragraph: Asking for an interview is the last step in the application letter. The interview is an opportunity to show samples of work, like designer's models or advertiser's copy, and to show the original certificates and testimonials.

These ideas can be used in the last sentence:

* *May I have an interview when I could show you some samples of my drawings?*

* *Although I have described my qualifications in detail, there must be many things you would like to ask me. I should be glad for an opportunity to answer your questions personally.*

* *I should be grateful if you would grant me an interview at which I can show you the originals of my certificates and answer your questions.*

Some illustrations of the conventional application letter are given below.

15 March, 2005

The Advertiser
Box No. 7004
The Times of India
Mumbai 400 001

Sir,

Please consider my qualifications, given below for the post of librarian which you have advertised.

I secured a first class degree of B.Sc. Lib. of — University in 1999, and also second class B.A. in Philosophy from — University in 1997.

My interest in library work began when I worked as a Library Clerk in XYZ College for two years while I was an undergraduate student. After graduation, I worked as Library Assistant in the ABC Memorial Library for three months in a leave vacancy and found the work so satisfying that I decided to take up Librarianship as my career.

During my study for B.Sc Lib. I completed a course at NIIT which familiarized me with the use of software packages, and I used the knowledge for my final B.Sc. Lib. project on Managing Library Inventories.

I am 25, unmarried, and in excellent health. My special interests are Indian classical music, French literature and photography.

The following have agreed to give you any information about me which you may require.

Dr. A.B. Mehta, Principal
X.Y.Z. College
Pune 411 004 Tel no.: ____

Mr. A.B. Blank, Librarian
ABC Memorial Library
Mumbai 400 001 Tel no. ____

Dr.C.A. D'Souza
Head of Library Science Department
University of ____
Nasik Tel no. ____

Copies of my certificates and testimonials are enclosed. May I have an interview so that I could answer any questions you may wish to ask me?

Yours faithfully,

(Miss) E.A. Mehta

Encls: Copies of 5 certificates

Sir,

Would you consider my candidature for the post of Assistant Manager in Sales Promotion, advertised in today's Economic Times? I am giving my detailed bio-data below:

Education:

B.Com. First class with Business Management as special subject; Sydenham College, Mumbai 19—.

Diploma in Marketing Management, M.I.T., U.S.A., 19—. Certificate Course in Publicity Photography, X Y Institute of Mumbai, 19—.

Experience:

Sales Representative, Himalayan Bouquet Cosmetics, 19— to date.

Free-lance advertisement copy writing for various advertising agencies in Mumbai. June, 19— to April, 19—

Personal Data:

Age: 28; Married; Languages: English, Hindi, Gujarati, Marathi; Hobbies: travelling, photography.

References:

Mr. A.B. Saldanha, Sales Manager
Himalayan Bouquet Cosmetics
Mumbai 400 008

Mr. D.B. Weling, Director
X.Y. Inst. of Management
Chowpatty
Mumbai 400 007

Mr. J.S. Mehta, Solicitor
260, Warden Road
Mumbai 400 026

I am seeking new employment in order to improve my prospects. My present salary is Rs. ____ per month and I am expecting a reasonable increment in the grade which applies to the post of Assistant Manager in your firm. I have enclosed copies of my certificates and shall produce the originals at the interview.

May I have a few minutes in which to give you any further details you may need about me?

Yours faithfully,

Sir,

Prof. A.R. Siddiqui of ____ School of Arts has suggested that I should apply to you for a post in your Advertising and Publicity Department.

My experience in printing work and in preparing advertising copies of various kinds, gives me confidence that I shall be able to shoulder a large amount of responsibility in advertising work.

My enclosed personal record sheet will show that I have been interested in a variety of activities which have given me useful experience. May I have an opportunity to meet you at your convenience? You can contact me at the address or telephone number given at the top of my personal record.

Yours faithfully,

Encl : Personal Record

Review

1. Write a statement of your skills and how you acquired them.
2. Are these statements true?
   (a) "Being given to understand that you have a vacancy for a market researcher, I beg to apply for the same" is a good opening for an application letter.
   (b) "If selected, I promise to serve to the best of my ability" is a poor ending for an application letter.
   (c) In an application letter, you should always mention the salary you expect to get.
   (d) Mentioning a large number of extra-curricular activities and interests gives the impression of a well-developed personality.

EXERCISES

Draft replies to the advertisements given below:

1. Young energetic fresh graduates required for Sales and Accounts work in our group of companies. Meet in person with application and bio-data at Laxmi Boards Ltd., Das Chambers, 16, Dalal Streel, Mumbai 400 001.
2. Wanted young, dynamic and result-oriented marketing personnel (Boys & Girls) for a reputed computer software company. No previous experience required. Must be degree college student. Successful candidates will get attractive compensation plus travelling allowance. Send application and resume along with passport size photograph before 23 October, 20... to Scill Consultants Pvt. Ltd., 8/A, Tall Tower, Nariman Point, Mumbai 400 021.
3. Canbank Financial Services Limited requires junior personnel. Candidates must be young (preferably students) with good communicative ability and marketing aptitude. Opportunity to work under professional Merchant Bankers and gain experience in marketing Financial Instruments. Come with application and bio-data for personal interview any day till 27 January, between 10 a.m. and 6 p.m. at 115 Atlanta, Nariman Point, Mumbai 400 021.
4. Wanted from 1st of June, for English Medium School, trained lady teachers with B.Com., B.Ed. Preference will be given to higher qualified and experienced teachers. Posts 2. Age below 35.

5. A plastic processing unit engaged in manufacturing various packaging products requires Marketing Executives. Graduates with 1 or 2 years' experience in marketing plastic/metal packaging products. Fresh graduates may also apply. Write to P.O. Box No. 882 Times of India, Mumbai 400001.
6. Wanted Accounts Assistants by an international Organization in Mumbai. Qualifications: Commerce Graduate with second class and minimum 3 years' experience in similar job. (1) Costing. Job: To assist in working out details. (2) Sales Tax. Job: To prepare statements of returns regarding sales tax. Selected candidates will be paid about Rs. 10,000/ per month. Those earning less than Rs. 8,500 per month should not apply. Please apply immediately to Box No. 1056, Indian Express, Nariman Point, Mumbai 400 021.
7. RFC India Limited require for their new Plant at Thane, Maharashtra, Clerk-Personnel. Education: Graduate, 2/3 years in a manufacturing unit. Should have handled personnel functions, such as maintenance of attendance records, time keeping and be conversant with E.S.I., P.F., Factories Act and other statutes. Apply giving age, qualifications, details of previous experience, names of firms and details of occupation. Applications should reach within 10 days to RFC India Ltd., P.O. Box 96, Thane, Maharashtra.
8. Wanted 2 Steno-Secretaries for permanent posts, one in Fort Office and other in Thane Works. Starting pay around Rs. 10,000 plus other benefits. Candidates should be at least HSC with at least 3 years' experience as stenographer with a speed of 100/50 w.p.m.; selected applicants will be tested at these speeds. Apply with full details to Personnel Manager, XYZ Pressure Cookers Ltd., Mahalaxmi, Mumbai 400 026.
9. Wanted for a permanent post at our Fort Office Receptionist-cum-Telephone Operator with ability to handle PBX switchboards. Salary will depend upon personality and ability. Applications giving full details of age, qualifications and experience, and enclosing a photograph should be addressed in writing to Personnel Manager, Pressure Cookers and Appliances Private Ltd., United India Building, Pherozeshah Mehta Road, Mumbai 400 001.
10. Prepare your bio-data in the style of Suresh Barot's biodata given in the chapter. What are the advantages and disadvantages of this style?
11. You are applying for admission to a Management College; you are required to write a composition of about 300 words stating your objective in seeking the admission. Draft the statement of your objective.

Prepare a bio-data and covering letter for the following walk-in interviews.

1. We are a fast growing finance company enjoying significant presence in car finance, home finance, personal finance and corporate finance segment. To further consolidate our ambitious growth plans, we are looking for Co-ordinators. You should be a graduate with at least one year of experience in co-ordinating with various departments, agencies, and individuals. Needless to add, you must have excellent interpersonal communication skills and be fluent in English. We offer excellent growth prospects. Salary and incentives shall not be a constraint for the right candidate. Walk-in between 11 a.m. and 5 p.m. from 16th to 19th June with your complete resume at: Esscom Marketing, 154-A Mittal Court, A Wing, Nariman Point, Mumbai 400 021.

2. ExCom, the number one institute imparting high quality computer education in India, is the best platform for you to build a great career. We have vacancies for Web Developer. Should have expertise in HTML, Javascript, at least one year experience in website implementation. Exposure to web administration and knowledge of DHTML, CSS would be an advantage. Walk-in on June 17, 1999, between 10 a.m. and 7p.m. at ExCom House, 17, Singhvi Road, Dadar, Mumbai 400 028.
3. Garment Export House needs Accountant. Female Commerce graduate with one year minimum experience of computer based Accounting apply: HiMark Exports, 44,Sahayog Industrial Estate, M.T.D.Marg, Vikhroli (West), Mumbai 400083.
4. A leading business associate of BPL Mobile is looking for young presentable go-getters with 1 – 2 years' experience in front line sales. Preference given to candidates from similar industry. Walk in on 16 and 17 June, between 12 and 5, at 48, Ashoka Shopping Centre, 1st fl, L.T. Road, Near Metro Cinema, Mumbai.
5. Required smart boys and girls on full/part time basis for Marketing, Field work, and Survey, BizSoftech (Pvt. Ltd., 269 Udyog Bhavan, Mulund (W), Mumbai 400080.

Chapter 20

PERSONNEL LETTERS

An organization has to write a number of letters related to employment and maintenance of staff.

Recruitment requires making enquiries about applicants, letters of appointment, confirmation, promotion and so on. Maintenance includes warning memos, letters of appreciation, letters of sympathy and so on according to the needs of the occasion.

Some of these letters are discussed in this chapter.

LETTERS TO APPLICANTS

The received applications are scrutinized by the Personnel Department or by the Head of the Department concerned. Applicants are short-listed for interview on the basis of the presentation of the application, qualifications and qualities. The shot-listed applicants are sent letters calling them for an interview. The letter mentions the application, the name of the post, and the place, date and time of the interview.

> Dear —,
>
> With reference to your application for the post of —, please be present for an interview on (day, date & time) at (place, address). Please bring your certificates with you.
>
> Yours sincerely,

Some companies write more personalized letters like the following.

> Dear Mrs. Walecha,
>
> APPLICATION FOR POST OF ASSISTANT TRAINING MANAGER
>
> Thank you for your application for this post.
>
> Please attend an interview with me and Ms Nalini Sheth, HRD Manager, on Tuesday, 15 September at 11.00 a.m.
>
> Please call Madhuri at tel no. 2222222 to say whether this date and time are convenient for you.
>
> Yours sincerely,

Very courteous companies also inform candidates who have not been included in the short-list so that they may not be kept in suspense.

> Dear —,
>
> Thank you for your application for the post of —.
>
> We have received many applications for this post. Unfortunately, your qualifications and experience do not match our requirement closely enough, and we are not able to include your name in our short-list.
>
> We understand that you will feel disappointed, but we appreciate the effort and time you spent in preparing your application. With your considerable experience you would soon be able to find a suitable position.
>
> Yours sincerely,

After the interview, the selected candidate is informed by a letter and asked to report at the office to take the appointment letter.

> Dear Ms ABC,
>
> I am happy to inform you that you have been selected for the post of ..., for which you were interviewed on the 27th last month. Please call at our office between 11.00 a.m. and 1.00 p.m. on any week day by the 18th and meet Mr. XYZ, Personnel Manager. He will hand you your appointment letter and also introduce you to your officer.
>
> Yours sincerely,

Other candidates who were interviewed but not selected are sent a letter informing them that the post has been filled, so that they may not keep waiting.

> Dear —,
>
> Thank you for coming for an interview on ... The post has been filled by a candidate whose qualifications were more suitable for our job requirement. We wish you the best in your efforts to find a suitable post.
>
> Yours sincerely,

Note how this letter maintains relations with a candidate who has not been found suitable after the interview.

> Dear —,
>
> It was a pleasure meeting you yesterday and having the opportunity to discuss your qualifications and career goals.
>
> I appreciate your frankness and feel that since your objectives are to work in the field of counselling you should attempt to obtain a position with an organization that will enable you to gain experience in your preferred area. Unfortunately, our firm does not afford this opportunity.
>
> I am sure you will soon find a position that suits you and I believe you have a great deal to contribute. Please accept my sincere wishes for your future.
>
> Yours sincerely,

References, Recommendations and Testimonials

When candidates are short-listed for interview, the employing organization needs to verify the claims that applicants make about themselves. Enquiries are made with references provided by the applicants; information and opinions may also be sought from persons in the institutions and organizations in which the applicant has been before. Candidates may also be asked to provide testimonials or recommendations.

A Reference is written in reply to an enquiry about a candidate or applicant. It is addressed to the person who has signed the enquiry.

A Recommendation is not necessarily in reply to an enquiry; it is written at the request of the candidate and is addressed to a prospective employer who expects the candidate to get a recommendation letter. Its style and content is the same as the reference letter.

A Testimonial is open, and not addressed to any specific person and is not for any specific post. It endorses the character and abilities of the candidate. It is a certificate and not written in letter form.

MAKING ENQUIRIES ABOUT CANDIDATES

Some companies have a form to be filled in by the reference, so that specific information about the candidate can be obtained. The form ensures that important aspects of the candidate's ability, intelligence, character, status etc., are included; it makes the reference give specified information instead of making vague general statements.

If no form is used, a letter is sent. The enquiry, as well as the reply, is confidential, and the word 'Confidential' is written on the letter and on the envelope.

Some specimens are given here.

Dear Mr. —,

Mr. J.R. Kavli who has applied to us for the post of assistant accountant, has given your name as reference. I would be grateful if you could give your opinion of his character and intellectual ability. Whatever information you may give or opinion you may express will be treated as strictly confidential.

Yours sincerely,

XYZ

Dear —,

We have received an application for employment from -(name), seeking a position as —. We understand the applicant was previously employed by your firm.

We would appreciate a reference about the applicant, including confirmation of the dates of employment with you, performance evaluation, and reasons for termination of the employment.

Your reference will be held in confidence.

Thank you for your co-operation.

Yours truly,

Dear —,

— (applicant's name) has applied to our company for a position in our bookkeeping department. He has given your name as a reference. Would you be kind enough to provide us with your written evaluation of this person? Please be assured that your response will be treated as confidential.

Yours faithfully,

GIVING INFORMATION ABOUT CANDIDATES

A Reference letter (and also a recommendation) depends, to some extent, on the relationship between the reference and the candidate, and particularly on the nature of the acquaintance. For example, a school/college Principal or teacher knows the candidate as a student in his teens; an employer knows his habits and ability as an employee at a later age. Both can give valuable information about the candidate.

An employer, past or present, would generally indicate the reason why the candidate left or is leaving the employment. It will be odd to speak well of an employee and then let him/her go without regret; it will reflect on the reference writer's quality as employer.

The letter should include:

(i) Candidate's name, length and nature of acquaintance

(ii) Brief account of conduct at the job, with colleagues, superiors, etc.

(iii) A few remarks about temperament and nature

(iv) Reason for seeking other employment

(v) Opinion on candidate's suitability for the post applied for

Dear Mr. —,

I have known Mr. — about whom you have enquired, since 1999 when he joined ABC Electrical Goods as Junior Sales Representative.

He proved himself quite able and was soon entrusted with the task of contacting important customers. He was able to get several valuable contracts for the company. His good personality and polite manners are an asset in the sales line, as well as in the office.

We should be sorry to lose his services but we cannot offer him promotion now and would not like to stand in the way of his career.

I feel that he will be able to do justice to the managerial post for which he has applied to you.

Yours sincerely,

Dear Sir,

Miss Lila Fonseca was employed in my office as telephone operator from 1999 to 2002—.

Her clear speech, pleasant voice and good temper were an asset in her job; she was also quick and alert with her work. Owing to her initiative and general ability, she undertook outdoor work in sales, and soon proved her skill in winning customers.

She left my office when she got a more suitable post as sales representative for Joy Food Products. She applied for the post with my knowledge.

I am sure that she will be able to handle the responsibilities of the post of senior sales representative.

Yours truly,

Here are some paragraphs from actual letters, which can be used with modifications, in any kind of reference or testimonial.

* *She has taken on a wide variety of projects and demonstrated the ability to manage several concurrent projects with ease. She has strong determination to finish what she starts, even when others become discouraged. She has exceptional organizational skills, allowing her to handle minute details without losing focus on more important tasks.*
* *She works independently with little or no supervision. In a group she facilitates compromise and builds consensus, and she has been instrumental in resolving several inter-departmental conflicts. She has excellent interpersonal skills and maintains a cordial professional relationship with all employees.*
* *She has strong hands-on experience with many different soft-ware packages, and she can make sense of obtuse computer manuals. She has designed a database for our — department which has proved a tremendous benefit both in productivity and convenience.*
* *In all, Lilian has been an asset to our department, and I feel she has the skills and attitude which will allow her to grow in any organization.*

A **Testimonial** is not a letter; it is a certification that the writer has known the subject for a certain period in a particular capacity, and has noted certain qualities of the person. It carries the title **Certificate** or **Recommendation**. A testimonial is handed to the subject, who may or may not use it. Its value depreciates rapidly, and a testimonial older than six months is hardly of any value.

A testimonial may be given by an individual officer personally, on a personal letterhead, or by a Manager on behalf of the company on the company's letterhead.

Examples of testimonials are given below:

To Whom It May Concern

Mr. J.R. Kavli has been known to me for the last four years during which he worked in this company as junior accountant. He did his work well and showed high ability in picking up new work assigned to him. He was also punctual and regular in attendance. His cheerful disposition and good manners were particularly noted by his colleagues as well as his superiors.

He leaves his present employment because his family has to shift from Mumbai owing to his father's health. Mr. Kavli will be able to handle responsible work in the Accounts Department of a large firm, and deserves to be given an opportunity to build up a good career.

XYZ
Manager

Certificate

This will confirm that — has been employed by — Corporation since 1 June, 19—. During his tenure, he has displayed unique ability to identify and solve problems. He has been instrumental in stream-lining our accounts department. His experience in accounting and finance has been a valuable asset, and can be of great value to any company that employs him. He is loyal and places the company's welfare above all else. His patience with his subordinates and relationship with the management make him an excellent employee. He is seeking new employment in order to enlarge his field and he can certainly count on re-employment with our firm. Any company considering — for employment has my most enthusiastic recommendation. If his performance here is any indication, he should achieve new heights in his career.

(Signature)
Title of signatory

Appointment Letters

Letters given by the employer to the employee are legal documents. In case of disputes about seniority, retirement benefits like Provident Fund, Gratuity, Pension, etc. these letters can be produced as proof of claim. Dates of appointment, of taking charge of the post, of confirmation, promotion, resignation, termination of service, etc. are an important deciding factor in computing the amount due to the employee when the appointment comes to an end.

Young persons on their first job are often unaware of the significance of the details contained in the letters given to them by their employers. It is advisable have the details of the appointment letter examined by a knowledgeable and experienced person before signing it. Once the acceptance is signed, both parties have to abide by the conditions of the letter.

The employee's signature is taken on two copies of the letter and the copies are filed in the office, one in the office records file and the other in the particular employee's service record file.

The personnel department has to be careful in preparing employment letters since the company which gives the letters is bound by the conditions stated in them. Most companies have pro forma letters so that uniformity is maintained, and no detail is forgotten; only the details applicable to each individual case need to be filled in.

These letters are printed out (or typed) on the official letterhead of the employer. The inside address must begin with the full name of the receiver since this letter is a proof that the particular person was given the terms of service mentioned in the letter. The salutation is by name, and the complimentary close is "Yours sincerely". The signature must be followed by the name and designation of the person who signs.

An Appointment Letter must contain the following details:

(i) Name of the post

(ii) Scale of pay and rate of increment. (This is written as Rs. 5000-100-7000-200-10,000 which means that the starting basic pay per month is Rs. 5000, the annual increment is Rs.100 till the basic per month reaches Rs.7000/-. Thereafter the increment is Rs. 200 till the basic reaches Rs. 10,000/-. After that there will be no further rise in the basic salary of the particular post.)

(iii) Basic salary to be given to the particular person; a person who has previous experience is often given a higher start.

(iv) Allowances applicable: These are: D.A. (Dearness Allowance), CLA (City Living Allowance), TA (Travelling Allowance for jobs involving travel), HRA (House Rent Allowance), Commissions, and so on.

(v) Date on which the person is expected to take charge of the post.

(vi) Provident Fund, or Pension and Gratuity benefits applicable to the post.

(vii) Period of probation if the appointment is on probation. The letter must indicate if the appointment is temporary or permanent or in a leave vacancy etc.

(viii) Period of notice required for termination by either side.

Dear Miss Kamal Mehta,

With reference to your interview on (date) for the post of Office Superintendent, I am happy to inform you that you have been selected for appointment to the post of typist. Your starting basic salary will be Rs. 5400/- in the scale of Rs. 5000-100-10,000/- and DA at state Government rates. The appointment is on probation for one year and will be confirmed on satisfactory completion of probation. Contributory Provident Fund benefits become applicable on confirmation. The appointment is terminable by a month's notice from either side during probation.

You are requested to take charge immediately. Please intimate your acceptance of the appointment.

Yours sincerely,

Dear Mr.—,

You have been appointed to the post of Sr.Clerk in the scale of Rs. 4000-75-8000/-. Your starting basic salary will be Rs. 4100/- plus D.A. at State Government rates. You will be on probation for one year and will be confirmed if your services are found satisfactory.

The post carries the benefits of pension and gratuity which become applicable on confirmation. During the probation period the services can be terminated by either side on giving a notice of one month.

You are requested to take charge on 1 July, 20xx.

Yours sincerely,

Manager

Confirmation Letter

A Confirmation Letter is given at the end of the probation period if the person's work is found satisfactory, or even earlier if the person is found very efficient. Confirmation is important because certain benefits like leave, Provident Fund, Pension etc. become applicable only after confirmation. Once confirmed, the appointment cannot be terminated by either side unless the required notice is given.

Since this is a binding, an employee who hopes to find a better place, or is not sure that s/he wants to continue in the post may request that confirmation should be delayed. Usually, the person concerned is informally interviewed before being given a confirmation letter, in order to find out his/her views and attitude to the job.

Points:

1. Brief reference to satisfactory completion of probation (or to good and efficient service) and decision to confirm
2. Date from which the appointment is confirmed
3. Benefits applicable after confirmation
4. Request for signature on copies, in acceptance

> Dear Ms —,
>
> In appreciation of your good service during the last four months, your appointment as Registrar is being confirmed from 1 November, 20xx, two months before the completion of the usual probation period. You will be eligible for P.F. and other benefits of the post from the date of confirmation. Please sign and return the attached copy in acceptance of the confirmation.
>
> Yours sincerely,
>
> Manager

> Dear Mr. —,
>
> Your appointment to the post of — is confirmed from 1 December, 20—., on satisfactory completion of your probation. The benefits of pension, gratuity etc., according to the service conditions, will now be applicable to you. Please sign and return the attached copy of this letter.
>
> Yours sincerely,

Promotion Letter

A Promotion Letter is given when a person is selected for a higher post. The letter should contain the following:

1. Date of promotion
2. Name of the new post and scale of pay
3. Basic salary to be given to the person
4. Reference to extra benefits, if any
5. Request for acceptance

Congratulatory expressions, as in the confirmation letter, may be included.

> Dear Ms —,
>
> I am happy to inform you that you are promoted to the post of Office Registrar with effect from 1 March, 20—. Your basic salary will be Rs... in the scale of Rs... which is applicable to the post. The post carries the benefit of Leave Travel Allowance in addition to Dearness allowance. You will be entitled to all the benefits of the post according to the service conditions.
>
> Please intimate your acceptance immediately.
>
> Yours sincerely,
>
> Manager

Dear —,

I am pleased to inform you that you have been promoted to the challenging and demanding position of —. This promotion is in recognition of the fine work you have done for this firm. I am quite confident that you will meet the new responsibilities which accompany the position of — with the same level of enthusiasm and enterprise which you have shown since you joined this firm.

Please accept my congratulations on your promotion.

Yours sincerely,

Warning Memo

A Warning Memo is given in confidence to an employee whose work is unsatisfactory or who violates rules and regulations, or behaves in an undisciplined manner.

Before issuing a written memo, the supervisor/manager meets the employee personally for a discussion of his/her unsatisfactory performance or behaviour. The written memo is in confirmation of the discussion.

In case there is no improvement, further memos may be given. Warning memos do not contain expressions of sympathy for any possible trouble which may cause the employee to behave improperly. But it refers to the previous oral warning.

The letter must give clear and exact details of the faults committed by the employee. There must not be vague statements; any statements about inefficiency or fault must be supported by recorded instances. The letter must refer to records or registers such as the attendance register, leave register, or the actual work done by the employee, to indicate that there is documentary evidence of fault.

A warning memo is not necessarily a threat of dismissal from service; it may only state firmly that better work/behaviour is expected, and that unless there is improvement, confirmation or increments or promotions, may be withheld.

The final warning must include a statement that dismissal would follow if there is repetition of the offensive behaviour.

The following examples illustrate the variety of ways in which a warning memo can be written.

Dear Mr. C.L. Achrekar,

It has been brought to my notice that your attendance at the office has been very irregular. You have reported late by more than half an hour, six times during this month, in spite of warning by your supervisor.

There have also been several mistakes in your work, indicating inattention and lack of application. These mistakes were pointed out to you by your supervisor on each occasion, yet you have not shown any concern to perform better. You are expected to be regular and punctual in attendance and to be careful and attentive in your work. If you do not improve your conduct and your work, disciplinary action in the form of withholding increments, may be taken.

Yours sincerely,

Manager

Dear —,

One of our long standing customers called my office today to inform me that he had been treated discourteously by you..

He was referring to a telephone call he made yesterday at 10.00 a.m. He claims that you stated that you were too busy to find the answer to his question at that time and you seemed totally indifferent to his problem.

This is, of course, completely against our policy, which is to make every effort to please and keep our customers happy. If there are no customers, we have no company.

I would like you to find the source of the problem in this account, call (customer's name) with the information he requested, and offer an apology.

Yours sincerely,

Date ____

To: (Employee's name)

Confirming our meeting related to certain unsatisfactory aspects of your performance, I expect that in the future you will improve your performance by: (list actions to be taken or improvements made)

I am confident that the problem will not be repeated.

(Signature)

Position

To (Employee's name)

You have been previously notified of certain problems in your performance as an employee; the problems appear to continue.

Any further violation of company policy or failure to perform in accordance with our standards will result in immediate dismissal without further warning.

(Signature)

To All employees

From Vice-President, HRD

I was disappointed and humiliated by the behaviour of some of our employees who attended the meeting on (day). The discourtesy shown to (name) was unforgivable. Some employees not only talked incessantly but also exhibited the height of rudeness by leaving the auditorium before the completion of his speech. To anyone who is guilty of these actions, I wish to remind that such behaviour is not tolerated by this organization.

It distresses me to have to write such a message as this to you, and I certainly hope that it will never again be necessary.

(Signature)

LETTERS OF GOODWILL AND APPRECIATION

Everyone likes to be appreciated. "Appreciating others" is a major function of a supervisor or a team leader. In a recent research study of employee motivation, it was found that personal congratulation by the manager ranked first among 67 possible incentives. The second was a personal note for good performance written by the manager.

Communication is important for employees. "Open communication" is considered an important reason for employees to like their organization. Employees need to be helped to reach their best potential in achieving their own and the organization's goals; recognition and rewards are among the primary ways of encouraging and motivating employees. Many firms have realized that their largest asset is their work force and that growth comes from asset appreciation.

Expression of good wishes and congratulation should be brief, direct and concise. Jargon or old-fashioned stereotyped phrases are totally out of place; natural expression is necessary for the letter to be sincere. Enthusiasm and genuine pleasure in the success and achievement of someone must be reflected in the letter. It must reflect the writer's pleasure in writing the letter.

Letters of congratulation and of appreciation are written on various occasions. Whenever an employee or a group makes an achievement, it is appreciated.

> Dear—,
>
> The displays you have created for the "Monsoon's Coming" promotion are just beautiful. Several of the sales staff have told me that they have received numerous compliments from customers.
>
> Congratulations on a job well done.
>
> Yours sincerely,

> Dear —,
>
> Your suggestion that we recycle the trimmings from our vinyl production has been examined and found to be highly viable.
>
> This recycling which will be implemented within eight weeks will result in direct savings to the company. We commend you for your resourcefulness.
>
> Please accept our congratulations on the adoption of your recommendation and our thanks for your enthusiastic attitude.
>
> Yours sincerely,

> Dear—,
>
> Your enthusiasm and your ability to motivate your team has resulted in a significant increase in productivity and profits of the firm.
>
> If we had an award to give, you would be the prime candidate. Please accept my sincerest appreciation for the fine job you are doing in the sales department.
>
> Yours sincerely,

> To: Sales Department Members
>
> From: A.C.Malhotra, President
>
> Subject: Monthly sales
>
> The numbers are in and I am proud to tell you that our total sales for the period of 15 June-15 September, amount to Rs.—— which represents a 10% increase over the sales for the previous period.
>
> You have achieved the goal we established in the first month, and you are all to be highly commended for your achievement. Congratulations!
>
> (Signature)

Here is a letter written to an employee who was quick to take action when a customer collapsed in the company's premises.

> Dear Emily,
>
> You are to be highly commended for the way that you handled the emergency that occurred yesterday. The doctor has informed us that if you hadn't acted as quickly as you did, our customer's attack might have been fatal. Thanks to your fast reaction, she is already out of intensive care and on the road to recovery.
>
> We are very proud of your association with this organization.
>
> Yours sincerely,

Here is a letter from the manager of a small firm to an employee who had been treated rudely by the truck driver of a supplier.

> Dear Rahul,
>
> Several of your associates in the shipping department have informed me of the incident that occurred last Tuesday with a representative of Grip Tools Suppliers. They have all agreed that this driver hurled some abusive language at you and that his actions were unjustifiably offensive.
>
> They also agreed that you remained a gentleman throughout the time, attempting to solve the problem. I compliment you on your self-control, and your handling of the situation in an exemplary manner.
>
> I have spoken to the owner of Grip Tools Suppliers and fully anticipate your receiving an apology from them.
>
> Yours sincerely,

Letters of Sympathy

Besides appreciation for achievements, other goodwill letters written to staff include letters of sympathy and condolence letters.

When an employee meets with misfortune of any kind, a message of sympathy should be sent. Such letters are difficult to write, but delay makes it even more difficult. It is easier to write a letter of sympathy immediately on hearing of the situation.

The two most important qualities required in a letter of sympathy are sincerity and tact. A letter written in simple language to express genuine feelings will carry warmth. Tact lies in taking care to avoid any words or sentiments which might distress the reader.

A letter of condolence should be short and simple; it is in bad taste to write a long letter philosophizing on death or quoting poetry or the scripture. It may include a suitable tribute, or a few words of praise for the person whose death has occurred.

In a letter of sympathy on the occasion of accident, illness or material loss, a consoling message, briefly expressed, may give some comfort or encouragement to the reader.

The examples given below show how letters may be written with varying degrees of formality.

> Dear Mr. Tiwari,
>
> We have just learned, with deep sorrow, of the passing away of your wife.
>
> We know there is little that one can say or do to lessen your grief, but we want you to know that the heartfelt sympathy of all your colleagues at Sheraton's is with you. We hope that time will replace present sorrow with a cherished memory.
>
> Yours sincerely,

> Dear Mrs. Setalvad,
>
> It is with deep sorrow that I learnt this morning of the passing away of your son, Sanjeev. I know that no expression of sympathy, however strongly felt, can lighten the grief that has come to you. I can only pray that God may give you the strength to bear this trial.
>
> Yours sincerely,

Accidents, injury and illness are occasions for letters of sympathy.

> Dear Amelia,
>
> I was sorry to hear about the fall you had, and I hope that by the time this letter reaches you, you will be feeling better. I am told that there is no serious injury but it must be painful and my sympathies are with you.
>
> Everyone in the office joins me in wishing you a speedy and complete recovery.
>
> Yours sincerely,

> Dear Mr. D'Souza,
>
> I was very sorry to learn that you had to be hospitalized yesterday. I do hope that you will be feeling better by the time you get this note.
>
> An active person like you will be impatient to get back to normal activity, but I am sure you will also realize the importance of complete rest until you get back your strength.
>
> My best wishes for your speedy recovery.
>
> Sincerely yours,

EXERCISES

1. A lady who has worked efficiently with you for six years as sales representative has applied to another company for the post of Assistant Sales Manager. You have received an enquiry about her ability. Draft a reference for her.
2. You have received an enquiry about a past employee in your Accounts Department. Draft an unfavourable reference in reply.
3. Draft an open testimonial for your telephone operator who is applying for the post of receptionist in a larger office.
4. A foreign university where you have applied for admission to a Management Course requires a recommendation from your college principal. Your principal has asked you to present a draft recommendation. Prepare the draft.
5. An accountant in your office has been repeatedly late in reporting to work, and careless in his work. Draft a memo to be given to him.
6. A senior salesman of your company has had a bad accident at Kolkata while on a sales visit, and has been hospitalized there. Write a letter assuring him of all care of himself and attention to his family's needs.
7. The Chief Accountant of your firm lost his son in an accident. Write a letter to be sent to him as from the owner of the firm.
8. An employee of your firm has been selected to be in the team of athletes representing the State in the inter-state athletics meet. Write her a letter of congratulation.

❑❑❑

Chapter 21

GOODWILL LETTERS

Businessmen and executives have to write a number of letters relating to their own and their organisation's social life. Most persons are members of professional organisations or fraternities; as office-bearers or committee members they need to write letters for organisational work. Letters of thanks and appreciation, letters of sympathy and condolence, letters inviting speakers at meetings and functions, accepting or refusing invitations to speak, etc. are some of the letters that people are required to write.

The pressures of business activities and the necessities of work make people neglect the little courtesies and the contacts that can add grace to business life and also build stronger personal relationships. The manager who gives as much attention to his social correspondence as to his official letters is really doing a service to his organisation's P.R. and is enriching his own personal life.

Opportunities for thoughtfulness are many. A few words of appreciation for a favour or help received from someone, an expression of sympathy for someone who has suffered, a letter of congratulation on the achievement of a colleague or an associate or an employee, can bring warmth and personal touch to the business life of a person.

Principles of Effective Goodwill Letters

There is no fixed plan or outline for such letters; it is better for each person to write in his own style. The following points may serve as a checklist of the requirements of effective personal and social letters.

1. The letter must be timed properly. Messages of appreciation, condolence, congratulation, and so on, are effective only if they are sent promptly, that is, immediately on learning of the event or occasion.
2. A short letter makes a better impression than a long one. The letter should be as brief as possible for its purpose.
3. The words must be carefully chosen. The writer's own natural vocabulary is the best. There must not be any words which may make the reader uncomfortable or unhappy.

4. The tone of the letter should be personal and suitable for the person who is to receive it. Flattery or lack of sincerity can be easily detected. A friendly and cordial tone suitable for the occasion and the person who is to receive the letter, makes the letter effective.
5. Jargon and "rubber-stamp" phrases are bad enough in business letters; they are worse in social and personal letters and must be strictly avoided.
6. The salutation and the complimentary close should be suitable to the message. It is proper to use the reader's name in the salutation. *Dear Mr. Limaye, My dear Harish, Dear Mrs. Shah, Dear Rekha*, are all suitable forms, to be used according to the relationship between the writer and the reader. The letter can be closed with Yours sincerely, Sincerely yours, Most sincerely yours, Yours most cordially, Yours cordially, or Sincerely, or Cordially.
7. All names and details of the occasion mentioned in the letter must be correct. Misspelt names, wrong dates, or any error in any detail will give offence to the reader, especially because the letter is personal.
8. Clarity comes from being sure of what one wants to say, and saying it directly and simply. It is difficult to be clear and simple in long and involved sentences.
9. The letter must have the power of feeling. The reader must sense that the feelings expressed are sincere.
10. The letter must be signed personally and not by a secretary or a P.A.
11. Courtesy requires that the letter should be well made up with neat typing, folding and addressing.
12. When the same message is to be sent to several persons (for example, a thank you letter to all participants in a programme, or a personal invitation to several guests to attend a programme), each one's letter must be a fresh copy. Carbon copies or Xeroxed copies must not be sent. It quite easy to get a fresh copy for each recipient with a computer.

A goodwill letter will be successful when you answer yes to the following questions:

1. If you were the reader, would you honestly like to receive this letter? (A goodwill letter does its job only if it makes the reader feel good)
2. Will the reader feel that you enjoyed writing the letter and that you mean everything you wrote?
3. Did you keep the spotlight on the reader?

Congratulatory Letters

In the normal course of business, there are many opportunities for writing congratulatory letters. The good fortune or achievement of employees, business associates and friends provides many occasions for writing letters of congratulation. Many people find it difficult to draft a short congratulatory note, and tend to postpone it; but then it loses its timeliness which is important for such messages. Expression of good wishes and congratulation should be brief, direct and concise. Jargon or old-fashioned stereotyped phrases and cliches spoil the message; natural expression is necessary for the letter to be sincere. Enthusiasm and genuine pleasure in the success and achievement of someone must be reflected in the letter. If the writer does not enjoy writing the letter, it is better not to write at all than to write a cold, businesslike letter of congratulation.

The letters below are examples of honestly felt joy in another's success.

> Dear Mr. Chaturvedi,
>
> It is a pleasure to congratulate you upon your election as President of the Grain Dealers' Association. Such a vote of confidence by your fellow businessmen is a high personal tribute to you.
>
> All the members of Damania & Company join me in this expression of hearty congratulations and good wishes to you.
>
> Yours sincerely,

> Dear Mr. Balsara,
>
> I learnt this morning of your election as President of Ahmedabad Chamber of Commerce.
>
> Congratulations on this splendid recognition of your ability. It shows the high esteem in which your fellow businessmen hold you.
>
> From our close relationship with you for almost twenty years, my colleagues and I know how well suited you are for this important work. We are sure your term of office will be one of great value to the business community.
>
> Sincerely yours,

> Dear Mr. Pardiwalla,
>
> Congratulations on the publication of your book "Notes on Legal Practice in India." I have been reading it with the utmost pleasure. All your rich experience has gone into the writing of the book and young aspiring lawyers as well as veteran senior advocates will find something useful, enriching and entertaining in it.
>
> Thank you for sharing your experience so freely.
>
> Yours sincerely,

A congratulatory letter need not contain the word "congratulation." It can convey the message by its tone and the manner in which it takes note of the achievement. The following letter was written by an employer to a member of his staff.

> Dear Mr. Vakil,
>
> Vincent Bedi told me of the fine talk you gave the other day at the meeting of the Bombay Suburban chapter of the Association of Cost Accountants.
>
> I want you to know that your participation in such professional activities means a great deal to the company in its relations with the professional community. I should be very glad to arrange for any clerical or other help and personal expenses you may incur, in accepting such engagements in future.
>
> Yours sincerely,

Dear Mr. Sethi,

I was very glad to learn that you have been appointed Secretary of the Thane Chamber of Commerce. I can think of no one better qualified for this important work; I know that you will make an outstanding success of it. If I can be of any assistance, I shall be glad to co-operate.

Sincerely yours,

Letters of Sympathy

When an associate, whether customer, colleague, employee or business acquaintance meets with misfortune of any kind, a message of sympathy should be sent. Such letters are difficult to write, but delay makes it even more difficult. It is easier to write a letter of sympathy immediately on hearing of the situation.

The length of the letter depends on three things: (i) the degree of friendship between the writer and the reader (ii) the particular incident on account of which the letter is being written (iii) the writer's knowledge of the temperament and taste of the reader.

The two most important qualities required in a letter of sympathy are sincerity and tact. If it is written in simple language to express what is felt, the message will carry warmth. Tact lies in taking care to avoid any words or sentiments which might distress the reader.

A letter of condolence should be short and simple; it is in bad taste to write a long letter philosophising on death or quoting poetry or the scripture. It may include a suitable tribute, or a few words of praise for the person whose death has occurred. In a letter of sympathy on the occasion of accident, illness or material loss, a consoling message, briefly expressed, may give some comfort or encouragement to the reader. The examples given below show how different situations may be handled with varying degrees of formality.

Dear Mr. Thomas,

We have just learned, with deep sorrow, of the passing away of your daughter. Though there is little that one can say or do to lessen your grief, we want you to know that the heartfelt sympathy of all your friends at Tristar Computers is with you. We hope that time will replace present sorrow with a cherished memory.

Yours sincerely,

Dear Mrs. Satyamurthy,

It is with deep sorrow that I learnt this morning of the passing away of your husband. I know that no expression of sympathy can reduce the sorrow that has come to you. I pray that God may give you the strength to bear this trial.

Yours sincerely,

A letter of sympathy written on the death of a company officer may be a little longer, and may pay a tribute to the person.

> Dear Mr. Shastri,
>
> I was shocked and saddened to hear of the sudden death of Mr. Haribhai Trivedi. I wish to convey to you and to the other members of your company, my deep sympathy on the loss of this trusted and dependable associate. I had the good fortune to know Mr. Trivedi for most of the years he served your company as Chief Accountant. He was a rare combination of personal charm, strict business ethics and untiring devotion to his work. Everyone who knew him will feel a personal loss in his death.
>
> Sincerely yours,

When a business associate suffers material loss, a letter like the following may be sent.

> Dear Mr. Dabholkar,
>
> All of us at Patel Transport were extremely sorry to learn this morning that a severe fire had damaged your warehouse, last night.
>
> If there is anything we can do to co-operate with you in overcoming your present difficulties, please do not hesitate to call on us. We have had a long association with you, and we shall be happy to extend a helping hand.
>
> Yours sincerely,

> Dear Mr. Mahopatra,
>
> I have just learnt of the heavy loss you suffered in the cyclone that hit your city last week.
>
> At a time like this, words of encouragement cannot bring relief. I sincerely hope that the damage proves less than you fear. If you can think of any way in which I can be of help in this emergency, please let me know. I shall be happy to give whatever help I can.
>
> Yours most sincerely,

Accidents, injury and illness are occasions for letters of sympathy.

> Dear Miss Contractor,
>
> I was sorry to hear about the fall you had, and I hope that by the time this letter reaches you, you will be feeling better. I am told that there is no serious injury but it must be painful and my sympathies are with you. Everyone in the office joins me in wishing you a speedy and complete recovery.
>
> Yours most sincerely,

Dear Mr. Divecha,

I was surprised and distressed to learn that you had to be hospitalised yesterday. I do hope that you will be feeling better by the time you get this note. No doubt an active person like you will be impatient to get back to your business, but I am sure you will also realise the importance of complete rest until you regain your strength.

My best wishes for your speedy recovery.

Most sincerely yours,

Dear Mr. and Mrs. Modi,

The loss of your daughter Pramila is a stunning blow, and I realise that no words of sympathy can lighten your grief. I am writing this note to you, nevertheless, to tell you how greatly we shall miss her lively presence in the college. She was one of our brightest and very responsible students. All the members of the staff join me in praying for strength and courage for you to bear this irreparable loss.

Sincerely,

Invitations

Invitations to functions, dinner, lunch may also be made by letter. Like other courtesy letters, the invitation should be cordial and gracious in tone. The degree of formality or informality depends on the relationship between the writer and reader, that is, personal friendship or only a business association. The letters given below illustrate different degrees of formality.

Dear Ms. Bajaj,

I am inviting a few friends to be my personal guests at an informal lunch to be hosted by my company, on Friday, 17 April, at which Mrs. Shobha Daftary will speak on "Bank Facilities for Women Entrepreneurs." The lunch will be at Oberoi Club in the Blue Rose Room. I do hope that you are able to join us. The lunch will be at one o'clock and will be followed by Mrs. Daftary's address. The programme will be of two hours.

Yours sincerely,

Dear Prakash,

I learnt with pleasure this morning that you will be in Mumbai next week for a conference of marketing managers. I would very much like you to be my guest at dinner on any day that best suits your programme.

Kailash Mazumdar and Dan Joseph are also looking forward to meeting you and will be joining us. I shall telephone to your hotel on Monday at eleven o'clock to fix our dinner appointment.

Yours sincerely,

> Dear Mr. Pauran,
>
> We have organised a programme of classical music at which six young and promising artists will perform. It will be held on Saturday, 18 April, from 4.30 to 8.30 in our college hall. Being aware of your interest in classical music and particularly your interest in encouraging young artistes, I am happy to invite you to the programme, along with your friends similarly interested. The enclosed brochure contains information about the artistes and other details of the programme.
>
> Yours most cordially,

> Dear Mr. Sanghoi,
>
> The ABC Audio-Visual Centre will be inaugurated on Sunday, 12 May, at 10.00 a.m., by Mr. Kumar Sinha, of Doordarshan, Mumbai.
>
> I am happy to invite you and Mrs. Sanghoi to the programme which will be held at the Centre, on the second floor of XYZ Building, Fourth Avenue, Santa Cruz (W), Mumbai 400 054. A short film by Bittu Sehgal will be shown after the inaugural address.
>
> Yours sincerely,

> Dear Mr. Doshi,
>
> I am happy to invite you and Mrs. Doshi to our Annual Day Programme on Tuesday, 20 December, at 6.30 p.m. at Birla Rangmandir, Bandra.
>
> Please also join us for tea with the Chief Guest at 5.45 p.m. in the conference room on the first floor of the Rangmandir office building.
>
> I am looking forward to meeting you soon.
>
> Yours sincerely,

Invitations to speak

Institutions, organisations, and professional associations hold meetings, seminars and conferences at which speakers are invited to address the audience. For such occasions, it is necessary to be able to write a good letter inviting a speaker.

The opening paragraph of the letter should give some information about the inviting organisation, and the purpose of the meeting or the nature of the function. The day, date, time and place of the function are very important details and must be included in the letter even if they have been conveyed orally. The subject on which he is expected to speak and the approximate time he is to have on the programme, should be given. If the choice of the topic is to be left to the speaker, this must be mentioned; a general idea of the type of meeting and participants will enable the speaker to choose a suitable topic. The letter should end with a request to confirm acceptance so that arrangements for the meeting can be completed.

Dear Mr. Thakur,

We hold a series of lectures annually, for our managers and senior executives, on subjects related to Management. The lectures will be held this year in the first week of September.

One of the lectures is to be on Creativity and I would like you to speak to us on the topic on Tuesday, 5 September. Your presentation would be of about one hour, followed by a discussion of about half hour. Overhead projector, TV and VCR are available if you are using transparencies and cassettes. The programme is held in our conference hall in this office from 11.00 a.m. to 12.30 p.m. I would like you to join us for lunch at the end of the session.

I do hope that you can accept this invitation. May I have your confirmation as soon as possible?

Yours sincerely,

Replies accepting or declining the invitation are illustrated below:

Dear Mr. Parekh,

Thank you for your invitation of 5 August, to speak to the managers of your organisation. I am pleased to accept the invitation and shall speak on The Conduct of a Meeting, as you have suggested. I will be using a video programme, and will need about 90 minutes for my presentation. I am looking forward to meeting you and other members of your organisation.

Yours sincerely,

Dear Mr. Pinto,

I am pleased to accept your invitation to speak at the B.M.A. annual meeting on 8 March at 2.00 p.m. What do you think of "Managing one's mind" as a topic? Since you have not indicated how long you wish me to speak, I shall limit my address to thirty minutes and shall be happy to answer any questions.

I am looking forward to meeting you.

Yours sincerely,

Dear Mr. Lall,

Thank you for your invitation to speak at your seminar on 9 August. I am sorry, however, that I am unable to accept on account of another engagement on that day.

Yours sincerely,

"Thank you" Letters

When someone has rendered a service, given help or participated as a guest in a programme, courtesy requires that a "thank you" letter should be sent immediately after the event. After paying an educational visit to a company or a factory, the institution which sent the students, or the group leader, must thank the office for their hospitality and reception. A guest speaker must also be sent a letter of thanks.

> Dear Mr. Miranda,
>
> I am writing to thank you for receiving our students and extending them a warm welcome. They were delighted with the attention and hospitality you gave them; they have also benefited immensely from the information you gave them about the working of the agency.
>
> I do hope that your relationship with our institution will continue and be beneficial to both.
>
> Yours sincerely,

> Dear Mr. Thakur,
>
> I write on behalf of T.A.A. to express our sincere appreciation of your time and trouble in participating in our symposium on Marketing of Tourism on last Friday. The fact that you changed your other appointments to be with us speaks highly of your commitment to the education and training of young people.
>
> We do hope you will honour us with your presence again at similar programmes.
>
> Yours sincerely,

Companies and associations which are given opportunities by organisations to make presentations to their members also send letters of thanks for the opportunity.

> Dear Madam,
>
> I appreciate the opportunity you gave me to speak to your students on careers in the Hospitality Industry, last Tuesday. It was a pleasant experience and has enriched my own information about student needs and expectations. I do hope the students also found it useful, and look forward to further interaction with members of your institution.
>
> Yours faithfully,

> Dear Mr. Govil,
>
> Thank you for the opportunity you gave us to make a presentation to your organisation members. We appreciate your help and the interest taken by your members in the problem of environmental health in industrial towns. We are sending a few copies of our brochure for the benefit of any members who might wish to have more information about environmental health and about our organisation.
>
> Yours sincerely,

Letters of Appreciation

Everyone likes to receive a letter of appreciation. Such letters do a great deal for the spirit of understanding, friendliness and goodwill. It is worth taking every opportunity to build up good relations with people whether they are subordinates or customers or associates.

Letters of appreciation should be written with genuine and sincere feeling; most persons can detect flattery. The letters given here illustrate the different opportunities and the varied styles of writing appreciation letters. They are similar to "thank you" letters; but they may be written by anyone, and not only by the person whose official duty it is to write a letter of thanks for a favour received.

Dear Ms. Nanavati,

This is not a business letter; only a few words to thank you for the excellent exposition of the subject of Training one's People, during the fifteen day course you gave. I have gained much that will be useful to me in my career. Above all, I appreciate the patience and the skill with which you ensured that each participant went through some practical experience.

Among the things I carry back with me is the remembrance of your interesting and informative lectures.

Most sincerely yours,

Dear Mr. Sethna,

I must express my appreciation of the excellent symposium on Personal Taxation you organised last week. It was highly stimulating as well as informative. I heard several persons who were present say how glad they were that they had attended. Thank you for the opportunity you gave us to hear the authorities on the subject.

Yours sincerely,

9 September

Dear Mr. Gosavi,

I am writing, most belatedly, to thank you for your excellent and enjoyable presentation on 30 August, to teachers of Business Communication. The delay, however, enables me to convey to you the delighted feedback I have been receiving from the participants.

Thank you once again.

Yours sincerely,

EXERCISES

1. The Planning Forum of your college is organising a symposium on The New Industrial Policy. Write to an eminent economist inviting him to speak at the symposium.
2. The Chief Accountant of your firm lost his son in an accident. Write a letter to be sent to him as from the owner of the firm.
3. You are celebrating the tenth anniversary of your company. Write a letter of invitation to be sent to your customers to attend a dinner being arranged to celebrate the occasion.

4. One of your customers has been elected President of his professional association. Write a letter of congratulation.
5. The daughter of a business associate has just started an export business of her own. Write congratulating her and conveying your best wishes.
6. An educational institution in your city was particularly co-operative in allowing you to use its library for a study that your company had to make. Write a letter to the Principal expressing appreciation of the co-operation and help given by the library staff, in particular.
7. You have been invited to speak at a meeting of the Bombay Management Association's quarterly meeting, on the management of non-profit organisations. Draft a reply accepting the invitation.
8. A business associate has invited you to attend his company's dinner meeting at which a well known tax consultant will be speaking. Write a reply regretting your inability to attend.
9. A senior salesman of your company has had a bad accident at Kolkata while on a sales visit, and has been hospitalised there. Write a letter assuring him of all care of himself and attention to his family's needs.
10. As the secretary of the Women Entrepreneurs' Association, you are expected to organise a training programme for young women. Write to an Education Society reserving their conference hall and lunch room for the programme.

❑❑❑

Chapter 22

ENQUIRIES AND REPLIES

The most common letters in business are buyers' enquiries about goods and services and sellers' replies giving information and quotations. Today, a good deal of information about goods and prices is conveyed by telephone or e-mail or fax; but all parts of the country and all people do not have these facilities and prefer to use letters so that they have a document and a record for reference.

In these letters, the direct approach is used to save time. The letters are short; formalities are not required, and you can get straight to the business.

ENQUIRIES

To ask for information, you can begin directly with a question or request like :

- Could you give us the following information ?
- Please send us the following information.
- I would appreciate receiving the following information from you.

The letter may also begin with an indication of the need. Indicating the purpose for which the information is needed helps the supplier to give relevant information, especially in the case of products with a vast variety of models. A dealer in computers will be able to give useful information and a quotation only when he knows the buyer's specific need.

* We intend to set up a computer laboratory with capacity for 40 students to work at a time. The room in which the laboratory is to be set up measures 6x7 metres.
* We have been awarded a contract for the construction of a railway bridge across River XYZ. This river is prone to tidal waves. The work is to be completed in four years. We would appreciate receiving the following information from you.

A series of direct questions may follow this opening paragraph.

End the letter with a friendly comment which will leave a sense of personal relationship. Endings like "an early reply would be appreciated" or "Thanking you in advance" are weak and outdated. It is more effective to end a letter with a more business-like sentence such as:

* We could discuss this personally, if you could meet me in my office next week.
* If you could get this data to me by Tuesday, I shall be most grateful.
* When replying, please include details of delivery.

The following letters illustrate these points.

Dear Sirs,

During a recent Trade Fair held here, I saw some samples of your new granite tiles for flooring. I would like to make use of them for the interiors I am designing for a new housing complex. Please give me the following information:

(1) In what sizes, colours and designs can you supply the tiles?

(2) Are the tiles likely to be affected by rising moisture?

(3) Is any special processing of the under-flooring required?

I shall be most grateful if you could send me answers to these questions by Friday, the 17th.

Yours faithfully,

Dear Sir,

We are opening a new school in New Panvel, with 36 classrooms and will be buying a large number of desks and chairs. We would be pleased to receive your catalogue of moulded plastic school furniture together with your price-list.

The school has to be fully equipped by the end of May, and we will expect supplies to reach us by 15 May.

If you can supply suitable goods, we may place further orders as we will be expanding some of our schools and also setting up new ones in other parts of the State.

Yours truly,

Dear Sirs,

We have received several enquiries for hand-made paper for printing cards. It seems to be a popular choice for wedding and other invitation cards among upper middle class people who make up most of our clientele.

It would be helpful if you could send us samples of a wide range of qualities and designs, along with a price-list.

Yours faithfully,

Points included in the letters are:

1. Courteous request for information, giving its purpose
2. Statement of what is wanted (or a list of questions)
3. Request that the information may be given by a certain date.

Reply to Enquiry

Always give prompt attention to an enquiry and make every effort to work it up to an order. Your reply must do a sales job. Tell the potential customer what he wants to know, and something more. You need persuasive skill and good judgment in giving information. Present the facts so as to show the customer the benefits of buying the product/service. When you send a brochure, catalogue, price-list or samples send a letter with it; give the relevant page numbers or models which will be suitable to the customer. Offer to send a salesperson to discuss it. It is not enough to say, "We hope that the samples will meet with your approval." You must show the advantages of the product.

The letters below illustrate these points.

> Dear Sir,
>
> Thank you for your enquiry of 22 October about our new granite tiles for flooring. We have enclosed a copy of our catalogue showing the designs and range of colours in which the tiles are available.
>
> Messrs. Dhruv & Co, 23 M.G. Road, Secunderabad, are a reliable firm and handle all our products in your area. We have asked Mr. Dhruv to get in touch with you; he will inspect the premises and advise you whether moisture would give rise to any problem. Our new PVC tiles are hard-wearing and, if they are laid according to the instructions provided by us, will give you lasting satisfaction.
>
> Yours faithfully,

> Dear Sir,
>
> In reply to your enquiry, we are happy to send you our catalogue and price-list of moulded plastic chairs and desks. They are enclosed.
>
> You will find models shown on pages 3-4 particularly suitable for schools. They are available in several sizes, so as to be suitable for children of different age groups. We have supplied these chairs and desks to many schools, both in Hyderabad and in small towns around Hyderabad.
>
> The schools have found them highly satisfactory as they require very little maintenance and are easy to clean. Their pleasant appearance adds to the attractiveness of the classroom. The variety of colours in which they are available gives you an added advantage.
>
> We shall be very happy to discuss your requirements personally. Please call us at any of the numbers given above for an appointment for our representative to meet you.
>
> Yours truly,

> Dear Mr. Keni,
>
> We are happy to learn that your customers have shown interest in hand-made paper for cards.
>
> We have dispatched separately, a set of samples showing our complete range, especially suitable for exclusive invitation cards and visiting cards.

For the high end market, we suggest sample number 7 which is available in several shades and is excellent for coloured printing. The subtle sheen and rich texture of the paper gives it an expensive look although its price is not much more than that of the other qualities. A special feature of this paper is that a touch of fragrance can be added to it.

We would be happy to send our representative to discuss details. The enclosed price list includes our terms of trade. Please contact me at tel. no. 555555 if you have any queries.

Yours sincerely,

Asking help or advice from business acquaintances

You may ask business acquaintances for information. If the information is likely to be confidential, you must be tactful; offer to help in other matters, whenever possible; address the enquiry to an individual rather than to a company.

Dear Mr. Venkateshwaraloo,

I learnt through a business friend, Mr. K.B. Acharya, that you have evolved a system for coping with the problem of rumours circulating among employees. Could you give me the details of your system and samples of any forms which you use?

As ours is also a Trading Company like yours, although in a different line, our problems would be similar to yours and we could learn much from your experience. Last month we had a team of personnel management experts make a study of our internal communication and I am sending you a copy of their report which may be of some use to you.

I am looking forward to whatever help you can give me.

Yours sincerely,

Dear Madam,

I am a T.Y.B.Com student of YYY College and am working on a project on the changes in advertising and marketing techniques for white goods over the last ten years. It would be helpful if you could let me have the sales figures for your white goods in the State of Kerala during the period 1995 to 200.

I shall acknowledge any help you give me and send you a copy of my report.

Yours faithfully,

Inability to give Information

Sometimes, you cannot give the requested information; it may be confidential or not available. A tactless refusal creates ill will; convey the negative message carefully. Courteously explain why the information cannot be given, and suggest some other source of information. Write in a helpful tone.

Points:

1. Appreciation of interest shown by inquirer
2. Apology and reason for inability to give information
3. Suggestion of other source of information, if possible.

Dear Mr. Joseph,

Thank you for paying us the compliment of asking our advice and help in handling Personnel problems. We do have a system for handling rumours. We regret, however, that this information cannot be divulged since we have an agreement with the Business Advisors' Bureau to maintain secrecy. You will find useful information and guidance in the book, "How to Handle Wayward Employees" by J.L. Smith; we have found the book very useful and have benefited immensely from the recommendations.

You can also consult the Business Advisors' Bureau in case of any serious problems. Their address is 272, Ivory Towers, J.N. Circle, Hyderabad 500 032.

We wish you success in your efforts to re-organise your office.

Yours sincerely,

Dear Ms Rao,

I am sorry that we do not have the data of sales during 1995-2000 which you requested in your letter of the 10th. Some information will probably be available with the Junior Chamber of Commerce. Their library may also be able to provide you with past issues of the Advertising Journal *Solus*.

I wish you all success with your project.

Yours sincerely,

Review

1. Are these statements true?
   (a) When you make an enquiry, it helps the receiver of your letter if you indicate why you want the information.
   (b) "Thanking you in anticipation," is an effective ending for an enquiry letter.
   (c) A reply to an enquiry has to do a sales job.
   (d) Even if you cannot give the requested information, you should try to be helpful to the person who asks you for information.
   (e) A good ending for a reply to an enquiry would be "We trust that you will find this useful."

ASKING FOR QUOTATIONS

When you intend to buy a product or service, you ask for quotations from several suppliers and then select the one most suitable to you. If your order is likely to be large or might lead to further orders, indicate it in your request; suppliers offer better terms to large buyers.

Mention all details of your requirements when asking for a quotation; if it is for a service like painting, renovation, air conditioning or any other installation, ask for a representative to visit you to discuss the details. If it is for a machine like Xerox or overhead projector, whose working you would like to see, ask for a demonstration to be arranged.

Points:

1. Polite request for quotation
2. Details of requirements with quality and quantity of goods
3. Place and time of delivery of goods required, carriage paid or carriage forward. Any special request about mode of delivery or packing.
4. Suggestion that the volume of business will be large if the quotation is favourable

Sirs,

We intend to purchase large stocks of notebooks for our newly opened Stationery section in our Departmental Store at Mehdipatnam, and invite you to submit your most competitive quotation.

If your prices and terms are favourable, and your goods and services of a high standard, we shall consider giving a five year contract for the supply of notebooks. Please send your quotation, carriage paid, within a week.

Yours faithfully,

Gentlemen:

The dining room and the conference room of our hotel are to be redecorated. We invite you to submit designs and estimates for carrying out the work. The building is on M.G. Road, Alkapuri, and is about 20 years old. The area of the rooms is 15 x 20 x 10 meters and 20 x 30 x 10 meters. Air conditioning is to be installed in both rooms. Please send your representative to inspect the rooms and discuss the matter personally. Please call us to fix an appointment for your representative's visit.

Yours faithfully,

Dear Sirs,

We have obtained a franchise for Sunshine Healthfoods, Indonesia, and will soon be starting production of various sweets and confectionery. Besides using exotic flavours from South-east Asia, we intend to present some of their traditional items with Indian flavours and colours for export to other countries.

We invite you to send us your quotation for your range of food colours and flavours of the very best quality. Please also send the full range of samples.

If you can supply suitable products and can keep to the required delivery schedule, we shall be placing large orders constantly, and are expecting a competitive quotation.

Please send your quotation and samples by the 28th of this month.

Yours truly,

GIVING QUOTATION

When market conditions are normal, the usual quotation is given. If the customer seems likely to place a large order, an exceptional quotation may be given. A tabulated quotation may be enclosed with a letter. Point out the advantages of the quotation and the benefit of buying the goods.

Points:

1. Thanks for the enquiry
2. Statement of prices and terms
3. Attempt to win the customer

Dear Sirs,

Congratulations on the expansion of your Department Store at Mehdipatnam, and thank you for giving us this opportunity to be associated with your business.

We are pleased to quote as follows:

100 page note-books	Rs. per hundred
200 page note-books	Rs. per hundred
300 page note-books	Rs. per hundred
500 page note-books	Rs. per hundred

These prices include packing and delivery.

We shall give a discount of 7% on orders of Rs. 50,000/ or more within the same calendar month. An additional discount of 2% will be given on every bill which is paid within 15 days from the date of the bill.

Regular customers can place orders with us on our website www. Rjnotebooks.com. Deliveries will be made within two days of receiving your order.

From the samples we sent, you must have noted that our note-books are made with good quality paper and have strong binding. They wear well even in the hands of small children.

We have enclosed an order form to enable you to place your first order conveniently.

Yours truly,

Dear Mr. Paul,

Thank you for your enquiry of 4 March.

Our representative Mr. Acharya will be visiting you next week after calling you for an appointment. Meanwhile, we are sending you a colour card for wall painting and some photographs of rooms decorated in different colours and designs. A study of these will help you to form some ideas of what you might like to have. Mr. Acharya, who is an architect, will also bring additional designs and discuss your requirements in detail.

We look forward to a pleasant and mutually beneficial relationship.

Yours sincerely,

Sir,

We are happy to learn that you have obtained a franchise for Indonesian Health Foods and we welcome the opportunity you have given us to introduce some of our products to you.

As you have requested, we have sent you samples of the complete range of our food colours and flavour concentrates. These products are exported to various Asian and European countries and are used by highly reputed hotels like Hyatt and Regent in India.

The enclosed price list will show you that our prices are competitive. We give 10% discount on orders of Rs. 100,000 and more, and 2% cash discount for payment in cash within 7 days of the date of the bill. All deliveries within the city are free, and made within 48 hours of receiving the order.

An order form is enclosed for your convenience. We are looking forward to the beginning of a pleasant business relationship with you.

Yours faithfully,

Firm offer: A firm offer is a quotation which is firm for acceptance by the receiver within a stated limited time. It is a promise to sell the stated quantity of goods at the quoted price provided the order is received within the given time, usually 3 to 7 days.

A firm offer is made when the price of a product is expected to rise or when the price is fluctuating, and quoting a definite price is difficult. It is also made when the supplies are short of the demand. The letter states the reason for making the offer firm, and the date up to which it is firm. A firm offer is a moral obligation but not a legal obligation. It builds goodwill with important customers.

Dear Sirs,

Thank you for your letter of the 13th, asking for a quotation for the supply of 3000 units of IFB microwave ovens.

Our price list is enclosed; we give a discount of 7% on all orders of 1000 units and above, and deliver goods carriage paid within the city of Mumbai.

Please note that this offer is firm only till 30 September. The demand for microwave ovens has gone up considerably, and the production cannot keep pace with the added demand just before Diwali festival. As your order is large, we shall hold the goods at your disposal for 5 days.

We urge you to take advantage of this offer and send us your order by 30 September.

Yours truly,

Offering a Substitute: If the requested goods are not available, try to get the customer interested in a substitute. An enquiry means a possible customer; make the effort to win him. The substitute you offer must satisfy the purpose and need of the customer. It must be the nearest in quality and price; if it differs, explain why. A substitute must be offered with confidence. Win the customer's confidence for the substitute product; send a sample with the quotation or offer a "trial lot" on approval.

Explain briefly why you cannot supply the product which the customer has asked for; just offering a substitute without explanation may give rise to mistrust. The letter that follows embodies these suggestions.

Dear Sir,

We thank you for your enquiry of January 12, about the supply of 20 facsimile machines.

The Corel machines which you have asked for are out of stock and not likely to be available for at least four months. We suggest the Twinkle Fax machines which have become very popular and have a good reputation for trouble-free service.

There is a range of six models which allows you to choose a different kind for each desk according to the needs. These machines also have the additional feature of storage of 100 addresses and telephone/fax numbers.

The prices of Twinkle Fax machine range are a little higher than the prices of Corel but the Twinkle machines have a guarantee of five years and can use several types of paper.

We would be happy to send our representative to your office to demonstrate the working of the Twinkle Fax machine on Wednesday at 11.00 a.m. Please call us at 235 XXX to confirm the appointment.

Yours faithfully,

Dear Madam,

Thank you for your letter of 10 February, asking about our Organics range of shampoos and hair care products.

We have discontinued this range and replaced it by Herbs of India products. You will see from the enclosed information brochures that these products have a wider range to suit a variety of skin and hair types as well as climatic conditions.

Our catalogues, price list, conditions of sale and terms of payment are enclosed. Although these products are a little more expensive than the earlier range, they have been well received in the market in the larger cities. The proven quality and our attractive packaging have enabled us to have them on the shelves of the best retail stores like Lifestyle and Berry's.

We are willing to offer you a special discount on a sliding scale basis, as follows:

On annual orders of between:

Rs. 1 lakh and Rs 3 lakhs	3%
Rs. 3 lakhs and Rs. 7 lakhs	5%
Rs. 7 laks and above	7%

It is not possible to give special discount on annual orders of less than Rs. 1 lakh.

An order form is enclosed for your convenience. We look forward to including your name on our list of regular buyers.

Yours faithfully,

Withholding quotation: If a particular customer repeatedly asks for quotations for the purpose of comparing with other quotations and does not place any orders, you may avoid giving a quotation. Write a tactful letter saying that the market is uncertain and you can quote only for a definite contract, or make a firm offer for a very short period.

Dear Sirs,

Thank you for your letter of 29 July, asking us to quote our rates for printing 5000 copies of your catalogue. As the price of paper is fluctuating and has to be negotiated for every order, we are unable to give a standard quotation. We shall be able to give a definite quotation only for a firm order. Our rates and terms for the printing job are the same as we had quoted for your brochures in April.

We shall be happy to negotiate the price of paper on your behalf as soon as we hear from you.

Yours faithfully,

Review

1. Fill in the blanks using as few words as possible.
   (a) A firm offer is made to a — customer when — for the purpose of —.
   (b) When you offer a substitute, you can win the customer's confidence by —.
2. Are these a good sentence to write in a letter?
   (a) Since you do not place any orders even when we send you a quotation, we do not wish to send you a quotation now, when the prices are fluctuating.
   (b) The goods that you requested are not available. We regret that we cannot help you in this matter.

BARGAINING LETTERS

On receiving a quotation, a customer may try to persuade the seller to offer better terms. If your order is likely to be large, you can point this out to persuade the seller to give better terms. You may also indicate that other suppliers are willing to give more favourable terms. The request should be specific.

Points

1. Expression of thanks for the quotation
2. Specific request for more favourable terms and attempt to show that the supplier will benefit if he gives the requested terms
3. Suggestion that large/frequent orders will be placed if the request is granted.

Dear Sir,

Thank you for your quotation for the supply of washing machines. We approve of your model Nos. X and Z and would like to place an order immediately for at least 20 machines, ten of each model, for our newly opened launderettes in Golconda.

However, we feel that your terms of sale are high. The discount of 12 ½% which you have offered does not compare well with what is offered by other suppliers. We have got our supplies at a discount of 15% before, and request you to reconsider your terms. We are planning to open launderettes in several more places, and will be placing further orders if we find your products and terms satisfactory. You will be compensated by the large orders we shall be placing.

As we are about to equip our new launderettes we would like to have your reply within a week.

Yours faithfully,

Dear Mr. Mirchandani,

Thank you for your quotation and samples of rexine schoolbags you sent me.

While I appreciate the good quality of the schoolbags, I must say that your prices seem to be a little too high even for products of this quality. In the locality in which I have my retail store, the demand is for goods of medium price range. If I accept your quotation as it is, my margin of profit would be reduced so much as to make it worthless for my business.

I do like the designs and quality of your products and would like to have them in my store. I would be happy to introduce the products to customers here. I suggest that you make a 10% allowance on your quoted price.

If you cannot make this allowance. I must regretfully decline your offer. I am hoping to receive a revised offer from you soon since I have to order stocks within a week for re-opening of schools.

Yours sincerely,

Seller's Reply

It may or may not be possible for the seller to reduce the quoted price. Either way, the seller must try to win the customer.

Agreeing too readily to reduce your price may give the impression that the originally offered terms were not fair, or that the sales are so poor that you are eager to get an order at any price. If you agree to the request, explain how it is possible to reduce the price.

The reduction might be offered on the condition of a specified large order or a long term contract. A request or a favour should be granted with dignity. A grudging or condescending tone will be resented by the customer.

Dear Sir,

We are glad to learn from your letter of 19 February that you have undertaken a project to establish launderettes in several places in the State, and we are happy to be able to co-operate with you in the project.

Since this is a long term project and there will be continuous business for quite some time, we are prepared to supply our washing machines at a discount of 15 % as you have requested.

Our machines are guaranteed for 5 years and are backed up by our excellent after sales service. We undertake to ensure your complete satisfaction with our products.

Our representative will visit you within four days to inspect the location and check the facilities for installation of the machines.

Yours faithfully,

If you have to refuse the request, remember all the skills of handling negatives discussed in chapter 13, Style of Business Letters.

Dear Sir,

We have given careful consideration to your request that we should give a discount of 15% on our washing machines.

Unfortunately, it is not possible for us to reduce prices to this extent without compromising on our standards of quality. We are sure you will understand that our pricing is worked out after taking into account the cost of maintaining high quality of products and excellent after sales services.

However, we are interested in being a part of your project to establish launderettes in the State, and though we cannot give a discount of more than 12 ½% as we have offered, we offer to deliver the consignments carriage paid on all your orders for five or more machines.

We request you to accept this offer and give us the opportunity of doing business with you.

Yours faithfully,

Dear Ms Jhaveri,

I am glad that you appreciate the quality of my rexine schoolbags, although you feel that the prices are high. I make every effort to keep the prices low without compromising on the quality.

The prices I have offered are quite competitive. However, taking into account the requirements of your locality, I am prepared to make you a special introductory offer of 5% on your first order of Rs. 10,000/-. I am making this offer because I would like to do business with you, but I must also point out that this is the best I can do.

I do hope that this revised offer will enable you to place an order.

Yours sincerely,
M.M.Mirchandani

Asking for Favours

A buyer may ask for a special concession or discount from a regular supplier for an occasion, like free gift packing during a festival sale, or reduction in price for a special customer. Show the seller that he has an advantage, such as publicity or increased sales.

Dear Sirs,

There is a good opportunity to sell a large quantity of your assorted chocolate boxes through our 96 branches in the states of Andhra Pradesh and Karnataka during the festival season.

We propose to offer the boxes as Diwali/New Year gift items and request you to give us gift packing at no additional charge. We will be ordering 6000 boxes to be delivered by 10 October.

It will give excellent publicity to your products in a wide market, and bring you good returns in increased sales.

Please let us know by the end of this week if you accept this proposal, as we would like to include the item in our publicity material which we will be printing next week. We are looking forward to adding your products to our list of special festival gifts.

Yours faithfully,

Seller's Reply

Granting a Request: This is a pleasant message; grant a favour cheerfully, without grudging. You may, of course, express expectation of benefit by granting the favour.

Gentlemen:

We are glad to say that we shall be able to give you the special gift packing you requested for our boxes of assorted chocolates at no extra charge.

Since your proposed order exceeds 5000 boxes we shall be able to get a substantial concession in the price of packing material which makes it possible for us to bear the cost. We appreciate your suggestion that our products could reach a wider market by offering them as gift articles.

Please place your order by 15 September so that we can order the special gift boxes before the festival season rush begins.

Yours faithfully,

Refusing a Request: Some requests have to be refused; a refusal must be conveyed tactfully so that chances of future business with the customer are not damaged. Customers can be persuaded to understand why the request cannot be granted and accept a reasonable explanation for the refusal.

Show that careful consideration has been given to the request. Take pains to explain why you are unable to grant it.

Dear Mr. Shah,

We appreciate your suggestion that our assorted chocolate boxes should be supplied in decorative packing for sale as gift articles during the festival season.

We made enquiries about the prices of decorative gift boxes but were disappointed to find that the prices are too high, and concessions are not available unless we order at least 10,000 boxes of the same design and size. As your requirement is only 6000 boxes, we will have to charge you an extra 2% for the gift packing.

For the next festival season, however, we expect to be able to negotiate the prices so as to give you the gift packing without charge. Thank you for the suggestion, and we are looking forward to carry it out for the next festival season.

Please let us know whether you would like us to send your current requirement in the usual packing or in special gift packing at an extra charge of 2%.

Yours sincerely,

Sir,

We have considered your request for a further discount of 5% on goods purchased during your Sales Week, but regret that we are unable to give any further discount.

Our paints are severely tested for high quality, and experience has shown that our paints do not peel off or flake even from walls which are in poor condition. The paints are packed in galvanised tins for longer durability, and the cost of these tins is quite high. The 7% discount which we have offered is the maximum we can give on purchases.

We allow an additional 2% cash discount if the bill is paid in cash within 7 days.

We are sure that you will understand that it is not possible for us to give further discounts, and will place your order on the originally offered terms.

Yours faithfully,

Review

Are these statements true?

(a) "We have a good opportunity to make additional profit by offering your products in a special packing for the festival season," is a good opening sentence for requesting a favour.

(b) Customers who make unreasonable demands should be told that they are being unfair.

(c) In asking for a favour, you should offer the supplier an advantage.

(d) You should readily grant any request made by a customer in order to win goodwill.

GETTING BACK LOST CUSTOMERS

Along with the effort to get new customers, you have to make efforts to keep old customers' goodwill. It is far more expensive to win new customers than to keep the old ones.

There are several reasons why a customer may stop buying:

1. Attracted by lower price or better service elsewhere
2. Dissatisfied because of unadjusted complaint
3. Influenced by competitor's sales effort
4. Drifted away to other sellers
5. Gone out of business or shifted to another area.

Only the last one is really lost; the others can be brought back. The commonest reason for loss of customers is that the supplier makes no effort to retain them and so they drift away to competitors.

A timely letter to a drifting customer can save a loss. A periodical check of records can show if any old customer has dropped out. A short letter should suffice; sending the latest catalogue, or samples of the latest designs/products may make an indifferent customer feel that he is remembered by you and ought to buy from you. In more competitive business, you may have to offer discounts/concessions, additional service etc. Also make a telephone call so that the contact is more personal. Address the letter to a specific person by name, and include these points:

1. Statement that the customer's communication has been missed (never mention "records") for some time
2. Tactful enquiry about why s/he has been silent
3. Information about new product/service or special offer
4. Request for order; assurance that satisfaction will be ensured.

Dear Mr. Mehta,

There has been no communication from you for a long time; I am anxious to know the reason. Did I unwittingly given you cause for dissatisfaction? If so, please tell me, and I shall gladly make adjustments.

I am able to offer the most competitive prices and terms now, owing to re-organisation of the business. The new price list is enclosed. Delivery is free for long standing customers like you.

I am enclosing a new easy-to-fill order form. Your requirements will reach you on the same day as I receive your order. Your convenience and comfort is my business.

Yours sincerely,

Dear Ms Porwal,

We have waited for the long period of six months without any communication from you.

As we always inform our old patrons first, of any new product that we start manufacturing, we have enclosed brochures of a new range of skin care products which we have just started manufacturing.

Our representative, Ms Rekha Shah will visit you on Monday, the 16th with our new catalogue and samples of the full range of our new cosmetic products and explain their special features.

A special concession trial order form, exclusively for longstanding customers, is enclosed. Rekha will help you to select the products for your trial order.

Yours sincerely,

Review

Are these statements true?

(a) Following up customers who do not place orders requires personalised letters.

(b) "We noticed from our records that you have not placed any orders with us for six months," is effective for winning back a customer.

(c) Most customers are lost because they are dissatisfied with the goods/services.

(d) Keeping in touch with customers helps to retain them.

EXERCISES

1. Invite Interior Decoration firms to submit a quotation for carrying out renovation work of your computer centre. They are to submit designs for interior decoration and to quote their terms separately for painting in Plastic Emulsion and for Oil Distemper.

2. Mahatma Computer Education Centre, Hyderabad, intend to advertise in the computer journal COMPUTECH. Draft their letter asking for a quotation for 12 back cover weekly advertisements.
3. Popular Tours ask New Image Graphics to quote their terms for the designing and printing 500 copies of a brochure of their package tours. They enclose a copy of a previous brochure. Draft the letter.
4. A college library intends to buy display boards and racks. Draft the college Principal's letter asking Jupiter Displays for their catalogue and quotation. The letter should stress that a substantial concession is expected as it is for an educational institution.
5. Write to a supplier of stationery articles that you are prepared to consider contracts for the supply of pencils, notebooks, paper and ink to your college co-operative stores, for a period of ten months, from June to March. Ask him to send a representative to discuss the terms.
6. A Pharmaceutical Products Company requires brown glass bottles of assorted sizes; they ask Borosil Glass Works Ltd. to submit a quotation, carriage paid, for the supply of 50,00,000 bottles, to be supplied at their factory in one month after the order is placed.
7. Invite a marketing agency to quote terms for designing a marketing campaign for a new product you intend to launch shortly.
8. Invite a firm of furnishers to submit their quotation for the upholstering of your college theatre with a capacity of 400. You require foam rubber for the seats. Ask for samples of leather cloth and request a visit from a representative.
9. Your class has decided to go for a picnic. Write a letter to the owner of a bus service, making enquiries.
10. You need an intercom system for your office. Draft a request for a quotation, giving all details of your requirements, to be sent to manufacturers of the system.
11. Unistar Computer Services need to get their premises treated for termites. They write to Pest Control (India) for a quotation, and request them to inspect the premises immediately. Draft their letter.
12. You have seen an advertisement for a new electronic Xerox machine which can be programmed to make up to thirty copies of 10 pages and sort the copies into sets. Write to them asking for a demonstration as you want to purchase one for your office.
13. Draft a letter to Godrej Boyce & Co. asking for information about their new ergonomic furniture for your office. Give detailed specifications of your requirements.
14. In reply to an enquiry from Mahatma Computer Education Centre publishers of COMPUTECH (a computer journal) send the schedule of advertising space rates and state the discount allowed on booking of space for 15 weeks.
15. Draft a letter confirming a quotation given by telephone. Give sales value to the letter and enclose an order form.
17. New Image Graphics reply to Popular Tours stating the price at which they will design and print 500 copies of their brochures in the design submitted. They also enclose samples of other designs.

18. A manufacturer of glass products has been asked for a discount and a special window dressing equipment and material, for an exhibition for one week, by a retailer in a small town. He can supply a sample lot of glass products and a standard window lighting plant at a rent of Rs. 3000/- per week. But he cannot give a discount of more than 5% because of a narrow margin of profit. Draft the letter.
19. In reply to an enquiry from a college co-operative store about the supply of ink and stationery for the period from June to April, write a covering letter to be sent with your price list and say that your representative will visit to discuss the details.
20. You have received a request for a quotation for the supply of examination answer books from a customer who often asks you for a quotation but uses it only to compare it with other quotations and never places an order. Reply tactfully avoiding giving a quotation.
21. Draft a letter to be sent to a College Principal who has not placed any order with you for two years, though she used to buy large quantities of answer books from you every year. Offer an inducement to get her to place an order.
22. You have received a letter asking if you can supply steel furniture within 15 days, for an office. Draft a reply stating that you can deliver only 10 writing desks immediately, and can send the rest a week later; computer tables and chairs are not in stock and can be delivered only after a month; filing cabinets with 4 drawers are not available at present, but you can supply cabinets with 5 drawers immediately.
23. A retailer has requested you to supply 6 fax machines at 20% discount for a valued customer. Draft a reply stating that the rate of discount cannot exceed 15%. Make an attempt to get the order.

Chapter 23

ORDERS AND REPLIES

Letters related to ordering of goods are central to a company's business; all other letters arise from orders for goods and services.

Orders are routine letters and their effectiveness depends on the accuracy of the details. Most of the contents of an order can be tabulated.

Replies to orders are treated as opportunities to build up goodwill and relationship with new customers, uncertain customers, regained customers as well as long standing loyal customers. Interest in replying to orders goes a long way in creating goodwill.

ORDERS

Before placing an order, get all the details of what you want to buy. Group the details under headings.

Product, its specifications and quantity

Give a full and accurate description of the goods you need. Some products come in a variety of sizes, colours etc. Identify the exact product you want by specifications like (i) size, (of product or the packing), (ii) colour, (iii) catalogue number, (iv) model number, (v) unit price.

State the correct quantity required. Different products are sold in different measures: liquids in litres; solids in kilograms, dozens or hundreds; large products like cupboards, in units.

Packing

Some products like liquids, grains and tablets, have packing of various quantities; shampoos are packed in 100ml, 200ml, etc; grains are packed in bags of 1 kg, 2 kg, and so on; tablets come in strips of ten or bottles of 50, 100, etc. Some products are available in different types of packing like bottles, tins and sachets. The required packing should be specified in the order. Packing goods suitably for transport is the responsibility of the supplier; buyer's instructions are needed only if the goods are to be specially packed for any special purpose.

Delivery

Give the full address at which the goods are to be delivered. Give the date if the order is urgent and you require the goods for a specific occasion and within a certain time. The mode of transport need not be mentioned unless it is carriage forward.

Settlement of Account

Mention the agreed prices and terms and refer to: (a) discount or concession given; (b) mode of payment of the bill.

Drafting Orders

Orders can be divided into three groups: (i) First or trial order (ii) Repeat order (iii) Routine order. There is a slight variation of opening and ending sentences in each of these; other details remain the same.

Points to be included in an order:

1. Reference to previous communication (for first order) and request to send goods
2. Details of required goods and other instructions, like place and time of delivery and reference to terms of payment
3. Goodwill message.

Printed Order Forms: Details to be given in an order are easy to tabulate, and hence many companies have printed order forms. Sellers prepare the forms with columns and printed headings for each detail required for their product. This ensures that no essential detail is left out; the form makes it easy for the customer to place an order.

Carbon copies as required, are arranged in the pad. Regular customers are given pads of the forms. A set of forms is sent with a quotation to encourage a potential customer to place an order.

First or Trial Order

Prices and terms are settled by a quotation and discussion, and samples are approved; but you have still to make sure that the seller gives efficient service, that is, proper packing, delivery of goods in time, prompt receipts for payments etc. A trial order is placed to check the efficiency of all this. A retailer may also place a trial order to find out the demand for a new product. A small quantity may be ordered for trial.

Any of the following situations may lead to a first order:

(i) Seller's samples and/or quotation are approved

(ii) A bargain has been concluded

  (a) request granted

  (b) buyer convinced to order on offered terms

(iii) Buyer is willing to try an offered substitute

(iv) Buyer intends to try a product in a new area.

The opening and the ending for each of these are given below:

(i) Open with a reference to the received quotation.

** Your quotation for ... is approved and we are pleased to place an order for the following:*

** Thank you for your quotation for.... We are glad to place a trial order with you as follows:*

When you have reason to be very particular about the quality of the product as in the case of medicines or precision goods, testing of samples leads to the order. Start the letter by mentioning satisfaction with samples.

** We have tested your samples of... and found that sample No. 099 suits our requirements.*

** We are glad to say that we approve of your samples of terry wool suiting, and would like to receive supplies as follows:*

End with the expectation that the trial order will be satisfactory and lead to regular business.

We hope to find everything satisfactory and are looking forward to placing frequent orders with you.

If you order goods on the basis of a sample, you expect them to match with the sample; you may refuse to accept the goods if they are different; mention this at the end of the order.

** We expect that your goods will be of the same high standard as the sample which has led us to place this order.*

** It is essential that goods supplied should be of the same quality as the selected sample and we reserve the right to reject goods which do not tally with the sample.*

(ii) (a) When the seller has agreed to a bargain, open the order letter with a reference to it.

** We thank you for agreeing to give us special packing at no extra charge.*

The corresponding ending would be:

** We assure you that a large amount of business will follow if the trial order is found satisfactory.*

(b) If you are convinced that the seller cannot give better terms, but still wish to place the order, mention this in the opening.

** We understand that it is not possible for you to give us export packing without charging extra, but we are wiling to take a trial lot of your Milk Powder tins.*

End with expectation of high standard of goods/services.

** We hope to find your goods and services of a high standard to justify our placing orders with you.*

(iii) If you decide to try an offered substitute, you may order a small lot.

** We are willing to try the A1 disinfectant cleaning fluid which you have offered instead of Yellow Bond phenyl we had asked for.*

End by suggesting that more will be ordered only if the trial order proves satisfactory.

* *We shall ask for further supplies if we find it suitable for our requirements.*

(iv) A buyer may place an order on his own initiative on seeing an advertisement if he feels that a certain product has a potential demand. The opening sentence refers to this.

- *There is a reasonably good demand for cotswool shirts in this town and we would like to have a trial consignment according to the following details.*
- *We have received several inquiries from local customers about your PVC tiles; as there is no supplier of your products in this area we would like to try the market. Please send us a trial consignment according to details given below:*

End with the hope that a regular demand will be established.

* *We hope to establish a good demand and expect to place frequent orders with you.*

An order placed by telephone or telegram is confirmed by a letter because a signed, written document is necessary for a contract. Open the letter with a reference to the order already placed, and the confirmation, for example:

* *We confirm our order for... placed by telephone this morning.*

Ending may be similar to that of (i).

Reserving the right to reject

A customer may reserve the right to reject delivered goods if

(i) they are not delivered within the specified time, when the question of time is very important, and the customer has no use for goods delivered late.

(ii) they do not tally with the sample when it is specified that the quality and/or the given specifications are important.

The condition is indicated at the end of the letter, for example:

* *As the monsoon cannot be expected to last very long we reserve the right to reject supplies received later than the 18th of this month.*

* *It is necessary that the goods supplied should be exactly of the same quality as the sample. We reserve the right to reject goods of any other quality.*

The following examples illustrate the points.

Dear Sirs,

We have tested your samples of adhesive paste and found that No. 27 is suitable for our requirements. We are glad to place an order for 500 large tins of this paste. Please deliver the tins at our factory at Andheri. Our cheque for Rs.— in advance payment, and our Sales Tax declaration form are enclosed.

The material supplied should be of the same quality as the sample and we reserve the right to reject material of any other quality.

Yours faithfully,

Dear Sirs,

We confirm our order for 5000 sheets of A4 size bond paper placed by telephone this morning.

Enclosed is our cheque for Rs.— as advance payment. Please deliver the package on the 16th at our address given above. The balance of Rs.— will be paid after delivery.

We shall be placing similar orders with you if we find that your products and services are of a high quality.

Yours faithfully,

Sir,

We are willing to try the range of A1 disinfectant cleaning fluids which you have suggested instead of the Yellow Bond phenyl we had asked for.

Please send a trial lot of 1 tin of 200 litres each of all the A1 disinfectant products, suitable for hospital use, to our address given above.

We shall consider placing an annual contract for the supply of the products if the quality is suitable for our requirements.

Yours faithfully,

The following is an example of an order placed on a form and a covering letter.

Blue Moon Hotel
Borivli
Mumbai

Order No. 126 3 August, 20—

Century Mills Ltd.
Rambaug
Bangalore

Please supply the following to the address given above.

Quantity	Item	Catalogue number	Unit Price
50	Bed sheets white (120 cms)	96	Rs. 250
50	Bed sheets blue (100 cms)	89	Rs. 300
100	Pillow covers white	42	Rs. 40
100	Pillow covers blue	45	Rs. 50
100	Bath towels green	67	Rs. 150
200	Hand towels green	69	Rs. 40

(Signed)
N.L.Rao
For Blue Moon Hotel

> Dear Sirs,
>
> We are happy to enclose our order number 126 for 6 items.
>
> As we need all these items urgently, please deliver them within a week. We understand that you will give us a discount of 7% on the total and a 2% cash discount if we make cash payment within seven days of delivery.
>
> Yours faithfully,

Repeat Order

When the buyer is satisfied with goods bought on a trial consignment he may place a repeat order.

The letter opens with a reference to the first order and the continuing demand.

- *We are glad to say that the A1 disinfectant cleaning fluids you supplied last week have been found suitable for our purpose and we would like to have another similar consignment.*
- *The PVC tiles we ordered from you last month sold very well and there is still a demand for them. We are glad to place a repeat order.*

Here are some examples:

> Sirs,
>
> We are glad to say that the Jay travel bags we purchased a fortnight ago have proved popular and are all sold out. We need another similar consignment immediately.
>
> Holiday travel season at this time of the year is very short and demand for travel bags cannot be expected to continue for more than a week. We must therefore receive the consignment by 22 December and we reserve the right to reject goods supplied later.
>
> Please dispatch immediately on carriage forward terms as before.
>
> Yours faithfully,

> Gentlemen:
>
> We are happy to inform you that the consignment of La Opala dinner sets sold out rapidly. Please send us another consignment on exactly the same terms and conditions as the first order.
>
> There is reason to be hopeful that a good demand can be created for your products in this town. We are expecting to place a larger order next time.
>
> Yours truly,

Routine Order

The most important thing to convey in a routine order is the details of requirements. Prices and terms are fixed by custom. These orders are usually placed by filling in order forms which may be accompanied by a letter. The letter opens with a courteous request for goods to be sent, for example:

* Please dispatch the following goods on the usual terms.
* Please send the enclosed order on your regular terms.

If there is any special requirement, state it at the beginning or at the end.

* The customer for whom we are ordering these products is to leave town on the 14th and must get them by the 12th. Please ensure delivery in time.

Some examples of letters follow.

Gentlemen:

Please send the following goods according to your usual terms:

Catalogue No.	Description	Price
3645 A	1 Wall cabinet, brown:	Rs. ___
367 - O	1 Computer table-cum-cabinet, brown:	Rs. ___
5462	1 Metal sink cabinet, brown:	Rs. ___

These products are required urgently as the customer for whom we want them has already removed the old cabinets and needs immediate replacements. Please arrange for quick delivery.

Yours truly,

An order placed on a printed form is usually accompanied by a covering letter like the following.

Sir,

We are enclosing our order form No. RO / 0845 for sports goods. As the colleges have opened and indoor games are very popular during the monsoon, we would like to have the goods delivered within a week's time.

Please bill our account as usual.

Yours truly,

Review

1. Collect the order forms of four or five companies selling different kinds of products and compare them. Order forms are also available on the websites of companies. How are these different from printed forms?
2. Fill in the blanks using as few words as possible.
   Details to be included in an order are — (give all points).

REPLIES TO ORDERS

A buyer's order is an offer to buy; when the seller confirms his acceptance of the order, it becomes binding on both parties.

The buyer has the obligation to accept goods supplied according to the terms of the order and pay for them as agreed in the order letter. He is also obliged to check the received goods as soon as possible and report any deviation from the terms of the order.

The seller, after he accepts the order, has to deliver the goods ordered, at the place and time agreed in the order. The seller also has to take responsibility to ensure that the goods are free from faults and deficiencies.

Always acknowledge an order as soon as it is received. The acknowledgement can be used to build and maintain good relationships with customers.

Include the following points:

1. Name and quantity of goods dispatched or being dispatched
2. Date of shipment and expected date of receipt or the date of delivery of goods
3. Mode of transport, and place of delivery
4. Mode of payment and reference to enclosed bill.

Reply to First Order

Assure the customer that every attention has been paid to the order, and that future orders will receive the same careful attention.

The letter given below includes the following points:

1. Expression of thanks for the order
2. Statement of terms etc.
3. Assurance of satisfactory goods and service and expectation that you will deserve further orders.

Dear Sirs,

Thank you for the cheque of Rs.—in advance payment for the supply of A4 bond paper. As agreed, we shall deliver your order for 5000 sheets to your address on the 16th.

We assure you that our products and services will come up to your expectations and look forward to a pleasant business relationship.

Yours truly,

Dear sirs,

We are happy to receive your order for our range of A1 disinfectants, and to welcome you as our customer.

We have dispatched the following goods by our van today:

Disinfectant Floor cleaner concentrate	10 litre can	4
Disinfectant Toilet cleaner	10 litre can	6
Disinfectant cleaner for trays, bedpans	10 litre can	6
Germicidal liquid soap	10 litre can	6
Germicidal cleaning fluid for kitchen	10 litre can	6

Our bill for Rs. — is sent with the goods. Payment in cash within 7 days of delivery entitles you to 2% discount.

We hope that our execution of your first order, and the quality of our products will be the beginning of a pleasant working relationship.

Yours faithfully,

Dear Sirs,

Thank you for your order for 15,000 cartons with corrugated partitions for packing biscuits.

We shall deliver your goods in 10 days, i.e., by the 20th as required. The bill will be sent with the goods; payment within seven days entitles you to a discount of 2 %.

You will find that our goods and services are of a high standard. We are looking forward to a standing contract for regular supplies of packing material for your biscuits and confectionery.

Yours truly,

Dear Ms Sibal,

I am happy to receive your order of 15 May for 500 schoolbags, and welcome you as our customer.

I confirm that the goods will be supplied on 31 May, at the prices mentioned in your letter. I am sure you will find that the schoolbags will be popular with your customers and will sell rapidly.

We manufacture a wide range of bags including sports bags and shopping bags as the enclosed catalogue shows. We can also make bags according to your specifications.

I am looking forward to a happy and mutually profitable business relationship with you.

Sincerely,

Geeta Kaul

Asking for extension of time: If goods cannot be delivered at the expected time, contact the customer to negotiate a new date. The purpose of the letter is to get the customer to agree to a later date of delivery.

Points:

1. Appreciation of the order and explanation of circumstances
2. Steps being taken to handle the situation, and approximate date by which normal conditions will be restored
3. Apology for the inconvenience and request for confirmation of the order for delivery at a later date.

Dear Sirs,

Thank you for your order for stationery items to be supplied by 5 June.

Owing to a rush of orders and somewhat slow supplies, we are not able to guarantee that we can supply your requirement by the required date. We are handling all orders in rotation, and expect to be able to deliver your consignment around 15 June.

We are making every effort to meet the requirements of all our customers and will get in touch with you as soon as we have the required supplies.

In the meantime, we request you to confirm your order for delivery by mid-June.

Yours faithfully,

Dear Ms Hansotia,

YOUR ORDER NUMBER 456

We are sorry to inform you that owing to a transporters' strike, there is some delay in the dispatch of our consignments. Your consignment against your order of 14 February is among those delayed.

In order to have your consignment delivered on time, we sent it by rail to Mumbai, five days ahead of the schedule. But we now learnt that it is still at the Bombay Central Station.

We are making private arrangements to transport it to Mahabaleshwar in time for the opening of your hotel on 20 March.

Please accept our apologies for this delay. We hope you will understand that it was due to conditions outside our control.

Yours sincerely,

Reply to Repeat Order

When the customer repeats his order, you can make a more definite attempt to win his confidence.

Points

1. Appreciation for success of the trial order
2. Statement of terms etc.
3. Expectation that regular business will follow.

Sir,

We are glad to learn from your letter of the 21st that the trial lot of A1 disinfectant cleaning fluids sent on the 7th are suitable for your purpose.

We are sending with this letter, the consignment of 200 tins of A1 floor cleaner you have ordered. Our bill of Rs.— is enclosed; cash payment within seven days will entitle you to a discount of 2 %.

We are looking forward to supplying our products to your hospital on a regular contract.

Yours truly;

Appreciating Regular Customers' Orders

Take every opportunity to maintain personal contact with all customers, specially, long standing ones. Use any special occasion like a festival or a large order to show appreciation of the customer's regular business. This is largely a goodwill letter, and not just a routine acknowledgement; address the letter by name.

Dear Mr. Parikh,

Thank you very much for your large order for 50,000 'Volga' cartons. We take this opportunity to tell you how much we appreciate your regular orders and prompt payments.

Business depends on customers like you, but unfortunately, while poor buyers and slow payers get letters, you receive only routine acknowledgements, bill and receipts. As a businessman yourself, you must have experienced the same problem of maintaining contacts with the best of your customers.

You will receive your goods as usual. Do accept our sincere thanks for the business you give us.

Yours sincerely,

Appreciating Orders from Regained Buyers

When an order is placed by a regained customer after a long interval, make an effort to re-establish the relations firmly. Show appreciation of a customer who has come back, and also assure him that he will be happy with his decision to return.

Points:

1. Expression of gratitude for the long-missed order
2. Statement of routine acknowledgement
3. Assurance of highly satisfactory service.

Dear Mr. Sanghvi,

We are indeed grateful for your order of the 10th which we have received after a long interval.

The drums of paint have been dispatched to you by truck and you will receive them by the 17th. The Transporter's Receipt is enclosed. Our bill of Rs.— — is enclosed.

We are anxious to make sure that our customers are satisfied with our goods and services; please feel assured that we shall take every care to see that you are happy with your decision to order goods from us again.

Yours faithfully,

Review

1. Are these statements true?
   (a) Replies to orders from long standing customers can be used as goodwill letters.
   (b) All orders should be acknowledged.
2. Fill in the blanks.
   A reply to an order should include — (give all points).

CHANGES IN ORDERS

A customer might have to make a change in an order which has been placed; it may be a correction on finding a mistake or a request for a change in the date or the place of delivery. In case of unforeseen circumstances, the customer may have to cancel an order.

Points:

1. Reference to order
2. Statement of change required, and explanation of the reason
3. Request seller's co-operation in making adjustment
4. Apology for the inconvenience caused.

The following example embodies these points.

Dear Sirs,

Please refer to our order No. XX03 dated 15 June, for steel shelves to be delivered on 15 September.

We are sorry we cannot take delivery of the shelves on 15 September owing to unforeseen shortage of storage space. Our warehouse was destroyed by fire this week, and we have had to remove salvaged goods to our show-rooms. It will take two months to arrange for storage space and unless you can store the goods for us, we shall have to cancel our order.

We are sure you will understand the situation and accept our apology for the inconvenience caused. Please let us know whether you can hold the goods for 2 months.

Yours faithfully,

Seller's Reply to Customer's Request for Change

If the change requested by the customer can be made without much inconvenience or loss, inform him that it will be made. If it involves disturbance, request the customer to co-operate.

1. Agreement to make the change as requested
2. Explanation of problem, if any, and how the customer can help
3. Statement of terms for purpose of acknowledgement.

Dear Sirs,

We are glad to inform you that we can deliver the washing machines you ordered, a week earlier than the date originally fixed, as you requested in your letter dated 15 May. Thank you for offering to pay additional charges, but we do not wish to charge anything extra for early delivery. However, as our delivery vans will be engaged till 15 June, we request you to release us from the contract to deliver carriage paid, and to make arrangements for the transport of the goods. We hope that it will be possible for you to make the arrangements.

Your consignment will be ready for collection by 10 June.

Yours faithfully,

Dear Sir,

We are sorry to learn from your letter of 7 September, that you are compelled to cancel your order for 50 rubber foam mattresses owing to delay in the completion of the hospital building.

Unfortunately, however, if you cancel the order at this stage, we shall be forced to charge a penalty of Rs. 5000 to cover the expenses we have incurred on making the mattresses to your specifications. As an alternative, we shall store them in our warehouse at a rent of Rs. 2000, if you wish. This will save you the penalty charge.

Please reply within a week. We hope that you will take advantage of the alternative which we have offered.

Yours faithfully,

Seller's Request for Change

Sometimes the seller may request the customer to permit a change in the date or the place of delivery; he may ask for extension of time if his production is held up; or he may request the customer to accept early delivery if he has more orders coming in and wants to free his space.

Adjustments are a matter of goodwill and understanding between the seller and the buyer.

Sirs,

Please refer to your order for the printing of 20,000 copies of your special tour brochures, to be delivered on 8 March.

Owing to a breakdown of one of our machines, there will be a delay in completing the printing work. Immediate repair work has been undertaken and the delay will not be of more than 4 days. Please accept our apologies for the inconvenience caused.

We already have 12,000 copies ready; please let us know whether you would like us to deliver these on the 8th and the rest four days later, or deliver all the 20,000 copies on the 12th.

Yours faithfully,

Gentlemen:

Please refer to your order of 15 January for 50 steel book-shelves. We are sorry that we have to request you to allow us an extension of time to deliver the goods.

Our supplies of steel sheets have been delayed by 15 days owing to shortage in the market, and this delay has affected our production schedule. We have been assured of our supplies by 15 February and will be able to complete your order within 20 days of receiving the supplies.

We are sorry for the inconvenience caused by this delay.

Yours truly,

If the seller is unable to fulfil an order owing to unforeseen circumstances, he may request the customer for release from the contract. The letter must explain clearly, the reason for inability to fulfil the order, and also keep open the possibility of taking up the order later.

Dear Sirs,

We thank you for your order dated 10 January, for 50 steel book-shelves to be delivered in 2 months. Unfortunately, owing to a strike in the steel industry, there is a shortage of steel sheets in the market. We shall not be able to deliver the shelves in 2 months as you have requested.

Negotiations with the Union leaders are in progress; however it appears that it will take a long time to reach a final agreement. As we shall be out of production for a fairly long time and cannot state any definite date, we must unfortunately request you to withdraw your present order.

We once again thank you for offering us your business and shall get in touch with you as soon as normal production is resumed.

Yours truly,

Customer's Reply

The customer has to make adjustments and may have to give instructions about delivery of goods in case of delay or early delivery etc.

Sirs,

We do not mind accepting early delivery of our steel shelves and cabinets which were to be delivered on the 18th. However, it is not possible to keep them at our show-rooms at Hutatma Chowk owing to lack of space and we therefore request you to deliver them carriage paid at our Thane show-room.

We shall expect delivery of the goods on the 11th as you have suggested, and hope that there will be no inconvenience in delivering them at Thane.

Yours faithfully,

Dear Sirs,

We are sorry to learn that a strike in the steel industry has caused you to be out of production. We appreciate your informing us in time to enable to make alternative arrangements.

We look forward to your resuming normal production.

Yours truly,

AFTER-SALES LETTERS

It is business courtesy and good business practice to contact a customer some time after he has bought a consumer durable product like a computer, a vacuum cleaner, a Xerox machine etc. Often, the salesperson visits the customer within a week of the sale to check whether the customer is making full use of it and is comfortable with it. An after-sales letter after three or four weeks reinforces the contact and the goodwill.

The after-sales letter performs three functions: (i) it checks that the customer is satisfied; if not, the seller has a chance to set matters right. Enquiring about the customer's satisfaction is the mark of a reputable seller; (ii) it reminds the customer about the after-sales service; (iii) it makes way for further business through the customer.

A customer who receives after-sales attention from the seller is more likely to speak well about the company to others. Word-of-mouth publicity through the customer is a very powerful image-builder. Address the letter by name.

The letter below is an example of an after-sales letter.

> Dear Mrs. Chitnis,
>
> We are writing to ask you about your experience with our Acme washing machine you bought last month.
>
> We want you to feel assured that in case you have any difficulty with any of the operations, we shall be glad to send our expert to help you. The booklet of instructions, supplied with the machine will, of course, be helpful in handling the machine.
>
> But please do not hesitate to call us if you need further help at any time. Once you buy one of our machines, you are our customer forever, and may claim our help and services at any time.
>
> Yours sincerely,

Review

Are these statements true?

(a) When a customer sends a letter making changes in an order, there is no need to acknowledge it if the changes can be implemented.

(b) After-sales letters can help to build up goodwill.

(c) Letters to regained buyers should be written with special care.

EXERCISES

1. Place an order for 300 boxes of coloured magic crayons subject to the manufacturer's agreeing to pack them in specially designed boxes for Diwali presentation for no additional charge.
2. You have received an order for 300 boxes of coloured magic crayons in special presentation packing for no additional charge. Write to the customer saying that you have dispatched the articles as required, tactfully suggesting that he should not, in future, ask for such concessions unless his order exceeds 5,000 boxes.
3. Place an order for 100 bar magnets for use in your factory of electrical goods, and reserve the right to reject them if they do not tally with the sample submitted.
4. Confirm an order given by telephone, for 100 pocket calculators for your school.

5. Popular Tours write to New Image Graphics that they approve of one of the brochure designs submitted by them, and wish to have 5,000 copies in that design. They will send their representative to the Press in the following week to settle the details of the contract. Draft the letter.
6. New Image Graphics inform Popular Tours that owing to the breakdown of their machines only 3,000 copies of their catalogue are printed; the remaining copies will be ready within five days. They ask the customer whether the copies that are ready should be sent at once, or retained till the rest are ready.
7. You had ordered 20 computers for a Computer Education class, to be opened shortly. A dispute among the partners has forced postponement of the opening of the class. Write cancelling the order unless the vendor is prepared to hold the order until your classrooms are ready.
8. Beam Personnel Services had placed an order for 100 conference chairs with Comfort Furnishers (Pvt.) Ltd. They now request them to deliver the chairs a week earlier than the agreed date. They are willing to pay for the extra work which will have to be undertaken.
9. Comfort Furnishers (Pvt.) Ltd. are willing to deliver 100 conference chairs ordered by Beam Personnel Services a week earlier than the originally agreed date as requested. They do not intend to charge extra for this but, as their own trucks will not be free at the time, they ask the customer to release them from their undertaking to deliver the goods free of charge. Draft the letter.
10. For the silver jubilee of your firm, you wish to present wall clocks to your staff. Write to a manufacturer of clocks giving details of your requirements and ask him to gift-wrap each clock at no extra cost. Point out how the manufacturer will benefit if he grants your request.
11. You have received an urgent order for 25 vacuum cleaners from a hotel. Owing to a rush of orders there will be a delay of three weeks in delivering the goods. Write asking for extension of time.
12. Rajesh Furnishers have received an order for six steel cupboards, based on an old price list. Prices have increased by 10% since then. Write a reply saying that you are willing to supply the goods at the old price, if the order is worth more than Rs.100,000/-. Mention that this special offer should not be treated as a precedent.
13. Quality Stationery Suppliers acknowledge the first order from Messrs. Mehta & Sons after a long interval, and try to build up goodwill. Draft the letter.
14. A long standing customer has written to cancel an order stating that there is no storage space in his warehouse. Write a reply offering to store the goods in your warehouse for a month, if he is willing to pay the warehousing charges.
15. Acknowledge an order placed by an old customer who has been regained by the efforts of the sales department.
16. You had given a specially low quotation to a potential customer for acceptance within fifteen days, as a price rise was expected shortly. The customer's order comes three days after the expiry of the firm offer when the prices have risen. Write to the customer persuading him to confirm his order at the raised prices.

17. A long standing customer has placed an unusually large order for designing and printing his company's office stationery. Write a letter acknowledging the order and showing appreciation of his regular orders and prompt payments.
18. You had ordered some goods to be delivered by a specified date. The goods did not arrive on time and are of no use to you now. Write to the supplier cancelling the order and pointing out that you have incurred considerable loss on account of his negligence.
19. Celina Cosmetics Suppliers have received an order from Camelia's Beauty Parlour three days after their firm offer expired. They write stating that they had only limited stock of the particular products and that they were sold out immediately after the expiry of the firm offer, two days before the order was received. Draft the letter, making an effort to get the customer interested in other products.

Chapter 24

COMPLAINTS, CLAIMS AND ADJUSTMENTS

In any business there will be some mistakes and mishaps; you may not get the goods and services as you had expected and ordered. If things go wrong on your order, you have to inform the supplier about the problem and see that the faults are corrected and adjustments are made.

Make a phone call as soon as the problem is noticed, to inform the supplier of the defect or deficiency, and then confirm it immediately with a letter. It is usually sufficient to point out the mistake in the execution of the order and leave it to the supplier to make the adjustment. In the case of a technological product, the seller is usually anxious to make sure that it functions properly with the customer.

When there is a mistake in the execution of your order, you may feel angry, but it is important to control your anger and speak and write calmly. You may have to bear inconvenience even though it is not your fault; but you are not necessarily the loser of money.

As a buyer you have to take steps to reduce the inconvenience, and you must make the supplier take steps to reduce your inconvenience and make adjustments.

Keep in mind the Cs of good letter writing:

- State the problem correctly and without exaggeration. Although anger sometimes makes you eloquent, be restrained, and give a factual account of the problem.
- Be clear and concise in describing. Suggest how the problem can be corrected; if you do not know what can be done, ask what the supplier proposes to do. Do not delay writing the complaint; delay weakens your position and also makes investigation difficult for the supplier.
- Courtesy is of great importance; resist the temptation to accuse the supplier of carelessness, negligence or inefficiency. Do not use offensive and discourteous words like *dishonest, careless, unfair, false, disgusted, useless, inefficient.* Use passive voice to mention errors. Saying,

"Our consignment of crockery was not packed with the necessary care," is more polite than saying, "You packed our consignment of crockery carelessly."

Do not attribute errors and faults to anyone unless you are sure. It is the seller's responsibility to find out who made the mistake. Firmness, emphasis and insistence on your rights can be done without discourtesy.

Review

1. Are the following statements true?
   (a) A complaint letter should be written in legalistic style in order to impress the supplier.
   (b) In a letter of complaint you should not accuse and blame anyone angrily even if you know whose fault it was.
   (c) Words like "cheating", "failure", "useless" should not be used while pointing out errors.
   (d) "Your negligent and careless attitude to my order has caused us a great loss and you will have to compensate us for it." is a good sentence to use in a complaint letter.

Occasions for Writing Complaints

A buyer may have one or more of the following reasons for making a complaint:

- Goods received in a damaged condition
- Unsatisfactory quality of goods
- Wrong goods received
- Quantity of goods different from what was ordered
- Goods delivered at the wrong place
- Delay in delivery of goods or completion of work
- Unsatisfactory work or service
- Discourtesy from staff of shop or office
- Mistakes in a bill, or reminders for payment after the bill has been paid.

Your claim and your expectation of the seller's response will depend on whether you are a commercial buyer or a consumer. As a commercial buyer you make adjustments, so that the inconvenience and the hindrance to business are minimised; there is more inconvenience than personal loss. You also have greater power to get adjustments and compensation because, as a regular buyer, you have a hold on the seller.

A small consumer may not find it easy to get adjustments; however, the Consumer Protection Act, 1986, has made it possible for small consumers to get compensation. Also, market forces and competition have forced sellers to make efforts to retain customers; they pay more attention to customer satisfaction when there is competition.

Letter of Complaint

The letter should include the following points:

1. Reference to the order, its date and number
2. Clear description of the mistake or deficiency

3. Clear statement of the inconvenience or loss caused, and the action the supplier should take to lessen the inconvenience
4. Request for adjustment and/or investigation.

The letters below illustrate how these points are included.

Complaint about damaged goods

Dear Sir,

The consignment of 5 Launderwell Washing Machines we ordered on 6 October was delivered to us today by a public carrier.

The crate was damaged. We pointed out the damage to your delivery staff and have entered a remark on the receipt. Three of the machines are damaged and the other two are slightly dented and scratched. It appears that the consignment was handled carelessly.

We cannot accept the damaged goods and expect you to replace them immediately. Please arrange for an immediate inspection and replacement.

Yours faithfully,

Dear Sirs,

OUR ORDER NUMBER C254

I had ordered 500 Melamine dinner plates on 8 October and received the consignment this morning. I am sorry that 29 of them are badly scratched and 3 are chipped.

Since the package containing the goods was in perfect condition, I accepted it and signed for it without raising objection. The damage was discovered only after opening the package. It appears that the goods were handled without care at some stage before they were packed.

I have kept the damaged plates aside for your inspection. Please arrange to collect and replace them immediately.

Yours truly,

Complaint about unsatisfactory quality of goods

Dear Sirs,

We have received a number of complaints from customers who bought your can openers. Most complain that they are very difficult to handle and tend to hurt the user or break in the attempt to use it. In some cases, when the opener was returned broken the next day after the purchase, we had to refund the price.

We tried the can openers ourselves when we received so many complaints and have to agree that they are defective.

You had supplied these can openers against our order number XN987 dated 16 September for 300 units. We had placed the order on the basis of a sample that your representative had given us. There are complaints only about the openers in the batch supplied against this order. There have been no complaints about earlier batches.

We have 218 can openers left from this batch and wish to return them. Please replace them with openers of good quality as of the earlier supplies.

Please inform us what arrangements we should make to return these openers.

Yours truly,

Customer's complaint to Manufacturer

Dear Sirs,

On 19 December, I bought a Dust Free vacuum cleaner from Victoria Home Appliance Sales at Andheri, Mumbai.

I am sorry to say that I am very disappointed with my purchase as the cleaner is not convenient to use. The extension pipes of the cleaner do not fix firmly and keep falling off.

The people at Victoria Home Appliance Sales were not able to correct the fault, and the Manager asked me to write directly to you. I have already called your service department.

Please let me know what arrangement you are making to correct the fault in the vacuum cleaner.

Yours faithfully,

Complaint about wrong goods

Dear Sirs,

We had ordered 4 filing cabinets, 3 shelves, 10 office chairs and 5 tables to be delivered to us here, on 23 September, in time for the opening of our new branch office.

The shipment has just arrived here and we find that 1 kitchen cupboard, 2 wardrobes and 3 garden tables have been delivered to us. It is probable that there was a confusion between two shipments and the wrong one was delivered to us.

Our branch office is to be opened on the 25th and we would like our furniture to reach us in time; the customer whose goods you have delivered to us must be equally unhappy with the office furniture delivered to her.

We expect that you will act immediately.

Yours truly,

Dear Sirs,

On July 30, we ordered 3 copies of *Dealing with Difficult People* by Cava Roberta and 5 copies of *Integrated Marketing Communication* by Robert Lauterborn by our order number LB432/99.

We received the parcel this morning, and on opening it we found that it contained 8 copies of *Principles of Marketing* by Philip Kotler. We cannot keep these books as we already have enough copies of it in our library. We are returning this parcel and want an immediate replacement as students urgently need the ordered books.

We expect you to credit our account with the invoiced amount of the returned books including re-imbursement for postage of Rs. 400/.

Yours faithfully,

Complaint about quantity

(a) Shortage

Dear Sirs,

OUR ORDER NUMBER SS492

Thank you for the prompt delivery of Washing Machines and Driers we had ordered on 16 September.

We had ordered 10 of each item but only 6 washing machines and 4 driers have been delivered. The person who delivered them was not able to explain the shortage. We have also not received any intimation from you about the shortage.

We need the full quantity we ordered and cannot proceed with our work of finalising the construction of the launderette without installing all of the machines. Please arrange to deliver the remaining machines immediately.

Yours truly,

(b) Surplus goods delivered

A buyer is entitled to refuse the surplus goods but is not obliged to return them. The supplier has to arrange for collection of the goods.

Dear Sirs,

OUR ORDER NUMBER YY432

Thank you for the prompt delivery of the red coloured coffee mugs we had ordered on 20 October. We have received 500 mugs instead of the 300 we had ordered.

We cannot make use of the 200 extra mugs that have been delivered and request you to arrange to collect them. The mugs are stored in our Head Office where they were delivered. Please let us know about your arrangements.

Yours faithfully,

Complaint about delay in delivery

Dear Mr. Parikh,

We had placed an order with you on 8 October for 60 pocket calculators to be delivered by the 20th of this month. Unfortunately, we have not yet received them. As we do not have any information from you about the delay, perhaps something has gone wrong somewhere.

Will you please find out the cause of the delay and let us know when we may expect delivery?

Yours sincerely,

Complaint about serious delay in delivery of goods

If goods are delivered so late as to be of no use, the buyer may refuse to accept them.

Sir,

We regret the manner in which our order for 5,000 pairs of sun-glasses was handled. Only 2,000 were delivered on the 21st and the rest have been delivered now, after the event for which they were required, is over.

We had placed such a large order only in order to take advantage of the opportunity to sell the sun-glasses on the occasion of the Air Force Day Celebrations held this morning. Your indifference in executing our order has cost us dearly.

As we no longer require the sun-glasses we request you to make immediate arrangements to collect the 3,000 pairs delivered to us today.

Yours truly,

Complaint about serious shortcomings in goods and delivery

Sirs,

The answer books we had ordered from you have just been delivered and I am sorry to say that I sorely regret having placed the order with you.

The consignment arrived without any prior notice, at 9.45 a.m. when the office staff and peons were engaged in the work of an examination to be started at 10.00 a.m. The candidates were arriving and were being gulded and helped to find their seats. The lobby and the space around the college office was crowded with candidates. The delivery persons refused to wait even until the examination was started and the space was cleared. They dumped the bundles wherever they could see space on the office floor.

The bundles are so badly packed that the wrappers of many of them are torn and the answer books are soiled and damaged.

When we protested to the delivery persons, they rudely replied that they were only the transporters and delivered goods as and when instructed and had no responsibility to inform the customer or for the condition of the packing.

An inspection of a few of the answer books revealed the following defects:

i. They measure 1 cm. less than the given size, both in length and in width, thus reducing the writing space.

ii. The quality of the paper is so poor that printing on the cover page is seen on the back of it making it impossible for candidates to write on the first page. We are led to conclude that the writing will be seen on the back of every page.

iii. The printing on the cover page is so poor that it can hardly be read, and gives the answer books a shabby appearance.

All this is not in keeping with the quality of material and service that we expect and receive from our suppliers.

It is not possible for us to use the answer books you have supplied. The bill will not be passed for payment. This incident will be taken up for discussion with our Education Society's Executive Committee meeting on next Saturday.

I expect you to arrange immediately to remove the bundles from the floor of the college office where they are causing serious inconvenience.

Yours truly,

Complaint about inordinate delay in completion of work

Dear Sirs,

RENOVATION OF CANTEEN AND LUNCH ROOM

We gave you a contract for this work on your assurance that it would be completed in three months. Six months have elapsed and the work is still not near completion.

The delay is causing great inconvenience to our office staff. It is also a continuous loss to us on account of our having to make alternative arrangements.

During our discussion of this issue last Monday, your representative made excuses which did not seem convincing. We must remind you that this unreasonable delay attracts a penalty on the contract price.

Please let us know within three days, when you expect to complete the work.

Yours faithfully,

Complaint about discourteous behaviour of staff

Dear Sir,

I am sorry to have to write this to you. When I visited your branch yesterday, the 8th at 11.30 a.m., I was astonished to find that I was kept waiting without any attention or even the courtesy of being offered a seat.

There were only two other customers in the bank at the time, but the staff appeared to be too busy with their computers to attend to visitors. When I asked for attention I was told that I would have to wait for some time before the concerned officer could attend to my need.

I have always used the services of your bank for all my needs for the last eight years, but after today's experience, I decided to open an account with another bank.

Yours truly,

Sometimes, a strong letter may be required. If the seller does not respond to a telephone call and a fax and a letter, this experience of the supplier's indifference justifies a strong letter. Rudeness is not justified; but a letter demanding immediate attention can be made effective by arousing the seller's self-interest. The following letter is an example.

Gentlemen:

It is over a fortnight since we informed you of the defects in the office table delivered to us on 12 August. When we telephoned to remind you on 25 August you promised to collect the table for the necessary modifications but the table is still here and it is of no use to us until it can stand on its legs evenly.

We do not think the treatment you are giving us will lead us to place further orders with you, or to speak pleasantly about your services to our business associates. In any case, the shaky table standing in our well laid-out office attracts many questions from every visitor and is eloquent testimony to the kind of service you render here.

You can at least prevent further damage to your image by replacing the table at once. We expect you to call for it within the next two days.

Yours truly,

Here is a **checklist** for writing complaints.

- Write promptly, without delay
- State the facts correctly, clearly and briefly
- Be courteous and restrained in the use of words
- Avoid accusation
- Say what action is desirable.

ADJUSTMENT LETTERS

Prompt attention and response to customers' complaints is an important part of customer service. With growing competition, increased customer awareness, and legislation to protect consumers, providers of goods and services have to ensure customer satisfaction and pay prompt attention to any dissatisfaction.

The success of a business depends on the satisfaction of the customers, and it is important for the company to know whether the customers are satisfied with its goods/services or not. Dissatisfied customers are likely to talk about their dissatisfaction with a product/service and may write to grievance columns of newspapers; this is bad for the reputation of the company.

When a customer complains, you get a chance to correct any faults, to make adjustment, to explain, and to help the customer to use the product properly; you get a chance to be in touch with the customers and to make sure that they are satisfied with your product/service.

"If you are dissatisfied, tell us; if you are satisfied, tell others." This is a very good message to convey to customers.

Offer of adjustment is used as a strategy for sales and for collections. Customers are offered goods/ services, and adjustment in case they are not fully satisfied. Customers who have not placed orders for a long time are asked if they are dissatisfied with products/ services; they may be won back by this offer.

Customers who have not paid their dues and not explained the delay in payment, are asked if they are not satisfied with the goods/services provided; it is a useful argument in persuading them to pay or explain.

Drafting an Adjustment Letter

Whether the claim is to be granted or not, the letter must follow certain principles in order to fulfil its function of maintaining good customer relations.

Customer is King; the letter must reflect the seller's respect for the customer's feelings and needs. When your customer finds something wrong with your goods or services, his/her confidence in you may be a little shaken; your reply to his/her complaint must restore the confidence. The customer may be feeling angry and cheated at not getting what he/she had expected for the money; your reply should regain any lost goodwill.

The Adjustment letter must first express regret for the inconvenience caused; it must state what is being done, speedily, to put matters right, no matter whose fault it was and then explain why things went wrong. You must have a proper frame of mind and a positive attitude for writing a good adjustment letter.

First of all, you must take an objective attitude to error; you must be able to:

(i) locate the error; find out where it occurred and who was responsible for it;

(ii) control the error; know what steps to take in order to put matters right speedily, and also know how to prevent such mistakes from occurring again;

(iii) forgive the error; use courteous words, and show human consideration while mentioning or describing the cause of the error, and not accuse either employees, associate businessmen, suppliers or the customer.

Secondly, be helpful and sympathetic. Sometimes, a customer who makes a complaint has the fear that he himself may be at fault.

If you re-assure him about using the product properly and help him to understand how to avoid trouble and get the best service, he will appreciate it. Use "You" attitude to get a favourable emotional response from the customer, for example,

- *You will get trouble-free service from the copier if you allow it to be used only by trained persons.*
- *You will not be inconvenienced in future, if you let us know in advance, the address of the place where you want the goods delivered.*

Thirdly, remember that the inconvenience is always suffered by the customer, no matter whose fault it was. It is the customer who has a broken-down machine to deal with, or damaged goods occupying space, or some other problem on account of not getting what was needed. It is therefore important to assure the customer about what action is being taken to reduce the inconvenience.

The question of who bears the loss is not to be confused with who takes action to satisfy the customer's need; the supplier must take the action to ensure the customer's satisfaction with the goods.

While answering claims,

DO NOT —

1. — say "your complaint", "you claim that", or "you complain that"; these are unpleasant phrases. Say, "your request for explanation" or "misunderstanding."
2. — express surprise on learning of the customer's dissatisfaction; you sound as if you doubted the customer if you say, "We are surprised to learn that you are not satisfied with our service." Also, it is rude to say that such an error has never occurred before, and that no other customer has complained. The customer will resent this attitude to his problem.
3. — pass on the blame to someone else, such as employee or carrier; admit any error on the part of the company without trying to avoid responsibility for it.

4. — repeat any ugly details of a mistake which the customer might have given; a customer may have complained that she found "two dead spiders in the packet of corn flakes," but if the reply repeats it saying, "We are sorry to learn that you found two dead spiders in one of our packets of corn flakes," the customer is needlessly reminded of it.
5. — give details of any confusion which might have led to unsatisfactory work. It is better not to tell the customer what a fine mess there was.
6. — sound unwilling or patronizing when granting an adjustment; the customer is not asking for favours; he only wants justice. Making the customer feel humiliated in any way will create ill-will.
7. — try to explain a refusal by saying that "company policy" does not allow it. The customer has the right to know why the claim is refused.
8. — make a promise that a fault will never occur again. The letter must assure the customer that steps have been taken to prevent the repetition of such errors.

Review

Are these statements true?

(a) Customers' complaints are a great inconvenience to a seller.

(b) A reply to a complaint must make every effort to regain the customer's confidence.

(c) "We are surprised to learn that you are not satisfied with our services" is a good sentence to begin a reply to a complaint.

(d) "We are sorry that we cannot help you in this matter" is a friendly way to end a letter.

(e) A reply to a complaint should always end with "Assuring you of our best services at all times."

Types of Adjustment Letters

Letters of adjustment may be classified as follows:

1. Granting customer's claim
2. Refusing customer's claim
3. Offering a compromise (partial adjustment)
4. Apologizing for errors when the damage cannot be put right
5. Stop-gap letter informing the customer that investigation is being made.
6. Offering to make adjustment on the assumption that the customer is dissatisfied
7. Answering a complaint in readers' grievances column.

Letters that grant customer's claim

A claim is granted when there is a fault in the execution of the order or the goods are defective or damaged.

Points

1. Express regret and sympathy for the customer's inconvenience
2. State the adjustment being made and what is being done to reduce the inconvenience

3. Briefly explain the error and the steps taken to control it
4. Show appreciation of customer's co-operation in maintaining standards.

> Dear Madam,
>
> We dispatched, today, 20 sets of Bone China Glassware to replace the damaged ones which you received on 31 January. We are sorry for the inconvenience caused to you.
>
> Temporary employees had been entrusted with the packing of the earlier consignment owing to a rush of orders and high pressure of work in the packing department. This time the packing has been done by the usual, experienced persons. Besides, more supervisors have been appointed to oversee the packing work.
>
> Please accept our apologies for this trouble and delay in getting your goods.
>
> Yours truly,

Review

Say whether these statements are true or false.

(a) A letter granting an adjustment should always promise that such a problem will never arise again.

(b) You should give a long and detailed explanation of the cause of the problem in order to convince the customer of your sincerity.

(c) A customer with a complaint is mainly interested in knowing what you are doing about his/her problem.

Letters that refuse customer's claim

Take a positive attitude even when you are refusing something. Refusing an adjustment means convincing the customer that the repair or replacement cost will have to be borne by the customer. You can never refuse service to the customer although you may not agree to bear the cost. It is poor customer relations to refuse to do any work such as repairing, or delivering goods again. You must willingly agree to render the service and explain why the customer will have to pay for it.

Points:

1. Express regret for the customer's inconvenience
2. State what the investigation shows as cause of the trouble
3. Politely explain that the customer must bear the cost of repair or replacement
4. Offer to repair, and reassure the customer that his trouble will be removed, make every effort to retain goodwill.

> Dear Mr. Thomas,
>
> We are sorry that you have missed your favourite TV programmes these two days because of the poor reception of the set you bought from us six months ago.
>
> Our mechanic has examined the TV set and found that it has been opened and some parts have been replaced. The replaced parts are not of standard quality and the repair work seems to have been done inexpertly. It is true that our TV sets are guaranteed

for five years against defective material or workmanship, but the guarantee ceases to be valid if the TV set has been repaired by unauthorized persons. We shall repair your TV set and replace the parts which have been changed; the cost of the parts will be Rs.—. There will be no charge for the work. It will take only one hour to complete the repair work.

The repair work will be done by the mechanic who brings you this letter, on receiving your instructions.

Yours sincerely,

Dear Mrs. Iyer,

We were sorry to learn from your letter dated 28 September, that the PC you bought from us in April has not been working properly.

Our service engineer, Mr. Srinivasan has examined it and found that there is extensive corruption of some of the files. The PC seems to have been used for playing games downloaded from some websites on the internet.

A PC used for business purpose should not be used for playing games; besides, downloading material from websites is definitely dangerous. It has been our experience that users of PC for entertainment do not take as much care as business users do, and files get corrupted and infected by virus in a PC used for playing games.

It will be necessary to carry out a de-virus operation; it will take about six hours and will be done on your premises, by our service engineer Mr. Srinivasan. The cost of the operation will be Rs. ____.

Please ensure that you use only your own floppies and do not allow any floppies from outside to be used by unauthorized persons. Also, it is advisable to keep the computer locked and inaccessible when your work is completed. This way it will remain free of any virus.

Our engineer will visit your office on Friday, 5 October to clean out the virus. Please confirm the appointment by telephone.

Yours sincerely,

Review

Fill in the blanks:

(a) When the customer is at fault and the claim is refused, the letter must convince him/her that — .

(b) Even if the claim is refused, the seller must offer to —.

(c) A good beginning for a letter refusing a claim would be "—

(d) "We are surprised by your complaint..." is a poor beginning because — and — (two faults in the sentence).

Letters that offer a compromise or a partial adjustment

A compromise is offered when there is a difference of opinion about the standard of service or quality of goods, or when the cause of the complaint was outside the control of either party, and not covered by insurance. It is done in order to maintain good relations and, sometimes, to avoid litigation.

Points:

1. Express regret that the customer has been inconvenienced
2. Explain the cause of the grievance and state the adjustment being offered
3. Make efforts to get the customer's agreement.

Dear Mr. Biswas,

We are sorry to learn from your letter of 20 July that four of the wall clocks in our shipment of 6 July were received in a damaged condition.

Ordinarily, we should replace any goods which a customer has received in a damaged condition. However, claims for damaged goods have to be made within seven days of the receipt of the shipment. When claims are made within seven days, we can make a counter claim on the transport company which is, in most cases, responsible for the damage.

Although we cannot replace the clocks in this case, we shall make the required repairs, charging you only 50% of the cost of repair. Our representative will collect the damaged clocks from your office this week.

We are sorry that you have been inconvenienced; we assure you that the clocks will be put into first class condition again.

Yours sincerely,

Letters of apology for irreparable loss

There are some unfortunate situations when an error is discovered too late for any adjustment to be possible. A customer orders goods for a special occasion and the goods reach him after the event; an important customer is treated discourteously by a clerk and you find out about it only after the customer has given a large assignment/contract to your competitor. Getting back the offended customer is a salvage operation. There is no hard and fast rule by which it can be done. Writing a letter of apology in such a situation needs tact, sincerity and humility.

Points:

1. Express regret for the customer's inconvenience and thank him for pointing out the error
2. Assure the customer that every care will be taken to prevent such errors
3. Request the customer to give the company another chance.

Dear Sir,

We are extremely sorry that the 5000 pairs of sunglasses you had ordered for 3 April reached you on the 5th. Please accept our apologies.

The sunglasses were packed and handed over to the transport agent on the 29th, but there was a flash strike of truck drivers which caused the transport to be delayed by 2 days. The goods were held up in transit.

We understand that this delay has cost you an excellent opportunity, and sincerely regret that we were not able to help. We must thank you for giving us this opportunity to explain our position.

> Since you do not wish to retain the sunglasses, we are collecting the consignment. Please hand it over to the bearer of this letter.
>
> We earnestly hope that there will be another opportunity, soon, for us to do business together.
>
> Yours faithfully,

Letters informing customer that claim is being examined

When a customer complains of non-delivery or delay in delivery of goods, or delivery in a damaged condition, you check in your office to see if anything went wrong. You may find that the goods left the company premises on time, and properly packed. The source of the trouble is outside your office (for example, the transport agency) and you have to take up the matter with a third party.

The customer cannot be kept waiting while you investigate and recover compensation from the carrier or any other party responsible for the problem. It is essential to take immediate steps to reduce the customer's inconvenience, and to write to the customer at once, informing him about it.

Any dispute as to who is to bear the loss can be settled after investigation is completed; meanwhile, business arrangements must not be allowed to get upset.

Points:

1. Express regret for the inconvenience caused and state what steps are being taken to reduce customer's inconvenience
2. Explain that the error is probably caused by a third party and is being looked into
3. Advise the customer if he has to take any action and what he should do with the damaged consignment.

> Dear Madam,
>
> We are sorry to learn that you have been inconvenienced because the sewing machine that you bought from us last month would not run properly.
>
> Our mechanic will visit you this Saturday at 11 a.m. to examine the machine. If there is any minor adjustment he will make it. In case there is any major work to be done, we shall let you know when we get the mechanic's report.
>
> Please be assured that everything will be done to see that you have a machine that is perfectly satisfactory.
>
> Yours faithfully,

Letters offering adjustment on the assumption that customer is dissatisfied

Offer of adjustment can be used as a strategy to regain a lost customer. Before trying to persuade the customer to buy, it is better to make sure that the customer has had no cause for dissatisfaction. Many customers do not tell the seller when they are dissatisfied; they simply go to another seller. In this letter, ask the customer if he has had any reason to be displeased, and offer to make any suitable adjustment.

Points:

1. Express regret that the customer's orders have been missed for a period of time
2. Ask for the reason for not buying, and offer to make satisfactory adjustment if there is a grievance
3. Persuade the customer to respond.

It is better to write these letters to a particular person, by name, rather than to the company. You can give the letter a personal touch if you write to an individual.

Dear Mr. Gohil,

I am sorry that we have missed your orders for the last three months.

Have we given you any reason to be dissatisfied with our goods or services? If so, please tell us and we shall be only too glad to make an adjustment. After all, business depends on long standing customers who not only buy and pay but also tell us when we err.

May I expect your reply within a week in the enclosed self-addressed envelope?

Yours sincerely,

Dear Mr. Gupta,

You will agree that it is poor business to let a long standing customer stray. You follow him if, after a reasonable period, he does not buy again.

You have not placed orders with us for a long time and we are beginning to fear that this may be due to some fault of ours. If so, we are anxious to take steps to put matters right.

Won't you please help us by answering the questions on the attached check-list? A stamped self-addressed envelope is enclosed for you to return the check-list.

Yours sincerely,

Offer of adjustment can also be used as a part of the strategy to collect overdue payments. You can send a letter to the debtor asking whether he has withheld payment because he has a complaint about the goods/services. These letters are discussed in the chapter on Collection Letters.

Review

1. Are these statements true?

(a) If a complaint has been caused by the negligence or fault of a third party, the seller should deny all liability in the reply to the customer's complaint.

(b) If the nature of a customer's complaint is such that it cannot be adjusted (e.g. the event is already over), there is nothing you can do to win back the customer's goodwill.

(c) In an adjustment letter, how you talk about the error is crucial to the effectiveness of the letter.

2. Fill in the blanks:
   (a) Writing a letter offering to make adjustment assuming that the customer is dissatisfied is a good strategy for dealing with — and —.
   (b) A dissatisfied customer is — for the seller; therefore a customer's complaint must be given—.

EXERCISES

Complaints

1. Tropical Fruits Company, Fruit Exporting Agents, placed an order with Sunripe Products, for 5,000 tins of Mango Pulp to be sent to a customer in China. On receiving the consignment they find that some tins are dented and some are punctured. Draft their letter to the supplier.
2. Sparkle Steel Goods Manufactures have found that knives manufactured from the material supplied by Brite Steel Suppliers, have rusted and caused dissatisfaction among their customers. Draft their letter claiming compensation.
3. Twice within the last six months you have received bills for goods for which you had paid cash. Write to the supplier.
4. Some steel cupboards and filing cabinets which you had ordered for your office have been delivered to your office in a damaged condition. You have reason to believe that they were carelessly handled while being transferred from the trucks to your office rooms. Write asking the supplier to get the goods repaired immediately and claiming compensation.
5. Deluxe Decorators were given a contract for the renovation of your computer class premises in a month's time. The work was completed one month late and the lighting arrangement is uneven. Write to the Decorators expressing dissatisfaction with the work and your intention to charge a penalty for the late completion of the work.
6. You placed an urgent order for office stationery, and the supplier promised to deliver the goods in 24 hours. They have not been delivered even two days later. Draft a letter to be faxed to the supplier.
7. Write to your supplier claiming compensation for shortage in a consignment of computer paper which you have just received. Give full details.
8. You have paid Rs 2,500/ for an annual maintenance contract with the firm from which you purchased a P.C. for your office. You find their service very poor; they do not send their engineer in spite of repeated telephone calls and letters. Write to the Customer Service Manager expressing your dissatisfaction with the service.
9. The trucks of a factory next to your office are parked in front of your gate, causing inconvenience to your staff and customers. Write to the manager of the factory, pointing out the problem and requesting his co-operation.
10. Write a letter to the Manager of a bank, complaining to him of the rude behaviour of the cashier. Inform him of your long standing as a depositor.
11. You placed a large order for art paper with Bombay Paper Mart. The quality of the paper supplied by them is inferior to that of the sample shown. Write a complaint letter, stating that you will be compelled to cancel the contract if they do not supply paper of the required quality.

12. After your Annual Social Gathering at Shalimar Hall, the Manager has sent you a bill for damage to seats. Draft a letter refusing to pay the bill, stating that the seats had been damaged earlier, and you had pointed out the damaged seats to the officer on duty when you took charge of the hall.
13. As a retailer, write a letter to the manufacturer, informing him that a large number of customers have complained about defects in the electric kettles supplied two weeks ago. Ask for suitable redress.
14. Premier Plastics write to Modern Graphic Art Printers that they are not satisfied with the first lot of their print order for catalogues which have been delivered. The catalogues have been printed on old paper. They are returning the stock and intend to cancel the entire order unless all the copies of the catalogue are printed on good quality paper.
15. ABC Building Contractors had ordered 500 tons of cement with specific instructions that it was to be delivered in 20-ton lots every three days, beginning on 10 October. Work was started with the arrival of the first lot, but although a week has passed, further supplies have not arrived. Write as from the contractors asking for immediate supplies and asking for an explanation of the slackness in executing their order.

Adjustments

1. Golden Square Housekeeping Equipment delivered a microwave oven to a customer a fortnight ago. She now claims that the oven was delivered in a damaged condition and demands a new one. Write a tactful reply as from Golden Square Housekeeping Equipment explaining why this is not possible.
2. Mr. Sohail Kapadia bought a video camera from you five months ago. He now claims that it is defective and asks for an exchange. Inspection shows that it has been carelessly handled. Write a suitable letter to the customer.
3. An organization whose staff you regularly train in using computers has suddenly sent its staff to be trained at a competitor's institute. Inquiries with your staff reveal that one of your new employees had been rude to the trainees during a training program. As proprietor of the computer institute, write to the Training Manager of the organization, trying to win back his goodwill.
4. A retail agent of Spry Hair Driers has written to the manufacturer that several customers have complained about the product in the last two months and demanded replacements. On investigation the manufacturer finds that there is a defect in one of the machines in the factory which caused the hair driers to be defective. Draft a suitable reply from the manufacturer to the retailer.
5. A customer has returned a bill stating that he has been charged for goods that were not delivered to him. Draft a letter to be sent with the corrected bill.
6. Blue Diamond Interiors have inspected the renovation work carried out by them in a Computer Centre on receiving a complaint about the work. They agree that the lighting is uneven and they will rectify it. But they do not accept liability for delay in completing the work because rains and moist weather had delayed the drying of the plaster and the paints. However, to avoid litigation, they are prepared to submit to a penalty of Rs. 50,000/-. Draft the letter.

7. Write a conciliatory letter to a customer who has complained that she received poor treatment when she visited in your office a few days before.
8. Messrs. Philip and Sons receive an angry letter from a lady customer who purchased a frost-free refrigerator five months ago. She claims that the refrigerator is a defective piece and has demanded a new one. Your technician has examined the refrigerator and reported that the settings have been repeatedly and carelessly changed over the last three months. Draft a tactful reply explaining why exchange is not possible.
9. You have received a complaint about the quality of answer books supplied to Presidency College, for their examination work. Your investigation shows that the complaint is baseless. Draft the reply.
10. A company which organizes its conferences in your conference room regularly, has complained about poor service during their last conference. Draft a reply as from the Customer Relations Manager.
11. A customer who had bought a washing machine from you three months ago has complained that it is defective, and demanded that it should be exchanged. Examination of the machine shows that the washing programme has been constantly changed midway during the process, thus causing damage to the programming system. Draft a reply explaining that the machine cannot be exchanged.
12. The Manager of a firm, which has an account in your bank, has complained that his peon is kept waiting when he is sent for the firm's bank work. Draft the banker's reply stating that generally, all counter transactions are completed without delay; explain why the peon had to wait for some time on some occasions.
13. An agent for pharmaceutical products has received a letter from the manufacturer complaining about the decline in the sale of the company's medicines in his region. Write a reply explaining that the decline has been due to the delay in receiving supplies from the manufacturer.
14. An important regular guest of your hotel has taken his annual conference to another hotel this year. Enquiries with your staff reveal that one of your new employees had been rude to him on his last visit to your hotel. As Guest Relations Manager of the hotel, write to the customer, trying to win back his goodwill.
15. A customer who had ordered a large quantity of flowers for the celebration of the office anniversary angrily telephoned to say that 6 of the 20 bouquets received were crushed. You sent 6 fresh bouquets, immediately. Draft a letter to be sent the next day, explaining the situation, taking care to emphasize the positive aspects.
16. You have received a letter from a customer, complaining that the carpet she has received for her drawing room does not match the sample shown to her. Write a tactful reply explaining that different lots / batches have a slight variation of colour in woollen carpets, and persuading her to accept the carpet at a reasonable discount as it has already been cut to the dimensions of her drawing room.

❑❑❑

Chapter **25**

COLLECTION LETTERS

Collection letters are written to customers who have purchased on credit and not paid their bill on the due date. Some debtors pay immediately on receiving a reminder, others may need to be pursued with a series of messages. Telephone calls, telegrams, fax and e-mail messages and personal visits are used in addition to letters. Most companies have a collection policy and procedure to be followed.

A collection letter has to do two jobs: get the money and retain the customer's goodwill. In order to do this, you need a good understanding of the particular customer, knowledge of how the customer usually handles his credit account, and knowledge of his present circumstances.

COLLECTION SERIES

Collection letters are written in a series. Most persons finally take action if they are reminded often enough, and with increasing pressure. A series makes it possible to increase pressure gradually and gently, from letter to letter. The collection series is both persuasive and constructive; it sells the customer the idea that it is to his own advantage to settle the account. The series allows you to try several approaches that may be suitable to a particular customer's nature and circumstances. Debtors are of several types and the reasons for non-payment can be many; the series can break down the reasons one by one. There is no point in assuming the worst reason for non-payment at the start. It is better to begin with a gentle approach and make every effort to save the relationship even if the customer must be finally lost.

Reasons for non-payment and types of debtors can be listed roughly in ascending order; the letters can tackle each one separately.

Group 1

1. Easy-going; forgets to pay
2. Very busy; overlooks payments
3. Muddled and cannot keep track
4. Has plenty of money; cannot understand that others need it
5. Kind-hearted/indulgent; cannot manage affairs/ employees

Group 2

6. Dissatisfied with goods/services; will not pay because he is angry
7. Troubled by sickness/misfortune; cannot pay because of temporary lack of money
8. Large buyer; thinks he is entitled to take time
9. Takes all the time possible; has other uses for his money
10. Has too many credit obligations and is not very particular about all of them

Group 3

11. Will pay only to avoid losing his credit reputation
12. Will pay only when frightened
13. Will pay only when convinced that he must, in order to avoid trouble.

The three groups roughly correspond to the three stages of the collection series. The first group will respond to repeated reminders with increasing insistence; this part of the series is the Reminder Stage. The second group has a variety that must be matched with a varied approach; it may not be necessary to go through every approach for every customer; this stage of the series is elastic and it may be shortened or lengthened by using less of more letters; this is the Enquiry-Appeal Stage. The last group is composed of tough people who will not yield easily to persuasion; with them the hard line is the only way, but you may still try to save the customer; this is the Warning-Threat Stage. A company usually tries to save its customers and will avoid coming to the last stage as long as possible. Besides, legal action is an expensive and bothersome process. Only very large debts are worth collecting by legal action; small bad debts are written off.

The number of letters to be written to a particular debtor will depend upon the company's collection policy and on the kind of risk the customer represents. The series, as well as each letter in the series, must be customized to match the circumstances and the nature of the particular customer.

Timing the Collection Series

Timing is an important factor in the success of the collection effort. The strongest pressure to pay should be applied at the time when the customer's business is in its best season and the highest profits are being made. For example, the owner of a book-shop selling textbooks has the best business in June-July; the owner of a hill-station hotel makes the greatest profit in April-May. It is expected that when there are profits the dues will be paid. If they are not paid at the best time, it is likely that they will not be paid unless persistent demands are made by the creditor.

The intervals between the letters can be arranged in such a way that the last three letters of the enquiry-appeal stage are sent when the customer has his best season. The number of letters to be used for a particular customer can also be decided according to the time available so as to reach the high pressure stage at the right time.

In the case of customers who do not have a seasonal business, the creditor has to decide how much time to allow a particular customer, and how fast he will come to the highest pressure point.

WRITING OF COLLECTION LETTERS

All collection letters can be written on this pattern:

1. Express regret that the account is still unsettled; refer to amount of bill, due date and reminders already sent
2. Try to persuade the customer to pay, (main argument depending on the stage)
3. Motivate action (enclose stamped envelope/ fix date for payment/ pointedly state customer's advantage etc.)

Collection letters must be written with care. Here are things to avoid:

DO NOT —

1. — be insincere in any of the arguments used.
2. — anger the customer by using "red pepper" words like neglect, ignore, fail, careless, debt, which hurt the customer's feelings.
3. — humiliate the customer by appearing superior.
4. — ever use dead commercial jargon phrases; collection letters are personal; ready-made phrases will never do.
5. — suggest two alternative actions at the end of the letter. If offered a choice between two actions, the reader often postpones the decision.

Reminder Stage

This stage can be lengthened by increasing the number of reminders and/or the interval between the reminders.

The **first** reminder is sent within a week of the bill or its duplicate copy. It may be a form letter which has the advantage of looking like mere routine with no personal implication.

A **second** reminder may be sent in a week or in a fortnight; this is a personal reminder that the bill has been rendered, and indicates expectation that it will be paid soon.

> Dear Sir,
>
> Your account today shows an unpaid balance of Rs.—. It is not a large sum, so we thought you had probably over-looked it.
>
> Will you remit the amount today?
>
> Yours faithfully

The following is another example, written in a different style.

Dear Ms Maya Patel,

This is a quick reminder to let you know that your account with us is past due. The amount of Rs. 3550.00 for services rendered on February 6, 2005 was due on March 15, 2005 per invoice number 2345. Please pay this amount by March 30, 2005 to avoid late payment penalties.

If you have already sent payment for this invoice, please disregard this letter and accept our thanks for your payment. We appreciate doing business with you and look forward to doing so in the future.

Yours sincerely,

V.R. Bizzmen

The **third** reminder is more pointed and urges the customer to settle his account early. The writer assumes that the customer has forgotten because of the pressure of business.

Dear Sir,

We reminded you earlier that your account is past due, as shown in the enclosed statement. We have not received the payment yet. May we remind you again to send your cheque as soon as possible?

If you have already sent your cheque, please accept our thanks and ignore this reminder.

Yours faithfully,

Another example of reminder letter which offers to co-operate if the customer has a problem.

Dear Ms Maya Patel,

This is the second reminder to inform you that your account with us is still past due. On March 20, I sent you a notice requesting payment for invoice number 2345 by March 30.

Since we did not receive your payment we have charged Rs. 50.00 late payment penalty to your account. You now owe Rs. 3660.00.

Please pay this amount immediately to avoid further penalties.

If there is a reason why you cannot make this payment immediately, please call me to work out a suitable payment schedule. I look forward to hearing from you.

Sincerely yours,

Humorous Collection Letters

Stunt collection letters are a part of the reminder stage. If there is no response after two or three reminders, you may try a letter with an out-of-the-way approach to get attention; an unusual letter has a better chance of getting a response. The letter may be unusual in its content or its layout. Collection letters can use the tricks and stunts of sales letters. The attention device may be anything like a picture, coloured paper or type, or a little article enclosed with the letter.

One picture is worth a thousand words. You can effectively use a little cartoon or any graphics; some ideas for this are given below:

* A picture of a man emptying the contents of a drawer or a waste paper basket; letter reading: *We're searching for your cheque everywhere.*
* A picture of a very fat man; the letter reads: *It's harder to reduce as we get older.—Yours sincerely, Old Bill.*
* A picture of a sailing ship dangerously out of balance; message reads: *S.O.S. Help! Most valuable asset aboard.*

A small object may serve as a good reminder when properly connected with the message.

* A rubber-band enclosed with a letter reading: *Stretch the rubber-band to this —x point and it will snap back, brand new. But stretch it to this—————— x point and S-N-A-P! Credit is like a rubber-band: you cannot stretch it beyond a point.*
* A small coin enclosed with a letter reading: *It's said, Money attracts money; we're sending this penny to attract your cash to pay our bill.*

Other devices include variation of the shape, size and colour of the paper, or the message of the letter.

* Typed on a letterhead ¼ of the usual size: *Your account is so small that we are sending this very small message to remind you of it.*
* Typed on a letterhead 4 times the usual size: *We're trying to make this silent messenger shout to get your attention to the bill.*
* Typed in red: *Help!—*

  — *Help us to get your account out of the red.*

Stunt collection letters are to be used with caution; use them only when you know that humour will be appreciated by the particular customer. Although humour is very valuable in business, it may not be appreciated by conservative customers.

Review

1. Are these statements true?

   (a) If a customer does not pay his dues, he should be immediately threatened with legal action.

   (b) It is possible to use humour in collecting debts.

   (c) You should try to keep the customer's goodwill even if the customer has to be reminded often, to pay his dues.

2. Fill in the blanks using as few words as possible.

   (a) Advantages of a writing collection letters in a series are:

   (i) —

   (ii) —

   (iii) —

   (b) Giving a choice of action at the end of the letter is not effective because —.

Enquiry-Appeal Stage

At this stage, the tone becomes serious and each letter has a definite argument for payment. The letters get progressively more insistent and there is a close connection between one argument and the next.

This stage has two aspects: first to ask about the customer's satisfaction and see if s/he has any problems with the products/services or with the business; and second to appeal to the customer's pride, sense of honour and sense of fear to motivate him/her to pay.

1. Enquiring about the customer's satisfaction: This serves a three-fold purpose: (i) it compels the difficult, 'silent' customer to say something; (ii) it makes sure that the customer does not complain later, about the product/service; (iii) it conveys the message of "customer first".

> Dear Sir,
>
> Our letters of the 10th and 18th, calling attention to our bill of Rs. 100,000 have not brought any reply from you. We are afraid that you might have some reason to be dissatisfied with our goods or services, and this probably keeps you from settling the account. If so, please let us know and we shall be glad to make a suitable adjustment. We want you to feel sure that you can buy from us with satisfaction.
>
> If, on the other hand, you are satisfied with our execution of your order, please send us the payment so that your account may be fresh for your next order. May we expect your reply within this week?
>
> Yours faithfully,

2. Enquiring about the customer's state of affairs: This has to be done tactfully. If some problem (like losses) affects the business, the customer may be embarrassed, and not willing to tell the creditor. It is useful to assume that the customer is anxious to be free from the debt; you can offer to help by accepting payment in installments or accepting return of any goods that the customer finds difficult to sell or use. Your desire to help must be strongly stressed.

> Dear Sir,
>
> Since you have not replied to our letter of the 25th asking whether you are satisfied with our goods, we assume that everything was all right. Our bill of Rs. 100,000, however, still remains unpaid.
>
> We are quite willing to accept payment by installments, if you are a little burdened at the moment. As a business associate, please do not hesitate to tell us if you are facing difficulties in disposing of the goods; we can also help by accepting back some unsold goods if you wish to return them. In any case, it would benefit both of us if you told us what the trouble is, so that we could together work out a plan for the settlement of the account without too much strain on resources. We are sure you will communicate with us so that we can tide over temporary difficulties in co-operation.
>
> Yours faithfully,

3. Appealing to sense of customer's sense of fairness: If offers to adjust and to help, both fail, an appeal to the customer's sense of honour may bring a response. Normally, a debtor would feel a little ashamed to misuse the trust placed in him by the creditor, and is likely to respond to an appeal to his sense of honour.

The essence of the argument is to point out that although you have done your part of the transaction satisfactorily, the debtor has not done his part. Such a long extension of time taken by the debtor is also not fair to other customers who pay on time. Besides, interest goes on accumulating if the payment is delayed. The following letter illustrates the use of some of these arguments.

> Dear Sir,
>
> We are sorry to see that you have not replied to our letters asking for payment of our bill of Rs. 100,000, outstanding since 20 March.
>
> You will agree that the bill is long overdue. We delivered your goods to your satisfaction but you have not done your part of the transaction with equal promptness. Usually, we do not extend credit for more than three months and in allowing your account to remain unsettled for so long we have been unfair to other customers from whom we collect payments in three months. Besides, you are not being fair to your own name as a reputed businessman, in this delay. We do hope that you will live up to your reputation and settle your account this week.
>
> Yours faithfully,

4. **Appealing to self-interest:** Some debtors may not be affected at all by appeals to honour; a harder line has to be tried with them. An appeal to self-interest may be effective. The success of the letter using this appeal depends on the fear aroused; the fear of losing credit may move such debtors to pay. This appeal can be used in letters of varying degrees of firmness as the following examples show.

> Dear Sir,
>
> We are surprised at your silence about our bill of Rs. 100,000/- due since 20 March, in spite of our several letters.
>
> Until now, all was well and our bills were paid promptly. Surely, at least an explanation of this delay is due to us. Non-payment combined with silence does not inspire confidence in creditors, as you must know from your own experience. Besides, creditors are sometimes asked to supply confidential information about their customers, and we would hardly know what to say if we were to be asked about your handling of your credit account with us. Please send your cheque in the enclosed envelope, so that your credit with us will remain clear as before.
>
> Yours faithfully,

Dear Sir,

We are really uncomfortable about your indifference to our letters about our outstanding bill of Rs.100,000/- for goods supplied in January.

This delay is not doing any good to your credit reputation and you know how difficult is to build up a good one. Will you now allow your credit to be tarnished by just ignoring our requests for payment?

We hope that you will not create an awkward situation by remaining silent even after receiving this letter. We are expecting your cheque by return of post.

Yours truly,

Warning-Threat Stage

When all appeals fail to bring any response from the debtor, the collection series enters the last stage. This stage is rigid, and can be extended to three letters, at the most. The **first** letter pleads with the debtor to settle the account and avoid legal action; no date may be set for the legal action. The **second** letter fixes the date for legal action but allows a period of time for the debtor to pay the bill. The **last** letter merely tells the debtor that the account has been handed over to the company's lawyer.

The tone and style of these letters varies considerably; the only fixed and inviolable rule is, never to forget courtesy.

Letter warning that legal action is contemplated

Dear Mr. Ghosh,

We have begun to feel that our judgement of you was too generous; you have maintained complete silence about our bill of Rs. 100,000/- in spite of every kind of effort we made to elicit some response from you.

If for any reason you were unable to pay, you would surely have informed us in order to protect your credit. But you have left us only one course of action — legal. That will be tiresome and expensive for both of us.

It is now in your hands to save the situation by sending your cheque within five days.

Yours sincerely,

Letter setting date for legal action

Dear Sir,

We have written to you repeatedly, calling your attention to your unsettled account of Rs. 100,000/- but unfortunately have not received any response.

We are sorry to inform you that, unless the account is settled by 30 May, we shall be compelled to place the matter in the hands of our solicitors.

We hope that you will not force us to take this unpleasant step.

Yours faithfully,

The following is a more personalized letter dealing with the same situation.

August 17, 2004

Mr. Dinesh Mane
150 Ambala Avenue
Pune 410 022

Hand Delivered By Courier

Dear Mr. Mane,

Final Notice: Invoice 168-04 – April 11, 2005 – Rs. 87,750.00

We regret that you have repeatedly ignored our written requests for payment of the above-noted invoice and you have not contacted us with any explanation.

Consequently, unless we receive payment in full by the end of the business day, August 31, 2005 we will have to take the unpleasant step of turning your account over to a professional collection agency. We would rather not be forced to do this since it will result in damage to your personal credit rating.

To prevent us from taking the final step of turning this matter over to a collection agency, could you please make payment in full by the end of the business day, Tuesday, August 31, 2005.

We urge you to please give this matter your full attention now, before it is too late, and send your payment to us immediately.

Sincerely yours,

B. R. Rangan
Accounts Manager

Final letter informing that account has been handed over for legal action

Note that the letter still makes a positive attempt to save the account.

Dear Sir,

You have not replied to our letters asking for a settlement 'of your account of Rs.100,000/-. It appears that you are not prepared to make a settlement.

We have today handed over your account to our lawyers for collection. However, we have instructed them to wait for four days before issuing you a legal notice.

We sincerely hope that you will take this opportunity offered and save both yourselves and us from irksome legal action. If your payment is received by Tuesday, we shall gladly instruct our solicitors not to proceed.

Yours faithfully,

Review

Fill in the blanks:

(a) It is useful to offer adjustment to a defaulting customer because —.

(b) The enquiry-appeal stage can be made shorter or longer by reducing or increasing — and —. Are these statements true?

(a) The warning-threat stage is flexible and can be lengthened.

(b) Letters in the final stage must be written courteously.

EXERCISES

1. Write a letter to a retail store reminding them that they have neither settled their account, nor replied to your earlier reminders. Offer to take installment payments to help them to settle the account.
2. One of your customers has failed to pay his dues in spite of several reminders. Write to him appealing to his sense of fairness and honour.
3. Messrs. D'Souza & Co. have not paid their bill of Rs. 50,000 although several casual reminders have been sent. Write to them to ask whether they have any complaint about your products or services.
4. All your reminders, requests and offers have failed to bring a reply from Messrs. Blank & Sons who owe you Rs. 1,000,000 for computers supplied three months ago. Write to them drawing their attention to their poor rating of their own credit reputation.
5. Draft a letter to Messrs. Mistry, Engineer & Co., firmly requesting payment of a bill of Rs. 300,000 for goods delivered some months ago. Make it clear that unless the bill is paid within a week, legal action might be the only solution.
6. A letter asking for immediate payment has been sent by mistake to a customer who has already settled his account in full. Write to him apologizing for the mistake.

Chapter 26

SALES LETTERS

Letters are commonly used for giving information about products/ services and persuading prospective customers to buy. With the use of computers the sales letter can be personalized to suit the needs and interests of selected groups or individual buyers. The letter is an extremely adaptable medium for contacting potential customers.

The sales letter is the most highly individualized form of advertising and publicity. It addresses an individual personally, and attempts to change the person into an interested, potential buyer. It is somewhat like a written sales presentation and follows the persuasion steps towards convincing.

STRUCTURE OF A SALES LETTER

The structure of a sales letter is designed to overcome the buying resistance that most people have. Customer comments, such as the following, indicate common buying resistance:

1. "You don't understand my problem"
2. "Why should I believe what you claim?"
3. "I don't need it just now"
4. "It won't work for me"
5. "What happens if I don't like it?"
6. "I can't afford it"

To be successful, a sales letter must address at least some of these objections. The sales letter closely follows the four stages of the selling process, viz.:

Attract attention

Create interest and desire

Win confidence

Motivate action

Each stage is a separate section and needs a different technique.

Attracting Attention

There are many ways of attracting attention. The attention device must be in the content and idea, and not just in the appearance. The attention must be favourable. The opening sentence must arouse curiosity and encourage the reader to read further.

You can use any of the following devices to grab attention.

(i) **Proverbs and quotations** from well-known writers are interesting for their pointed style which can focus attention at once.

- *It is the busiest man who has the time to spare. (to sell a book or a course on time management)*
- *"No pains, no gains" is an old proverb. But today's technology has taken the pains out of most things. (to sell any gadget)*
- *"Work expands so as to fill the time available for its completion." Since the formulation of this Parkinson's Law in 1958, busy executives, managers, students and career-pursuing house-wives have devised ways to expand time for the completion of work.*

(ii) **Striking information** often includes figures.

- *By the middle of the twenty-first century, India will have the largest population in the world. .*
- *The noise level in metro cities has already reached 95 decibels; the tolerance limit is 45 decibels.*
- *The number of road accidents in the city last month was 2,286 and 294 of them were fatal.*

(iii) **Stories and anecdotes** must be used with great care. In the first place, the story must be told in an interesting manner. Then, it must be related quickly to the product being sold and to the main appeal being used in the letter. Well-known animal stories, stories from mythology, anecdotes about well-known personalities, can be used effectively. You can also narrate an interesting experience like the following:

> Dear Professor,
>
> We once received the following application from a candidate. "With refrence to you adverteasement in "The times of India' for Acoints trainy, plise cunsider me..."
>
> Well, we did consider him.
>
> We sent him a copy of the Longman Dictionary of Contemporary English (LDOCE).
>
> Yours sincerely,

(iv) **Split opening** is a trick of layout. A statement or a question or a command, can be divided in such a way that the first few words are startling, though the sentence as a whole is simple. An unexpected negative idea in the first half of the sentence can make a good split opening.

* *You can't buy everything in the world —*
— but you CAN buy the best of some things.

* *Listen—*
— to the world's masters in music

* *Did you know that—*
—India has over one and a half million net users—
—and there will be over 8 million by 2007?

* *STOP——*
——gaining weight before it is too late.

* *Arrest—*
— declining sales.

(v) **A conditional sentence** can be exciting provided the suggested condition is a possibility within the reach of the reader. A conditional phrase can be used to begin *a statement, or a question, or a command.*

**If you have intelligent children, they will ask questions which adults never dream of.*

**If you want your office to function efficiently, it is not enough to have an efficient secretary.*

The conditional phrase can suggest uncomfortable possibilities and leave the rest to the reader's imagination by leaving the sentence incomplete.

* *If your mind goes blank in the middle of your examination...*

A comfortable situation may be suggested as dependent on a condition.

* *Performance is sure to be good if the preparation has been thorough.*

* *If you take care of the pence, the pounds will take care of themselves.*

Sentences beginning with **When** are effective for calling attention to a sure future event.

- When you complete your college education, you will find yourself in a highly competitive world.
- *When the vacation begins, why not visit some of the wild life places you saw on the Discovery and other Nature channels?*

(vi) **Questions** have the power to arouse thought; they set the mind thinking to find an answer. There are three types of questions; each type of question creates a different response in the reader's mind:

1. Questions beginning with a **Wh**- word require information to be given as answer.
2. Questions beginning with a helping verb like *can, would, are* require **yes** or **no** or **not sure** as answer.
3. Tag questions beginning as a statement and ending with a question tag ask for confirmation of the statement (e.g., You will write the CET exam, won't you?).

The question must be related to the reader's interest as well as to the product. Also, it should not provoke an unfavourable answer.

Which three places would you like to visit if you got a free trip as a prize?

(This requires the names of the three places as answer)

* *Will you be able to take a vacation this summer?*

(This requires **yes** or **no** or **not sure** as answer; it can make the reader conscious of the desire to take a vacation.)

* *You would like to take the family for a grand vacation this summer, wouldn't you?*

(This requires **yes** or **no** or **not sure** as answer, but also creates slight discomfort because the question expects the answer to be **yes**. A tag question clearly expects the suggested answer.)

A question can also be used with an **if**- or **when**- clause.

* *If you had to take the examination your daughter is taking, how good would your performance be?*
* *When you interview candidates for jobs in your office, what is the most important thing you look for?*

Striking information can be introduced by a question like:

* *Did you know that ....*
* *Have you considered that ....*

(vii) **A command** can startle the mind into thinking of something new; for example:

* *Take your ruler and mark off 1/1000 of an inch.*
* *Get the best out of your computer.*
* *Find the ten traffic hazards in the enclosed picture.*

To be effective, the command must ask for an action within the possible reach of the reader. Commanding the impossible, or something unrelated to normal life does not arouse interest unless you immediately show the possibility or the relation to normal life.

(viii) An **exclamation** is an expression of an impulsive feeling. In a sales letter, the exclamatory sentence must reflect the reader's feeling, not the writer's. For this, a situation has to be described so as to put the reader into imagined action. An exclamation may follow the description as an observation or a remark on the reader's projected situation.

Exclamations are colloquial, and suitable for conversational style. They are not of much use by themselves and are to be used very sparingly.

However, common feelings, suitable for the season or an annual event, may be put in the form of an exclamatory sentence:

* *Here comes the festival season!*
* *Three long power failures in the same fortnight!*

The function of the opening paragraph is to grab attention and arouse enough emotion to make the reader read further. It should be short and should lead at once to the next stage.

Review

1. Write down 3 products of your choice. Write an opening sentence to sell each of them. Use a different style for each one.

Creating Interest and Desire

You need an understanding of human desires and feelings, good knowledge of the product, and a clear mental picture of the prospective customer in order to develop an effective chain of interest, desire, confidence and willingness to buy (or at least try) your product/ service..

There are two things that really stimulate people: the hope of gain and the fear of loss. The fear of loss is the stronger of the two. Hope of gain and fear of loss are basic to common human desires. Whatever product/ service you are selling, you have to position it so that its benefits satisfy one or more of these universal desires.

- To be wealthy
- To look good
- To be healthy
- To be popular
- To achieve social status
- To have security
- To attain inner peace
- To have free time
- To have fun

In order to arouse interest and create desire, you can spell out the readers' problem and describe how it feels to have that problem. The reader should think, "Yes, that's exactly how I feel." Stir up the emotion further by vividly describing the pain and distress of enduring the problem. People are not willing to change fixed habits unless there is great pain.

After you have built up the readers' emotion by making them feel the pain, **provide the solution**. Make a confident statement that you can solve the problem. Introduce yourself and your product/ service. Relieve the readers' anxiety by showing that they need not struggle with their problem since your product/ service will solve it for them.

The reader may doubt your claim; therefore, include one or two short sentences to establish your credentials. Mentioning the names of one or two of your prestigious customers or the length of your experience in the field should be sufficient.

Show the benefits of the product/ service; tell the readers how they will personally benefit from it. Talk about the benefits first and most; talk later and less about the features of the product. People are more interested in what a product/ service will do for them, not so much in its features. Bullet point each benefit to make it easier to read.

Here is a useful exercise. Divide a sheet of paper into two, lengthwise. On the left side, write all the features of your product / service. On the right, write every possible benefit (the obvious and the not-so-obvious) of each feature.

Describe vividly, the pleasure and comfort of the benefits and of having the product/ service. The letter must make the reader feel that he needs the product.

The following paragraphs from sales letters illustrate methods of creating interest and desire.

- *This is a household reference book to which you will constantly refer to answer your children's questions, for help in entering contests, for writing letters, for following current events, for guidance in understanding important documents. It will explain technical terms, medical terms and legal terms so necessary for peace of mind amidst whirling, rapid developments in which, as citizens, we get involved.*
- *Everyone has an urge for movement. If you suppress this urge you become irritable, nervous, dull, or FAT. When you are tired, you stretch to get fresh blood into your muscles, or yawn heartily to fill your lungs with fresh air. When you are happy you want to run or dance. Muscles are crying out to be used, and insist on moving. Walking or week-end sport is not enough and does not call all the muscles equally or regularly into action. In fact, this irregular and sudden demand on muscles may prove shattering rather than constructive.*

The following vivid picture of the suffering of a sleepless night makes the reader conscious of the need for sound sleep and a comfortable night. Several products like a health tonic, a mattress and pillow, a cot, a blanket, an air conditioner, a room-freshener, night clothes, mosquito repellent and so on, may be sold by the appeal to the need for a comfortable night's sleep.

Why spend sleepless nights, tossing and turning in bed, wishing that the day would come? Why should you have to stay awake when some lucky people can put aside their day's tasks and drift happily into the land of dreams. Lack of sleep is known to lead to premature aging, blood pressure and other ailments besides making a person irritable and unable to concentrate.

Wake up bright and fresh in the morning, instead of just beginning to doze off when the alarm rings. Our course of Twelve Weekly Special Massages has helped hundreds of executives in such prestigious organizations as xxx and yyy to regain their night's restful sleep. You will begin to feel the difference within one week of the first massage.

The letter must show how the product can satisfy the aroused need. Information about the need-satisfying benefits of the product must be stated. The brand name of the product is used as often as possible, and is printed in capitals, in colour or in a distinctive type so that the name impresses itself on the reader's mind.

** In the old days they laid straw on the floor and at the doors to keep noise out of the sleeper's room. Now DREAM mattresses guard your sleep and your precious dreams from the world's disturbing noise. And DREAM remains a faithful guardian of your comfort all your life. It's a DREAM of a mattress.*

Fear of loss is an emotion that needs care in handling. The feeling of fear may become unconsciously associated with the source of the letter and thus give rise to unpleasant feelings towards the company and the product. Many people have a 'defensive' resistance to appeals to fear. It is better to hint at the danger and dramatize the reassuring aspect of the recommendation.

Review

1. In three sentences, describe what you miss if you do not have a calculator.
2. Explain in two sentences, why it is attractive for customers to take your holiday package.

Creating Conviction and Winning Confidence

While you present your solution and try to make readers accept what you say, they go through different emotions. The initial interest and desire for a product/ service gives place to strong doubts and uncertainty of different kinds and on different accounts.

The first doubt may be aimed outward at the seller and/or at the product. The reader may think of such questions as: Is the seller to be believed? Does the company support its product and stand by the buyers? Is the product really so good? durable? satisfactory? trouble-free? What about after-sales service? What if I find the product unsatisfactory?

The reader is likely to think, *"Yah, he thinks he can fix my problem. They all say that!"* Therefore, immediately present your credentials, that is, the reason why you can be trusted and the proof that your claims are true.

Evidence or proof of worth is of two types: (1) facts and (2) opinions.

Facts include:

- figures of sales
- medals, prizes and certificates won in competitions
- accreditation by certifying bodies such as Ag Mark, ISI mark, ISO 9002 certification
- results of tests made by independent bodies
- samples, demonstrations and trial offers
- cost of operating in case of machines.

The facts must be from a reliable source, they must be verifiable, and they must be clearly stated and shown to be relevant to the reader. What you say should make a clear impression that your products/ services have been successful and recognised, and that the reader can expect the same results.

Opinions of satisfied users add social proof. There may still be doubt in the readers' mind, even though they may secretly hope that the stated benefits are true. Some of the doubt is directed inward towards oneself by the reader: How does this fit into my life-style, my economic choices, my values and my budget? These doubts are personal; testimony of persons who are perceived as trustworthy as well as on level with oneself, is likely to be acceptable.

To build up credibility, present testimonials from satisfied customers. Letters of appreciation received from satisfied users are the best testimonials. You may get such letters from customers to whom you send after-sales letters.

Testimonials give proof of the truth of your claims. Testimonials are more powerful if you can include names and addresses and telephone numbers of customers. Most readers will not call up the given numbers, but it is a powerful statement to include customers' complete contact information. It shows that the testimonials are genuine. **Note, however, that this can only be done with permission of the concerned customers.**

Using too many points as proof of worth is not effective. Present just one or two relevant facts, strengthened, by an opinion. If the main appeal has been the desire for social status, figures of sales among people of social standing together with the opinion of a leading member of society will be effective.

The style must be business-like and rational. Here are some examples:

* Too good to be true? Even we thought so till we received the enclosed congratulatory letter from the well-known wrestler Black Sam who used our Trugrit Exerciser to build up his muscles and still uses it to keep them in shape.

* 'Sunripe' fruit sauce won a gold medal in the Dessert Sauces category at the International "Food for Health" Exhibition held in Bonn last year. And of course, our company has ISO 9002 certification.

* To substantiate these statements, I am enclosing our mailing list of customers in your locality. A number of them have written to us expressing their satisfaction with 'The Woman of Today' as the most comprehensive ladies' magazine.

* You need not take our word for it; or anybody's word, for that matter. A box, containing a sample bottle, is waiting to be sent to you as soon as we receive the enclosed postage-paid card with your signature on it.

Make Your Offer: Your offer is the most important part of your sales letter. Your offer must be irresistible; a poor offer cannot be supported even by the best written sales letter. The reader must feel, "I have a real advantage in this deal."

The most attractive offers combine discounted prices, comfortable terms and free gifts. For example, if you were selling a kitchen gadget, your offer might be a discounted retail price, exchange of an old gadget for a further discount, and additional spare parts, or free service up to five years.

Always try to raise the value of your offer by adding on something, not by lowering your price. Include short, vivid descriptions of the benefits of the additions in order to enhance the perceived value of your offer.

Give a Guarantee: Most people are worried about the risk of buying a new product; they fear that they may be stuck with it if the supplier does not accept it back. To make your offer really irresistible you have to remove the risk of the purchase.

Give the strongest possible guarantee you can. In order to be able to win the reader's confidence, you must yourself have confidence in your product or service to give a strong guarantee. In fact, most small businesses give a very strong guarantee; they tell their customers that they will take back the product if the customer is not satisfied. It is very rare for a customer to return a product.

Here is an example of a guarantee that is offered for some products.

"100%, No Questions Asked, Bring-it-back-to-us Guarantee"

This guarantee that they will get specific benefits from the product, may extend for six months or even a whole year. If they don't get what they expect, they get their money back with no questions asked. This almost eliminates all the risk for the buyer.

Hint: The reader may feel that the offer is "too good to be true." To avoid this, explain why and how you are able to give such an offer; for example, you might want to clear up your stock.

Review

Name four types of facts which can convince a customer about the value of a product.

Inducing Action

The most important function of the sales letter is to get action from the reader. The entire structure of the letter is built up so as to make the reader take a step towards the product.

Introduce Scarcity in order to make readers take a decision. Most people put off responding to offers. People delay their decision to buy something new for several reasons such as,

- They don't feel enough pain to make a change
- They are too busy and just forget
- They don't feel that the value outweighs your price
- They are simply lazy.

An extra incentive is needed to make people take action. The incentive of fear of loss works well; it can be brought in by introducing the idea of scarcity. When people think there is a limited supply of something that they want, they usually rush to get some of it. You can create a sense of shortage by limiting the offer in some way, such as by stating that the quantity is in limited supply, or by making your offer valid for only limited time. For example,

* If you purchase by (a stated last date) you will get the entire set of free bonuses.

* Our supply is limited to only 40 (product name). It will be sent to you on a 'first come, first served' basis. After they are exhausted there won't be any more available.

* This offer is good only until (stated last date) after which the (product or service) will return to its original price.

Note that you have to come up to your offers in every way, the benefits as well as the limitations. If you make the benefit available after the deadline, you will wear away the customers' trust.

The **concluding sentence** must tell the reader exactly what action to take and how to do it. The sentence must be extraordinarily clear and precise. For example, any one of the following:

- Call (give toll free number) and ask for (give name of the person).
- Return the enclosed postage-free card with your signature
- Send e-mail to (the given address).

The action to be recommended depends on the previous section; if you are making a free-trial offer, the reader should ask for a free trial; if you are sending or enclosing a sample, the reader should use it; if you are enclosing a price-concession coupon which is attached to the sample, the reader should buy the product in exchange for the coupon. It should be easy for the reader to take the suggested action; for example, just a telephone call or just signing and posting an enclosed card.

Some commonly used inducements are:

- Gift/price-concession coupon valid up to a given date
- Reply-paid post card for the reader to sign and mail
- Reduced price if the purchase is made by a given date
- Free service/gift for visiting stall/showroom/demonstration.

The effectiveness of the inducement to take action also depends upon the kind of sentence used: a direct command clinches the persuasive argument; a friendly question is suitable for a letter which depends on friendly persuasion for its effect. Here are some examples.

- *Just sign and mail the enclosed pre-paid card today, and get a free, ten-day trial of our JOOSER.*
- *Walk into your grocer's shop with the enclosed coupon to get your packet of Yummy Breakfast Food at 25% discount. Hurry! the offer expires on the 6th.*
- *Don't you also want to be one of this distinguished little circle? You only have to fill in and return the enclosed form.*
- *Won't you use the enclosed form so that we may add your name to our list of Helpers of Neglected Children? An exclamatory imperative would be an effective Hook for a letter which creates an atmosphere of interest and desire by describing a merry bustle of activity; for example:*
- *Hurry to join the dancers! The special rates close on the 18th!*
- *It's not too early to start thinking about a renewal. Act now and you can be sure not to miss a single week of the world's only truly international news magazine. And get an exceptional bargain besides.*
- *Give it a thought. Drop us a line. A handy order form is enclosed with its own self-addressed envelope for your convenience.*

The conclusion of the sales letter can be effective only if it urges the reader to take action, and makes the action easy to take. It must tell the reader, firmly and definitely, what action to take. Leave no doubt in the reader's mind about the action to be taken, and also make it easy to take the action.

Avoid—

- words like *if, may, hope, trust*; they weaken the force.
- offering a choice; a choice between two actions causes a divided urge; the reader may postpone the decision, and either forget about it or change his mind.
- saying anything about the product after urging action. If description or proof appears after the "action" sentence, the reader is diverted from the action.

Close with a Reminder: Always include a postscript (P.S.) in a sales letter. The P.S. is one of the most read elements of the sales letter. In your postscript, remind the readers of your special offer. If you have used scarcity in your letter, repeat your call to action and remind them of the limited time (or quantity) offer.

Review

1. Which of these sentences is most likely to make the reader take action?

(a) We hope you will visit our stall at the exhibition.

(b) For a demonstration, visit our stall or our showroom.

(c) See a demo at our stall and collect your surprise gift.

(d) Please visit our stall at the exhibition.

Some examples of sales letters are given below:

Dear Housewife,

STOP——

————scrubbing pots and pans. Let us do that for you.

There's no need to get back to the kitchen after the meal, to wash the dishes. You can put all your used dishes and pots into the Sparkle Dishwasher, put in the soap, turn on the tap and the switch. The machine will do the rest, even for the stickiest, greasiest pots. You can rest while it works to make your dishes, cutlery and glassware sparkle. It will scrub, rinse and dry them.

Then it will quietly turn itself off. You'll find your dishes clean, bright and dry when you go to the kitchen. Sparkle Dishwasher is manufactured by Tulip, the trusted name in kitchen machines, in collaboration with the Japanese Mitsubishi Home Aid Co. It is guaranteed for five years and is backed by expert and prompt lifetime after-sales service. As an introductory offer, we are giving a handsome discount of 20% on orders placed with our agents during the Demonstration Week from 12 to 19 April.

Banish dish-washing! Get yourself a Sparkle Dishwasher.

Come!—See it work! Order one for yourself!

Yours sparklingly,

Tulip Kitchen Machines

Dear Madam,

What's the word you associate with "Kitchen"?

If you're like most Indians, it's "Work". Now you can eliminate most of the work and make your kitchen the most attractive room in your home by installing modern equipment tailored to your individual needs. And at surprisingly low cost.

My job as contractor for kitchen installations is to help you select your equipment, design it for greatest efficiency, and follow your wishes in colour and location. You can have your choice of cabinets, gadgets, and sinks; my experience with dozens of installations will be at your service while you choose what best suits your needs. I personally supervise the work and can guarantee that your modern kitchen will be efficient, economical and attractive.

By modernizing your kitchen you'll be making an investment with low or no maintenance cost. And the investment will save your time and energy for many years to come. I would be pleased to show you any of the installations I have made. You will also get an opportunity to talk to my clients who know my work.

I'd like to call for an appointment in the next few days to tell you about the joys of having no dishes to wash, no garbage to be collected and no weary miles to walk in your kitchen.

May I submit a design and estimate for your kitchen without any cost or obligation on your part? Call me at 2626262 or fax 2626261.

Sincerely,

Neesha T.

Dear Executive,

Who'd insure an elephant riding on a raft? We did! You'd think a raft-riding elephant was too kookey for a company like ours to insure. But true to our reputation for imaginative insurance, we said we'd try. It seems elephants are good swimmers, so it was a good risk and we covered it. Why did the elephant people come to us anyway? Well, because Morning Star Insurance Co., is known for insuring things never insured before.

Haven't you got an elephant? Don't fret. We also give good Non-elephant insurance. Electronic data processing equipment, farm crops against locusts, expensive clothes against theft, to name some. What do you want insured? Your house, your business, your car, your health, your reputation? The elephant is not important, our broad minded approach to insurance is.

The day you want creativity and derring-do in insurance you want Morning Star.

Yours Around-the-World,

Morning Star Insurance Co.

Dear Executive.

If you don't have an Instamatic camera in your business, how can you take it home for the week-end? The Instamatic camera does something no ordinary camera can do. Just shoot. Pull out the film pack. Wait one minute: Peel cover off a finished picture. No developing tanks or liquids; photos develop themselves.

Advantages in business? Construction progress can be studied on the same day; competitors' displays shot for immediate reporting; damaged goods proved immediately for claims; site photos ready for instant mailing. No long descriptions involving hours of time in typing and reading, with much piling up of papers. Instant photographs of whatever you want. The fun at home at week-ends? We leave it to the Lady-of-the-House to imagine.

Photographs are enclosed to show you how life-like are the colours and how sharp the details. You'll wonder how you got along without it when you've used it for a week.

Sign and mail the enclosed card and you will receive one for a free seven-day trial, loaded with a free sample film.

Yours cordially,

Dear Friend,

The mouth is the weapon with which we kill ourselves. It opens and shuts too often. For food. Too much food leads to fat.

Fat can cut life short. High blood pressure, strokes, heart diseases, diabetes are all dangerous, alone or in combination; they can all be caused by fat. A disturbing number of people in their late twenties and thirties are overweight. And they did it to themselves.

But it need not happen to you. Watch for the first signs of fat: belt moves a notch, a hook needs a new eye; a zip needs extra effort. That's proof you have stopped burning calories like a teenager; so stop eating like one. You don't have to starve. A weight control programme starts with a sensible low calorie breakfast. The Gold Coin K-Plan Special Breakfast is the result of much careful study of nutritious but non-fat food for sensible people. A complete slimming programme diet is packed with every carton of 500 grams of Gold Coin K-plan Special Breakfast. The enclosed card entitles you to a free health check-up before the 15th of next month, at any of the clinics mentioned on the card, and also to a free sample pack of Gold Coin K-plan Special Breakfast.

Get your free health check-up and sample pack before the 15th of December.

Yours sincerely,

Dear Madam,

Eyes are the most direct way to the mind. Clutter and confusion before the eyes means clutter and confusion within the mind.

How can one hope to have a clear relaxed mind for attending to one's work, for thinking, or even for enjoying oneself, with chairs, tables, bookshelves, bedsteads, everywhere? No space to stretch the legs, no space for a potted plant. Throw away all the furniture and spread mats? If only we could go back to the good old days of the multi-purpose mats which can be neatly folded and put away!

We too have felt this way, and suspecting that there are others who share our feelings, we set ourselves to find a solution to the problem of space in modern city flats .... And we have the answer! Dining table which will fold invisibly away to cover your kitchen shelves; sofas that will quietly open themselves into beds; shelves that will grow up along the wall as your needs multiply. FOLD-IT MULTI-PURPOSE FURNITURE that's the answer.

We'll take measurements to suit your flat and your requirements; we'll get the colours you want and design your own secret hinges. It's for this versatility that we won the gold medal for interior decoration at the All-India Furniture Designing Exhibition held in New Delhi last October. Our representative will come to your home and submit designs and estimates for your flat, without any obligation. Just sign and mail the enclosed prepaid postcard.

Yours cordially,

Dear Preferred Subscriber,

You'll agree, there's no dearth of news today. Newspapers, magazines, satellite TV—it's a deluge of information. But that doesn't necessarily make you better informed. Precisely where TIME enters the picture, especially to put news in perspective for you by giving you not just the 'what', but the 'how' and the 'why' as well. TIME interviews, interprets and reports all that's happening across the globe so that our readers can better understand events and personalities that are shaping the world. I'm sure that like TIME subscribers all over the world, you too like your news in true perspective. So, I hope you'll avail yourself of our special introductory subscription offer—save up to 46% off the cover price of Rs. 52/- per copy PLUS your free gift, the exclusive TIME Over-night Bag.

Hurry! This exclusive offer is open only till December 31. Send in your order by filling the order form and mailing it in the enclosed Business Reply Envelope, today. Don't lose TIME!

Sincerely,

Regina Ng
Circulation Director—South Asia

P.S. To take advantage of this offer and get your free gift, your order must reach us by December 31.

28 July 2004

Ms Nirmala Naidu
[Address] [City],
[State] [PIN/Postal Code]

Dear Ms Naidu,

Don't lose this letter, or you'll lose your free gift!

At Golden Bow Store we are having our Annual Festival Sale, and we want you to be there, for outstanding savings on everything in the store.

And a FREE gift everyone will love.

Beginning 8 August 2005 and Ending 8 September 2005, Golden Bow Store will have huge discounts, up to 60% on items like these:

60% off all Ready Made Garments or 45% off all Footwear or 30% off all Glass Ware. And not only will you save, but if you bring in this letter during the Annual Festival Sale, we'll also give you a Travel Set of Lakme Beauty Products, absolutely free.

Mark your calendar now for the Annual Festival Sale: 8 August – 8 September 2005. Come to the sale early, and don't forget to bring this letter, because our supplies of Travel Set of Lakme Beauty Products are limited.

And there's no telling when we'll run out.

Sincerely,

Akshata Krishna
Golden Bow Store

P.S. Tape this letter to your door—mail it to yourself—put it in the glove compartment of your car—just don't lose it or you won't get your Travel Set of Lakme Beauty Products for free.

[Date]

[Mr./Mrs./Ms./Dr.] [Customer's Full Name]
[Address] [City],
[State] [PIN/Postal Code]

Dear [Mr./Mrs./Ms./Dr.] [Customer's Last Name]:

The More You Buy The More You Save!

Now you can save even more on all items in the Summertime Catalogue. And the more you order from the catalogue, the more of a discount you'll receive.

It's simple to save.

If you place an order of Rs. 50,000/, we'll take 35% off your entire order.

If you place an order of Rs 40,000/, we'll take 25% off your entire order.

If you place an order of Rs 30,000/, we'll take 15% off your entire order.

But never mind the arithmetic. The easiest way to save is to find what you want from the catalogue, make sure it adds up to at least Rs. 50,000/, Rs. 40,000/, Rs. 30,000/, then give us a call. We'll make sure you get just the right discount.

Our toll-free number is 600 2222. So call now and save as much as 35% on your order from Red Star Catalogue Stores. With this offer, you just can't help but save money.

Sincerely,

P.S. Remember, all you have to do to qualify for the highest discount is order Rs. 50,000/ or more. So plan ahead for birthdays, holidays and other special occasions, and save money now on items you need to buy anyway.

FOLLOW-UP LETTERS

A sales letter is not the only thing in a sales campaign. It is a part of a programme which includes high pressure advertising, concession offers, salespersons' visits, shows, demonstrations, and gifts.

The role of a sales letter in this programme may be to invite potential customers to a sale or demonstration; to follow up contacts made by visits, or as a follow-up of an earlier sales letter.

A "follow-up" letter is written with reference to something that has gone before; it follows up on the previous contact. The customer's attention is secured by reference to the previous event. The letter is short since desire and conviction have been created before, the function of the follow-up is to remind the customer to take action.

The timing of the follow-up is important; for example, the season or any current event which concerns everyone. The follow-up usually points out that time is running out and the reader should hurry to take advantage of the limited offer.

Writing good sales letters requires a flair for writing, good command of the language, and ability to turn out interesting words and phrases. Lively imagination is very useful for sales writing as for advertisement copy writing. Sales writers should make good use of books of anecdotes, quotations and humour.

EXERCISES

1. Write a sales letter to promote the sales of the following:
   (i) Home exercise equipment. Prospect: women.
   (ii) Folding clothes-drier with attached heater. Prospect: small laundries and hotels.
   (iii) Microwave oven. Prospect: housewives.
   (iv) Laser printer. Prospect: office managers.
   (v) Accounting software package. Prospect: Accounts managers
   (vi) Laptop. Prospect: college teachers.
   (vii) Pocket calculator; Prospect: students.
   (viii) Safe Deposit lockers service. Prospect: local residents.
   (ix) Fax-cum-xerox machine. Prospect: professionals.
   (x) Computer programming course. Prospect: college students.

(xi) Display boards. Prospect: school/college Principals
(xii) Holiday Tour Package. Prospect: students
(xiii) Mobile phone with internet facility. Prospect: journalists
(xiv) Digital camera. Prospect: editors of magazines.

2. As agent for a chain of hotels at hill stations and holiday resorts, draft a sales letter to be sent to high income group persons, offering special off-season packages.
3. Draft a letter to be sent to housewives to induce them to join the following courses:
   (a) A six weeks' course in baking by a Catering Technology Institute.
   (b) Distance Education Courses for adults.
4. Business executives, managers, proprietors & professionals are to be sent a sales letter for the following products. Draft the letters.
   (i) Space-saving filing cabinets
   (ii) Air-purifiers
   (iii) Stationery
   (iv) Electronic diaries
   (v) Set of office handbooks
   (vi) Voltage stabilizers
   (vii) Vacuum cleaners
   (viii) Advertising space on websites.
5. Write a paragraph to win confidence for the following:
   (i) Food processor: to office canteens
   (ii) Books and Magazines: to students and teachers; librarians; general readers
   (iii) Washing machines: to housewives; retailers
   (iv) A set of children's books: to parents; schools; book shops
   (v) Laminating machine: to Schools and College Principals
   (vi) Vocational courses: to H.S.C. students
   (vii) Transport services: to Super markets.
6. As the Manager of a bank, write a sales letter to your customers to promote the credit cards introduced by your bank.
7. You have started a computer centre. Write a sales letter to business houses in your city, offering to train their staff in using computers.
8. You have got a franchise for teaching computer courses of a well-known computer training institute. Draft a sales letter to be sent to potential students in your locality.
9. You have an agency of a well-known international group of magazines. Write a sales letter to be sent to educational institutes.

❑❑❑

Chapter 27

CREDIT AND STATUS ENQUIRIES

Letters related to credit must be written with the greatest tact; otherwise you may either damage your sales or invite trouble for yourself with collection of dues.

You have to get information about the credit standing of customers who ask for credit, and also give credit information about your customers when others make enquiries. Sometimes you may have to tell a customer that credit cannot be granted. You also have to write letters to collect dues from customers who do not pay on time.

With increase in the use of credit cards and debit cards, and development of e.commerce, the procedures for establishing credit will change; however, it will be quite some time before the use of credit cards becomes common.

SOURCES OF CREDIT INFORMATION

A buyer's credit standing depends on his Capital, Capacity and Character. In addition, Circumstances also play an important part in a buyer's credit position.

Capital is the cash as well as the stock, the building, the machinery and other property that the buyer owns.

Capacity is the person's skill and ability to use resources properly and run the business/profession profitably. This may be partly affected by the line of business and the location of the business.

Character is what really makes a reputation; it consists of honesty, ability to work hard, and self-respect.

Circumstances are outside the person's control; political conditions, government's financial and economic policies and industrial relations in the region or in the whole country may affect any business or profession. Currently, computerization of business as well as globalization is causing changes in many organizations. Circumstances can change and may either improve or worsen the standing of a business enterprise.

All these aspects of credit are taken into account before granting credit.

The enquiry begins by asking for information from references given by the credit applicant, and may extend further to sources found out from the first references or agencies.

The usual sources of credit information are the credit applicant's bank and suppliers. Organizations like Credit Agencies, Merchants' Chambers and Trade Associations can help in ascertaining the credit standing of potential customers. A somewhat elusive but useful source is market gossip from which organizations gather information. For the purpose of letter writing we are concerned with the bank and other suppliers as sources of credit information.

A bank knows several things about the customer. The scale of the customer's business is assessed from the amounts paid out and deposited. The business circle of the customer is indicated by the names of the parties on the incoming and outgoing cheques. The customer's peak season and lean season of business are indicated by the timing and frequency of incoming and outgoing cheques. The general standing and conduct of the customer can be gathered from the manner in which the account is operated. The bank is generally the most reliable source of credit information.

Other suppliers with whom the customer has already established credit, can give information about the customer's credit standing, general respectability and regularity in settling accounts.

Asking Customer for Credit Information

If a customer sends an order to be executed on credit, without giving credit references, you have to ask the customer to give credit references. A Credit Application form may be sent. Otherwise, you can send a letter asking for specific information, like name and address of the bank, account number and names and addresses of two other creditors. Also explain the need for this procedure.

Points:

1. Appreciation of the order
2. Explanation of routine enquiries to be made, credit references to be given and the time it will take to complete enquiries
3. Offer to send goods c.o.d. if customer's requirement is urgent

Sir,

It is a pleasure to welcome you to our large circle of customers. Your order for 500 tons of cement is being attended to in our dispatch department.

Meanwhile, we need some information on which our credit manager can base his records. The names of two of your suppliers with whom you have already established credit and the name of your bank will be suitable.

We expect to be able to complete the enquiries within a week's time. If your need is urgent, please let us know if we should send a part of your order on C.O.D. terms immediately.

Yours truly,

Sir,

Thank you for your order of 29 September for 1000 boxes of our Camel Crylin Colours, to be delivered on 30 days' credit.

As it is customary to have some records on our files about our credit customers, we are sending you, enclosed, our credit application form. Please fill and return it to us in the enclosed envelope, as early as possible. It will take some time to collect the required information; it usually takes a fortnight to complete the enquiries.

In case you need some of the boxes urgently, would you prefer to send us a cheque so that we can make shipment immediately?

Yours truly,

Encl: Credit Application form

Making enquiries About Credit

Information about customers' financial standing and paying habits of the customer is got from the references. The enquiry should be specific and clear. Status enquiry questionnaires are quite useful since the definite questions can bring definite and clear answers from the references.

The reference gives information only as a favour; courtesy demands that the information should be requested politely and with an offer to return the favour.

Assure the references that whatever information they give will be kept in strict confidence. These letters are marked "Confidential" and are addressed to an individual official, and not to the company in general.

Points:

1. Name and address of credit applicant stating that their name has been given as reference; amount and period of credit requested.
2. Request for information on specific points (e.g., amount and period of credit allowed by the reference, details of delay in payment by customer), and opinion on the advisability of the proposed transaction.
3. Offer to help in return in similar situations and promise to keep the given information confidential.

Dear Sir,

Your name has been given as a credit reference by Messrs. Sanghavi & Pai of 87, Green Street, Bangalore 560004 who have asked us to supply goods worth Rs. 100,000/- on credit.

This is our first contact with them and it would help us in assessing their credit if you could give us some information about their credit standing and your experience in doing business with them. A credit information form is enclosed; please fill and return it in the enclosed postage-paid envelope.

We would be glad to help in a similar way whenever we can. Please be assured that the information you give will be treated as strictly confidential.

Yours faithfully,

Dear Mr. Parikh,

We have received a request for credit of Rs. 1,50,000/- for 2 months from the firm of Messrs. J.K. Shah & Sons, 710 Wallace Street, Ballard Estate, Mumbai 400 001. They have given us your name as credit reference.

We would be grateful if you could help us to assess the credit application by giving us information about the number of years they have been your credit customers, the amount and period of credit you grant them, and whether there has been any difficulty in collecting dues from them.

Whatever other information you may have about the firm's general reputation in the business circles would also be appreciated.

The information you give will be used with the utmost discretion, in strict confidence and no liability on your part.

Yours sincerely,

Sir,

The Ball Printing Press, Dadabhoy Road, Hyderabad 2, have given your name as credit reference and requested us to supply paper worth Rs. 300,000/- on 3 months' credit.

We do not know much about the proprietors but we have an impression that their business is not large enough to expect a credit of Rs. 300,000/-. Of course, we may be quite mistaken, and would be glad to know your opinion of their business and your experience of collecting dues from them.

We would be glad for an opportunity to return this courtesy and help in ascertaining the credit standing of our customers who may approach you for credit. Whatever information you give will be kept in strict confidence.

Yours truly,

Bank References

Banks do not give information about their customers to the public. You have to write to your own bank to take up the enquiry with the prospective customer's bank.

The letter to the bank is formal and short. It includes the following points.

1. Name, address and business of credit applicant, with amount and period of credit
2. Name and address of credit applicant's bank and A/c number
3. Request that the bank should take up the reference and advise on the safety of the risk
4. Assurance that the information given will be treated as confidential

The Manager
Bank of India
Mahatma Gandhi Road
Bangalore 560 001

Sir,

We have been asked for credit of Rs. 75,000/- by Messrs. Sanghvi & Pai of 87, Green Street, Bangalore 560 004, who have given the same of Canara Bank, Lal baug Gardens Branch, Bangalore, as their credit reference. Their A/c No. is 4870.

Please take up the reference on our behalf and inform us whether the proposed transaction is a safe risk. The information you give will be treated as strictly confidential.

Yours faithfully,

Review

Are these statements true?

(a) To find out about a customer's credit standing, you should write to the customer's banker.

(b) In order to get information about a credit applicant's status from the customer's bank, you must write to your own bank.

(c) A letter asking for credit information about a customer may be addressed to "Image Graphics" with the salutation "Sirs".

Giving Status Information about Customers

Letters giving credit information must be marked "Confidential" and addressed by name to the individual who has signed the enquiry letter.

The information given must be helpful to the enquirer as well as fair to the credit applicant. The behaviour of a customer may not be the same with all his creditors; besides, with a long standing credit relationship, many little faults on either side may have become accepted as routine. The reference can help by giving information about the scale of the customer's business, reputation as a skilled businessperson and habits with regard to payment of bills.

Talking about a person's credit is a delicate matter; the letter must be tactful. It is advisable to keep to facts like the length of business relationship with the customer, the amount and period of credit granted, and the longest extension of time the customer has taken to settle the dues. General market opinion can be given to balance personal experience.

The credit standing of a customer depends upon the strength or weakness of each of the four Cs of Credit. Some information can be given about the customer's capital, capacity and circumstances. It is important to be tactful in indicating any weakness. Character should never be mentioned in the letter.

Points:

1. Reference to inquiry indicating name (or enclosed slip with name) and length of business relation with the customer

2. Information about personal experience; general market opinion
3. Reminder that information is given in confidence and should be treated with the utmost discretion

These examples show how different kinds of customers can be described.

> Sir,
>
> We are glad to be of help in ascertaining the credit standing of our customer, Messrs. Sanghvi & Pai of 87, Green Street, Mumbai 400 004.
>
> They have bought from us on credit for the last five years, and we grant them credit up to Rs. 200,000/-. They have always been prompt in paying their bills and are known in the market for their integrity and business acumen. We ourselves would readily grant the credit they have asked for from you.
>
> This is our personal opinion of the firm and we request you to treat it as such. We are not responsible in any way for any decision you may take in this matter.
>
> Yours faithfully,

> Dear Sir,
>
> The party about whom you enquired in your letter of the 6th (name is on the enclosed slip), have been our customers for the last 3 years.
>
> We grant them credit up to Rs. 50,000/- and have not tried higher limits; we have had no difficulty in collecting dues from them. One of the partners who has recently joined the partnership, has had a good training in business administration, and the firm may be expected to develop rapidly.
>
> Please note that our experience with the firm is limited, and whatever decision you may take is without any responsibility on our part.
>
> Yours truly,

> Dear Sir,
>
> We have known the party you mentioned in your letter of 30 August, for seven years.
>
> Our credit dealings with them have been few and they have paid, usually, after a delay of fifteen days. We have had little opportunity of observing their habits of payment with their regular creditors. We suggest that you make further enquiries, and not consider our opinion as anything final or decisive.
>
> Please treat this letter as strictly confidential.
>
> Yours faithfully,

Review

1. Are these statements true? If any statement is not true, give the correct statement.

(a) The name of the party should always be mentioned in a letter giving information about their credit standing.

(b) Credit information letters are marked "Confidential."

(c) Letters giving information about a party's financial status must be addressed to an individual.

(d) In a reply to an enquiry about a customer's credit standing, you should give definite advice whether to grant credit or not.

2. Choose the correct alternative.

When talking about a person's credit standing, we should avoid mentioning the person's—-

(a) capacity (b) capital (c) character (d) circumstances

INFORMING THE CUSTOMER

Your decision to grant or refuse credit will depend on several things. Your own financial position and credit limit is an important factor. Besides, you have to consider whether you can afford to take the particular risk, and to take the trouble to collect dues from debtors who need constant reminders.

When the decision is taken, the customer is informed.

Granting Credit

This is a pleasant message to convey and should be written with a note of welcome. The letter gives information about the routine terms of shipment of goods and payment of bills.

Points:

1. Statement that credit is approved
2. Information about regular terms
3. Message of goodwill

The following letter illustrates the suitable tone:

> Gentlemen:
>
> We are happy to inform you that your application for a credit account has been approved.
>
> Your account has been opened on a monthly basis. You can either pay the bill for each consignment within seven days of the delivery of goods and take advantage of the 2% cash discount, or you may pay the entire bill amount in the month following your purchase. We send our monthly bills in the first week of each month; the payment is to be made by the 10th of the month.
>
> We are looking forward to receiving your first order which will mark the beginning of a long and pleasant business relationship.
>
> Yours truly,

You may decide to give credit for a lower amount than asked for by a customer. If you have a small working capital, you may not be able to give a large amount of credit. A letter conveying that credit is granted for a lower amount may include these points:

1. Statement that enquiries have been completed and explanation of the position as seen from the enquiries (e.g., competition is tough; demand for the product is not very high)
2. Decision to grant credit up to a given limit
3. Expression of confidence that the customer will understand the situation and agree to the proposed terms.

> Sir,
>
> We have examined your request for credit of Rs. 750,000/- for 3 months to stock microwave ovens and other kitchen equipment. It appears that the proposal should be re-examined in the light of the recently announced exim policy.
>
> In the long run, the demand for Indian kitchen equipment will pick up, but at the moment we feel that it is somewhat risky to invest a large sum on stocking goods which may be a little slow moving for some time. We suggest that you buy goods worth Rs. 3,00,000/- on credit and the rest on cash basis in small amounts as and when you require them. You will, of course, have the benefit of cash discounts. Besides, you will have part of your working capital free to enable you to make any quick changes that will be necessary because of rapid changes in the market.
>
> We are sure you will see that this advice is given in a spirit of friendly co-operation between businessmen. Your consignment will be dispatched as soon as we receive your confirmation of these terms.
>
> Yours faithfully,

Refusing Credit

Of all the negative messages, this one is the most unpleasant for the writer as well as the reader.

You must take care to analyse this situation carefully before conveying the message. If you show personal interest, you have a better chance of persuading the customer to place his order on cash. Make every attempt to win the customer.

It is better not to give vague reasons for the refusal; it is more useful to discuss it in a friendly way with the customer. Conditions and circumstances do not remain the same; they may change so as to become more favourable to the customer. An offer to reconsider the application at a later date can soften the refusal.

Look at the situation from the customer's point of view, understand his needs and point out the benefits he can get by buying on cash, like

(a) saving capital by getting discounts for cash payments

(b) ensuring fresh stock by buying in small lots (fashion goods, medicines and technological products become out-dated rapidly)

(c) lower expenditure on cash buying and passing on the advantage of low prices to valued customers to build up goodwill

(d) freedom from commitments

Taking a positive attitude makes it easier to persuade the customer to buy in small lots on cash.

Points:

1. Statement that enquiries related to credit are complete
2. Explanation of what seems to be strengths and what are the weaknesses of customer's position
3. Statement of refusal, with apology
4. Suggestions for improvement, showing advantages of present cash buying
5. Inducements to buy on cash and assurance of co-operation
6. Expression of confidence that the customer will understand the situation and place orders on cash.

Sir,

We have made complete enquiries in connection with your request for credit. With the development of the locality in Bhoisar, we are sure that your business will grow well.

At present, however, owing to the risk of over-stocking we cannot grant the credit. Stocking large quantities of medicines in an area with a small population is risky, especially since medicines have an expiry date.

We, therefore, suggest that you buy on cash, but in smaller lots, as and when required. You will have the benefit of 5% bulk purchase discount if you buy medicines worth Rs. 300,000/- in 3 months. We shall deliver the medicines within 24 hours of receiving your orders.

We are sure that you will understand that small cash purchases are to your advantage until the market grows large enough for larger stocks.

Your consignment will be dispatched as soon as we receive your instructions.

Yours faithfully,

Sir,

We have completed enquiries in connection with your credit application and our understanding of the situation is as follows:

As you are going to open a new shop you will have to face a good deal of competition, and it will take some time for you to build up a sound business. The risks at the initial stage are greater and we feel that it is advisable to avoid commitments at this stage.

As soon as you have established yourself firmly, we shall be glad to reconsider credit terms. At present, we suggest that you spread your large order into small cash orders over a period of four months. This will give you the benefit of discounts which we offer on cash purchases. The goods will be delivered promptly when you require them.

We are sure that you will understand why we are refusing your request for credit now, and that you will let us have your instructions for dispatching your first consignment.

Yours faithfully,

Dear Mr. Ahuja,

We have completed enquiries in connection with your application for credit of Rs. 300,000/-

Considering the location of your shop in Wajreshwari we feel that the risk that you are taking is not very safe. Fashion goods and cosmetics cannot have much sale in your area yet. We must therefore request you to place your order on cash terms. The cash discount of 7% will be a saving which you can pass on to your customers.

We shall give you a special bulk discount even if the purchases are spread over a period of 6 months. We also guarantee prompt delivery of goods ordered.

We are sure that you will agree with us and find it to your advantage to buy on cash at this stage. May we have your instructions for the dispatch of the first consignment?

Yours sincerely,

Review:

1. Fill in the blanks in these sentences:
   (a) In a letter refusing credit, it is better to show the customer the advantages of __ .
   (b) Taking a positive attitude while refusing means that you have to __.
   (c) A letter granting credit should include information about __.
2. Choose the correct alternative:

   The reader is most likely to respond favourable if we write –

   (a) We regret very much that we cannot grant your request for credit since the market conditions are not favourable.
   (b) We are extremely sorry that we are unable to grant credit terms at present; we shall re-consider your request when the present conditions improve.
   (c) We greatly regret our inability to help you by granting credit terms owing to unfavourable market conditions.
   (d) It is a matter of regret for us that we are unable to grant you credit because the market conditions are unfavourable to us.

CREDIT IN THE SALES CAMPAIGN

Credit is offered to customers of long standing in order to create goodwill. It is also offered to individuals or firms of high repute and known credit standing to win them as customers. The following is an example of a letter offering credit.

Dear Sir,

You have been buying from us for over five years now, and we feel that you would like to enjoy our credit privilege.

With credit facilities you can keep good stocks and pay for the goods only after most of the goods have been sold, and your profits made. You can also buy in large quantities and take advantage of bulk purchase discounts. We hardly need to enumerate further, the various benefits that credit customers enjoy.

Please fill in and return the enclosed card and we would be glad to open a charge account for you.

Yours truly,

A lost customer may be offered credit terms to win him back as this letter does.

> Dear Mr. Sanghavi,
>
> It is a long time — over six months — since we received your last order. Perhaps you did not need stocks of stationery as this is not the peak season for these goods. We expect your order soon, however, and are glad to inform you that we are offering credit terms to a few of our customers. You can now place your orders on credit, with bills payable every three months, or when the amount comes up to Rs. 50,000/- This will enable you to benefit from bulk purchase discounts and also to put your capital to other uses.
>
> We are sure you will take advantage of this offer and place your order soon.
>
> Yours sincerely,

EXERCISES

1. A customer has placed an order for goods to be supplied on credit of thirty days, but has not given any information about himself. Write to him asking for credit information.
2. A prospective buyer has referred you to his banker for information about his financial position. Draft the letter you would write taking up the reference.
3. You have been asked about the financial standing of a customer whose credit facility you have temporarily stopped owing to repeated delays in payment. Write a reply which is fair to both the enquirer and the applicant for credit.
4. You have been asked about the credit standing of a partnership firm which has bought from you on credit for 8 years. There has been a recent change in the constitution of the partnership and this has led to some lowering of their credit reputation and you have tightened your credit facilities to the firm. Draft a suitable confidential reply to the enquiry.
5. Tristar Electronics have asked you to supply goods worth Rs 1,000,000/ on credit. Enquiries show that they have a limited working capital and are probably trying to expand too rapidly; their credit seems to be good up to Rs. 500,000/-. Draft a suitable reply, persuading them to buy in smaller lots.
6. You have received an order for the first time, for goods worth Rs. 250,000/- from Messrs. Naidu & Sons. Enquiries you have made indicate that their financial position is not satisfactory. Draft a suitable reply.
7. A newly trained diploma holder of a Computer Programming Course, intending to open a computer training class has asked for credit from a supplier of computer furniture. Draft the supplier's reply suggesting that she should reduce her order by half and pay 50% on delivery and the rest a month later. Full credit terms may be considered after six months; meanwhile she would be granted the suggested limited credit.
8. A credit customer who was regular in making payments for three years, has been delaying payments for the last one year, owing to difficulties in business. Write to him tactfully pointing out that in such circumstances, he should stop buying on credit for some time.

9. Inform a customer that owing to his repeated delay in paying his dues you are compelled to deal with him on cash basis only.
10. A highly placed official in Wipro Ltd. has just been transferred to your city. Write as from a well-known department store offering him credit terms in an effort to win him as a regular customer.

□□□

Chapter 28

BANK CORRESPONDENCE

Banks render a number of financial and security services. Commerce and industry cannot run without their assistance. Banks collect spare funds from members of the public and make them available to businessmen & others who need funds. They provide safety for money and valuables, and also render services in connection with shares and stocks, payments of bills, premiums and rents, and establishment of credit in domestic and international trade.

As the services are varied, the customers of banks are equally diverse. They range from experienced and knowledgeable financiers and industrialists to the simplest and most uninformed individuals who may have a little surplus money which they want to keep in the bank.

In a developing country like ours, nationalized banks have been rendering more services to the financially weak and helping them by providing finances for setting up a business or a small handicraft unit. Members of the public often do not understand that bank loans and overdrafts are governed by rules; they are likely to approach banks with requests for money or unrealistic plans for business which they want the bank to finance. Customers may also approach banks for services, help and advice on financial matters of which they do not understand much.

Conditions for opening accounts and also for granting of loans vary according to the circumstances of the locality in which a branch functions; the conditions in rural and agricultural areas are quite different from those in urban and industrial areas. Banking is governed by the laws of the country; the Reserve Bank of India announces new regulations from time to time according to the economic policies and requirements of the country. Rates of interest, regulations about granting of loans and overdrafts, collection of dues, savings and investment schemes, etc. change in accordance with the decisions taken by the Reserve Bank on these matters.

Writing of bank letters requires skill and patience as well as some knowledge of bank operations. A part of the bank manager's function is to educate the public in banking and to help people to make use of the services offered. The bank's letters must be written with an understanding of this situation. The language, style, and details of explanation, vary according to the type of person who is to receive the letter.

Answering Customers' Enquiries

Since banks render various types of services, customers make enquiries when they need the bank's services. Enquiries about safe custody, investments, procedure for getting a loan, etc., are made by different types of customers whose knowledge of these matters may be limited. It is good practice to request the enquirer to visit the bank for a personal discussion, after giving some essential information. With the increase in the number of branches, it is easier for customers to visit the bank office and make enquiries personally. Very few enquiries are made by letter. Replies to some of the enquiries that customers might make are discussed below.

(a) Safe Custody Services

Banks give several types of safe custody services. Lockers are rented to customers; also valuables in sealed covers or boxes are accepted for safe keeping. Safe Custody Savings Accounts link the safe keeping of shares and stocks with the Savings Account; collection of dividends, bonus shares, right shares, and other work in connection with shares is also undertaken by the bank. A layperson is likely to be confused if all this is explained in detail in a letter; it is better to invite the person to visit the bank for a personal discussion of requirements so that suitable arrangements can be made according to needs.

> Dear Madam,
>
> Thank you for your letter enquiring about our safe custody services.
>
> We have several types of safe custody services. You can hire lockers at rents ranging from Rs.— to Rs.— per annum, or you can hand over to the bank, your valuables in a sealed box for safe keeping. We also open Safe Custody Savings Accounts for customers who wish to hand over to the bank, all work in connection with shares and stocks such as collecting dividends, bonus shares etc.
>
> If you visit the bank on any week day between 9.30 a.m. and 12.00 noon, we shall gladly discuss your requirements personally.
>
> Yours faithfully,

(b) Advice on Investments

Banks have a number of schemes for investment of savings like Perennial Pension Scheme, Super Savings Package Scheme, Recurring Deposit Scheme, etc., besides Fixed Deposit Scheme. The scheme which seems to be the most suitable for the needs of the enquiring customer, is suggested and explained. The following is a reply to a lady, working as a personal secretary, who has asked for advice on investing her savings.

> Dear Madam,
>
> We are happy to help you in choosing a suitable investment scheme for your savings. There are several investment schemes for the benefit of persons with different needs. Since you have a regular income, you will find the Recurring Deposit Scheme the most suitable.

In this scheme, you make a fixed amount of deposit every month; the amount should be in multiples of 100. You can choose the period of time from two years to seven years according to your convenience. During the period, you deposit the agreed amount every month.

Compound interest is paid on the collected balance. This is an advantage over the Fixed Deposit Scheme in which only simple interest is paid. The enclosed folder shows how the interest is calculated in the Recurring Deposit Scheme. If you need any further clarification or information, please do visit our office; we shall be glad to work out the details for you.

Yours faithfully,

(c) Information about a Customer's Creditworthiness

A bank gives information about its customers only to another bank. The actual position of the account is never disclosed. A general opinion based on facts may be given in noncommittal terms. The bank makes it clear that it accepts no liability for any decision that may be taken by anyone on the basis of the information.

The enquiring bank then advises its customer on the basis of the information received. The name of the credit applicant is not mentioned in the letter. A brief report of the customer's credit standing is written on a separate sheet of paper which is enclosed with the letter. The letter is marked "Confidential".

Banks take several precautions to avoid legal complications which might arise from giving credit information about their clients. They reply only to another bank and never to a member of the public. The bank's reply is non-committal. The client's name is not mentioned; a note giving information/assessment of the customer's credit is written on an enclosed sheet of plain paper. The letter mentions the enclosed note and points out that the Bank has no liability in any way.

Dear Sir,

The party about whom you enquired in your letter of the 10th, and whose name is on the enclosed slip, have been in this business for the last 9 years.

Their scale of business seems to be quite small although in recent years they have built up some good contacts. It might be safer to reduce the amount by half and grant credit for one month.

Please note that the bank is not responsible for this information which should be used with the utmost discretion.

Yours faithfully,

Sir,

From the enquires we have made in connection with the credit application made to you by the party mentioned on the enclosed slip, it appears that their financial standing is quite good. Their dealings usually exceed the amount you have mentioned and their business contacts are wide and respectable. There seems to be no great risk in the transaction you propose.

This information is given in strict confidence and the bank or any of its officials are not responsible for whatever decision you may take.

Yours truly,

Dear Sir,

We have made enquiries about the party mentioned in your letter dated 29 October. The party's business appears to be seasonal, with the best period during October-November. The contacts are limited and the scale of business modest. The credit asked for seems a little ambitious and may be reduced by half.

This information is strictly confidential and given without any responsibility on the bank's part.

Yours faithfully,

CONFIDENTIAL

The Credit Manager
XYZ Co. (Pvt.) Ltd.
Bombay - 6

Dear Sir,

From the information we have collected about the credit standing of the party mentioned in your letter of 17 September, 2003, it appears that the credit transaction of Rs.1,50,000/- which you propose is safe. The party's normal business is on a much larger scale.

Please note that this information is given in strict confidence and without any responsibility on the part of the bank or any of its officials.

Yours faithfully,

XYZ (Manager)

(d) Customers' requests for Overdrafts and Loans

Banks lend money to customers according to rules and regulations laid down by the Reserve Bank of India, and by their own policies. There are some priority sectors like farmers, small scale industries, women entrepreneurs and small businessmen, that get special consideration from nationalized banks with regard to loans. Advances to other entities like Partnership firms and Public and Private Limited Companies are governed by different considerations and regulations.

Banks usually insist that the borrower must deposit some security with them; the advance is granted up to a certain percentage of the value of the security ranging between 30% and 90% depending on the kind of security. In accepting security, banks are mainly concerned with steady value and easy convertibility into cash so that, in case of insolvency, the loan can be recovered. If an advance is to be granted without any tangible security, the bank requires two guarantors who will be responsible for the repayment of the loan. In all cases, banks take into account the creditworthiness of the applicant for the loan.

The property which is offered as security must be owned by the borrower as a separate entity. A partnership firm cannot pledge any individual partner's property; it must be property owned by the firm, and not by individuals who constitute the firm.

Small businessmen, small scale industries, etc., are required to submit Profit & Loss Account and the latest Balance Sheet certified by Auditors. Cash budget, projected profit and loss account and projected balance sheet may also be asked for. Small businessmen can get an advance of a small amount without security, against hypothecation of stocks in the shop. In case of a partnership firm, the bank also requires Partnership Deed and authorization signed by all partners authorizing one or more partners to apply for the loan. Companies have to submit Memorandum of Association, Articles of Association and a signed copy of the Board Resolution authorizing the Secretary or a Director to apply for a loan, and a certificate from the Registrar of Companies that the proposed borrowing is within the un-exhausted limit of the company's borrowing power. A statement of the purpose for which the loan is required must also be submitted.

Loans are granted on the following securities:

(1) Shares of public limited companies, which are listed on the Stock Exchange.

(2) Goods which are not perishable, which are insured and carefully warehoused. It is troublesome for the bank to keep constant watch on the goods; banks accept goods as security only if they are convinced of the integrity of the customer.

(3) Machinery and other equipment which belongs to the borrowing entity, provided that it is insured.

(4) Life Insurance Policy up to its Surrender value provided the insured's age has been admitted; the latest premium receipt must be submitted.

(5) Buildings/houses are avoided because of depreciation, difficulties of valuation and difficulties of checking that the insurance policy on the building is kept up-to-date.

(6) Banks are often reluctant to accept rural land as security because of difficulties of assessment, and complications arising from varied systems of ownership and rules of succession. Validity of title to land is also difficult to ascertain. Besides, in case of bankruptcy, the banker often finds that forced sale brings lower value, particularly in rural areas.

After the bank has completed its credit enquiry and considered the suitability of the security offered, the customer is informed whether his loan application is granted or not. The letter given below informs the customer that his loan request has been granted.

Dear Sir,

We are pleased to inform you that your request for a loan of Rs.2,000,000 against the security of the following shares has been granted.

500 equity shares of XYZ Co. Ltd.
1000 equity shares of PQR Co. Ltd.
2000 equity shares of ABC Co. Ltd.

As it was already discussed with you, the rate of interest will be 16% per annum. The loan will be repaid over a period of three years.

A margin of 30% on the market value of the shares must always be maintained, and in cse of any shortfall, you will have to make the required adjustment when you are notified about it. The shares will be held under blank transfer, but you are required to notify the concerned companies. We are happy to be of service to you. Please meet me in the branch office with the share certificates, to sign the loan documents.

Yours faithfully,
Branch Manager

If the loan is refused, the reason for the refusal must be explained. The letter may indicate that the request can be considered later and, if possible, make a counter-proposal.

A letter like the following serves the purpose.

> Sub.: Your application for loan of Rs. 500,000/-
>
> Dear Mr. Sharma,
>
> Our loan committee has considered your application but has declined the proposal as the security you have offered is not acceptable.
>
> The shares you have offered are not quoted on the Stock Exchange. The building is over fifty years old, and will depreciate rapidly. If you can offer some other security, the loan committee will reconsider your application. Please visit the bank at your convenience for a personal discussion.
>
> Yours sincerely,

The bank may also refuse a loan if it has had previous experience of delayed repayment by the customer.

> Dear Mr. Verma,
>
> Your request for an additional loan of Rs. 600,000/- has been considered.
>
> The bank records show that a loan of Rs. 500,000/- had been granted to you in May, 2002, to be repaid by 15 December, 2002. The loan was repaid only on 26 March, 2003, after several letters from the bank asking you to repay.
>
> The balance sheet of your business also indicates losses during the past three quarters.
>
> We regret that, in view of your difficulty in repaying the earlier loan and the prevailing conditions, your present request cannot be granted.
>
> Yours sincerely,

Replies to Customers' Complaints

Customers sometimes misunderstand services rendered by banks, and having made arrangements for one type of service, they expect to get the benefits of another type of service. Banking is a specialized service and many of a bank's customers are people who have no idea of banking practice at all; they need a careful and clear explanation. When a customer complains, the bank's position must be clearly explained; the customer may also be told that the bank will render the desired services under a different arrangement.

Replies to some complaints are discussed below:

(a) Complaint about Bank Charges on Current Account

Banks levy incidental charges on accounts in which the deposits are so small that the bank cannot invest them to earn any interest. If the deposits are larger, the cost of banking service is covered by the income earned by investing the funds. A courteous explanation of this may be given to the customer.

Sub.: Your Current Ac. No....

Dear Sir,

This is in reply to your letter of 15 July, about service charges debited to your account for the period April to June.

Banks usually charge a small amount as service charges on the accounts in which the average balance is less than Rs.5000/- for more than three months. The charge is for covering the expenses of running the account. Generally, the amount of expense is covered by interest earned from the funds; it is only when the balance falls below Rs.5000/- for more than three months that the charge is debited to the customer's account.

You will notice that the balance in your account during the period 28 March to 3 July, 2000, was less than Rs.5000/-.

A copy of the Rules of Current Accounts is enclosed for your reference. We are sure that you will see that the small charge made by the bank is justified.

Yours faithfully,

(b) Complaint about Dishonour of Cheque

When a customer complains that his cheque has been dishonoured, it is because he thinks that there was sufficient balance in his account to pay out the cash on the cheque. The bank has to explain why there was not sufficient balance. It may be that a cheque which was deposited for credit had not been credited to the account. There are several reasons why this can happen, for example:

(i) Strike of employees in this or the drawee bank may prevent prompt collection;

(ii) Cheques on banks in other states take 5 to 6 days for collection; a bank holiday in another state causes further delay;

(iii) The deposited cheque may have been referred to drawee for some reason.

This letter talks about two cheques: the issued cheque which was dishonoured and the deposited cheque which was not credited. Be careful not to confuse the reader between the two cheques.

Dear Sir,

We regret the inconvenience caused to you by the refusal of payment of your cheque of Rs.16,000/- dated 8 September, issued in favour of C.K. Mehta. The cheque could not be paid out as the balance to your credit when it was presented on the 9th, was only Rs. 10,481/-.

The cheque of Rs.25,000/- which you had deposited for credit on 7 September was on Gujarat State Cooperative Bank, Baroda. Cheques on banks in other states usually take about five days to collect; in addition, 10 September was a bank holiday in Gujarat and this caused further delay. Your account was credited with Rs. 25,000/- only on the 11th. Since there was no overdraft arrangement, the issued cheque could not be paid out.

The present balance in your account is sufficient to pay out the cheque drawn in favour of C.K. Mehta. In order to avoid such situations in future, we advise you to allow at least five days between depositing a cheque for credit and withdrawing the amount and, in any case, to ascertain the balance before issuing a cheque.

Yours faithfully,

The bank may advise a customer of good credit standing to arrange for overdraft facilities to avoid an awkward situation.

(c) Complaint about Bank's Failure to Render Some Service

The bank is liable if a customer suffers loss through the negligence of the bank in carrying out the customer's standing instructions. Customers sometimes fail to give clear instructions and then hold the bank liable for losses incurred. A careful explanation must be given to show that the bank has not failed in its duty, and also clearly indicate that the bank is willing to render the services which the customer wants.

Dear Sir,

We regret that you lost the opportunity to apply for right shares owing to non-presentment of the coupons which are kept in the box given to the bank for safe custody. We must point out, however, that the bank is not liable for your loss.

The bank is not authorized to open any sealed containers given by customers for safe custody, unless there are written instructions from the customer that the bank should take out the contents for a particular purpose. Since there were no instructions from you that we should present your coupons, the bank is not liable for your loss in this instance.

We would be glad to render you whatever services you need in connection with your shares and stocks. You only have to give instructions, in writing, in order to avail yourself of the various services we render.

Please visit the bank on any week day during banking hours for a personal discussion of your requirements.

Yours faithfully,

Letters about Overdrawn Accounts

If the customer is important and has been known to the bank for a long time, the bank may pay out an occasional cheque in excess of credit balance even though overdraft arrangements have not been made. The customer is informed at once that the account is overdrawn and courteously requested to deposit the amount required and to check the balance before issuing cheques. If a valued customer overdraws again, the bank may suggest making O/D arrangements. Usually a customer is warned that cheques will be dishonoured if there is not sufficient balance or if O/D arrangements are not made. These letters are marked "Confidential".

Dear Sir,

We paid out, today, your Company's cheque for Rs. 15,000/- dated 10 October, issued in favour of Messrs. Kotecha Bros. although there was insufficient balance. Your company's account now stands overdrawn by Rs. 8,000/-. The cheque was honoured in spite of shortage of funds in the account in view of your Company's long standing relations with this bank. However, it is advisable to arrange for overdraft facility in case the Company requires additional funds at its disposal.

Please arrange to verify the balance before further cheques are issued.

Yours faithfully,

XYZ

Manager

If a customer frequently overdraws the account without making any overdraft arrangement, the bank takes a tough stand after a few occasions.

> Sub.: Cheques issued in excess of balance
>
> Dear Sir,
>
> Your cheque of Rs.22,000/- dated 8th December drawn in favour of Messrs. ABC and Co., has just been paid out even though the credit balance in your account was not sufficient. The cheque was honoured because you are one of our valued customers. Please arrange to deposit Rs.8,000/- into your account immediately.
>
> Your account has been overdrawn several times in the last three months. Since the issuing of a cheque without sufficient balance in the account has been made a cognizable offence under Section 138 of the Negotiable Instruments Act, we could not afford to return your cheques unpaid in spite of the lack of balance, keeping in view your status as a businessman.
>
> However, there are restrictions on the powers of a branch manager, and it is not possible to allow overdraft beyond a certain limit and it will not be possible to continue to pay out cheques in excess of your credit balance. I request you to maintain sufficient balance in your account to provide for the cheques you issue.
>
> Yours faithfully,

Dishonour of Cheque

If there is no balance in a customer's account when the cheque is presented for payment, the bank may dishonour the cheque. The customer is informed immediately about it. The letter is marked "Confidential".

> Sub.: Your cheque of Rs.— issued in favour of ...
>
> Dear Sir,
>
> We are sorry to inform you that the above-mentioned cheque had to be returned unpaid when it was presented for payment today, on account of lack of credit balance in your account. The credit balance was Rs.— only.
>
> Please ensure that you maintain sufficient balance to cover the cheques issued on your account. It is embarrassing for the bank as well as for you if a cheque has to be returned unpaid for want of balance.
>
> Besides, you must be aware that issuing a cheque when there is no balance in the account has been made a cognizable offence under Section 138 of the Negotiable Instruments Act. We hope that there will not be any repetition of such a situation.
>
> Yours faithfully,

If a customer's cheque has to be dishonoured more than once, the letter is written in a stronger tone.

> Sub.: Your cheque no.— in favour of Vinod Steel Ltd.
>
> Dear Sir,
>
> The above-mentioned cheque of Rs. 18,000/- dated __ had to be returned unpaid today on account of lack of balance in your account.
>
> This is the second time within fifteen days that you have issued a cheque without keeping sufficient balance in your account to meet the cheque. I have already brought

to your notice the provisions of Section 138 of the Negotiable Instruments Act related to issue of cheques when there is no balance in the account.

Issuing cheques in this manner can have a serious effect on your business reputation. Banks also take a serious view of this.

Please make it a point to maintain sufficient balance and to make provision for every cheque you issue.

Yours faithfully,

Closing a Customer's Account

A bank requests a customer to close the account if it is operated unsatisfactorily; that is, if the required balance is not maintained or cheques are frequently issued in excess of balance without overdraft arrangement, or stop payment commands are issued frequently. An account cannot be closed by the bank without adequate notice to the account holder; usually one month is considered adequate notice. The bank informs the customer that deposits for credit will not be accepted after a certain date; and that the customer should arrange to withdraw the balance and return unused cheques within a month's time. The letter is marked "Confidential".

CONFIDENTIAL

Sub.: Your Current A/c No....

Dear Mr. Dalvi,

I am sorry to inform you that your cheque of Rs.15,000/- dated 7 September, 2003, drawn in favour of S.S. Shah, had to be returned unpaid because there was insufficient credit balance in your account.

Since 3 June, 2003, the bank has had to dishonour five of your cheques for the same reason. Besides, you have countermanded four cheques in the last two months. Such irregular conduct of the bank account is viewed unfavourably by the directors of the bank as it reflects badly on the bank's reputation as well as the customer's. I must therefore request you to close your account with this bank within a month.

The balance to your credit is Rs.5,300/-. Further credits to your account will be accepted only for 15 days from today and your cheques will be paid out, according to the balance, till 10 October.

Please arrange to withdraw your balance and return unused cheque forms by 10 October.

Yours faithfully,

XYZ

Manager

Overdraft and Loan Accounts

Customers who have borrowed loans or have overdraft arrangements have to be informed if there is any change in the existing or original conditions. Some examples are given below.

(a) If a customer does not use the overdraft facility for a long time, the bank may decide to close the facility because the bank's funds are tied up. This is different from closing a customer's account; only the overdraft facility is to be stopped, the current account continues. There is absolutely no reflection on the customer's credit.

Sub.: Overdraft facility on your current account No. ...

Dear Sir,

We find that you have not made use of your overdraft facility for over six months, and conclude that you are not in need of the facility now. We are therefore withdrawing it from 1 January, 2004.

The lending capacity and power of a bank and its branches are limited by various regulations; it is therefore necessary for us to distribute overdraft facilities among customers who are in need of finances. Since we have overdraft applications pending, we are closing the unused facilities.

Please be assured that this has no personal significance, and the bank will be willing to consider a loan application if you should be in need of finances, at any time. The credit balance in your A/c is Rs.... In case you have issued a cheque in excess of that, please make provision for the payment of the cheque.

Please arrange to collect your securities deposited with the bank against the O/D facility.

Yours faithfully,

(b) If there is substantial depreciation of the security deposited by a borrower against a loan, the bank may recall part of the loan, or ask the customer to make good the shortfall in the security.

Sub.: Your loan of Rs.1,50,000 granted on 17 July, 2003

Dear Sir,

I am sorry to inform you that the security deposited with the bank for the above-mentioned loan has depreciated.

The shares of XYZ Co. Ltd. which were valued at Rs.— have now fallen to Rs.—. It will, therefore, be necessary for you to deposit additional security of the value of Rs.—.

Alternatively, you can reduce the loan to Rs.— by repaying Rs.— so that the present value of your security will be sufficient. The adjustment must be made within fifteen days. In case you have any difficulty, please call on me for a personal discussion, during banking hours.

Yours faithfully,

LETTERS BETWEEN HEAD OFFICE AND BRANCHES

Branch Managers and Agents of banks have certain powers with regard to granting loans and overdraft facilities; but if there is an unusually large loan to be granted or if a customer is to be accommodated on unusual terms, it must be sanctioned by the Head Office.

The General Manager
Dena Bank
Bombay 400 001

Sub.: Customer's request for loan

Dear Sir,

I have received an application for a loan of Rs.2,000,000/- for one year from Messrs. Gulabdas & Sons of Everest Launderers, Kalyan. They are unable to deposit any security; they require the loan for modernizing their laundry and installing high-powered washing machines.

They have had their trading account with this branch for the last eight years, and have always been careful in the conduct of their account. Their business has grown rapidly in the last four years as they have been able to capture almost all the upper class clientele in this locality. The partners themselves enjoy a considerable social reputation.

The application, along with their Balance Sheets and Profit and Loss Accounts for the last three years, is enclosed. They have agreed to arrange for two guarantors. I recommend that their application should be granted.

I would appreciate receiving an early reply since the clients are anxious to have the work completed before the monsoon begins.

Yours faithfully,
XYZ
Manager

The following is a reply from the Head Office:

Dear Mr. Murthy,

I have examined the proposal of Messrs. Gulabdas & Sons, of Everest Launderers, Kalyan, for a loan of Rs. 2,000,000/- for the purpose of modernizing their laundry.

The loan application may be granted with the following modification. A letter of hypothecation of the machines to be purchased should be obtained from the clients, in addition to guarantees from two persons of good financial and social standing. Also, they should be requested to submit a copy of their monthly Profit & Loss Account to the bank until their loan is repaid.

It is also advisable to ensure that this concession does not become a precedent in future.

Yours sincerely,
XYZ
General Manager

EXERCISES

1. Write a letter as from the manager of a bank to a customer, informing him that his facility to overdraw his account is being withdrawn since he has not used it for over eight months.
2. A letter drawing attention to an overdrawn account was addressed to a valued client whose account is in credit. Draft the bank manager's letter of apology and explanation.

3. A fancy goods dealer has asked his bank for an overdraft facility up to Rs. 50,000/- for two months, without security. He has pointed out that he has excellent business prospects during the approaching festival season. Draft the bank's reply.
4. A loan of Rs. 80,000/- was granted two years ago to a customer, on the security of shares valued at Rs. 120,000/-. Since then, the value of the shares has fallen by 20%. Write to the customer, informing him what should be done in the matter.
5. A lady customer has written to her banker asking for advice on the investment of Rs.2,000,000/-. She had pointed out that she wants a safe investment with a steady income. Draft the bank's reply.
6. A customer has enquired of his bank whether he can get a loan of Rs.45,000/- against the security of his insurance policy. Draft the bank's letter explaining that the Life Insurance Policy can be considered up to its surrender value, provided that his age has been admitted by the L.I.C. and the policy has not been assigned.
7. A taxi-driver has approached his bank for a loan of Rs.600,000/- to purchase a new car as his old taxi is worn out. Draft the bank's letter explaining how the bank will help him.
8. A customer writes to complain that his cheque was dishonoured although, according to his books, there was sufficient balance to his credit. Draft the bank's reply, explaining why the bank was compelled to dishonour the cheque.
9. Write a letter as from the manager of a bank to a customer who does not maintain the required balance and often countermands his cheques, asking him to close his account.
10. A man with influential friends and relatives in the locality requests a bank to open an account in his name and to grant him a small overdraft without any security. The branch manager knows that he has no means and is little worthy of confidence. Draft a tactful reply to be sent to him by the branch manager.
11. A girl who has recently got a job as a clerk, has asked your bank for advice on investing her savings. Write a reply giving some information about suitable savings schemes of the bank.
12. The Manager of a firm, which has its account in your bank, has complained that his peon is kept waiting when he is sent for the firm's bank work. Draft the banker's reply stating that generally all transactions are completed without delay, and explaining why the peon had to wait for some time, on some occasions.
13. As the branch manager, you have granted a loan to a customer without prior sanction from the head office. The head office has asked for a justification for granting a loan in a hurry. Draft a reply.
14. As the manager of a branch of a bank, write to the Head Office asking for additional furniture/computers/more facilities for the staff.
15. As the branch Manager, write to the Head Office asking for larger premises and more staff.
16. As the branch Manager, write to the Head Office asking for more services in your branch.
17. A branch manager has granted a loan to a customer without proper security. Write her letter to the Head Office giving reasons to justify her action.

18. The Head Office of a bank has received a complaint from the Bank Depositors' Association about delays in counter transactions and mistakes in filling in customers' passbooks at a certain branch. The manager of the branch has been asked for an explanation. Draft the branch manager's reply.
19. Write a reply to a customer who has complained that the bank has failed to make payment of her electricity bill in spite of standing instructions.
20. Write a tactful letter as from the branch manager to a customer requesting him not to issue cheques in excess of the balance in his savings account, and suggesting that he should open a current account with overdraft facility.
21. Draft a circular to be sent to all customers of your branch informing them that the loans department is being shifted to a neighbouring building owing to lack of space in the branch office.
22. Your branch has installed a safe deposit vault; lockers will be available from the first of next month. Draft a circular to all your customers, informing them about the new facility.
23. ATM facility has been started at your branch. Draft a circular informing all customers of the branch. Use the opportunity to build up goodwill.

Chapter **29**

INSURANCE LETTERS

FIRE INSURANCE

Fire insurance is a contract by which an insurance company, in return for a premium paid by the insured party, agrees to make good any loss or damage caused by fire, during a particular period. The maximum amount which the insured party can claim from the insurance company is fixed at the time of making the contract, and is specified in the contract. But this is not the measure of the actual loss; the actual loss can be estimated only after the fire has occurred.

A person who wants to insure his or her property makes a proposal to the insurer on a printed Proposal Form. The form requires the proposer to give all information about the property, such as situation, construction, and occupation of the building, previous insurance, history, etc.

If the proposal is accepted by the insurance company, a Cover Note is issued indicating the granting of protection for the period from the date of acceptance till the policy is issued. A Cover Note is valid for 30 days if the insurance period is one year and for 15 days if the period is shorter.

Request for insurance, enquiries about premium rates etc., may be made by letter. The letter asking for insurance premium rates must give all details of the location, address and value of the property to be insured.

Dear Sirs,

We wish to insure our stock of cotton bales worth Rs. 10,00,000 stored in 3 warehouses at 16, Hospital Road, Parel, Bombay 400 012. Please send your surveyor to inspect the goods and the premises. The Keeper of the warehouses has been instructed to assist the surveyor; he may visit the warehouses on any day between 9 a.m. and 6 p.m.

Yours faithfully,

Dear Sirs,

Enclosed is the Proposal Form giving details of our woollen mill and warehouses at Thane. A cheque for Rs.— is also en-closed in payment of the first premium. Please arrange to issue the policy as early as possible.

Yours faithfully,

In fixing the rate of premium, the insurer takes into account the physical hazards of the risk. The following physical hazards are considered.

(a) Construction of the building is an important consideration. Reinforced concrete, stone or burnt brick with cement or mortar binding, and hard roof of tiles or slate are good risk. Mud walls, wooden frames, bamboo, plaster etc., are high risk. A thatched roof is by far the most risky. Wooden flooring and floor openings for stairs and lifts are considered a bad physical hazard as fire and hot gases rise upward and the flooring can collapse easily. The fire also spreads easily to upper floors. Height of the building is taken into account as it adds to the difficulties of fire-fighting because water pressure decreases at higher levels. Water damage to lower floors is also increased.

(b) Lighting, heating and power systems represent another aspect of physical hazard. Electrical installations may be faulty, dampness may lead to combustion or there may be faulty circuits. Where there is lighting by gas or oil, the open flame and possibility of fuel leakage adds to the risk of fire. In industrial premises, the hazard is greatly increased if there is night work, owing to artificial lighting, possible carelessness of workers and continuous use of machinery which may result in fire by friction.

(c) Occupation is a very important factor in assessing the hazard. A dwelling house is a lesser risk than a shop; a warehouse used for the storage of combustible or inflammable goods is a greater risk than a warehouse used for non-inflammable goods. A printer's shop is a great hazard because of the heat given out by high-speed machinery and the presence of oily rags and paper adds to the risk of spontaneous combustion and spread of fire.

(d) Situation of the building, that is, the nearness of other buildings, the nature of the adjoining buildings, the degree of congestion in the area, are also taken into account; if there is a coal shop, kerosene shop, timber yard, or petrol pump nearby, the risk is increased. On the other hand, nearness to a fire brigade station or to a source of water supply decreases the risk and attracts a discount in the rate of premium.

The rates depend on the degree of the physical hazard. The risks are classified according to trade and occupation; the basic rate for each class and sub-class is laid down in the Tariff; extra charges are added for bad features and discounts are given for good features. Rules, regulations and rates are laid down by the Insurance Association of India. Rates for the common classes of risks, are given in the Tariff; rates and regulations for the inclusion of extraneous risks of Riot and Civil Commotion or Earthquake, are also given in the Tariff.

Though the Tariff provides the rates and the rules, the risk is assessed by the insurer on the basis of the survey report given by the insurer's representative after inspecting the premises.

In addition to physical hazard, there may be a moral hazard in a proposal. It arises from human nature and depends on the character of the insured, his relations with employees, neighbours, tenants, etc., his efficiency in management, general carefulness, and honesty. If the insurer feels that the moral hazard is bad, he may refuse to accept the risk.

The letter below illustrates the insurance company's quotation of rates after inspecting the premises to be insured.

> Dear Sir,
>
> We had our surveyor inspect your godown at 16 Hospital Road, Parel, as you requested in your letter of 8 September. The survey report indicates that the building is 50 years old and has wooden flooring. Besides, there is a kerosene shop in the adjoining building. Thus, there are internal and external hazards.
>
> In these circumstances, we shall cover your stock of cotton at 8%. Our risk begins as soon as we receive the enclosed Proposal Form, duly filled in, with your first premium.
>
> Yours faithfully,

A client may try to bargain for a lower rate. The client's bargaining letter should point out circumstances and conditions which reduce the risk of fire.

> Dear Sir,
>
> We have received your quotation of rates for covering our stock of cotton stored in godowns at Parel. We would like to point out that a stock of cotton textiles in another godown in the same building has been insured at 7%. The electric wiring in the building has recently been completely renewed, and Fire Extinguishing Appliances have been installed in the building. This should entitle us to a discount in the rate. We, therefore request you to reconsider your quotation.
>
> Yours faithfully,

Any change in the occupation of the building or shifting of the goods from the place where they are stored at the time of taking out the policy, must be brought to the notice of the insurer. As a consequence of the change, the premium rate may be increased or reduced. In either case, the insurer informs the client. If the client does not inform the insurance company of the change, the policy becomes invalid.

> Sir,
>
> Sub: Fire policy No. F 70689 covering silk yarn
>
> valued at Rs. 3,00,000 stored at
>
> 710, Waudby Street, Lalbaug.
>
> We have transferred the entire stock mentioned above, to another godown at 15, Library Road, Bandra. The building is new and has fire extinguishing appliances installed on all the three floors. We, therefore, expect a reduction in the premium rate. Please send your surveyor to inspect the premises and confirm cover for the goods in the new godown.
>
> Yours faithfully,

The insurance company's reply informs the client about the new rate of premium and arranges for adjustment of premium already paid.

> Sirs,
>
> Sub: Your Policy No. 70689
> Goods shifted to new godown
>
> Our surveyor has inspected your new godown at 15, Library Road, Bandra, as you requested in your letter of 17 February, 2001. We confirm cover for the goods. As the new godown has been rated higher than the old one at Lalbaug, the rate of premium will be reduced from Rs. 7% to Rs. 4%. We have en-closed a Receipt Form for Rs. 2500/- to be signed by you. We shall send a cheque for Rs. 2500 in refund of the excess premium already paid by you.
>
> Please attach the enclosed Endorsement Slip to your Insurance Policy.
>
> Yours faithfully,

Losses and Claims

An ordinary fire policy covers damage caused by (i) accidental fire in a place where there ought not to be a fire; (ii) lightning; (iii) explosion of gas used for domestic purposes in a building which is not a part of a gas works.

Losses resulting directly from fire are also paid under the policy; generally these are damages caused by:

(1) water or other fire-extinguisher used in fighting the fire;

(2) any act of the Fire Brigade in extinguishing the fire;

(3) falling of parts of the building because of the fire;

(4) breakage during removal from a burning building;

(5) exposure to rain or bad weather because of lying in the open after removal from a burning building.

Other risks can be covered by a special endorsement, on payment of additional premium. Some of these are : Earthquake Shock and Fire Damage, Strike Riot and Civil Commotion (SRCC), Explosion (especially for industrial units), and Flood.

When property covered by a fire policy is damaged or destroyed by fire, the insurer must be informed within 24 hours of the event. A claim on the prescribed Claim Form is to be made within 15 days, and must be supported by documents to prove the loss and the values stated in the form.

The insurance company sends its representative or a surveyor to estimate and investigate the loss and negotiate with the client to arrive at a settlement; he submits a Survey Report to the insurance company. The company examines the report and settles the claim according to it.

Sirs,

Sub: Fire Policy No. 3842 covering cotton bales stocked at 16 Hospital Road, Parel.

We are sorry to inform you that a fire broke out about 11.30 last night in the godown mentioned above. The night watchman called the fire brigade immediately and the fire was put out about 1.00 a.m. It has not been possible to establish the cause of the fire.

According to our estimate the loss is Rs.—. Please send your representative to inspect the damage. As we are anxious to have the godown repaired and to re-stock as soon as possible, we request you to settle our claim immediately. Please let us know what particulars we should furnish for making a claim.

Yours faithfully,

Sir,

Sub: Your claim under Fire Policy No. F. 3842

We have received your letter dated 8 February, stating that there was a fire in your godown insured under the above- mentioned policy.

Our Surveyor, Mr. R.G. Samant has been instructed to survey the loss. Please make your Account books and other relevant records available to him. A Claim Form is enclosed for you to fill in and return. We shall proceed in the matter as soon as we receive the claim form and the survey report.

Yours faithfully,

Claims Manager

The insurer may accept, dispute, reduce or refuse the claim after making various enquiries as to the cause and extent of the damage, and taking into account the terms of the contract.

A dispute may arise about the value of the goods damaged or destroyed, or about the possibility of salvage of some goods (like cloth damaged by water) or about the repair of goods which got broken in the confusion caused by fire, and so on.

If the insured has made any changes in the storage or occupation of the property without informing the insurer, the policy becomes invalid. The insurer will refuse to pay if the insured goods have been transferred to a different place, or night work has been started without endorsement of the insurer.

Fire insurance is a contract of indemnity; the insured is to be put in the same financial position as he held before the occurrence of the fire; he is not allowed to make profit from the insurance. The insurer may make good the loss either by cash payment or by replacing or reinstating the property. The measure of indemnity is estimated by the surveyor. For a building, the measure of indemnity is the cost of repairing the damage so as to restore it to its pre-fire condition; allowance for depreciation is also calculated. For stock and merchandise, the insured is entitled to the market value of the goods at the time and place of the fire; this is naturally different for a manufacturer's stock and a retailer's stock. In case of under-insurance, the insurer is protected by the condition of average. The insurer's maximum liability is the amount insured; if there is partial loss, the insurer pays a rateable portion of the loss.

Some letters dealing with claims are given below:

Sirs,

Sub: Your claim: Fire Policy No. F. 3842

Our surveyor Mr. G. K. Sawant has submitted his report after inspection of the damage caused to your stock of cotton. The damage has been assessed at Rs.3,800,000/-. We have enclosed our cheque for the amount, on Bank of India, Mumbai. Please sign and return the enclosed receipt.

Yours faithfully,

Sub: Fire Policy No. F. 4584

Dear Sir,

We have received your letter of 10 May, 2001, notifying us of a fire in your godown covered by the above-mentioned policy.

We regret that the policy, which was for a period of six months, expired on 30 April. In our letter No. F/47/27 dated 28 April we drew your attention to the expiry date of the policy and requested you to renew it, if necessary. As you did not renew it we had to allow it to lapse. In these circumstances we are not liable to make good your loss.

Yours faithfully,

Sirs,

Sub: Your Fire Policy No. F/3842/91

We have received your claim form and documents related to the damage caused to your stock of cotton bales insured under the above-mentioned policy. The survey report submitted by our surveyor Mr. G. K. Sawant, on inspection of the damage, indicates that the destroyed and damaged goods were of the value of Rs. 3,800,000/-.

Though the total value of the stock in the godown was Rs.8,000,000/- your policy was taken for only Rs. 4,000,000/-. By the condition of average stated in Clause 2 of the policy, we are liable to pay only a rateable portion of your loss. We therefore, accept your claim for Rs.1,900,000/-. A cheque for the amount will be sent as soon as we receive the enclosed receipt form with your signature.

Yours faithfully,

ABC

Claims Manager

MARINE INSURANCE

Marine insurance is generally effected through an insurance broker. A merchant who wants to have his risk covered writes to a broker giving details of the risk. The Insurance Company determines the acceptability of the risk, quotes the rate and issues the policy after considering the details of the risk. The Insurance Company requires particulars about (1) the client; (2) the ship (or conveyance); (3) the voyage; (4) the goods and mode of packing; (5) the risks required to be covered; (6) the value of the goods for the purpose of insurance.

(1) The client: The moral hazard of a client is considered very important in marine insurance because carelessness in packing, and selection of forwarding and clearing agents causes the risks to be higher. Experienced and reputable exporters get more favourable rates.

(2) The conveyance: It is usually enough to give the name of the ship by which the goods will be sent; if the quotation is required for an open policy, it is sufficient to state that goods will be sent by "an approved steamer" or "a first-class steamer." If the goods are to be sent by rail or by road, details like goods or passenger train, open or closed wagon, date of railway receipt or carrier's receipt and registered number of the truck must be given.

(3) The voyage: The route and length of the voyage is an important factor; the premium rate is also affected by the condition of the ports at both ends of the voyage. In many small ports in India, ships have to stand out at sea, and the loading and unloading of cargo is done by lighters (small boats); this exposes the cargo to risk of loss and damage. Insufficient warehouses, poor cranes, poor facilities for moving cargo away from the port, etc., expose the cargo to pilferage, theft, rain and other risks. The ports of sailing and of destination must be mentioned.

(4) The goods and the packing: Each product is liable to different kinds of damage from different causes like ship's sweat, climatic conditions at various stages of the voyage, rough handling, taint from other cargo, etc.

Packing is of great importance since different kinds of packing attract different risks. Cotton or jute packed in bales is exposed to hook damage, but not so much to pilferage; cased cargo can be pilfered but is not exposed to hook damage. Iron-bound bales are safer than rope-bound bales. Tea packed in lead-lined cases is considered a good risk. Bagged cargo like flour, cement, sugar suffers from hook damage, bursting of bags, pilferage etc.; new double gunny bags are considered better than single or old bags. Liquid goods are packed in drums; the condition of the drums is important.

Technological advances in containers and packing methods have significantly reduced the risks of damage to goods during transport.

(5) The risks: The plain form of policy covers the following marine perils: (a) perils of the seas include damage by sea water, storm, waves, wind, lightning, collision, stranding and such dangers which are unforeseen and are normally guarded against by the ship owners and the crew. (b) Damage or loss caused by attacks of pirates and rovers (i.e., sea robbers). (c) Jettison, i.e., throwing over-board, any cargo to lighten the ship in order to save it from danger. This risk is automatically covered for cargo which is normally carried on deck, like timber or corrosive acids; but for cargo which is normally not carried on deck, this risk has to be specially covered. (d) Barratry, i.e., wrongful acts committed by the ship's master or crew.

In addition to these, other extraneous risks can be covered by paying additional premiums. Some of these are: Theft, Pilferage and/or Non-Delivery (TPND), Hook Damage, Heating, Sweating, Damage by other cargo, Country Damage, Leakage, Breakage, and Fresh Water/Rain Water damage when inland transit is involved.

A policy may be FPA (Free of Particular Average) or WA (With Average). (In marine insurance, the word "average" means loss). If the policy is extended to cover one or more of the additional extraneous risks it is called "wider cover." A "comprehensive cover" is on W.A. conditions, including the normal extraneous risks except leakage and breakage. All Risks Cover includes all extraneous risks but not War or SRCC (Strike, Riot, Civil Commotion); if any of the risks is to be excluded from All Risks cover, it must be specifically mentioned as excluded. War and Strike, Riot, Civil Commotion includes capture, seizure, arrest, civil war, revolution, etc., and damage caused because of such disturbances.

(6) The value: The value of the goods for the purpose of insurance needs to be carefully considered. The goods are in transit and in the course of being delivered under a contract of sale. The goods appreciate in value as they reach near the destination because cost of transport is to be added; also, customs duty and other factors make the market price of a particular cargo different, in different countries. The uncertainty is avoided by issuing "agreed value" policy. All losses are then settled on the basis of the agreed value irrespective of market value.

Types of Policies

There are two main types of policies for cargo, viz., specific and open.

Specific Policy or Voyage Policy is issued for a single shipment when all the details are known, such as date and ports of sailing and destination, the route, the cargo, its packing and its value.

Open Policy or Declaration Policy is issued for a large amount, to cover a series of consignments for a period of six months or one year. The details are specified at the time of each shipment, which is declared against the policy. The full amount of the premium is paid at the time of taking out the policy; this kind of policy saves premium on small consignments and also saves stamp duty which the client has to pay. A particular consignment is covered only if the Declaration Form is sent to the insurer within 24 hours of the shipment.

Time Policy is usually issued for ships (and vehicles); it covers the ship for a stated period of time, usually one year. It has nothing to do with voyage; the ship may take any route and make any number of voyages. But there are warranties, i.e., prohibition on entry into certain zones during certain seasons, e.g., Baltic warranty prohibits entry into the Baltic sea from 15 November to 28 February.

Some specimen letters are given here.

Dear Sir,

Please issue in our name an F.P.A. All Risks policy to cover a shipment of Kashmir Woollen Goods valued at Rs. 5,000,000/. The consignment is to be shipped on account of Messrs. Dickinson & Sons, London, by S. S. "Jaldoot" sailing from Mumbai on 25 September.

The goods will be packed in double hessian over waterproof paper, and metal-strapped. There will be five bales each valued at Rs.1,000,000; the bales will be numbered from 1 to 5 and will be marked with the enclosed figure.

We would appreciate receiving the policy soon, as we wish to send it to our consignee with the shipping documents.

Yours faithfully,

Dear Sirs,

The ship S.S. "Jalmayur" of XYZ Shipping Corporation has been chartered by us and will sail from Mumbai for London on 15 October, with a cargo of tea. The tea will be packed in lead-lined cases.

Please arrange for insurance cover for the ship and the cargo for Rs. 2,000,000 and Rs. 3,000,000 respectively. We request you to keep within a limit of a premium of 3% for the ship and 3.5% for the cargo. This should not be difficult considering the excellent reputation of the shipping corporation and the expert crew manning the ship.

Yours faithfully,

XYZ

Export Manager

Tea Board of India

Sir,

We have entered into a contract to supply Kashmir Silk and Woollen goods to New York, to the extent of Rs. 6,000,000/ from August 2001 to March 2002. Please issue in our name, a W.A. Open Policy for the amount, covering All Risks including S.R.C.C.

The goods will be packed in bales and shipped by approved steamers, from Mumbai. The first consignment will be shipped in the first week of August. Please send us the policy by 3 August.

Yours faithfully,

When the insurer gets all the details of the proposal, he quotes a rate of premium. A large number of marine risks are tariffed in India but there is still a great deal of non-tariff business which accounts for the variation in the quotations of different companies. In judging a risk, the company goes by its past experience of the particular type of business. Besides, all clients do not get the same rates; a new client whose volume of business is small will get a higher rate than a regular client with a larger account.

Dear Sirs,

According to your instructions in your letter dated 4 October, 2001, to arrange for insurance for the ship s.s. "Jalmayur" and your cargo of tea sailing for London on 15 October, we made enquiries with insurance companies, but find that it is not possible to get your terms of 3% and 3.5%. We therefore, request you to raise your limit to 3.5% for the ship and 4% for the cargo as these are the terms offered by New Assurance Co.

Please fax your reply immediately.

Yours faithfully,

XYZ

Insurance Broker

Sirs,

We thank you for your letter of 25 July asking us to issue an Open Policy for Rs.6,000,000 for your shipments of Kashmir Silk and Woollen goods to New York, from this August to April next year.

The Policy No. M 124365 covering All Risks including SRCC, as required, is enclosed, together with our Debit Note for Rs.— to cover the premium @ 3% and stamp duty of Rs.—

Each shipment dispatched must be declared giving details of the number of packages, value, marking, destination, name of the ship, and number and date of the B/L. A particular shipment is covered by the policy only if we receive the relevant Declaration Form which we must receive before the ship sails. Eight Declaration Forms are enclosed.

Yours faithfully,

ABC

Marine Manager

Encls: Policy No. M. 124365
Debit Note for Rs.—-
Eight Declaration Forms

When an open policy is fully declared, the company informs the client.

Sirs,

Your Open Policy No. M. 38427 stands fully declared by your last declaration dated 7 January. We shall be glad to issue a fresh Open Policy in your name on the same terms and conditions as soon as we receive your instructions.

Yours faithfully,

Losses and Claims

In marine insurance, loss may be total or partial. Total loss is of two kinds: (1) actual total loss is destruction of the subject matter insured or such damage as to make the article unfit for use or beyond repair; (2) constructive total loss is loss caused because of abandonment of ship or goods which have been so badly damaged that recovery or repair will cost more than the actual value of the goods. If the insured abandons the ship or the cargo he must give notice of abandonment to the insurer and surrender his claim to the goods.

Partial loss is of two kinds: (1) Particular Average is a partial loss caused by the usual perils insured against. (2) General Average loss is a sacrifice made or expense voluntarily incurred in time of danger, to avoid total loss of the ship. The ship's captain or officers may take an action to protect the ship, its passengers, crew, and cargo; for example, jettison of heavy goods to lighten the ship, or hire a tug to re-float a stranded ship. All those whose interests are saved have to make rateable contribution to make good the sacrifice or the expense. General average losses and contributions are recoverable from respective marine insurers of the ship and the cargo.

A claim is made by the party who has an insurable interest in the goods at the time of the damage. This depends on the type of contract of sale; in FOB and CF contracts the goods are at the buyer's risk from the time they are loaded, while in a CIF contract they are at the seller's risk during the voyage. However, since the damage comes to the notice of the consignee first, the policy is usually assigned to him. The consignee can prefer the claim to the insurer's Claim Settling Agent at the port of destination, or to the agent nearest to the place of claim, or to the office which issued the policy or to the Head Office of the insurance company; all these have the power to settle a claim.

The consignee has to get the damage surveyed by authorized survey agents. The name and address of the authority whose survey report is to be obtained is usually given on the policy. At ports where there is no surveying facility, Lloyd's Agents are authorized to act as surveyors.

Sirs,

Sub: Marine Policy No. 15886

Declaration No. 7

We regret that the consignment of Kashmir Silks which we shipped to New York by s.s. "Jalprakash" on 17 October, 2001, insured as above, has been reported missing at the port of destination. Our consignees, Messrs. John & Bailey, have sent us their statement and the certificate from the ship's captain.

Please inform us what documents are to be sent to you, and arrange for an early settlement of the claim.

Yours faithfully,

XYZ

When a claim is received, the insurer calls for the required documents from the client and also collects reports from other sources; for example, meteorological report for the day and place required, the ship's log and records from port authorities to check whether any accident or damage had occurred at the ports.

The insurer has to establish the cause of the loss. For cargo claims, an independent surveyor may be appointed to check the cause and extent of the loss. In case there is a possibility of recovery from the carriers, the insurer will ask for a damage/shortage certificate from the ship's captain. The insurer also checks whether the claim is admissible under the terms of the policy.

Sir,

Sub Your claim: Policy No. M. 684489.

We received your letter dated... informing us of the damage to your consignment of... insured under the above-mentioned policy, and have examined your claim and your damage report. The loss is payable under the policy. Please send us the following documents:

(1) Original Insurance Policy duly endorsed

(2) A copy of the Bill of Lading

(3) Letter of subrogation (draft enclosed)

(4) Damage certificate from ship's captain

Your claim will be settled as soon as the documents are scrutinized.

Yours faithfully,

XYZ

Claims Manager

Claims may be accepted, or reduced or refused for various reasons. Letters given below, deal with claims.

Sirs,

Sub: Your claim: Policy No. M. 684329 Declaration No. 6

Your claim form and other documents in connection with the claim mentioned above have been scrutinized and your claim of Rs. 840,000/ has been accepted in full. A loss voucher for Rs. 840,000/ is enclosed for you to discharge and return. A cheque in settlement of your claim will be sent as soon as we receive the voucher from you.

Yours faithfully,

XYZ

Adjuster of Claims

Sirs,

Sub: Your claim: Policy No...

Declaration No...

We have received the damage report from our surveyors, in connection with your claim of Rs. 840,000/ as indemnity for damage caused by sea water to your consignment of paper which arrived on board the HMS "Olivia" on 17 September.

The Survey Report indicates that the contents of three of the ten cases are not touched by water at all, and are in perfect condition. The contents of only seven cases have been damaged. We, therefore, cannot accept your claim in full.

According to the statements in your Declaration Form, the value of the contents of the seven cases is Rs. 580,000/. Please submit a revised claim voucher to enable us to settle the claim.

Yours faithfully,

XYZ

Adjuster of Claims

Sirs,

Sub: Your claim under Policy No. M 823045

We have examined your claim for loss of your consignment of tea shipped to London on 17 November, 2003.

The reports we have received, show that the ship S.S. "Jalprabha", by which the consignment was shipped, did not meet with any accident or run into any trouble on the voyage which might have caused the loss of the consignment. The loss is evidently due to some other cause. We are liable for such losses only if the policy includes the Theft, Pilferage and/or Non-Delivery clause. As your policy does not include this clause, we cannot accept your claim.

We suggest that you present your claim to the shipping company for compensation.

Yours faithfully,

XYZ

Adjuster of Claims

LIFE INSURANCE

Life insurance is not a contract of indemnity; the event insured against, namely, death, is a sure event. In other types of insurance, the event insured against is only a possibility; it may or may not happen. Life Insurance is a kind of investment and saving, and security for the family. The person who wants to take out a policy decides the amount and the period of the policy.

The rate of premium is based on the age of the subject, the amount of insurance desired, the term and the nature of the policy; since age is an important factor, proof of age has to be submitted to the L.I.C. When the proof is submitted, the words "Age admitted" are entered on the policy document. If the age is not admitted, proof of age will have to be produced later, at the time of repayment or claim or surrender or assignment of the policy.

A policy taken out at a young age has a lower rate of premium than a policy taken out later, since the rate is directly related to the age of the subject.

Premiums are to be paid according to schedule, i.e., monthly, quarterly or annually. The policy lapses if three consecutive premiums are not paid in spite of reminders; a lapsed policy has no value. The L.I.C. makes efforts to get the policy-holders to keep up their policies, and a lapsed policy can be revived on paying a nominal revival charge and the premiums in arrears.

If a policy-holder finds it difficult to continue payment of premiums, the policy can be converted into a paid-up policy for a reduced amount; but the term of the policy cannot be reduced, and the amount will be paid to the policy-holder on the original date of maturity of the policy. The value of the paid-up policy is calculated on the basis of the proportion between the originally insured sum and the premiums paid. The bonus up to the date of the conversion is credited to the paid-up policy. The L.I.C. makes efforts to prevent lapsing of policies and dissuades policy-holders from converting their policy to paid-up.

Dear Sir,

Re: Your Policy No. 78426 : own life

We regret that the above-mentioned policy stands lapsed as you have not paid any premiums since 7 August, 2000, although we sent you several reminders. We informed you in our letter dated 28 November, 2000, that the policy would lapse if three consecutive premiums were not paid. No benefits are payable on a lapsed policy.

The policy can be revived on a payment of a nominal revival charge along with the premiums in arrears. We are sure you will realize that it is a loss to allow a policy to lapse, and will pay the amount shown below, immediately.

Arrears of 3 months' premium:	Rs. 9800:00
Revival charges:	Rs. 50:00
Total:	Rs. 9850:00

Please call on us personally if you need any explanation or assistance in this matter.

Yours faithfully,

XYZ

Divisional Manager

Dear Sir,

We are sorry to learn from your letter dated 18 November, 2001, that you wish to convert your policy to paid-up owing to difficulties in paying premiums.

We urge you to avoid conversion of your policy. The sum cannot be paid to you till the policy matures, even if it is treated as paid-up. There are obvious advantages to you and your family in having a life insurance policy in force. Since your policy was taken out at an early age, you have had the advantage of a low rate of premium, and it would be loss of this advantage if you did not complete the full term of the policy. Besides, a policy can also be used as security for a loan from the L.I.C.

Your policy has lapsed because of non-payment of the last three premiums; it can be revived on the payment of a revival charge of Rs. 100/- along with the premiums in arrears and interest on the amount of the premiums. The total amount you will have to pay is Rs. 9900/- only. You will also have to submit a medical report from an authorized L.I.C. medical practitioner.

Please take immediate steps to revive your policy, as a lapsed policy can be neither converted nor continued until it is revived. We earnestly request to keep your policy in force for its full term.

Yours faithfully,

ABC

Divisional Manager

A policy-holder in urgent need of money may wish to surrender the policy. A policy acquires a surrender value only after premiums have been paid for three consecutive years. A policy cannot be surrendered if it has been assigned to a minor, since a minor cannot give a valid consent. In order to surrender the policy, the policy-holder has to submit the original Policy, bonus certificates, proof of age if age has not been admitted, and assignee's consent on the prescribed form, if the policy has been assigned. As the surrender value of a policy is less than the total amount paid by the policy-holder, it is a loss to surrender a policy. The LIC makes efforts to dissuade policy-holders from surrendering their policy.

Dear Sir,

Re: Your Policy No. 7800452

We are sorry to learn from your letter dated 18 November, 2001, that you wish to surrender your policy owing to adverse financial circumstances. It is more advantageous for you to take a loan from the L.I.C. on the security of your policy than to surrender the policy.

The amount you get on surrendering a policy is much less than what you have paid in premiums. Besides, a life insurance policy is a good investment as well as a security for your dependants. Even if you take out a fresh policy later, to provide for your family, you will have to pay a higher rate of premium as the rate is directly related to your age at the time of taking out the policy. Considering the disadvantages of surrendering the policy, we strongly recommended that you arrange for a loan on the policy.

If you should finally decide to surrender your policy, you will have to send the following documents:

(1) Original Policy

(2) Bonus Certificates, if any

(3) Consent of assignee on the enclosed form

(4) Proof of your age if age has not been admitted.

The surrender value of your policy is Rs...; the cash value of bonuses already declared, will be added to this amount.

You can get a loan of Rs... on the security of the policy, i.e., 90% of the surrender value. Terms and conditions of the loan are given on the enclosed form.

Yours faithfully,

XYZ

Divisional Manager

Loans

Loans are granted by L.I.C. up to 90% of the surrender value of the policy. A policy which has no surrender value is not acceptable as security for a loan. If the policy has been assigned to a minor, a loan cannot be granted on it because the assignee also has to execute the loan bond, and a minor cannot legally do so. A loan from L.I.C. is for a minimum period of six months. If the loan is granted, the L.I.C. requires the policy-holder to send the Original Policy, proof of age if it has not been admitted, the assignee's consent on the prescribed form and the amount of stamp fee for the loan bond. The policy is to be assigned to the L.I.C. If it matures before the loan is repaid, the outstanding amount, interest due, and incidental charges in connection with the loan will be deducted from the amount payable to the policy-holder.

Dear Sir,

Sub: Your application for loan on Policy No. 1784620

We are glad to inform you that a loan of Rs. 30,000 can be granted on your policy. The terms and conditions of the loan are given below:

1. The policy must be assigned absolutely to the Corporation. The Corporation will hold the policy until the loan is fully repaid, with interest.
2. Interest will be charged at the rate of 16%.
3. The loan cannot be repaid in less than six months after it is paid.
4. The loan is to be repaid, with interest, on your being given three months' notice by the Corporation.
5. In case the policy matures or becomes a claim before the repayment of the loan, the outstanding amount, with the interest and incidental charges, will be deducted from the amount payable on the policy.

Please send the following documents to enable us to prepare the loan bond.

(1) Your Original Policy

(2) Proof of your age if age has not been admitted

(3) Assignee's consent on the enclosed form

(4) A cheque for Rs.250/- as stamp fee.

Yours faithfully,

XYZ

Divisional Manager

Dear Sir,

Sub: Loan on Policy No. 84364: own life.

We have received your request for a loan of Rs.200,000/- on the security of your life policy. Unfortunately, it is not possible to advance a loan on the policy since it has not yet acquired surrender value.

A policy acquires surrender value only after premiums have been paid for two consecutive years excluding the first year. Your policy will acquire surrender value only after three more quarterly premiums have been paid. Even then, the surrender value will be Rs. 140,000/- which will not be sufficient for the loan of Rs. 200,000/- which you require. You can get a loan of Rs... after 3 more premiums have been paid.

We regret that it is not possible to grant the loan, at present.

Yours faithfully,

ABC

Divisional Manager

Claims

Claims

If the policy-holder survives the date of maturity of the policy, L.I.C. sends the policy-holder a letter asking for the required documents. If the policy-holder dies, a claim to the benefits of the policy is made by the nominee. On receiving a claim letter, the L.I.C. informs the claimant about the documents to be sent. The claim is scrutinized and paid out if all details are correct and the claim is justified.

Dear Sir,

We are sorry to learn from your letter dated 18 August, 2001, of the death of your father, Mr. S.P. Velankar. Please accept our condolences. Please be assured that the claim of Mr. Velankar will be settled immediately on completing the routine formalities of scrutiny and verification.

The enclosed claim form is to be filled in and returned with the signatures of all persons legally entitled to the benefits of the policy.

Please send the following documents with the claim form:

(1) Original Policy

(2) Bonus certificates issued so far

(3) Death certificate

(4) Proof of age of the deceased if age has not been admitted.

Yours faithfully,

XYZ

Claims Manager

EXERCISES

1. A fire policy holder has instituted a claim of Rs. 800,000/-. On the basis of the surveyor's report the insurance company refuses to admit the amount claimed. Draft the company's letter to the policy-holder.
2. Draft the letter you would write to the Insurance Co. asking for an Open Policy to cover your annual export business amounting to Rs. 9,000,000/-. Give all necessary details.
3. A policy-holder informs the Commonwealth Insurance Co., that the cotton goods stored by him in his godown at Matunga and covered for Rs. 3,000,000/- have been transferred to another warehouse at Sewri. Draft a reply on behalf of the insurance company advising a higher rate of premium as a consequence of the transfer.
4. A customer writes to the Regal Insurance Co., that he considers the rate quoted for the insurance of his godown against fire, too high. As the Fire Manager of the insurance company, write a suitable reply, pointing out that, for the reasons given, the company has to charge him a rate higher than the standard rate.
5. Steel Works Ltd., Mumbai, have entered into a contract with Bradford Engineering Company Limited, Bradford, U.K., to purchase machinery worth Rs. 5,000,000/- for their new factory at Bhandup. The machinery is to be shipped in five monthly batches, beginning June, 2003. They ask the Western India General Insurance Co. to suggest a suitable policy. Draft a reply from the insurance company suggesting an open marine-cum-erection policy pointing out its advantages.
6. Write a letter from an Insurance Company to their agents in Nairobi, instructing them to scrutinize very carefully, all claims submitted by a local importer, who seems to be making false claims. Mention all the necessary details.

7. A consignment of cotton shipped to Mumbai from Port Said by s.s. "Habiba" by Abdeally & Sons, Cairo, was damaged during the voyage. Draft the consignee's letter to the insurance company, giving the necessary details and supplying the required documents.
8. A merchant applies to the Orient Insurance Company, Mumbai, for insuring his godown used for storing grains, at Surat. The insurance company replies that on enquiry they find that the godown is situated near the river and that they will have to charge the applicant a higher rate than usual. Draft the company's letter.
9. An insurance company has received a claim from a merchant in Vengurla for damage by heavy seas to a consignment of sugar while being taken to the shore in small boats from the steamer standing at some distance from the shore. The company's claims manager replies to the merchant that they have official evidence that, on the day in question, the sea was dead calm, with no wind, and that the claim cannot be considered unless the two conflicting statements are reconciled.
10. A policy-holder who wishes to buy an ownership flat in a Cooperative Housing Society writes to the L.I.C. of India, asking for a loan of Rs. 1,000,000/. Draft a letter on behalf of the L.I.C., explaining why the loan cannot be granted.
11. Draft a letter on behalf of the L.I.C. to a policy-holder who wishes to convert her policy to paid-up, dissuading her from doing so.
12. A life insurance policy-holder wants to know the surrender value of his policy. Draft the reply from L.I.C. explaining why the policy has no surrender value.

Chapter 30

MEETINGS: NOTICE, AGENDA AND RESOLUTIONS

An official meeting is supported by several written documents. For the smooth functioning of a meeting, the supporting documents must be prepared carefully. Usually, they are prepared by the Secretary, in consultation with the Chairman. The most essential documents are: Notice of the meeting, Agenda, and Minutes. The notice of the meeting and the agenda, together with the minutes of the previous meeting, are sent to members well in advance of the meeting. Meeting rules of different bodies lay down the number of days of notice required to be given for a meeting.

NOTICE OF MEETING

The notice of a meeting is typed or printed on the organizations' letterhead; it must always include the following points:

(i) Name of the body/group which is to meet

(ii) Day, date and time of the meeting

(iii) Place of the meeting, i.e. the address and the specific room/hall

(iv) Agenda of the meeting.

The following are examples giving these essential details:

- *There will be a meeting of the Executive Committee on Wednesday, 8 April, 2005, at 11.00 a.m. at the Registered Office, in the Conference Room, to discuss ...*
- *A meeting of the Managing Committee will be held on Saturday, 9 November, 2005, at 10.00 a.m. in the Committee Room at the Registered Office, to discuss the following items.*

Public companies and many registered voluntary organizations use a legal form of notice for general body meetings. The notice is accompanied by the agenda for the present meeting and the minutes of the previous meeting. There may also be notes and background papers related to different items on the agenda. The notice of the meeting must be sent well in advance, according to the requirements laid down in the organization's rules. Usually, at least a week's notice is required. If members have to come from different places to attend the meeting, longer notice is required.

Here is an example of the annual general meeting notice of a large registered voluntary organization.

Notice of Meeting

To

All Members

Notice is hereby given that the Annual General Meeting of Members of the Bombay Managers Association will be held on 22 September, 2005, at 4.00 p.m. at the Taj Mahal Hotel, Mumbai, 400 039, to transact the following business:

- To receive and adopt the Income & Expenditure Account , the Balance Sheet, the Report of the Auditors, and the Report of the Committees for the year ended 31 March, 2005;
- To declare the results of the election of the President, Vice-President, Hon. Secretary, Hon. Treasurer, and Four Ordinary Members of the Executive Committee for the years 2005-2006 and 2006-07, in accordance with Rule 34 (iii) of the Rules and Regulations of the Association:
- To appoint Auditors for the year 2005-2006 and fix their remuneration;
- To consider any other matter that may be brought forward of which written notice of at least seven days has been given.

By Order of the Executive Committee
(Emile Gala)
Honorary Secretary

Mumbai
September 3, 2005

TATA ENGINEERING AND LOCOMOTIVE CO. LTD.
Bombay House, 24, Homi Modi Street, Churchgate,
Mumbai 400 023

Ref. No. 123/MJ/92 16 July, 2005

Mr. Mahipal Jain
A-3/15, Mahesh Nagar
S.V. Road,
Goregaon (W)
Mumbai 400 062

Mr. Jain,

A meeting of the Board of Directors will be held on 5 August, 2005, at the registered office of the company at 2 P.M. THE AGENDA for the meeting is enclosed. Please be present at the meeting.

Yours Sincerely,

P. A. Thakore
(Secretary)

Encl.: Agenda

Items No.	Particulars
1.	To confirm the minutes of the last meeting.
2.	To grant leave of absence of Mr. Atul Vaidya and Mrs. Raksha Shah
3.	To produce list of accounts for payment and sign the cheques for payment
4.	To approve transfer and transmission of shares
5.	To put the proposal to appoint Messrs. Surdiwala and Sons as agents in Mumbai
6.	To fix the date of the next meeting

R.R. Mehta
Chairman

If a meeting is expected to go on for a long time, it is customary to indicate in the notice that tea/lunch will be served. It is also necessary to indicate whether travelling allowance will be paid to those who attend the meeting.

AGENDA

Agenda is a list of items to be discussed at the meeting. It is also called Business. It is usually sent with the notice of the meeting, but it may be sent later if it takes time to prepare it. Items included in the agenda depend on the type of meeting. According to rules of conduct of a meeting, apologies for absence received from members are taken up and recorded before the Agenda is taken up.

The agenda begins with the item "Approval of Minutes" because the minutes of the previous meeting must be approved and signed before any matter can be taken up by the present meeting. This item may be written in the agenda as "Minutes" or in greater detail as Approval of minutes of previous meeting. The second item is usually matters arising out of the minutes. This may be indicated in the agenda as "Matters arising"; however, it is not necessary to indicate this item in the agenda. The new items are set out after this. Some of the items are routine requirements, like payments to be passed and cheques to be signed, Progress reports, Review of activities, etc.

There are two ways of writing the points in the Agenda:

(i) In the form of nouns, for example,

* *Appointment of sub-committee to look into losses...*
* *Proposal to open a branch in...*
* *Membership drive*
* *Fund collection*
* *Review of the month's activities*

(ii) With an infinitive verb, for example,

* *To appoint a sub-committee to look into...*
* *To consider a proposal to open a branch...*
* *To organize a membership drive*
* *To collect funds*
* *To review activities of the month.*

All the items in an Agenda must be written in the same style.

Different organizations use different styles of writing the items in the agenda. Public Limited companies and some organizations use a very formal and detailed style while some use informal style and describe the items in short. When all the items on the agenda have been dealt with and decisions recorded, the chairman of the meeting may allow members to raise any items which are not on the agenda, if time permits. The chairman may himself raise a matter which is not included in the agenda. To allow for this, the item "Any other business with the permission of the Chair" (also written as "Any other business") is usually included at the end of the scheduled business items. The final item is usually, "Date of next meeting" (also written as Next meeting). It is the usual practice to fix the date of the next meeting before the current meeting is ended. The order of the items on the agenda cannot be changed during the course of the meeting except by consent of the members. The chairman of the meeting must take great care to decide the order in which the items are to be put on the agenda, especially if there are likely to be controversies over any of the items. It is desirable to have urgent items and non-controversial items first.

A specimen Agenda is given below:

1. To confirm the minutes of the meeting held on 25 July, 2005 (enclosed)
2. To approve the Revised Budget for 2004-05 and the Budget Estimates for the year 2005-06, with or without modifications (will follow)
3. To consider applications for Life Memberships (list enclosed)
4. To review the working of the Society and its Institutions
5. Any other matter permitted by the Chair
6. Next meeting

Review

1. Fill in the blanks using as few words as possible.
   (a) An agenda is —
   (b) Notice of a meeting must include — (give all the points).
   (c) The first and the last items on the agenda are — and — respectively.
2. Are these three items on an agenda correctly written?
   (1) Appointing a sub-committee to survey ...
   (2) To review the working of the standing committee
   (3) Fund collection.

MINUTES

A record of the decisions taken at a formal meeting is called Minutes. All companies, statutory bodies, social organizations, associations (whether registered or unregistered) and committees have to maintain a record of the meetings. Minutes are the official record of work done and decisions taken at the meeting of members; they must be precise and clear. They record what was decided and done.The minutes of companies and statutory bodies are written in formal style. Other organizations may write minutes in informal style.

At the next meeting, the minutes are read out by the secretary or may be taken as read if a copy was sent to members; the minutes are then approved and signed by the chairman and the secretary as a correct record of the meeting.

Minutes are a legal document and can be produced in a court of law as evidence.

The details given below are an essential part of minutes, and must always be included:

(a) Name of the body and nature of the meeting

(b) Day, date, time and place of the meeting

(c) Name of chairman of the meeting, names of members present (list is attached if there are many names)

(d) Names of persons "in attendance", that is, any invited officials like the auditor, the solicitor, who are not members of the meeting

(e) Leave of absence to those who are not present.

These are laid out as shown below.

Minutes of the first meeting of the Board of Directors of Sadguru Trading Corporation, Ltd., held at the Registered Office on 12 February, 2005, at 4.00 p.m.

The following members were present:

Shri ABC, Chairman & Director
Shri DEF, Director
Shri GHI, "
Shri JKL, "
Shri MNO, "

In attendance:

Shri XYZ, Secretary
Shri PQR, Solicitor

Shri LIC and Shri PNR had intimated their inability to attend, and were granted leave of absence.

Minutes of the meeting of the Managing Committee of Friends of Trees, held on Friday, 18 June 2005, at 5.00 p.m. at the Registered Office of the Society

The following members were present:

Shri G.E.Bhabha, in the Chair
Smti Priti Shah
Dr. S.N.Velankar
Dr.(Smti) Avan Setalvad
Shri Rajesh Mehra
Shri S.N.Sheth

Shri Shamak Dorabji was present by invitation.

Smti Lily Sengupta had intimated inability to attend and was granted leave of absence.

The minutes are recorded below these details. The first minute is always the reading and confirming of the minutes of the previous meeting. Examples are given below:

- *Minutes of the meeting held on 18 June, 2005, which had been circulated earlier, were taken as read, and were approved and signed.*
- *The Secretary read out the minutes of the last meeting held on 18 June, 2005. They were signed as a correct record of the meeting.*

If there is a condolence resolution, it is passed before the confirmation of the minutes.

The last item of the minutes is the ending of the meeting with a vote of thanks to the Chair.

- *There being no other business, the meeting ended with a vote of thanks to the Chair.*

Other items in the minutes depend on the agenda. Every item on the agenda must have a corresponding item in the minutes.

Review

1. Fill in the blanks using as few words as possible.
   (a) The first item in the minutes is —.
   (b) The last item in the minutes is —.
   (c) A condolence resolution is always—.
   (d) The title of the minutes includes — (give all the points).
   (e) Minutes are written for the purpose of —.

Method of Writing Minutes

Minutes may include only the resolutions without details of the discussion which took place before the decision was taken; or it may include a short summary of the discussion and a statement of the reason for the Resolution. Very formal minutes include the proposal with the name of the proposer and the seconder, a short summary of the discussion and finally, the resolution.

The style and method of writing minutes is fixed by custom and practice by each organization.

Language of Minutes

(i) Minutes are written in simple past tense; for example:

- *The Secretary read out.....*
- *The Chairman informed.....*
- *The meeting ended......*

(ii) Many of the items are written in passive voice; for example:

- *The minutes....were taken as read, and confirmed and signed.*
- *The progress report for December was presented...*
- *The Secretary was authorized....*
- *The next meeting was fixed for ......*

(iii) Impersonal passive voice is used for recording decisions and resolutions. The impersonal passive voice is used only for verbs of mental action like decide, resolve, suggest, recommend, etc. These are not physical actions; they can be taken by a group collectively. Here are some examples:

- *It was decided that a committee be appointed...*
- *It was resolved that the meeting be adjourned.*
- *It was decided to create a separate fund for the purpose.*
- *Resolved that a separate fund be created for the purpose.*

(iv) The verb is in the subjunctive mood. Subjunctive mood of the verb describes an action that is proposed or intended or planned or thought of, but not yet completed. It is used only for the verb to be, and only with verbs of command or desire; for example:

- *I move that Mr. Samant be appointed...*
- *I propose that the Secretary be authorized...*

When the suggestion is adopted by the meeting, the common decision is recorded as a resolution to take action; for example:

- *It was Resolved that Mr. Samant be appointed...*

But this is still only a decision to appoint; it does not indicate that the appointment was actually made at that time. To indicate that the appointment was actually made, the resolution must be written as follows:

- *It was Resolved that Mr. Samant be and is hereby appointed...*
- It was decided that the Secretary be and is hereby authorized to...
- *Resolved that a committee consisting of Mr.ABC, Mr. DEF and Mr. PQR, be and is hereby appointed to...*

A complete resolution indicating that a decision was taken and action is to be started, will be expressed as follows:

- *Resolved that a new building be constructed on the north side of the factory for the staff welfare centre. It was further resolved that the Secretary be and is hereby authorized to invite tenders for the construction and to make any other arrangements required for getting the building constructed.*

A Resolution has a heading indicating what it is about; e.g.

- *Appointment of Secretary*
- *Appointment of Bankers*
- *Endorsement of cheques*
- *Signature on Negotiable Instruments.*

Review

1. Fill in the blanks.
   (a) Minutes are always written in the — tense.
   (b) The subjunctive mood of a verb describes an action —.
   (c) The passive form of "They approved of the minutes" is — —.

2. Are these statements true?
   (a) Every resolution has a heading.
   (b) Group decisions are recorded in impersonal passive voice.
   (c) Minutes are recorded in present tense.

SPECIMEN RESOLUTIONS

*Chairman of Board of Directors: It was Resolved that Shri N.F. Engineer be and is hereby elected Chairman of the Board of Directors.

*Appointment of Secretary: It was Resolved that Shri K.T. Swami be and is hereby appointed Secretary of the Company at a monthly salary of Rs. 7500, the appointment being terminable by either side on three months' notice, and that an agreement be prepared by the Company's Advocate embodying these terms.

*Common Seal: The Seal was produced at the meeting. It was Resolved that the Seal produced be and is hereby adopted as Common Seal of the Company, that an impression of the Seal be made in the Minute Book, and the Seal be kept in safe custody under lock and key.

*Appointment of Solicitors: It was Resolved that Messrs. Udwadia, Bharucha and Merchant, Solicitors, Parikh Chambers, Dalal Street, Mumbai, be and are hereby appointed Solicitors of the Company.

*Appointment of Auditors: It was Resolved that Messrs. Mehta, Sanghavi and Lakhani, Chartered Accountants, "Chhaya", Hamam Street, Mumbai 400 001, be and are hereby appointed Auditors of the Company till the conclusion of the first Annual General Meeting of the Company.

* Appointment of Bankers: It was Resolved that Bank of India, M.G. Road, Mumbai 400 020, be and is hereby appointed Bankers to the Company, and that the Secretary be and is hereby authorised to open the company's account with the bank.

*Endorsement of Cheques etc.: It was Resolved that all cheques and other documents requiring endorsement of the Company be endorsed by any one Director and the Secretary. It was further Resolved that the Secretary be and is hereby authorised to send specimen signatures of the Directors and the Secretary to the bank.

*Signature on Negotiable Instruments: It was Resolved that Bills of Exchange, drafts or other negotiable instruments issued or executed by the Company be drawn or accepted on behalf of the Company by any one Director and counter-signed by the Secretary.

*Books and Stationery: It was Resolved that the Secretary be and is hereby authorised to obtain the books, forms and other material required by the Company.

*Appointment of Sales Agent for Pune: Resolved that Messrs. Chandog & Co., of Budhawar Peth, Pune, be and are hereby appointed the Company's sole agent for Pune on the following terms:

(i) Period of contract — 3 years
(ii) Commission of 7% to be paid annually
(iii) The agency may be terminated by either party by giving a notice of 3 months.

*Resolved that the Secretary be and is hereby authorised to draw up the agreement in consultation with the Company's Solicitors.

*Appointment of sub-committee to investigate decline of sales in Kolkata Branch: The Managing Director informed the Board that the sales had declined considerably in the last two years in the Kolkata branch.

*After some discussion, it was Resolved that a sub-committee of the following Directors be and is hereby appointed to investigate the causes of the decline of sales in the Kolkata branch and to report with recommendations, by 15 May:

(1) C.S. Iyengar, Convener

(2) P.A. Saraf

(3) S.V. Gupta.

*Transfer of Shares: The instruments of Transfer Nos. 86 to 94 as they appear in the Transfer Register were submitted together with Ordinary Share Certificates Nos. 1780 to 1822 in favour of the transferees given in the Transfer Register. The transfers were passed by the Board, and it was Resolved that the said Certificates be endorsed in accordance with the rules.

*Payments: Lists of payments due and the required vouchers were submitted to the Board by the Secretary, and it was Resolved that the cheques be signed as required.

*Date of Annual General Meeting: It was Resolved that the third Annual General Meeting of the Company be held on 20 September, 2000, at 2 p.m. at the Registered Office of the Company.

It was further Resolved that the Secretary be and is hereby authorised to get accounts, reports, notices and other documents signed and printed, to send them to the shareholders and others who are entitled to receive them, and to arrange for the publication of the notice of the Annual General Meeting in the press.

*Report and Accounts: Drafts of the Directors' Report, Profit and Loss Account and Balance Sheet as at 31 March 2000, were laid on the table and it was Resolved that the Directors' Report and Annual Account and Balance Sheet be adopted and signed as required, by the Chairman.

*Dividend: It was Resolved that, of the total net profit of Rs. 8,660,000 and Rs. 11,60,000 be credited to the Dividend Equalisation Fund, and Rs. 660,000 be credited to the Taxation Reserve Fund, that balance of Rs. 6,84,000 be distributed as dividend to shareholders and that the dividend on Equity Shares be and is hereby recommended at the rate of 9% per annum.

*Closing of Share Transfer Book and Register of Members: It was Resolved that Transfer Books and Register of Members be closed from .... to .... both days inclusive, and that a public notice be issued to that effect, by the Secretary.

*Appointment of Director: Resolved that Shri K.M. Tahilramani, retiring by rotation, being eligible for re-election, be and is hereby appointed a Director, of the Company.

Decisions taken at meetings of voluntary organisations and associations are written in informal style as in the examples below:

*Special Award of the Year: It was suggested by Shri M.S. Morani that the Fund undertake to give a substantial sum as aid to the most needy student of the current year.

*The suggestion was put to vote and carried unanimously. It was decided that Shri G.B. Gokhale of S.Y.B.A. Class, Morning Session, be given a wheel chair or any other aid as the student might choose.

It was further decided that a box collection be held for this purpose on 8 August and that the award be declared at the Flag Hoisting meeting on 15 August.

*Film Show for Raising Funds: It was decided to arrange a film show in November in order to raise funds.

Prof R.Q. Siddique, Kum. Kamala Gupta, Shri Rakesh Goradia, and S.V. Iyer were to act as a sub-committee to work out the complete details of the arrangements for the film show.

*Books and Stationery Aid to Students: Kum. J.N. Gavaskar suggested that some deserving students be given aid in the form of textbooks, notebooks, paper and pens, these articles being collected by voluntary contribution from other students. After some discussion, a sub-committee consisting of Prof. S.M. Sanghvi, Kum. Rita Vora, Kum. J.N. Gavaskar and Shri Harish Shah was appointed to examine the possibilities of starting Books and Stationery Aid.

Condolence Resolutions

A condolence minute is in three parts. The first part states that the Chairman referred to the demise and that a resolution was passed.

The second part mentions the person's achievement, nature, ability, etc. It also expresses the sorrow and sense of loss felt by the members of the meeting. The length of this part depends on the personality and the relationship with the members. A condolence message, whether a resolution, a letter or a speech, should be brief and yet express sufficient appreciation of the person. Sincerity is the most important requirement of the resolution. A copy of this portion of the minute is sent to the bereaved family. Good taste is the only guide in writing a suitable condolence resolution.

The third part mentions that the meeting stood in silence and that it authorized the Secretary to convey the condolences of the meeting to the bereaved family.

A few examples are given below:

(a) Homage to Shri Komal Shastri: The Chairman referred to the sad demise of Shri Komal Shastri and spoke of his contribution to the theatre and dramatic literature in Hindi. The following Resolution was passed.

This General Body meeting of the Bombay Natya Sangh records its deep sense of loss and grief at the demise of Shri Komal Shastri. The world of literature and the theatre has lost a great patron and leader in his passing away.

As a mark of respect of the departed dramatist, the members stood in silence for two minutes. The Secretary was asked to convey the condolences of the Natya Sangh to the family of Shri Komal Shastri.

(b) The Chairman referred to the death of Mr. Murlidhar Jagani, on 15 September, 2000. He said that Murlidhar had been a promising cricketer, and his death at the young age of 21, was a great loss to the game of cricket. The meeting passed the following resolution:

The Chairman and members of the College Youth Sports Club are deeply shocked and grieved at the untimely and tragic demise of Murlidhar Jagani, on 15 September, 2000. He was a highly valued and beloved member of his college cricket team. Last year, he contributed to the victory of the college in Bombay University Inter-collegiate Cricket Tournament. Murlidhar will be greatly missed by all cricket-loving people, and particularly by his team-mates. He will be remembered by all who knew him as an affectionate, courteous person and cricketer both on and off the field.

Members of the College Youth Sports Club convey their heartfelt condolences to the bereaved family of Murlidhar, and pray to God to give them courage and strength to bear this loss. May his soul rest in peace.

The meeting stood in silence as a mark of respect to their departed fellow member. The Secretary was asked to convey the condolences of the College Youth Sports Club to the family of Murlidhar Jagani.

The following are examples of the middle paragraph:

(a) We, the office bearers and members of Society for Clean Air deeply mourn the shocking, untimely demise of Shri Rajiv Gandhi, former P.M. of India. The country has lost a promising young leader who was loved and respected. We offer our condolences and deep sympathy to the bereaved family and pray to God to give them the strength and courage to bear this grief. May his soul rest in peace.

(b) We, the staff and students of XYZ College are deeply grieved and shocked at the sudden demise of Sundeep Patel of S.Y.B.Sc., who passed away on April 5, 2000 in a tragic road accident.

May God grant strength and courage to his family to bear the grief and irreparable loss. May his soul rest in peace.

(c) The Chairman, Directors and Staff of Zarina Plastics (Pvt.) Ltd., express their heartfelt grief and sense of loss at the sad and premature demise of Mr. Pandurang Phule who was a peon in this company's office for the last 18 years. He passed away at the age of 39, on 16 June, 2000, after a brief illness.

He was loved and appreciated by all members of the company on account of his sincere and cheerful temperament. His demise is an irreparable loss to this office, and especially to the production department where he had spent most of his years of service.

May God grant strength and fortitude to the members of his bereaved family to bear their grief. May his soul rest in peace.

(d) The Principal, staff and students of the college are deeply shocked and grieved at the sad and untimely demise of Prof. T.C. Ahluwalia, on 28 June, 2000.

He was a founder member of the college, and has contributed to the culture of the college, by setting an example of discipline and academic devotion. Prof. T.C. Ahluwalia, as the Head of the Sociology Department, built up a homogeneous team of teachers. He was loved and respected by his colleagues and his students.

The Principal, staff and students express their grief at the irreparable loss of one of the pillars of the institution, and their gratitude to the late Prof. T.C. Ahluwalia for the heritage of discipline, devotion and hardwork he has left behind.

May God give his bereaved family the strength to bear this loss. May his soul rest in peace.

EXERCISES

1. Draft a notice calling a meeting of the Managing Committee of a college association of which you are the secretary.
2. Write down the preliminary parts of the minutes of the following meetings:
   (i) Statutory meeting
   (ii) Routine meeting of Board of Directors
   (iii) Annual General Meeting
   (iv) First Board Meeting
   (v) Managing Committee meeting of a Gymkhana, held prior to Annual General Meeting.
3. Write down the first two required items of the minutes of the following meetings:
   (i) First Board Meeting
   (ii) Annual General Meeting
   (iii) Routine meeting of any Body.

4. You have to hold a condolence meeting on the demise of one of your colleagues on the Managing Committee of your club. Draft the Resolution to be adopted at the meeting.
5. Write down the last two items of minutes which indicate the conclusion of a meeting.
6. Draft Resolutions on the following items which may be on the agenda of different meetings:
   (i) to appoint a sub-committee to examine the proposal to open a branch factory in Gujarat State
   (ii) to consider appointing an agent for sales in West Bengal
   (iii) to appoint bankers to the company
   (iv) to fix a date for Annual General Meeting
   (v) to consider ways and means of raising funds for a proposed women's hostel
   (vi) to fix the date of the next meeting of the Board of Directors
   (vii) to appoint auditors for the following year at the Annual General Meeting
   (viii) to appoint a director on the retirement of an existing director
   (ix) to close Share Transfer Book and Register of Members
   (x) to declare dividend on Equity Shares at Annual General Meeting.

❑❑❑

Chapter 31

REPORTS

A report is a logical presentation of facts and information. The information is needed for reviewing and evaluating progress, for planning future course of action and for taking decisions. Reports provide feedback to the managers on various aspects of the organization.

Every organization has a system of routine periodical reporting on the progress and the status of different activities. Besides, management may assign certain special studies for the purpose of taking decisions. Special Reports may be written by an individual or by a group of persons to whom the task has been assigned. The report is submitted to the authority that has assigned it.

Reports are written for various purposes. They may be required to review performance, keep a check on a continuing activity, plan for the future needs of the organization, survey the market, submit standardized information, etc.

TYPES OF REPORTS

Reports may be routine or special. Routine reports are periodical and are usually prepared by filling in printed/cyclostyled forms, to convey information about the progress or status of work/tasks. They are submitted at regular intervals or soon after the completion of the task.

Special reports are required when a special situation or problem arises. An individual or a committee of persons who have knowledge and understanding in the field / subject, is appointed to investigate and study a specific problem, collect information related to it, and make suggestions to help the management to take a decision.

The following diagram gives an idea of the types of reports:

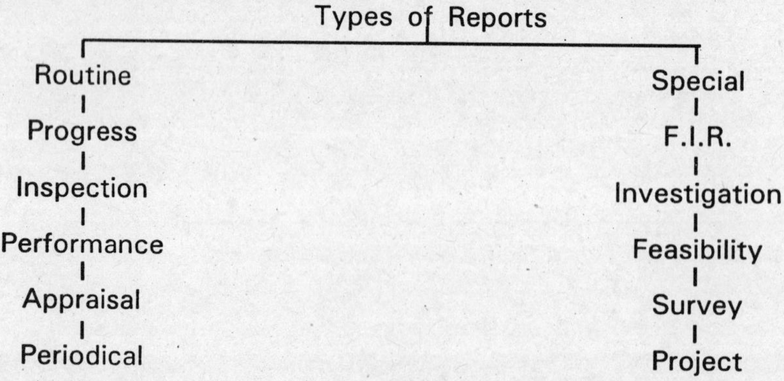

Routine Reports

Routine reports are usually forms in which blanks have to be filled in or multiple choice statements are to be ticked. Report forms must be prepared carefully to ensure that the management gets complete information.

The following are routine reports:

(a) **Progress report** gives information about the progress of a project or a task which is in the process of being completed, such as construction of a building or manufacture of products or implementation of a scheme. This report is also prepared by filling in a standard form periodically.

(b) **Inspection report** is submitted as soon as an inspection is carried out. It is necessary for detecting any irregularities or deviations from standard practice, in day-to-day work; for example, internal audit reports. Inspection of machinery, buildings, and property may be done at regular intervals. Audits and inspection of work and systems may be done by surprise check in order to ensure that they work properly at all times.

Printed forms and guidelines for checking may be provided by the authorities; otherwise, experts in the field, like engineers, auditors, etc., use their own guidelines and formats for inspection reports.

(c) **Performance Appraisal** report is periodical and is usually prepared by filling in a form. It is meant for assessing and recording the performance of an employee. Every supervisor has to fill in an assessment report for each of the subordinates annually. Performance appraisal helps the superiors to assess performance of individual employees. It also helps employees to get feedback on their performance. On the basis of these reports, decisions about promotions and other benefits are taken.

(d) **Periodical report** is prepared at regular intervals on the working of a section or a department. The information required is of a routine nature and can be easily tabulated; hence it is prepared by filling in a form.

Special reports

(a) **First Information Report (F.I.R.)** is required when there is a disaster like fire, building collapse, robbery or accident in an organization. It is prepared by a responsible person on-the-spot or the person in charge, for submission to a higher authority, for example the branch manager prepares it for submission to Regional Office or Head Office. The report has to give all the information which is available immediately after the incident occurs. It must state what happened, about what time, who first noticed it, and what steps were taken immediately. It also states the extent of destruction or loss of life, property, important papers, etc. as can be estimated immediately.

A First Information Report is always written by an individual.

(b) **Investigation report** is written after making a thorough study and inquiry. An investigation is made when there is a problem and the management needs to find out the causes of the problem, and needs suggestions for solving it. For example, falling sales, declining deposits in a bank, many customer complaints, losses in a branch, etc.

A committee may be appointed to find out the causes of the problem, and suggest measures to solve it and prevent it from occurring again. It requires collection of facts which are not always easy to get. The collected information has to be analyzed; conclusions have to be drawn and recommendations may have to be made.

Since such reports require a great deal of work, thinking, discussion and consideration, they are usually assigned only to a committee of competent and experienced persons. A simple investigation of a small problem may be assigned to an individual who has knowledge and experience in the field.

(c) **Feasibility or Survey Report** is required when an organization intends to launch a new product in the market, introduce a new service, or make any major changes that may affect the company's customers. The proposed field or area has to be surveyed, and its conditions observed and recorded. The factors to be examined and recorded depend on the purpose of the survey. The purpose may be to consider the suitability of a site for a factory, to evaluate the feasibility and financial viability of a proposal, to survey the market, to estimate damage.

For some purposes only a physical survey and inspection of the area may suffice; for others, availability of essential requirements in the area, attitude of the local people, State Government's policies, possible expenses, etc., will be needed.

A survey may be made by an individual or by a committee, depending on the size of the survey to be made. For example, if a factory is to be established, the survey involves a great deal of work, and a committee would be appointed; if damage to a piece of machinery is to be surveyed for the purpose of estimating the loss, an engineer can do it alone.

(d) **Project Report** is written after a proposal takes shape, and after the preliminary survey has been completed. It describes the proposal as projected into the future, showing the cash flow and expected results. It is used for planning and also for convincing others, especially sanctioning and funding authorities like government departments and banks.

A project report may be prepared on their own by persons who want to get their proposal approved or sanctioned.

STRUCTURE OF A REPORT

A report is divided into sections with headings so that the collected information can be presented in a form that is easy to read and refer to. A covering letter usually accompanies the report.

Reports are read by different persons for different purposes. Some are interested only in the findings and/or conclusions; some may want to know only the recommendations; yet others may want to check the procedure followed for data collection; most might want to know with what terms of reference the report writer was working. All these details have to be included and presented in a logical format.

A report may be written by an individual or by a committee. Both are formal and must follow a logical order. An individual report may be a little more personal in tone, while the committee report is impersonal in tone.

A **report by an Individual** is written by one person. It follows the same logical presentation as the committee report.

If the report is short, it is written in letter form with numbered and sub-titled paragraphs. It is addressed to the person or the body that has authorized /assigned the report; it does not have the complete inside address as it is internal communication and is typed on the organization's letterhead. It is dated on the day of submission or a day earlier. The salutation is Sir, or Madam, as required, and the complimentary close is Yours faithfully. If the report has enclosures, these must be indicated. At the end, the report usually records acknowledgement of the help received in making the study.

I am grateful to Mr. Rajendra Sen, Chief Accountant, and Ms Naina Biswas of the computer department, whose help enabled me to access past and current records of the company.

The last line offers to make further study, if necessary:

I shall be glad to undertake further study if required.

If the report is long and includes complex details, it is written in the schematic form with sub-headings, and is submitted with a covering letter.

A **Committee Report** is written by a group of persons who have been assigned the work as a committee. It is impersonal in style and written in the passive voice. The words we or our are not used; the committee is used when necessary. It is never written in the form of a letter; it must always be presented in schematic form with sub-headings. The report is typed on plain paper and submitted with a covering letter.

The **Covering Letter** is typed on the organization's letterhead. It is addressed to the appointing authority, and has the date of submission of the report. It is signed by the convener/ chairperson of the committee. The letter states what work was assigned, that the work has been completed and is being submitted. It ends with a courteous message, offering to undertake further study if required.

Review

1. Name the types of routine reports.
2. Name the types of special reports.
3. Fill in the blanks using as few words as possible:
   (a) Reports are required by an organization for—.
   (b) An individual report may be in — form.
   (c) A committee report must be accompanied by a —.
4. Are the following statements true?
   (a) A committee report may be written in letter form.
   (b) A committee report must be signed by all the members of the committee.
   (c) An individual report may be in letter form or in schematic form.

PARTS OF A REPORT

A report has several parts which enable the writer(s) to lay out all the complex information in an easy-to-read form. All reports do not require all the parts; but long reports need to include all the parts. The parts from the title to the signature are essential and must be included in all reports.

Title

A report must always have a title indicating the subject of the study, the period and the location of the study. A long report has a full title page which gives the title, the name of the person who assigned the report and the name/s of the person/committee who prepared it, with month and year of submission. In a short report, the title appears at the top of the first page, before the text of the report, as follows:

Report of Committee
appointed to investigate
the decline in sale of cycles
in
Tamil Nadu
between January and June, 2005

In an individual letter form report, the title is in the form of subject line, indicating only the topic, for example:

Subject: Decline in Sale of Cycles in Tamil Nadu between January and June, 2005

Terms of Reference

This is the first section of the report and is numbered I. It gives (i) details of the assignment and, (ii) the purpose and scope of the study.

(i) Details of assignment include: who assigned the report (and/or appointed the committee), on what date and how the appointment was made (that is, by a resolution at a meeting, or by letter or office order). In the case of a committee, the names of the members of the committee are included. It also states what is the assignment, what is the date for submitting the report, and whether the report is expected to make recommendations. For example:

The committee was appointed by the following resolution adopted at the meeting of the Board of Directors, held on 8 July, 2005:

Resolved that a committee consisting of Mr. A.(Convener), Mr. B. and Mr. C, be, and is hereby, appointed to investigate the decline in the sale of cycles in Tamil Nadu between January and June, 2005, and to report with recommendations in one month's time.

If the assignment is made by letter by the CEO or any other authority, the terms of reference must give the number and date of the letter, the name and title of the appointing authority, the purpose of the report, and the time allowed.

According to the D/O letter no. xxx, dated xxx from Ms Zarine Chowna, M.D., a committee consisting of Ms ABC, Mr DEF and Ms PQR was formed to examine the complaints of customers in xxx region. The committee was asked to report with recommendations in three weeks.

An individual writing a letter form report includes the authorization in the first paragraph of the letter.

- *In accordance with your letter no. xxx dated xxx I have examined xxxx and am presenting the report below.*
- *As you requested, I have investigated xxx and am happy to present my findings as follows.*

(ii) Purpose and Scope includes: information about the area surveyed/problem examined, and the limitations imposed on the study by constraints like time, finance, non-availability of data.

- *Owing to constraints of time, the committee limited its study to five most populous cities in Tamil Nadu.*
- As data related to xxx was not available, this study is limited to xxx only.

Procedure

This is the second section of the report and is numbered II. Methods used for collecting information are stated in this section. It begins with the meetings held by the committee, for example:

* *The committee met three times, on 26 July, and 12 and 20 August, 2005.*

Other methods of collecting information depend on the nature of the study. There are several methods.

(i) Records of the organization can provide data on production, sales, recruitment, marketing, expenditure, etc. A comparison of figures for different periods may suggest useful conclusions.

(ii) Observation consists of watching certain phenomena involved in a problem, and recording what is systematically observed. This method is useful for problems like wastage of time in movement of material in a factory, or the circulation of traffic during certain hours or buyers' behaviour at the point of purchase.

(iii) Interrogation is the method of asking questions. It may be done by (a) interviewing, if the number of persons to be questioned is small, (b) getting questionnaires filled in, if the number is large, (c) meeting experts and asking for their opinion, (d) informal talks with randomly selected concerned persons can be used for collecting information, provided that questions are asked skilfully.

(iv) Reference to books, directories, standard publications.

(v) Visits and personal inspection are necessary when suitable sites are being surveyed.

(vi) Experimentation is done by various kinds of tests for different kinds of inquiries.

The committee's work of investigation is recorded in passive voice, for example,

- Meetings were held with the members of the panchayat.
- All the three sites were visited by the committee.
- Buyers' choice decisions were observed for three days.

The value of the findings, conclusions and recommendations depends on the thoroughness of the investigation, and the methods used. Therefore, a report must indicate the methods used for collecting information.

Findings

This is the third section and is numbered III. Presentation of findings is the main part of the report. The collected facts and information have to be organized into a presentable form, with headings and sub-headings.

The mass of collected information is analyzed and divided for easy and readable presentation and the units are joined by a numbering system. The usual form of numbering is:

I. first division

A. sub-division

1. second sub-division

a. third sub-division

(i) fourth sub-division

The basis for division into units may be time periods, or geographical location, or cause-and-effect or any factors which enable classification of the data.

The sub-divisions must be named carefully; they should be only one or two words for example, Raw material, or Competing products. Sub-titles of equal importance must be in the same grammatical form, preferably a noun phrase, for example:

(a) Lagging machine output

(b) Increase in marketing cost

(c) Difficulty of attracting skilled labour

Details may be in the form of numbered statements, for example:

(i) Unemployed villagers are migrating to cities in search of jobs.

(ii) Failure of the monsoon, leading to drought conditions, has encouraged migration to cities.

(iii) Exposure to city life-styles has popularized the use of consumer durables. As a result the villagers have little surplus income left to deposit in bank accounts.

This section may end with a brief summary of the most important findings or some conclusions which emerge from the findings. If the conclusions are very important and significant, there may be a separate section with the heading Conclusions.

Use of Illustrations

A report becomes much more readable, clear and effective if the findings are explained with relevant illustrative data like diagrams, graphs, charts, plans or maps. There are several advantages in using illustrations.

* They clarify and support the verbal analysis.
* They can present a large amount of complex data in a compact form and with precision.
* Comparisons of data can be seen at a glance in a graph or chart.
* Pictorial representation is more attractive and interesting to most people.

Every illustration should have a number and a title and should be mentioned in the text of the report. A table has a Roman number (I, IV, IX are Roman numbers) and title placed above it. A figure has an Arabic number (1, 4, 9 are Arabic numbers) and title placed below it.

An illustration should be placed as near as possible to the point where it is mentioned for the first time in the text. Complicated illustrations are given as Appendices. All diagrams, graphs, charts, maps etc., used as illustrations must have:

* proper labels to show what information is being represented
* the scale used
* the key to colour/shading/symbols used
* the date of the information it contains.

Recommendations

This is the last section and is numbered IV (or V or any required number depending on the number of previous sections). Recommendations are proposals for action suggested by the report writer(s) to the appointing authority.

This section is included only if the assignment has asked for it. Sometimes, an assignment may be only to present findings without recommendations. Usually, very senior persons in responsible positions are asked to include recommendations. A person or committee of persons in junior position may make suggestions; since they have studied the problem in depth, they are in a position to suggest ways to solve the problem.

Recommendations should be written in the same order as the problems are stated in the findings, as far as possible. They may be numbered, and must be in the same grammatical form. Recommendations may be introduced with a sentence like,

* *The committee makes the following recommendations.*
* *The sub-committee recommends the following steps:*
* *The following steps are recommended:*

The recommendations may also be written without any introductory sentence, for example,

* *A scheme of loans to educated boys and girls should be introduced to encourage self-employment.*
* *Loans should be given for minor irrigation projects to combat the drought conditions.*
* *The possibility of establishing a hire-purchase scheme through the bank for consumer durables should be explored.*

Signature, Place, Date

A committee report must be signed by all members of the committee. The signatures are on the right. The place and date are on the left. The date is the day of submission of the report.

Place : Kolkata	R.B. Das Gupta,
Date : 23 May, 2005	Convener
	C.K. Puranik
	J.J. Mitra

These are the essential parts of a report.

Other Parts of a Report

A long report which is divided into several chapters or sections has some ancillary parts to make it easy for the reader to find different parts or sections.

Table of Contents is given after the title page. It is a list of the chapters by number (and name if any), with the page number on which the chapter begins. It is like the table of contents in any book.

Acknowledgements can be written in one paragraph or a few short paragraphs; it is a list of names of persons who helped the writer of the report with information, references, discussion, etc. It appears before the first chapter.

Appendix (plural: appendices or appendixes) is supplementary material given at the end of the report. This may be a copy of a questionnaire used, or plans of buildings, maps or other material which is referred to in the body of the report, but need not appear in the body. Any interested reader can refer to it since it is mentioned in the report. If there is more than one appendix, they are numbered.

Bibliography is the list of books and articles used by the report writer. It is arranged in alphabetical order of the surnames of the authors.

Review

1. Name the essential parts of a report.
2. Explain in two or three sentences, the following parts of a report. (a) bibliography (b) appendix.
3. Name some non-verbal methods of presenting information in a report.

SPECIMEN REPORTS

15 June 2005

The Managing Director
XYZ Paints Ltd.

Sir,

Re: Working of Nagpur Branch

In accordance with your instruction by telephone, on 4 June 2005, I visited the Nagpur Branch for a surprise inspection last week. I observed the working of the branch office for three days and also inspected the office and the records. I am sorry to report that the branch office is run in a most unsatisfactory manner.

When I reached the branch office on 10 June at 10.15 a.m., which is 15 minutes after opening time, I found that there were only a peon and two clerks. Taking me for a client, they informed me that office work started only at 11.00 a.m. The manager, Mr. R.S. Tatki arrived at 11.30 a.m.; lacking discipline himself Mr. Tatki is unable to maintain any discipline among the staff.

The stock register and the account books have not been properly maintained for the last three months. It also appears that office stationery and small articles are freely used and taken away by the staff. The general indiscipline, if not controlled at once, is likely to result in heavy losses. Already there is loss of business since many of our clients have turned to our competitors owing to the poor service rendered by our branch office.

Since the situation is quite bad, it will be necessary to take drastic steps to restore discipline in the branch office. I recommend that Mr. Tatki should be brought to the H.O. and kept in a subordinate position. Mr. G.K. Nayyar, Assistant Manager of Pune branch has proved himself quite able; he may be promoted as Manager and posted at Nagpur.

Yours faithfully,

ABC
Secretary

Date ....

The Managing Director
Glazed Tiles (Pvt.) Ltd.

Dear Sir,

Sub: Decline of Sales of Tiles

In accordance with your instructions I have enquired fully into the causes of the decline in the company's business in the last two years till July 2005, and submit my report as follows:

Several new companies have put out glazed tiles in the market. Some of the companies have introduced artistically designed tiles in a variety of colours. Besides most companies make square tiles in four sizes and rectangular tiles in two sizes. We have limited our production of tiles to six standard colours without design, and to only two sizes.

Tiles are used extensively in kitchens of homes and hotels but the demand is for designed tiles, and for sizes other than those we make. Hence, while the market for tiles has gone up, we have not been able to keep our share of the business.

Recommendations

1. An experienced designer should be appointed to create new designs for our tiles.
2. A colour technician should be appointed to assist the designer.
3. Some of the more popular sizes and shapes should be introduced.
4. An intensive advertising and sales campaign should be launched in order to win back the lost market.
5. Follow-up correspondence should be maintained with all former customers in order to regain and build up old contacts.

Yours faithfully,

XYZ
Secretary

The following report by Auditors to Directors of a company where indiscipline has led to losses was assigned to a firm of Auditors.

15 September, 2005

The Directors
Rosa Glass Works (Pvt) Ltd.
Mumbai

Sirs,

In accordance with the instructions in your letter dated 1st September, 2005, we had two experienced persons from this firm observe the working of your company for two weeks to investigate the methods of running the business, and the daily conduct of the staff.

From the observation, the following defects were noted:

1. The Secretary's age and continued poor health has made him lose interest; the Registrar is too indecisive to control the office staff who disobey his instructions. As a result, the work as a whole is not carried out according to the instructions of the Managing Director, and is often seriously delayed. Customers complain about delays and some have cancelled their orders owing to the delays in delivery.
2. The section heads at the works, with the exception of the Head of the Stores Department, have become too friendly with the workers. Their authority is thus weakened, and the workers waste a great deal of time. The production is seriously slowed down, and the goods are not finished to the required high standard. This has resulted in rejection by customers, and general loss of business, apart from the loss of man hours, power and raw material. This matter has been reported twice to the Secretary by the Works Manager, but no action has been taken.
3. The Accountant has not kept his professional knowledge up-to-date, and has made no effort to find the best system of costing to suit the company's business. Prices quoted for some contracts have sometimes been below the actual cost, and some of the contracts carried out have resulted in losses. When an attempt was made to correct this, unreasonably high prices were quoted, leading to loss of business.

The following recommendations are made:

1. The Secretary should be superannuated. The Registrar designation may be changed to Superintendent. The positions of Secretary and Registrar should be filled by competent and well qualified persons who are able to impose discipline on the staff.
2. All the departmental heads at the works, except the Stores Manager, should be given notice of termination on the basis of their appraisal and performance reports.
3. The Accountant should be superseded, and a qualified accountant with up-to-date knowledge should be appointed to take charge of the accounts department.
4. The staff should be addressed by the General Manager to explain the need for changes in the working of the organization and the need for improving production and customer service.
5. A well planned training programme will have to be designed and carried out for re-orientation of the staff.

Yours faithfully,

XYZ
Partner, Sanghvi and Shah
Auditors

The schematic form may be used for presenting a complex report. The details are arranged under headings. The passive voice is used for most statements in a formal style.

Report on Workers' Unrest at Pyramid Plastic Works Factory, Wadala, Mumbai

I. Terms of Reference

To report on the workers' unrest and make recommendations to remedy the situation. The report was assigned by Board of Directors at its meeting held on 2 December, 2005.

II. Procedure

A. The Works Manager of the factory, Mr. D.C. Mehta, was met twice, and detailed discussions were held, once alone, and the second time in the presence of his Assistant, Mr. A.J.Guha.

B. Two meetings were held, one with the foremen alone, and one with the foremen in the presence of the Assistant Works Manager.

C. Twenty workers, chosen at random, were interviewed personally, and their views ascertained.

III. Findings

A. Extent of Unrest: The discontent and apathy, and the unrest that followed were observed among the workers in the month of September for the first time. To begin with, there were only signs of occasional outbursts of ill-temper or lack of interest in work. These were followed by group meetings and discussions of workers. Finally at the end of October a meeting of all the workers was held and a memorandum was presented to the Works Manager. A report was sent by the Works Manager to the General Manager, but the workers' representation was not sent.

Several foremen felt that unless remedial steps were taken, the situation might get out of hand, with the possibility of total strike.

B. Causes of Unrest: Resentment was felt by workers at the insistence of the new Works Manager on punctuality and greater efficiency while conditions in the factory have become too uncomfortable for efficient functioning. Complaints were made by workers that:

1. There was no suitable bus service available from the Railway station to the factory. Even a slight delay in starting the machines was ticked off by the Works Manager.

2. There was not enough room in the canteen; workers' strength has been doubled during the last two years.

3. Machines were kept too close to each other and workers were unable to operate them with ease as they used to, before additional machines were installed.

IV. Conclusions

The complaints made by the workers seemed just.

(i) Workers who travel by train find it difficult, occasionally, to arrive in time, owing to irregular bus service from the station to the factory. However, the delay has never been more than seven minutes.

(ii) Owing to lack of space in the canteen, workers have to spend part of their lunch hour in waiting for a seat in the canteen. They are often forced to eat hurriedly to be in time after the lunch hour.

(iii) Additional machines installed in the month of August have been installed in violation of the Factories Act which lays down the minimum space between machines.

V. Recommendations

1. A bus service should be operated between the factory and the station, to be run four times daily to coincide with the two shifts.
2. The store-room adjacent to the canteen should be cleaned up and handed over to the canteen for additional space.
3. The Works Manager should be advised to keep some of the machines in the crowded parts of the factory unused, so as to prevent hazardous occupation of workers at the machines, until the machines are moved to new premises. Work should be suitably rescheduled.
4. The contractor should be advised to hasten the construction work so that the extension of the factory is completed within two months.
5. The Works Manager should be advised to take a more humane view of the problem until the extensions are completed and conditions are made more comfortable.

18 December, 2005 James Mason
Secretary

A committee's report is always in the schematic form. The following are examples of a report in schematic form.

Report of Sub-committee on Decline in the Circulation of the Company's Magazine "The Indian Woman"

To the Board of Directors
Popular Magazines Pvt. Ltd.

I. Terms of Reference

The sub-committee was appointed by the following resolution of the Board passed at the meeting held on 8 February, 2005.

"Resolved that a sub-committee consisting of Marketing Executive, Mr. B.C Dalal, convener, editor of "The Indian Woman" Dr. Neena Gulzar, and Finance Officer Mr. P.T. Ahuja be, and is hereby, appointed to investigate the causes of the decline in the circulation of "The Indian Woman' and to report with recommendations in a month's time."

II. Procedure

(i) The sub-committee met three times, on 11th and 23rd February, and 5th March.

(ii) Three of the large distributors in Mumbai were contacted and their views noted.

(iii) Twenty small magazine shop owners were questioned to find out their experience with the sale of women's magazines.

(iv) Fifteen hundred questionnaires were collected from various readers including our past and present subscribers and members of women's associations. Ten interviewers were sent out for getting the questionnaires filled in.

(v) Other women's magazines available in Mumbai were carefully compared with our magazine.

(vi) Circulation figures of the last 3 years for our magazine were studied.

(vii) The company's budgeting policy was reviewed in consultation with Mr. Murthy of the Finance department.

III. Findings

From the investigation, the sub-committee arrived at the following conclusions:

The decline in the circulation became sharp in May 2004 although there had been a gradual decline over the six months before that. The fall by over 30% in January 2005 coincided with the arrival of a new women's magazine, 'Eve's Era,' on the market. While our two competitors, 'Women Today' and 'High Fashion' were able to withstand the impact, our magazine failed to retain its share of the market. This is largely due to the fact that the quality of our magazine had already begun to deteriorate.

The deterioration in quality was traced to the decision to make no increase in the expenditure on paper and to purchase paper in bulk for all the company's publications. The women's magazine editor had always been given freedom to select the paper in view of the sophisticated readership of the magazine and the need for good reproduction of photographs, drawings and various other illustrations. The magazine suffered an immediate set-back when it was allotted the ordinary paper.

As a result of using the ordinary paper, the photographs and illustrations became poor in reproduction. This caused reputed photographers, artists and illustrators to refuse to contribute to our magazine. Reputed writers who used to write regularly for our magazine were attracted by competing periodicals. Hence, there was a general fall in the quality of the magazine.

IV. Recommendations

(i) Adequate funds should be allocated to the magazine. The present allocation of Rs. —/ should be raised by 40% to Rs. —/.

(ii) Paper of good quality should be ordered immediately and used for the next issue.

(iii) Honorarium to reputed writers should be made more attractive. The rate should be at least double the present rate.

(iv) The services of good artists and photographers should be attracted by offering higher incentives.

(v) An intensive sales campaign should be launched to regain lost readership and gain new readers.

Sd-
A.G. Dalal, Convener
Neena Gulzar
P.T. Ahuja

Date : 12 March, 2005
Place : Mumbai

Report of Sub-committee on the choice of a suitable site for a branch factory in Maharashtra

To the Directors

Crystal Glass Works

I. Terms of Reference

The sub-committee was appointed by Resolution No. 845 adopted at a meeting of the Board of Directors, held on 10 January, 2005. The sub-committee, consisting of Mr. Pea, convener, Mr. Que and Mr. Are, was authorised to choose a suitable site for a branch factory for producing glassware in Maharashtra and to report in two months.

II. Procedure

The sub-committee held three meetings, on 13 and 29 January and 28 February.

The members of the sub-committee visited Mumbai, Pune and Nagpur between 20 January and 10 February, and saw several sites available for industrial units.

The members also met the Government and Municipal authorities to enquire about permission, licences, water and power connections.

III. Findings

The sub-committee felt that Mumbai is the most suitable city for a glass works factory, owing to the local market as well as export facilities.

Other conditions are described below:

A. Raw materials: All the components for the manufacture of glass are available in Mumbai since there are several other glassware factories. Fine sand is regularly supplied by specialised agents, from the banks of the Narmada, the Tapi, and the Godavari rivers.

B. Staff and Workers: Supervisory staff, and skilled and unskilled labour are available. The salaries and wages are higher than in the other cities but the quality of the work is of a high standard. Highly qualified technicians and designers receive very high salaries in Mumbai, but the expense of such staff will be compensated for by the market.

C. Power and Water: The Government authorities have agreed to give electricity and water connections and to supply the required quantities of power and water.

D. Scope for Expansion: The company's market can be extended to foreign countries through the Export Promotion Council as well as the consulates in Mumbai.

E. Site: There are three suitable sites of 4, 5 and 6 acres at Vikhroli, Borivli and Mulund respectively. All are available on a 99 years' lease. Details of the 3 sites are in Appendix I.

IV. Recommendations

The sub-committee recommends that:

1. One of the sites be chosen in consultation with the Company's Architects.
2. Negotiations be started immediately to acquire the selected site.
3. The Secretary be authorised to invite tenders for the construction of the factory and to apply to the Government of India for licence to import the required machines.

Date: 5 March, 2005, N.O. Pea
Place: Surat O.P. Que
P.Q. Are

EXERCISES

1. The Chief Marketing Executive of Udai Garments, visited Germany to explore the possibility of entering the European market. He found that the company's garments were criticized for dull colours, and limited range of sizes. Write the Executive's report to the company's Directors recommending changes to be made in the production designs to enable the company to sell in the European market.
2. There has been some unrest among the employees of a pharmaceuticals firm. The employees are all women. Write the report of the Human Resources Manager who was asked to make an inquiry.
3. There has been remarkable decline in the sale of sports goods manufactured by a company. The Marketing Manager has been asked to report with recommendations for stopping the decline. Prepare the report.
4. Many complaints have been received about delays in delivery, and shortage in the consignments of a company's edible oils dispatched to Gujarat. A senior marketing official from the company has been asked to look into the causes of the complaints and report to the Board of Directors within fifteen days. Write the report.
5. The Principal of a college has appointed a committee of two teachers and three students to suggest new directions in which students' co-curricular activities can be developed. Write the committee's report.
6. As the Librarian of your college, you have been asked by the Principal to suggest reorganization of the college library so as to make the maximum use of space and facilities available. Prepare the report, recommending computerization of the library's catalogues and lending system.
7. The results of a college have been very poor for the last five years. The Managing Committee of the Society which runs the college has asked the Principal to make a recommendatory report for improving the results. Write the report including a brief statement of the finance required.
8. Three management trainees have been appointed to a committee to look into the problem of theft and pilferage from the factory premises. Write their report.

9. A manufacturing company proposes to start a Welfare Centre for its employees. The Personnel Officer has been asked to make a report presenting a plan for the Centre. Write the report.
10. A manufacturing company (product of your choice) from Himachal Pradesh proposes to open a sales depot in Pune in Maharashtra. Prepare the report to be submitted to the Board of Directors by a subcommittee of three of the Directors.
11. Madhusagar Fruit Canning Company, Nagpur, proposes to open a branch factory in Goa in order to take advantage of the different variety of fruit available in the region. A sub-committee of Directors has been appointed to examine the feasibility of the proposal. Write the report recommending a suitable location for the factory.
12. There has been significant decline in the business of the urban branches of a nationalized bank. A committee of five Regional Managers has been appointed to look into the causes. Write the report recommending computerization of the branches and customer relations training for the staff.
13. It has been proposed that the working hours of your bank branch be changed to morning and evening hours, for the banking convenience of customers. You have been appointed convener of a committee to look into the feasibility of implementing the proposal. Prepare your report with recommendations.
14. A committee consisting of the Factory Manager, the Personnel Manager, and the Chief Engineer has been asked to look into the possibility of holding regular refresher courses for all supervisors of the factory workers. Draft the report to be made after completing the survey, giving recommendations.
15. There have been constant complaints from your customers about late delivery of goods and shortage in the goods supplied. As Head of the dispatch section you have been asked to look into the matter and report with recommendation. Draft your report.

Chapter 32

SUMMARISATION

A summary or precis is a condensed version, usually one-third of the length of the original piece of writing.

Uses of Summarising Skills

Summarising tests your ability to understand what you read and to express yourself concisely. These two skills are essential for work. Countless occasions arise when text needs to be re-phrased to take up less space, as when you have to —

compose a telegram or telex message

write minutes of a meeting

write telephone messages

draft an advertisement or notice for the press

write synopsis of a report

summarise correspondence

fit a blurb on the jacket of a book

adjust desired information on a package

avoid adding four pages to a booklet

save a sheet to fax

and above all, to store information for future use.

Busy executives are always in need of summaries and abstracts of articles in order to absorb important information quickly. Some organizations offer executive summaries of important new books as a service to companies. Summarising involves reading skills, understanding, judgement in selecting the important points, and ability to write in simple and clear style for easy reading.

Oral summary skills are most essential at discussions and meetings. A summary of proceedings of the discussion or meeting is expected from the leader or chairman. Participants can be much more effective if they can summarise the discussion before making their own contribution.

Summarising a Passage

Summarising is generally done orally at the end of a meeting by the chairman/leader of a discussion group; it is also required at the conclusion of any business meeting like a briefing, a sales talk to a customer, negotiation of a deal, or negotiation with staff.

A precis is a concise written re-statement of the main ideas of the original passage. It does not contain special expressions and entire sentences from the original text.

The completed precis must—

- be a good piece of composition, presenting ideas logically and concisely
- maintain the point of view of the original
- be in the same tense as the original
- not be in the words of the original
- not contain quotations or data or examples
- not use the first person I.
- make no comment on the views expressed in the original
- always have a title indicating what it is about
- always be in only one paragraph
- usually be one-third of the original in length; a few words more or less are acceptable.

You should be able to express an idea in several types of sentence constructions; practice in transformation of sentences (negative/assertive, interrogative/affirmative, active/passive, replacement of parts of speech, etc) is helpful.

The following steps should help in learning summarising skills.

1. Read the passage carefully; mark the difficult words.
2. Write down at least one word to say what the passage is about; for example, Advertising, Population, Technology, Marketing, Money. The title is to be built up and framed around this word; a one-word title is inadequate.
3. Try to infer and derive the meaning of the difficult words by reading the sentences in which they occur. Usually, it is possible to make out the meaning of a word from the context and the general sense of the passage; if this is not possible, use a dictionary; it will help increase vocabulary. With practice, it will be possible to make a good guess at the meaning of a word, for the purpose of writing a precis.
4. Read the passage again, with good guesses of the meaning of the difficult words. Take notes of the main points as you read.
5. Expand the collected main points into full sentences in simple, clear style, in your own words. A precis must be written as far as possible in your own words and sentences.

The following must be taken care of:

(a) Quotations, repetitions, details are to be left out.

(b) Illustrations, examples, statistical data are to be replaced by a generalisation drawn from them.

(c) Flowery, figurative expression is to be changed to simple prose.

(d) Exclamations and questions are to be left out.

(e) Unfamiliar, long words or phrases are to be replaced by simple words.

(f) Abbreviations like don't are not acceptable.

6. Write the rough draft in your own words in a complete paragraph with the help of the notes.

7. Count the number of words; this is easy if the rough draft is written after dividing the page into four/five columns for writing one word in each column. While counting the words, remember the following:
   - Words of the title are not counted.
   - The articles, a, an and the are counted.
   - The word *"and"* must be written in full and counted.
   - Words joined by a hyphen like job-oriented or government-financed are counted as one word.
   - A number (e.g. the year 2005) is counted as one word.
   - If the number of words exceeds by more than five, make local revisions to compress. If it is short, read the passage again to check for points which might have been left out or compressed too much.

8. Revise the precis carefully to make sure that ...
   - no important point has been left out,
   - it reads like a good composition,

9. Frame the title. The following steps are useful in framing a title:

(a) Expand the one word written in step 2, into a sentence which gives the main point of the passage; for example, "Time is modern man's tyrant", "History teaches us lessons for future conduct", "Growth of population was rapid after the Industrial Revolution", "Advertisements are effective only when they appear in proper places".

(b) Compress the sentence to a phrase, like "Time—Modern Man's Tyrant" or "Lessons of History" or "Population Growth after the Industrial Revolution". The title never begins with *"The."* Articles and prepositions need not be capitalised, but other words should begin with a capital letter. Note that a good title is a noun phrase.

10. Make a fair copy with the title written at the top. Write the number of words used in the precis, at the end.

Here are some methods to compress your writing:

(a) One Word Substitution:

It is worth developing a good vocabulary; it is often possible to reduce the number of words by finding a single word for a phrase. The following are only some examples.

1. One who is out to subvert a government: Anarchist
2. One who is recovering from illness: Convalescent
3. One who is all powerful: Omnipotent
4. One who is present everywhere: Omnipresent
5. One who knows everything: Omniscient
6. One who is easily deceived: Gullible
7. One who does not make mistakes: Infallible
8. One who can do anything for money: Mercenary
9. One who has no money: Pauper
10. One who changes sides: Turncoat
11. One who works for free: Volunteer
12. One who loves books: Bibliophile
13. One who can speak two languages: Bilingual
14. One who loves mankind: Philanthropist
15. One who hates mankind: Misanthrope
16. One who looks on the bright side of things: Optimist
17. One who looks on the dark side of things: Pessimist
18. One who doubts the existence of god: Agnostic
19. One who pretends to be what he is not: Hypocrite
20. One incapable of being tired: Indefatigable
21. One who helps others: Good Samaritan
22. One who copies from other writers: Plagiarist
23. One who hates women: Misogynist
24. One who knows many languages: Polyglot
25. One who thinks only of himself: Egoist
26. One who thinks only of welfare of women: Feminist
27. One who is indifferent to pleasure or pain: Stoic
28. A man who is quite like a woman: Effeminate
29. One who has strange habits: Eccentric
30. One who speaks less: Reticent
31. One who goes on foot: Pedestrian

32. One who believes in fate:	Fatalist
33. One who dies without a Will:	Intestate
34. One who always thinks himself to be ill:	Valetudinarian
35. A Government by the people:	Democracy
36. A Government by a king or queen:	Monarchy
37. A Government by the officials:	Bureaucracy
38. A Government by the rich:	Plutocracy
39. A Government by the few:	Oligarchy
40. A Government by the Nobles:	Aristocracy
41. A Government by one:	Autocracy
42. Rule by the mob:	Mobocracy
43. That through which light can pass:	Transparent
44. That through which light cannot pass:	Opaque
45. That through which light can partly pass:	Translucent
46. A sentence whose meaning is unclear:	Ambiguous
47. A place where orphans live:	Orphanage
48. That which cannot be described:	Indescribable
49. That which cannot be imitated:	Inimitable
50. That which cannot be avoided:	Inevitable
51. A position for which no salary is paid:	Honorary
52. That which cannot be defended:	Indefensible
53. That which is not likely to happen:	Improbable
54. People living at the same time:	Contemporaries
55. A book published after the death of its author:	Posthumous
56. A book written by an unknown author:	Anonymous
57. A life history written by oneself:	Autobiography
58. A life history written by somebody else:	Biography
59. People who work together:	Colleagues
60. One who eats too much:	Glutton
61. That which cannot be satisfied:	Insatiable
62. One who questions everything:	Cynic
63. A flesh eating animal:	Carnivorous
64. A grass eating animal:	Herbivorous
65. One who lives in a foreign country:	Immigrant
66. To transfer one's authority to another:	Delegate
67. That which is lawful:	Legal
68. That which is against law:	Illegal

69. A game in which no one wins:	Draw
70. A study of ancient things:	Archaeology
71. Murder of a human being:	Homicide
72. Murder of a father:	Patricide
73. Murder of a mother:	Matricide
74. Murder of an brother:	Fratricide
75. Murder of an infant:	Infanticide
76. Murder of self:	Suicide
77. Murder of the king:	Regicide
78. To free somebody from all blame:	Exonerate
79. To write under a different name:	Pseudonym
80. A thing no longer in use:	Obsolete
81. A handwriting that cannot be read:	Illegible
82. One who is greedy for money:	Avaricious
83. Something that cannot be imitated:	Inimitable
84. One who doesn't know how to read and write:	Illiterate
85. A person's peculiar habit:	Idiosyncrasy
86. An animal who preys on other animals:	Predator
87. Violating the sanctity of a church:	Sacrilege
88. One who can throw his voice:	Ventriloquist

(b) Reducing a sentence by reconstruction

Sentences can be transformed from one kind of construction to another kind to shorten them. For example, active voice sentences are shorter than passive voice sentences:

Passive: The ABC company suddenly realized that they were being watched by the XYZ company

Active: The ABC company suddenly realized that XYZ company was watching them

Positive sentences are shorter than negative ones:

Negative: We did not realize that our designs were being copied by our competitors until ——

Positive: We realized that our designs were being copied by our competitors when —-

Negative: People often do not think of checking the facts.

Positive: People seldom think of checking the facts.

Other methods of transformation sentences such as changing the degree of comparison, substituting a noun or verb for a phrase, and substituting a phrase for a clause, are also useful in shortening as well as in giving variety to style.

(c) Removing redundant words

Many people develop bad writing habits like repeating an idea in another phrases, for example, "true fact", "I saw it with my own eyes", "twelve noon" "Uneducated people who have never had schooling." Take care to avoid such repetitions.

Redundant	Trim Version
12 midnight	midnight
12 noon	noon
3 am in the morning	3 am
absolutely spectacular/phenomenal	spectacular/phenomenal
a person who is honest	an honest person
a total of 14 birds	14 birds
biography of her life	biography
circle around	circle
close proximity	proximity
completely unanimous	unanimous
consensus of opinion	consensus
cooperate together	co-operate
each and every	each
enclosed herewith	enclosed
end result	result
exactly the same	the same
final completion	completion
frank and honest exchange	frank exchange or honest exchange
free gift	gift
he/she is a person who . . .	he/she
important/basic essentials	essentials
in spite of the fact that	although
in the field of economics/law enforcement	in economics/law enforcement
in the event that	if
job functions	job or functions
new innovations	innovations
one and the same	the same
particular interest	interest
period of four days	four days

personally, I think/feel	I think/feel
personal opinion	opinion
puzzling in nature	puzzling
refer back	refer
repeat again	repeat
return again	return
revert back	revert
shorter/longer in length	shorter/longer
small/large in size	small/large
square/round/rectangular in shape	square/round rectangular
summarize briefly	summarize
surrounded on all sides	surrounded
surrounding circumstances	circumstances
there is no doubt but that	no doubt
usual/habitual custom	custom
we are in receipt of	we have received

EXERCISES

Make precis of the passages given below. Some questions are given at the end of the first few passages to help in understanding the passage. A precis should always be given a title.

1. Trees are useful to human beings in three important ways: they provide wood and other products; they give shade; and they help to prevent drought and floods.

   Unfortunately in many parts of the world people do not realize that the last point is the most important. In their eagerness to make quick profit from the trees, they cut down a large number of trees and do not realize that they are losing their best friends.

   Two thousand years ago a rich and powerful country cut down trees to build warships and hoped to gain itself an empire. It gained the empire but without tress, the soil became hard and poor. When the empire fell to pieces, the country found itself faced with floods and starvation.

   Even where the government understands the importance of having a large number of trees, it is difficult to persuade the villagers to see this. They want wood for cooking their food, they can earn money by selling the wood to townspeople. They are often too lazy or too careless to plant and take care of new trees. Unless the government has a good system of control, or can educate the people, forests will gradually disappear.

   This means that people have fewer trees; but more seriously, it means that there will be floods and the soil will eventually turn into desert. Where there are trees, their roots break up the soil and allow the rain water to sink in and bind the soil, thus preventing it from being washed away easily. If there are no trees, the rain falls on hard ground and flows away on the surface, carrying away with it the rich top-soil in which the crops grow. When the top-soil is gone, nothing remains but useless desert.

Explain in your own words the effect of trees on the soil and the result of removing the trees. Do not use more than 50 words.

2. To be a good teacher, you need some of the skills of a good actor. You must be able to hold the attention and interest of your audience; you must be a clear speaker with a strong pleasant voice which you can control well. You must be able to act what you are teaching in order to convey its full meaning.

   Watch a good teacher and you will see that she does not sit motionless before the class. She stands most of the time, she walks about, she uses her arms, hands and fingers to help in explanations, and her face to express feelings. Listen carefully, and you will hear the quality, the tone and the rhythm of the voice changing according to what she is speaking about.

   Though the teacher needs and has some of the gifts of a good actor, it does not follow that the teacher can necessarily perform well on the stage. There are some important differences between the teacher's work and the actor's work. The actor has to speak words which he has learnt by heart, and repeat exactly the same words every time he plays that part. Even his movements and actions and expressions are fixed. What he has to do is to make these previously learnt words and actions appear natural on the stage.

   A good teacher works quite differently. Her audience has to take an active part in the play; they ask and answer questions; if they do not understand something they ask for explanation. So, the teacher has to suit her act to the needs of the audience which is the class. She cannot learn her part by heart; she has to invent as she goes along.

   Many teachers who do a fine job in the classroom cannot act on the stage because their brains refuse to be limited to the words and part written by someone else and learnt by heart.

   Answer these questions in your own words, using one complete sentence for each answer.

   (a) What skills of the actor does a teacher need?

   (b) How does a good teacher use her voice while teaching?

   (c) How does a teacher's audience participate in the "play"?

   (d) What does an actor have to do with his part when he is on the stage?

3. Growing at an annual compound rate of 40% for the past five years, the information technology (IT) industry has become one of the largest foreign exchange earners in India. During this period, the growth blazed by the IT industry seems unattainable for many others in the current economic scenario.

   The past five years have seen the Indian IT industry go through fundamental changes. Earlier, the IT industry was equated with hardware, which was then the major bread earner. But now, software accounts for more than half of the industry's total revenue. The transition hasn't happened overnight. Some factors aiding the downfall of the hardware sector have been the lack of government spending, adverse policies, and the Y2K problem which has pumped in millions of dollars into software. The hardware sector faced with high tariffs, was forced into a corner in the early nineties when manufacturing became unviable. This goaded Indian hardware companies into joint ventures, with international majors for marketing their products in India. The sector still faces stiff competition from the unorganized sector. (174 words)

Write five questions which should cover the major points in the passage and help you to make a summary of it.

4. Organizations are trying to redefine their role and mission in society. Many organizations have found their purpose in society as a service to community and the effort is to provide an improved quality of service, irrespective of whether it is a manufacturing organization or a service organization. The emphasis is on a better understanding of people and their behaviour, and caring more for them and their needs.

   Research studies emphasize the fact that what customers want is personalized service. The personal touch is considered a high priority for enhancing customer satisfaction. several executives of America's largest companies have said, in a survey, that how much an airlines cares about its customers is as important to them as prompt baggage delivery and efficient check-in.

   Several companies have started revamping their hiring and pay practices. They now try to compensate their employees on the basis of how well they have served their customers. They inspire their employees with 'service ethic' and they believe in the fact that contented employees make for better-served customers. There appears to be a direct relation between customer retention and employee retention. Satisfied and well-served customers not only lead to higher profits but also to enhanced employee retention and lower costs of training since good employees stick around longer. (211 words)

5. Banks expect that bancassurance — selling insurance through bank branches— will generate large commission earnings which will compensate for declining profits in traditional banking. Insurance companies view banassurance as a new channel which will be cost-effective. Banks feel they have a competitive edge over other channels due to their proximity to customers, a large data-base of the existing customers and their image. Yet, the global track record of bancassurance in the global market is not bright and most successes are in life insurance, not in general insurance. The most glittering example of success in bancassurance is France, where 55% of life insurance is sold through banks. But in other mature markets bancassurance has failed with distribution of insurance products through bank branches accounting for less then 10% of the market. Even in India, bancassurance will face many road blocks. Here, banks will be more comfortable with life insurance products which have synergies with things like fixed deposits. But bancassurance is likely to face several hurdles in India.

   One, life insurance is different from fixed deposits, because the former has no liquidity for the first three years, followed by limited liquidity, whereas the latter has total liquidity as well as an assured interest rate. Besides, the yield on life insurance in the form of bonus is not guaranteed. It is much more difficult to sell a life insurance product on the basis of its main benefit — risk coverage. So, the past experience of bank employees may not be relevant in selling insurance. Two, selling strategies differ across banking and insurance. People buy banking products, whereas insurance products have to be sold. Insurance agents have to visit customers an average of three times to persuade them to purchase. Banks expect to close insurance sales on the first visit, — a practical impossibility. Three, banks hope to sell insurance when customers visit branches, but with the growth of credit cards and ATMs fewer customers visit branches with fewer opportunities for employees to meet customers. Four, India's insurance market is polluted with rebating of customers by agents. Although rebating is prohibited by law, it is rampant. Individual agents can offer rebates but banks cannot. Finally, complacent bank employees will need a drastic change of mindset to sell insurance aggressively. (376 words)

Chapter 33

PUNCTUATION

Punctuation marks are essential in written composition; in oral communication, the inflection of the voice, its rise and fall, its pauses and its stresses make up the punctuation of the spoken word.

Incorrect punctuation or missing punctuation marks can confuse the meaning of a sentence.

Punctuation Marks

All the marks are not of equal importance for all types of writing; a story with dialogue requires quotation marks, exclamation marks, question marks, dashes and apostrophes while a piece of business writing needs full stops, semicolons and commas with a few apostrophes and colons and question marks. A report requires very few punctuation marks; a letter needs more.

The following are a few general rules for punctuation.

Full Stop (.)

(a) The full stop is the basic mark of punctuation; it marks the end of a complete sentence.

(b) It is also used after an abbreviated form of a word, like *Messrs., Co., Ltd., Pvt.*

It has now become acceptable to omit the full stop after the common abbreviations like *Mr* or *Mrs* even in print; however, many standard books still use it.

Full stop is not used for words coined by using initials like

UNESCO, SAARC, WTO, GATT

Full stop is not required at the end of each phrase in a list of items like an agenda.

Comma (,)

The comma is the most used punctuation mark; some common uses are given below:

(a) Commas are placed between three or more items in a series:

I intend to visit France, Germany, and Switzerland.

Also correct:

I intend to visit France, Germany and Switzerland.

(b) In letters, a comma is placed after the salutation as in *Dear Sir,* and after the complimentary close as an *Yours truly,*

(c) Commas are used to separate the elements of a date:

Friday, 15 October, 1998

No comma is required if only the month and the year are given:

October 1998

(d) If an address is written as part of a sentence, commas separate the elements of the address, except the city and PIN code.

279, Cochin Street, Fort Market, Mumbai 400 002

(e) If a sentence begins with an adverbial phrase or adverb, a comma follows it.

Notwithstanding the rise in prices, many people placed large orders for our products.

(f) In large numbers, groups of three digits, beginning with the unit, are marked off with commas: *61,000,000,000*

(g) Words or phrases which are parenthetical need a pair of commas.

*We shall inform you, however, as soon as we get some news.

*Please note that, for the purpose of our record, we need the following documents:

Semicolon (;)

The semicolon is almost a full stop in the sense that it can be used only after a sentence is grammatically complete; but the following sentence continues the same idea since it is not a complete break.

(a) It can be used in place of a conjunction to make the sentence more emphatic, for example:

You have not replied to our reminders; we fear you are dissatisfied with our goods.

(b) The semicolon conveys the sense of *therefore,* or *hence,* or *and so.* The semicolon is often followed by words like *therefore, hence, thus, besides, consequently, however.*

Colon (:)

(a) The colon is used to introduce a list or series or an explanation, for example:

Articles available with us are: refrigerators, washing machines, TV sets, and VCRs.

The different kinds of marine insurance policies are: Open, Voyage, and Floating.

(b) The colon is used after the phrases *as follows: the following: given below:*

(c) Colon is used for separating the figures of hours and minutes, *12:15*; for separating initials of dictator and typist, *AWP:DPK*; for separating title and subtitle of a book, *Black Money: A Study of its Impact on Indian Economy.*

(d) Colon is used after the salutation in a letter in American practice.

Question Mark (?)

(a) A direct question ends with a question mark.

*Have you applied for a loan to any other financing institution?
*How many copies of the circular will be needed ?

Note: An indirect question does not have a question mark at the end:

*Please state whether you have applied for a loan to any other institution.
*I want to know how many copies of the circular will be needed.

(b) A polite request in the form of a question requires a question mark.
Will you please settle the account this week?

Apostrophe (')

The Apostrophe has two functions: (i) in possessives and (ii) in contractions.

(i) **Possessive apostrophe:**

(a) For singular nouns, the possessive apostrophe is placed before **s**;
Manager's office, accountant's table, our company's products.

(b) For plural nouns which do not end with **s**, the apostrophe is placed before **s**:
children's park, women's hostel, men's tailor.

(c) For plural nouns which end with **s**, the apostrophe is placed after **s**:
workers' overalls, customers' requirements, Companies' representatives.

(d) Possessive adjectives, *his, its, whose* and possessive pronouns *his, hers, yours, theirs* do not have any apostrophe. In the complimentary close of a letter, *Yours faithfully,* there is no apostrophe.

(e) The possessive apostrophe is used in phrases like
a week's holiday, half an hour's interval, ninety days' credit, three months' time.

Note 1: The exception *one's* a possessive adjective has an apostrophe.
Note 2: The possessive form of *it* is *its. It's* is a contraction of *it is.*

(ii) **Non-possessive apostrophe** is used in contracted words to indicate that letters have been dropped, as in *it*'s (it is), *can't* (cannot), *we'll* (we shall/will), *don't* (do not) etc. These forms are used only in oral communication and are not used in formal business writing like letters, reports, and minutes.

Quotation Marks ("...")

(a) Quotation marks are used to begin and end statements which are the exact words spoken or written by someone else.

(b) Quotation marks also enclose a word or phrase which is not in common use, but has become known or accepted among a group of people.

A full stop is usually inside the quotation marks; a question mark is inside if it is a part of the quoted sentence, but it may be outside if it is not a part of the quoted sentence.

It is common practice to use single quotation marks. But if there is a quotation within a quotation, the main one has double and the one within has single quotation marks.

Hyphen (-)

Hyphens are not used for commonly compounded words like *layout, inputs, outlay, subcommittee, nowadays.* If a hyphen is to be used, it should be at the main break, e.g., *sub-committee.*

Compound adjectives are hyphenated.

sales-oriented, Government-financed

Business titles like *Vice President, Vice Chancellor, Deputy Secretary* are not hyphenated. But if a person holds dual position, the combined title like *treasurer-secretary* is hyphenated.

Exclamation Mark (!)

An exclamation shows strong feeling like surprise, admiration, enthusiasm. It is not used in official writing except in sales letters and in drafts of speeches where the style is free.

Review

Choose the correct alternative for filling in the blank.

(a) That's what you'll need — a notebook, a pencil, and a clip.

to buy,
to buy:
to buy;

(b) She has a — daughter.
two-year old
two year-old
two-year-old

(c) — I'm not sure I believe that.

Really?
Really:
Really—

CAPITALS

A capital letter is used:

(a) At the beginning of a sentence, after a full stop.

(b) For proper nouns: Names of persons, countries, cities, rivers, mountains, names of months and days, names of institutions, titles of books and magazines, names of festival/holy days, names of trains, ships, companies.

(c) Titles of public officials, like *President, Prime Minister, Governor.*

(d) Official positions and designations in an organization, like *Marketing Manager, Chief Accountant, Managing Director.*

(e) Courtesy titles like *Mr. Mrs. Miss Dr.* whether in full or in abbreviated form.

(f) The first person singular pronoun *I.*

(g) In a letter, the words in the salutation, *Dear Sir, Madam, Gentlemen,.*

Note:In the complimentary close, only the first word is capital. *Yours faithfully, Very truly yours, Sincerely yours.*

(h) Names of bodies, made up of initials, *OPEC, UNO, IDBI* have all capital letters.

(i) Some words have a different meaning if written with a capital letter.

State is the organized community with a government; *state* is condition or plight; *Government* is the governing body: *government* is the function of governing. *East/West* is used to indicate countries in one or other part of the globe: *east/west* is the direction.

(j) Names of collective bodies are in capital when referring to a particular one:

This decision was taken at a meeting of the Board of Directors.

and in lower case when used in general:

A public limited company is managed by a board of directors.

ABBREVIATIONS

An abbreviation is a shortened or contracted form of a word or phrase, used to represent the whole. The contraction may be made by omitting letters as in *ft* for *foot/feet*, or by substituting as in *Xmas* for *Christmas* or by using only the first letter as in *N-W* for *north-west* or by using the first syllable as in *Mon.* for *Monday.* Abbreviations are useful for writing notes, inter-office memos and other informal papers; they save time. They are only for writing and are always pronounced in full; *Prof.* is always read and spoken as *Professor,* and *Dr.* as *Doctor.*

Every trade and profession has its abbreviations. If they are used in documents meant for the public, the layman may not understand them. A reasonable method is to write the word in full the first time it occurs in a document, give the abbreviation in brackets and then use it in further occurrences.

Some abbreviations like *Mr., Mrs., Dr.* are commonly accepted. So also are the symbols for dollar ($), rupees (Rs) and other currencies. Abbreviated words like *Ltd., Inc., Co., Pvt.,* which occur in names of companies are commonly known.

Abbreviations for months and days are not considered polite in a formal letter or report. Names of days and months must be spelt out fully whether in the date or in the body of the document. The word *and* must be spelt out.

It is not considered proper to abbreviate personal titles like *Honourable* or *Reverend;* they should be spelt out in full.

Some abbreviations have more than one full form. They are to be used with care for the reader's knowledge and for the formality required in a particular document. When in doubt about the meaning of a particular abbreviation, consult a dictionary.

Acronyms

An acronym is a word formed from the initial letters, or groups of letters, of words in a set phrase, as UNO from United Nations Organization. The words formed in this way are written in all capitals and do not have full stops.

Acronyms become words in their own right; words like *UNESCO, SAARC, ASEAN,* are pronounceable and are used in speech as well; while abbreviations are only for writing and are always pronounced in full.

Some commonly used abbreviations are given here.

Days

Sun.	Sunday
Mon.	Monday
Tue.	Tuesday
Thurs.	Thursday
Fri.	Friday
Sat.	Saturday

Months

Jan.	January
Feb.	February
Mar.	March
Apr.	April
Sept.	September
Oct.	October
Nov.	November
Dec.	December

May, June and July are not abbreviated.

Titles before Names

Smt.	Shrimati
Kum.	Kumari
Mr.	Mister
Messrs.	Messieurs
Mrs.	Mistress
Dr.	Doctor
Prof.	Professor

Weights and Measures

A unit of measure is abbreviated only when it follows a figure; for example, we write *30 kg* but *thirty kilograms; 15 yds* but *fifteen yards.*

Some short terms of measure like *acre, day, mile, ton,* etc. are not abbreviated.

The more commonly used abbreviations of units of measure are given below.

amp/A	ampere
cal	calories
cc	cubic centimetre
cm	centimetre
doz	dozen
gm	gram
hp	horse power
hr	hour
Hz	Hertz
kg	kilogram
km	kilometre
kW	kilowatt
lb	pound (weight)
mg	milligram(s)
mm	millimetre
min	minute
sec	second
sq ft	square foot
oz	ounce

Miscellaneous

a.c.	alternating current
a/c	account
ad/advt.	advertisement
approx.	approximately
arr.	arrival (in time-tables of railways,etc.)
Ass/Assoc	Association
Ave.	Avenue
B.A.	Bachelor of Arts
B.B.C.	British Broadcasting Corporation
B.C.	Before Christ
B.Com.	Bachelor of Commerce
bldg.	building
B.F.	Brought Forward (in accounts books)
Bros.	Brothers (in names of business firms)
C.	Centigrade/Celsius
C.A.	Chartered Accountant
C.F.	Carried Forward (in account books)
cf.	compare (Latin confer)
Capt.	Captain
Ch./Chap.	Chapter

c.i.f.	cost, insurance and freight (commercial use)
Co.	Company
c/o	care of (used in addressing letters)
C.O.D.	Cash on Delivery
Co-op.	Cooperative Society
Cr.	Creditor (in account books)
d.c.	direct current
deg.	degree
do.	ditto
Dr.	Debtor (in accounts books)
E.& O.E.	errors and omissions excepted
ed.	editor/edited by
F.	Fahrenheit
fig(s).	figures(s)
f.o.b.	free on board
G.P.O.	General Post Office
H.Q.	Headquarters
ht.	height
Inc.	Incorporated
ISD	International Subscriber Dialling
ISDN	Integrated Services Digital Network
ISP	Internet Service Provider
Ltd.	Limited (in names of companies)
mph	miles per hour
M.P.	Member of Parliament
MS(S)	manuscript(s)
Mt.	mountain
N.B.	(Latin: nota bene) please note
No(s).	Number(s)
O.K.	all correct, agreed
p.a.	per annum
pl.	plural
p.	page
pp.	pages
P.T.O.	Please Turn Over
Pvt.	Private (in names of companies)
Q.E.D.	(Latin: quod erat demonstrandum) which had to be proved
qr.	quarter
R.S.V.P.	(French: repondez s'il vous plait) Please reply
Sec.	Secretary
STD	Subscriber Trunk Dialling
Supdt.	Superintendent
temp.	temperature
V.I.P.	Very important person
viz.	(Latin: videlicet) namely
Vol(s).	Volume(s)
V.P.P.	Valuc Payable Post
wt.	weight

www	World wide web
yr(s)	year(s)

In many cases the same abbreviation is used both for singular and plural. A few examples are given below.

in.	inch or inches
ft.	foot or feet
lb(s).	pound(s)
mm	millimetre or millimetres

Most dictionaries have a section on abbreviations. Whenever necessary consult a good dictionary.

Abbreviations are not used in formal communication like business/official letters and reports; only the most common ones, like Mr., Mrs., Dr. as titles before a name or common symbols related to measures and figures like $, Rs, %, kg., etc, are used in formal communication.

EXERCISES

1. Fill in the blank with the correct alternative.
   (a) I don't expect to be back until— call before that.
   Friday, don't
   Friday; don't
   Friday — don't
   (b) This is — I have no room for it in my house.
   too expensive: moreover,
   too expensive, moreover,
   too expensive; moreover,
2. Put an apostrophe where required in these terms:

ours	6 oclock	students books
4 months leave	an hours interval	shouldnt

   it fell on its face
3. Put a question mark where required
   (a) Please inform me where I should deliver the consignment
   (b) Have you applied for any other course
   (c) We want to know how many applications have been received
   (d) You have not sent the letter, have you
4. Are these acceptable in formal documents?
   Jan., Tues., Vice President (HRD), UNESCO, Ltd. & %

❑❑❑

Chapter 34

NUMERALS

Numbers form a part of most texts and it is necessary to know the correct form of writing numbers for different purposes like dates, the time, amounts and measures.

CARDINAL NUMBERS

1 one	11 eleven	21 twenty-one	31 thirty-one etc
2 two	12 twelve	22 twenty-two	40 forty
3 three	13 thirteen	23 twenty-three	50 fifty
4 four	14 fourteen	24 twenty-four	60 sixty
5 five	15 fifteen	25 twenty-five	70 seventy
6 six	16 sixteen	26 twenty-six	80 eighty
7 seven	17 seventeen	27 twenty-seven	90 ninety
8 eight	18 eighteen	28 twenty-eight	100 a hundred
9 nine	19 nineteen	29 twenty-nine	1,000 a thousand
10 ten	20 twenty	30 thirty	1,000,000 a million

600	six hundred
130	a hundred and thirty
1,008	one thousand and eight
70,237	seventy thousand, two hundred and thirty-seven
9,000	nine thousand

(a) Notice the following points:

(i) When writing in words or reading a compound figure, the word **and** is placed before the last word.

e.g. 4,614 *four thousand, six-hundred and fourteen*

6,204 *six thousand two-hundred and four*

478 *four hundred and seventy-eight*

(ii) The words **hundred**, **thousand**, and **million**, when used of a definite number, are never made plural:

e.g. eight hundred students; four thousand and ten rupees.

But note the phrases:

- *Hundreds of trees; thousands of students*

Here the words are used to convey the idea of a large number; in this use they must be made plural. Also, the preposition *of* is placed after *hundreds*, *thousands*, etc. A definite number is never followed by **of.**

The words **dozen** (12) and **score** (20) follow the same rule. The word **gross** (144) has no plural form and is always followed by **of.**

a dozen eggs six dozen eggs (definite number, no **s**)

but dozens of eggs (indefinite number, with **s** and **of**)

a gross of pins, two gross of paper clips

(b) When the numbers 100, 1,000, 1000,000 stand alone, it is more common to say

a hundred, a thousand etc,

rather than one hundred, one thousand, etc.

But when more numbers are added it is more common to say:

one hundred and four, one thousand, one hundred and forty

WRITING NUMBERS IN A TEXT

The following rules are used for writing numbers in a text:

1. Numbers 1 to 9 are spelled out and numbers 10 and above are written in figures.
   five years *seven tables*
   18 days *49 cars*
2. Any number that occurs at the beginning of a sentence is spelled out.
   Two hundred and thirty-four students took the examination.
   Twenty miles is a long distance to walk.
3. Numbers which are a part of a compound word are spelled out
   three-year-olds
   sixty-year-olds
4. Figures are used for technical units, *whatever the number.*
   6 kHz 500 hp 100 kw
5. Two zeros are placed before the decimal point if there is no integer in a figure.
   00.089 00.479 00.007
6. Amounts of money are written in figures except when they appear at the beginning of a sentence.
   Rs 3 Rs 44,307 Rs 2,13,97,000

Note that amounts have to be written in words as well as in figures in documents related to transactions. Two zeros are placed after the decimal point when amounts of money are tabulated.

	Rs.
	14.00
	39.00
	67.25
	74.50
	94.25
Total	289.00

7. A fraction which appears at the beginning of a sentence is written in words.

One-eighth of an inch

Two-thirds majority

One-hundredth of this quantity

8. Figures with more than three digits require a comma after every three digits counted from the right.

4,400

79,670

7,843,705

58,462,455

Note that *lakh* and *crore* are not English words; 100,000 (one lakh) is a hundred thousand and 10,000,000 (one crore) is ten million.

9. If there are a series of numbers in a sentence, they can be written in figures.

They can give us 200 chairs, 100 tables and 10 desks.

10. Figures are used for numbering chapters, pages, items in a list, illustrations, and models in a catalogue. Telephone numbers, insurance policy numbers, examination seat numbers and other identification numbers are always written in figures.

Fig. 11	*S.No. 6*	*Roll no. 694*
page 482	*Chapter 34*	*File No. C/56/319*
Telephone No. 299132	*Insurance Policy No.8806483*	
Model No. KL52		

11. Plot numbers, house numbers, flat numbers in addresses are written in figures.

12 A, Cadell Road	*103, Lodi Street*
9, Anand Nivas	*C/8, Lok Housing Society*

Street numbers are spelled out if they are below 10.

Fifth Avenue

12. Percentages, and measurements are written in figures.

75% *5.00 a.m.* *10.00 p.m*

8½ in × 12 in. *8 cm × 16 cm × 48cm*

ORDINAL NUMBERS

first	eleventh	twenty-first	thirty-first, & c.
second	twelfth	twenty-second	fortieth
third	thirteenth	twenty-third	fiftieth
fourth	fourteenth	twenty-fourth	sixtieth
fifth	fifteenth	twenty-fifth	seventieth
sixth	sixteenth	twenty-sixth	eightieth
seventh	seventeenth	twenty-seventh	ninetieth
eighth	eighteenth	twenty-eighth	hundredth
ninth	nineteenth	twenty-ninth	thousandth
tenth	twentieth	thirtieth	millionth

(a) **Points to be noticed:**

(i) The irregular spelling of **fifth, eighth, ninth,** and **twelfth.**

(ii) When ordinal numbers are written in figures, the last two letters of the written word must be added:

first = *1st* *twenty-first* = *21st*

second = *2nd* *forty-second* = *42nd*

third = *3rd* *sixty-third* = *63rd*

fourth = *4th* *eightieth* = *80th*

(iii) In compound ordinal numbers the rule about *and* is the same as for compound cardinal numbers:

101st is read **as** *a hundred and first*

The article **the** is normally placed before ordinal numbers.

the sixtieth day *the fortieth visitor*

Titles of kings/queens are written in Roman figures:

Charles V *Elizabeth II*

but are read as **Charles the Fifth** **Elizabeth the Second**

Dates

Names of days of the week and months of the year are spelled out in full in formal writing. They are always written with a capital letter.

Days of the week	*Months of the year*	
Sunday	January	July
Monday	February	August
Tuesday	March	September
Wednesday	April	October
Thursday	May	November
Friday	June	December
Saturday		

The date is written in cardinal numbers in modern practice, especially in official letters;

12 June or *June 12*

However, the date may be written in ordinal numbers, and in any of the following styles:

12th June   *June 12th*   *12th of June*

The year must be written in all four figures. When speaking or reading we use hundred (not thousand) for the year.

1999 is read/spoken as **nineteen hundred and ninety-nine** or **nineteen ninety-nine.**

The year 2000, is read as **two thousand.**

Time

The time of the day can be expressed in different ways.

(i) It may be stated in terms of one 24-hour period or in terms of two halves of the day as shown by the clock.

09.00 hours or 9.00 a.m.

21.00 hours or *9.00 p.m.*

The 24-hour style is used for timings of trains, flights, TV and radio programmes, etc which run for 24 hours. For daily official business, use the 12-hour style. It is important to write **a.m.** or **p.m.** correctly.

Note that 12 o'clock in the day is **12.00 hours** or **12.00 noon** and at night, is **00.00 hours** or **12.00 midnight**.

(ii) The word "o'clock" follows only the exact hour without any minutes.

three o'clock   *eleven o'clock*   *twelve o'clock*

9 o'clock   *11 o'clock*

The context indicates whether it refers to the hour before or after 12.00 noon.

(iii) For formal writing, the time is expressed by stating the number of minutes after the hour, even if it is close to the next hour.

2.20 (a.m. or p.m.) 8.45   11.50

In reading or speaking, we may say

two twenty *eight forty-five* *eleven fifty.*

In informal speech the time can be expressed in terms of the nearest hour.

twenty past two *a quarter to nine* *ten to twelve*

In official documents, the time may be written either in 24-hour terms or in 12-hour terms with a.m. or p.m. Uniform style must be followed throughout the document and set of documents related to a matter.

ROMAN NUMBERS

Arabic numbers 1,2,3,... are used for most purposes. Roman numbers I, II, III,... are used for a few purposes and it is useful to know the numbers at least up to 20 and to be able to recognise the rest. Unless required or necessary, use Arabic numbers rather than Roman numbers.

Roman numbers are given below:

Arabic numbers	Roman numbers	Arabic numbers	Roman numbers	Arabic numbers	Roman numbers
1	I	55	LV	400	CD
2	II	59	LIX	500	D
3	III	60	LX	600	DC
4	IV	61	LXI	700	DCC
5	V	65	LXV	800	DCCC
6	VI	69	LXIX	900	CM
7	VII	70	LXX	1,000	M
8	VIII	71	LXXI		
9	IX	75	LXXV		
10	X	79	LXXIX		
15	XV	80	LXXX		
19	XIX	81	LXXXI		
20	XX	85	LXXXV		
21	XXI	89	LXXXIX		
25	XXV	90	XC		
29	XXIX	91	XCI		
30	XXX	95	XCV		
35	XXXV	99	XCIX		
39	XXXIX	100	C		
40	XL	150	CL		
49	XLIX	200	CC		
50	L	300	CCC		

It is advisable to have and adhere to a house-style for writing dates, time, and all other numerals.

❑❑❑